The Empress and the Architect

YALE UNIVERSITY PRESS
New Haven & London

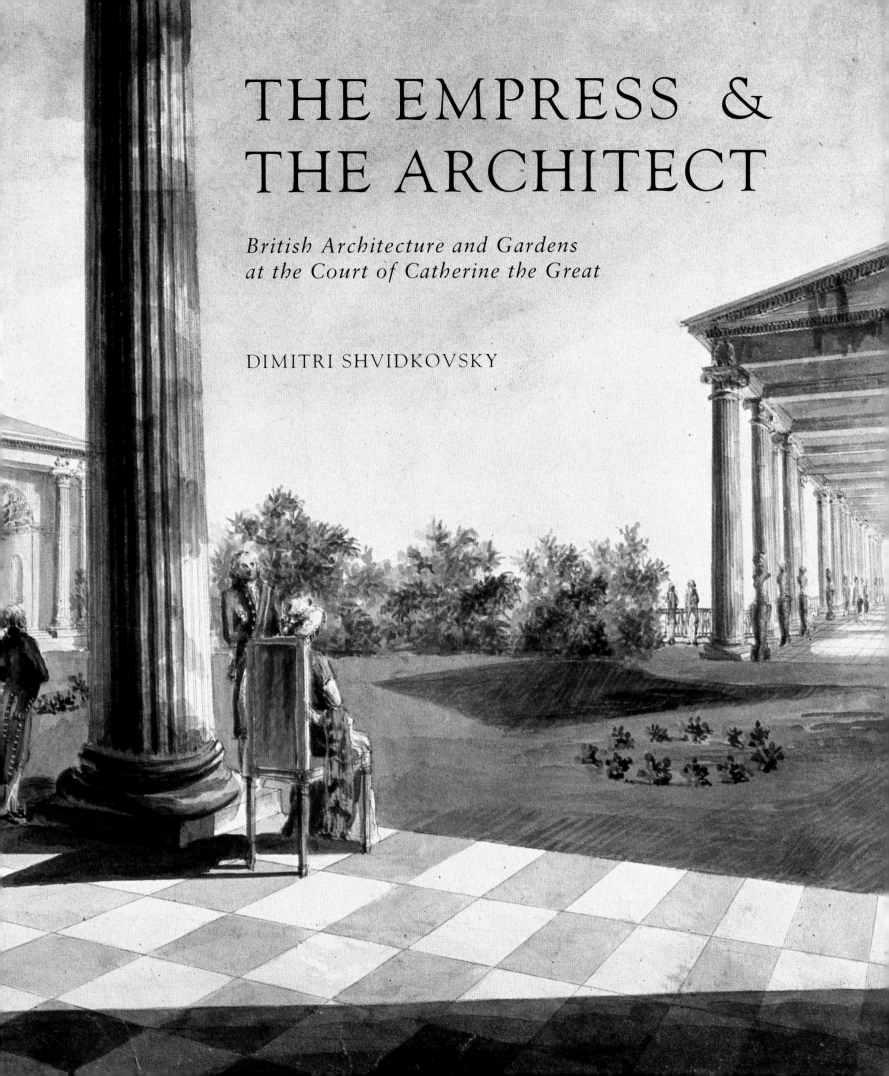

THE EMPRESS & THE ARCHITECT

*British Architecture and Gardens
at the Court of Catherine the Great*

DIMITRI SHVIDKOVSKY

Translated from the Russian. The publishers are grateful to Dr Catherine
Cooke for her work on the preparation of this book for publication, and to
the following for their assistance with various aspects of the translation:
Felicity O'Dell, Vladimir Vnukov, Julia Whitby, Robin Whitby, and
Rachel Gomme.

Colour photography by Alexander Viktorov
Designed by Gillian Malpass
Set in Linotron Bembo by Best-set Typesetter Ltd., Hong Kong
Printed in Hong Kong through World Print Ltd

Library of Congress Cataloging-in-Publication Data

Shvidkovsky, D. O. (Dmitri Olegovich)
    The empress and the architect: British architecture and gardens
at the court of Catherine the Great / Dimitri Shvidkovsky.
    Translated from the Russian.
    Includes bibliographical references and index.
    ISBN 0-300-06564-7 (alk. paper)
    1. Neoclassicism (Architecture) – Russia (Federation) – Saint
Petersburg.   2. Architecture – England – Influence.   3. Architecture,
Modern – Russia (Federation) – Saint Petersburg.   4. Cameron, Charles,
ca.1743–1812 – Criticism and interpretation.   5. Catherine II,
Empress of Russia, 1729–1796 – Dwellings – Russia (Federation) – Saint
Petersburg.   6. Architecture and society – Russia (Federation) – Saint
Petersburg.   7. Gardens, English – Russia (Federation) – Saint
Petersburg.   8. Saint Petersburg (Russia) – Buildings,
structures, etc.   I. Title.
NA1196.S54   1996
720′.947′453—dc20   95-46576
                                                          CIP

A catalogue record for this book is available from The British Library

Page i illustration: Andrei Ivanovich Chernyi, *Catherine the Great*, miniature in enamel
and copper after Feodor Rokotov, frame from the Imperial Porcelain Factory,
St Petersburg. Hermitage, St Petersburg/Bridgeman Art Library, London.

Frontispiece: Charles Cameron, *View from Catherine the Great's Apartments towards
the Hanging Garden, the Agate Pavilion and the Cameron Gallery* (detail), 1790s.

CONTENTS

Acknowledgements   vi

Introduction   1

1   Charles Cameron   11

2   The Artistic Worlds of Tsarskoye Selo   41

3   Pavlovsk   117

4   Orientalism in Russian Neo-Classical Architecture   167

5   Russian Neo-Gothic in the Age of Classicism   185

6   Adam Menelaws and William Hastie   225

Abbreviations   252

Notes   253

Bibliography   262

Index   268

ACKNOWLEDGEMENTS

I WORKED FOR MANY YEARS – about twenty – researching both the links between Russian and British architecture and gardens in the eighteenth and nineteenth centuries and also the biography of Charles Cameron. During this time I received vital help from different people and institutions both in Great Britain and in Russia. Without that help, this book would not have been possible, and I am most grateful.

I am grateful particularly for the continuous support throughout this long period of research that I received from the directors, academic council and the rest of the staff of the Institute of Theory and History of the Fine Arts of the Russian Academy of the Fine Arts.

I owe thanks to the State Hermitage, and especially to Dr Melitsa Korshunova, the Hermitage's expert in eighteenth-century architectural drawings, whose advice and help was always extremely valuable; to the Museum of Pavlovsk and all its staff, especially Dr Nina Stadnitchuk; to the Museum of Tsarskoye Selo and especially to Dr Larisa Bardovskaya; to the staff of the library of the St Petersburg Institute of Railway Engineers; and to the staff of the Shusev Museum of Architecture in Moscow. I would like to thank academician Tatiana Savarenskaya, my former teacher, the late Professor Andrei Tchegodaev, Professor Michael Libman, Professor Olga Evangulova, Dr Igor Riazantsev, architect Olga Grushevaya, and Dr Galina Otarova.

I am grateful to Alexander Viktorov, the principal photographer of the magazine *Russian Heritage*, for the excellent colour transparencies he made, and to Professor Ulij Orsa for his friendship and considerable contribution to the black-and-white photographs.

I regret that I cannot list all the people in Russia whom I would like to thank, because so many were kind and helpful that their names would fill another book.

The book could not exist without much support from Great Britain also. First, I thank Peter Hayden, former chairman of the Garden History Society, who organised my first visit to Britain and did everything to help me become acquainted with gardens all over the country and to further my research. I am grateful also to the Garden History Society itself, so many of whose members collaborated with me in my research, and most of all to Mavis Batey, MBE, president of the Society. It is impossible for me to overemphasise the support – intellectual, moral and social – that she gave me: she opened up to me the many secrets of English gardens.

The most valuable help during my research was received from Dr John Simmons of All Souls College, Oxford. My work was made possible only because of his extraordinary energy and talent for organising even the most difficult things. I dare to dedicate this book to him.

I thank 'from the whole heart', as Russians say, Sir Keith Thomas, president of Corpus Christi College, Oxford, and the fellows of Corpus Christi for their hospitality, friendship and help during my two long stays in Oxford. I am grateful also to All Souls College, Oxford, for support and hospitality, and especially to the staff of the Codrington Library.

The research and preparation of the book was supported by the Mark Fitch Fund and the Aurelius Fund, without which support the work could not have been completed. I am especially grateful to Roy Stevens.

I received substantial and very valuable help and advice from many British scholars. I owe great thanks to Professor Anthony Cross, the leading authority on British–Russian connections, for his kind collaboration over many years. Extremely important was the influence on my work of the late Sir John Summerson, as was the support of Sir Howard Colvin. I am grateful also to John Cornforth, Ian Gow, John Harris, Eileen Harris, Charles MacCalum, Robin Middleton and Andrew Saint.

Sir Donald Cameron of Lochiel, chief of the Cameron clan, gave me access to his private archive, for which I am very grateful. Likewise I thank Dr and Mrs Alexander Currie, Mr and Mrs Brian Knox, Marion Waller, Philip Hackett and Anna Rafael for their help and kindness.

I owe special gratitude to Dr Catherine Cooke of Cambridge for her help with my research and with the translation of the manuscript into English. An old friend of my family, she is someone who has made her own impact on contemporary developments in British–Russian links in architectural history, transmitting Russian architectural ideas to the West.

For all the help and friendship I have received during work on this book I shall be eternally grateful.

My family was patient and kind while I was engaged on my research. My father, the late Professor Oleg Shvidkovsky, my mother, Professor Vera Kalmykova, and my wife, Dr Ekaterina Shorban, helped me greatly in many different ways, including professionally: all the members of my family are architectural historians.

Dimitri Shvidkovsky

INTRODUCTION

THE SCENE OF ACTION IS Tsarskoye Selo, Catherine the Great's favourite country estate not far from St Petersburg. It is the middle of 1785. A summer's day. The empress is passing through her private apartments on the first floor, decorated for her by Charles Cameron who had arrived from London five years before. 'He is a master, a master who excites the imagination', she had written of him a few years earlier.[1] Wedgwood medallions are set into the walls of her luxurious rooms; silver candlesticks – the work of British craftsmen – are placed at intervals.

The empress appears on the open terrace of the Hanging Garden and, without descending to ground level, she passes into the Cameron Gallery (pl. 1), which has been designed specifically for her walks. Below is an English landscaped park, the work of John Bush, the former owner of a nursery garden in Hackney. In the distance, over the lake, is a marble bridge, just like the one on Lord Pembroke's Wilton estate. Nearer, but a little to the side, the Chinese Village and the pagoda now being built are in the spirit of William Chambers's constructions for Kew Gardens. The canal beyond the village and the little bridge over it are based on the drawings of William Halfpenny.

In the gallery there is a long row of bronze statues of ancient statesmen and philosophers. Stopping in front of Demosthenes, Catherine declares to her secretary Khrapovitsky that the person she would consider equivalent to Demosthenes today would be the British politician Charles Fox, and that his portrait, too, should be in the gallery. 'Pitt will be jealous', she adds.[2]

This evocation, assembled from a variety of historical sources, suggests how many elements of British culture were present in Russia in the eighteenth century. Moreover, only Tsarskoye Selo has been described, and only a small part of that. Not yet mentioned is the nearby palace of Prince Potemkin at Bablovo, which resembles Walpole's Strawberry Hill at Twickenham, or the ideal city of Sofiya, erected by Charles Cameron on the edge of the park of Tsarskoye Selo. Neither must the neighbouring Pavlovsk be forgotten – another large Russian estate created by Cameron and closely linked with the Neo-Palladian tradition running from Chiswick House to Kedleston Hall; or those Cameron interiors that are comparable to the work of the Adam brothers.

As well as examples of the English classical tradition, there are numerous constructions in the 'Chinese' or the 'gothic' taste in Russia: hundreds of buildings, including the largest ensemble of exotic architecture in eighteenth-century Europe, at Tsaritsyno near Moscow. Its 150-metre façade demonstrates on a massive scale the linking of medieval, ancient and fantastic motifs on which was based the Gothic language of the eighteenth century, invented, according to Sir John Summerson, by William Kent.[3] Nor is Tsaritsyno the only large creation of romantic architecture in Russia. More than ten constructions of a comparable size either still stand or are preserved in plans, most important among them being the ensemble at Khodynka; the Konkovo and Bulatnikovo estates and the Petrovsky castle near Moscow; and the Chesmensky Palace near St Petersburg.[4] It is important to remember also all the 'English embellishments'

1 Tsarskoye Selo: Cameron Gallery. Perspective drawing, 1790s.

1

to be found on almost every one of Russia's numerous country estates: the chivalric towers, the stables in the form of castles, the various kinds of pavilions dotted about parks as hermits' huts, dairies and ice-houses, and the summerhouses resembling mosques. All these bear some connection with sketches of buildings at Kew or Stowe, Wilton or Chiswick. Almost all of them, either through ignorance or lack of sympathy, have been undervalued by architectural historians, or, even worse, have been consigned to the backyard of Russian architectural history and denied a role in the history of European architecture. As we look increasingly to the cultural links across borders, such a position is, it seems to me, unacceptable.

Of course, it is not easy to represent the character, evolution and significance of the connections between British and Russian architecture. The researcher is faced with an unusually colourful mosaic consisting of an enormous amount of information of varying significance. The temptation is to represent each link between the two countries as accidental, and this has frequently occurred. Thus we hear of an illustrated book published in London falling by chance into the hands of a Russian architect; or of a landowner just happening to have brought to his attention a dinner service depicting British buildings; while another might have an English wife or friend. While I accept the obvious truth that any example of a building on Russian soil connected with an British model or idea must have had some specific source, the main argument of this book is that the establishment of close links between Britain and Russia in the late eighteenth century was a natural element of European cultural history, and was indeed essential to its development.

These links were first forged at the end of the 1760s, and they were at their strongest at the end of the century. They continued to develop until the 1830s, when their character changed. Thus they affected the whole period of neo-classicism in Russian architecture, and the relationship changed only at the point when the eclectic was established in Russian architecture. This change in no way prevented interaction with British architecture, but British ideas mingled with the abundance of other ideas characteristic of the period of many styles. The British influence was from then on only one of many.[5]

By contrast with this later period, the British influence on the architecture of Russian classicism is characterised by a sharp individualism, which clearly distinguishes it from other parallel developments in Russian architecture at the end of the eighteenth and the beginning of the nineteenth centuries. The particular charm it brought to Russian architecture derived from the fact that the buildings that resulted seem to speak in their own, special language. The era of classicism produced such magnificent work as the ensembles of Tsarskoye Selo, Pavlovsk, Tsaritsyno, the Chesmensky Palace and many others. The period under consideration, from the 1760s to the 1830s, is one of the most interesting epochs in the development of Russian architecture.

It is important to emphasise that the influence of British architectural culture came to Russia through several quite different means. The first and simplest of these was through the direct imitation of buildings or architectural elements that Russian architects had seen in plans, drawings, paintings or engravings. There are, however, fewer such examples in Russia than in many of the European countries where the British idea of the landscaped garden with its architectural ornaments penetrated. Among such works of direct imitation by Russian architects are the wrought-iron gates in Tsarskoye Selo, created to Yury Velten's design in 1780 in accordance with sketches published by Charles Over;[6] the Chinese cross-bridge on the same estate built by Ilya Neyelov to J. and W. Halfpenny's design;[7] and the mosque-summerhouse erected at Count Chernyshev's Yaropolets estate to an English design.[8] Such examples were not a rarity in Russian architectural practice, but they were certainly not in the majority. More direct links were of far greater significance.

The second, extremely important level of interaction was through British architects who came to work in Russia. Without question the leading role here was played by Charles Cameron, a Londoner of Scottish origin, who is one of the greatest architects of Russian classicism. Cameron gave Russian classicism a new character, introducing into it a fanatical passion for antiquity. He created a special mood in his imaginative interpretation of classicism. His buildings and gardens exerted such a powerful influence on those who saw them that they were enraptured and, consciously or unconsciously, succeeding generations of architects in Russia were influenced by them. Even such a scholarly and self-confident architect as Giacomo Quarenghi, who arrived in Russia at the same time as Cameron, was fascinated by his works, which he described as 'as splendid as they are original'.[9]

Of the younger generation of classicist architects, it was Andrei Voronikhin, architect of Kazan cathedral in St Petersburg, who felt a particular enthusiasm for Cameron's work. He repeated the design of the Cameron Gallery at Tsarskoye Selo in his Stroganov *dacha* on the Chernaya river near St Petersburg.[10] Cameron was admired also by the great decorator, park-builder and architect, Pietro Gonzago. After Cameron's death Gonzago wrote in a letter to Tsar Alexander I: 'I am submitting to Your Majesty the request that I might have the honour to serve you as architect in place of Mr Cameron who is no longer in this life and whose erudition and library have enabled me to replace him. I dare to claim . . . that, if I cannot compare with the late Mr Cameron in talent, I am his equal . . . in zeal.'[11]

In his lifetime as well as after his death, Cameron's talent was highly valued in his adopted country. In one record of the early nineteenth century he is referred to as one of the three or four best architects in Russia.[12]

However, more surprising than the high opinion held of Cameron by his contemporaries is the fact that his fame has remained constant in Russia ever since his death in 1812. The works of the first Russian art scholars in the nineteenth century drew readers' particular attention to the perfection of the Cameron Gallery at Tsarskoye Selo.[13] In 1885 one of Russia's first serious architectural historians, P. Petrov, wrote an article entitled, 'The significance of the architect, Cameron';[14] at that time articles about individual architects working in Russia were extremely rare. At the end of the nineteenth and beginning of the twentieth centuries, with the renewed interest in neoclassicism, such architects as Ivan Fomin and Nikolai Lansere adopted Cameron's legacy in their own works.[15] In the Soviet period, particularly from the 1930s to 1950s, when Socialist Realism specified 'a critical assimilation of the architectural heritage', Cameron's name was synonymous with the highest precision in the reproduction of antique forms. This is remembered by many Soviet architects of the older generation to this day.

All this makes Charles Cameron the central figure in the account that follows; but he was not the only British architect working in Russia during this period. William Hastie and Adam Menelaws, both Scots, answered Cameron's advertisement for craftsmen to join him at Tsarskoye Selo, and both earned considerable reputations in their own right in the early nineteenth century. They, too, occupy a significant place in the history of Russian architecture. Moreover, although their careers may have been less eventful than Cameron's, they were happier. Certainly Cameron's is the finer work, but Hastie and Menelaws built a great deal, and their roles were very varied.

Hastie became first and foremost a town planner and the creator of standard designs for residential buildings which were very widely applied. At the beginning of the nineteenth century he occupied a key place in Russian urban planning by virtue of his high position in the Ministry of Internal Affairs, where he dealt with the drafting of town plans. Suffice it to say that it was he who put his signature to dozens of master plans for various settlements. His designs for Yekaterinoslav and Tomsk are famous. In addition, he worked out no less than a hundred designs for model houses, and these were the only ones that Russian law permitted to be built in Russian towns. Hastie's greatest achievement was the creation of a new plan for Moscow, following its destruction during the invasion of Napoleon's great army in 1812.[16]

While Hastie consistently developed the principles of strict classicism in all areas of his architectural activity, Menelaws had very different passions. In the history of Russian architecture the figure of Adam Menelaws stands on the border between classicism and the eclectic style, with a leaning towards the latter. He was primarily a court craftsman, a creator of garden pavilions and small palaces. At Tsarskoye Selo Menelaws designed buildings in Egyptian, medieval and Turkish styles. His most intriguing creation is the intimate little palace of Nicholas I, called the Kottedzh, the Cottage, in the picturesque Alexandria Park.[17] His work is interesting, but it lacks the range and brilliance of Cameron's.

A somewhat different line of influence on Russian architecture came through British craftsmen. Notable here was David Cunningham,[18] who worked with Cameron on the construction of the Admiralty buildings in St Petersburg at the beginning of the nineteenth century.

Much more significant was the whole galaxy of English gardeners who were employed in the famous imperial parks. The best known of these are the Tsarskoye Selo gardeners, John Bush and his son, Joseph.[19] From 1779 they were engaged in creating the park at Tsarskoye Selo, particularly the planting and care of the flower gardens. They were not responsible for any architectural work. There does exist a plan of Tsarskoye Selo made probably by Joseph Bush, but it is a depiction of what had already been built rather than a working design for the builders.[20] It hardly justifies any claim that Bush determined the structure of the park or the disposition of its pavilions. Nevertheless, the Bush household, which was based in a wing attached to the Orangery in Tsarskoye Selo, was one of the most interesting little islands of English culture in Russia at the end of the eighteenth century. The hospitable home and its virtuous mistress, distinguished by her culinary talent, attracted many guests,[21] including the two British Physicians in Ordinary to the imperial household, Thomas Dimsdale and John Rogerson.[22] Bush was not only a friend of the gloomy Cameron, who lived nearby, but he gave him his daughter, Catherine, in marriage.[23]

Enjoying perhaps greater freedom in his work than the Bush father and son did was James Meader, a gardener in the park of the English Palace at Peterhof. Meader was one of the most significant popularisers of British ideas on landscaped parks in Russia. In England he had been the gardener at Alnwick Castle in Northumberland.[24] He came to St Petersburg in May 1779 and continued working for ten years at Peterhof. Drawings of his compositions for the park still exist.[25] This ensemble, which has not been preserved, was conceived by Catherine the Great herself, together with several other parks, and was the result of her passion for the English garden which manifested itself at the end of the 1770s. Quarenghi started to build a comparatively modest Palladian palace here in 1781. Apparently his work did not stimulate the empress's imagination as strongly as did Cameron's luxurious creations. The palace did not receive much attention, its construction was long drawn out, and it was completed only shortly before Catherine's death in 1796.[26] Work in the park, however, was carried out with great intensity, so that it became one of the first landscaped gardens in Russia.

The creation of the park at Gatchina Palace near St Petersburg was primarily the responsibility of John Bush and two other British gardeners, James Hackett and his assistant James Sparrow.[27] In 1765 Catherine the Great gave this estate to her favourite, Prince Grigory Orlov, who had been one of the prime movers in removing her husband Peter III from the throne and in murdering him in 1762. John Bush worked here from 1779 to 1783. After Orlov's death Gatchina came into the possession of the heir to the throne, Grand Duke Paul Petrovich. In his time Hackett and Sparrow worked on the garden with the German, F. Helmholtz. Not all of Gatchina park was executed in the English style. The Island of Love and the Konnetabl and Sylvia areas, for example, were reminiscent of the Prince de Condé's park at Chantilly, and there were elements taken from Italian and Dutch gardens. However, the central part with its large lake with picturesque banks and an entire archipelago of islands was the work of Bush, Hackett and Sparrow.

During Paul's reign as tsar (1796–1801) yet another landscaped park was created at Gatchina, called Prioratsky. This name was given in honour of the Prioratsky Palace, the headquarters of the Great Priory of the Russian Order of Malta, whose title of Grand Master the tsar took for himself. Unfortunately, it has not proved possible to find detailed information about the work of the English gardeners at Gatchina.

The role of two other natives of Britain, Francis Reed (or possibly Reid or Read) and John Munro, also remains obscure. They were summoned from England by the tsarine no later than 1782, to work on the park of the imperial palace of Tsaritsyno near Moscow.[28] Work had begun on the ensemble nine years before, and much had been completed in the park. The Russian architect of the palace, Vasily Bazhenov, wanted to preserve large areas of the regular garden which had existed there in the first half of the eighteenth century, but he also wanted to recreate other parts in the English style.[29] He greeted the appearance of the Englishmen with considerable lack of enthusiasm, even with annoyance, seeing them as further reinforcement of the English influence: 'Over a nine-year period [Tsaritsyno] has become so attired in pleasant glades . . . that it would hardly be possible to find such a place in England itself.'[30] Nevertheless Reed and Munro continued to work here for several years until they were replaced by the German, K. Ungebauer.

Many legends abound about the gardener of Prince Potemkin. Potemkin was one of Catherine's favourites and the most powerful Russian grandee at the end of the eighteenth century. He had a talent for administering grandiose projects and was in charge of the reconstruction of all southern Russia. At the same time, his life was characterised by wild and extravagant behaviour. He would send officers to Paris to get shoes for some beautiful lady, or make them rush by post-chaise across the whole of Russia with a barrel of cucumbers marinaded to a particular recipe; on the other hand, in a rage he could trample on a diamond necklace of fabulous value. Reflections of this unusual personality also fell on his gardener. Potemkin acquired the very best for himself: he was served by a pupil of Lancelot (Capability) Brown, named William Gould. Gould frequently had to contend with the unexpected. An English traveller, Sir John Carr, told how Potemkin, when journeying in the Ukraine, was accompanied by Gould and several hundred workers.[31] Wherever they stopped, it was said, the prince had a collapsable palace erected, and, in the course of twenty-four hours, an English garden with picturesquely winding paths would be created. In fact, this was not the exact truth. Potemkin had the responsibility of building temporary palaces and gardens during the course of Catherine the Great's journey through southern Russia with Joseph II, the Holy Roman Emperor. Moreover, it was not only palaces and parks that were constructed: entire villages, with full facilities, were erected. The phrase 'Potemkin's villages' became synonymous with the notion of deception through theatrical effects.

Potemkin had also acquired the title of Tauride Prince after the unification of the Crimea (formerly Tauria) with Russia. Gould was given the task of creating the garden of the Tauride Palace, which was built by Ivan Starov at the end of the 1780s in the suburbs of St Petersburg. The park itself was not large, but it was full of exotic plants. The indoor Winter Garden was particularly luxuriant. It could be entered from an

enormous hall of columns, and its roof was supported by more columns, in the form of palms. The heating stoves were concealed and the walls disguised, all to create an illusion of a romantic southern landscape. At every turn the paths revealed new surprises: a Greek statue, a pool with amazing fish, a huge crystal vase. It was Gould who was responsible for the organisation and upkeep of all these effects and for the welfare of the great variety of exotic plants. Without doubt his activity was remarkable, but the less extravagant compositions of the Bushes at Tsarskoye Selo, of Cameron at Pavlovsk, or of Meader at Peterhof exerted a more significant influence on the development of the Russian garden.

English architects and masters of park design were to be found scattered in numerous parts of Russia. Their relationship with the landowners and their position in state service were equally diverse, just as they themselves were very different types of people. Yet their work, almost without exception, was connected to one specific and relatively limited phenomenon in the development of Russian architecture: establishing the architectural culture of the Russian country house in the era of neo-classicism. All the component parts of this new conception of the stately home were affected by the British craftsmen: the formation of a new house-type for the great rural estate, the establishment and development of a picturesque garden and the working out of a system of architectural embellishments for a landscaped park. In these areas, thanks to the practical strengths of the British architects and gardeners, works were created which provided a mature expression of quite specific artistic traditions.

As far as the main house was concerned, these traditions called for neo-Palladian, of which the most impressive embodiment in Russia was Cameron's palace at Pavlovsk. After this, estates with a principal building of similar structure and character began to appear all over the country. The most famous of these are Lyalichi near Bryansk, Marino near Orel, Gorenki and Yaropolets near Moscow, and Znamenskoye-Rayok and Nikolskoye in the Tver region. All adhered to the traditional neo-Palladian format: the main house with the obligatory formal portico, and wings connected to the centre by a colonnade or passages; the entrance to the estate often marked by small, 'feudal' towers in a neo-gothic style, which was also a sign of a particular architectural orientation. In the late eighteenth and early nineteenth centuries such building complexes were associated in the Russian consciousness with English estates, and this association was interwoven with curious tales about Anglophile landowners. An account of one such estate, Nikolskoye in the Kazan region, is characteristic. It was described by the writer Sergei Aksakov in his memoirs of his childhood:

> A stone two-storeyed building connected by colonnades to its wings provided one side of a square courtyard with round towers at each corner . . . I had never seen anything like it and so . . . now I have added to the reality of the house which lives in my memory descriptions that I have read of knights' castles or of stately homes of English lords . . . the owner loved to boast of his house, its garden and all its buildings . . . 'I've got pigs here, the like of which you've never seen; I brought them from England in a hut on wheels. Now they have their own house. Would you like to have a look?'[32]

Such an account reflects the typical enjoyment of wit and eccentricity in their parks which Russian landowners associated with Englishness.

Without doubt, the creation of a new relationship between the stately home and its park was enormously significant. In Russian park art the principle of reflecting nature achieved classic perfection in the Slavyanka valley in Cameron's park at Pavolvsk, and in the English park at Peterhof created by Meader. Ideas about the landscaped garden quickly spread throughout Russia. The empress herself was their main propagandist. She even tried herself to translate books about British parks.[33] But it was a humble

2 Pavlovsk: the palace and the Centaur Bridge.

person with no elevated rank or wealth who did most to define the characteristics of the landscaped park. This was Andrei Bolotov, who served as manager on the Bogoroditsk estate of Count Bobrinsky, the illegitimate son of Catherine the Great and Count Grigory Orlov. Bolotov created a magnificent park and a nursery for plants, and he acted as consultant for numerous neighbours. Furthermore, thanks to the initiative of Nikolai Novikov, a major figure of the Russian Enlightenment and a prominent personality in Moscow's masonic lodges, he published the journal, *Ekonomicheskiy magazin*. This reported on the most famous gardens around the world, paying particular attention to those in England, and gave advice on planning and decoration as well as practical tips for the creation of a garden.[34] In addition to Bolotov's journal, several other works on British gardens were published in Russia at the end of the eighteenth century.[35] An essential feature of the British garden was its architectural decoration, which was characterised by a diversity of style. This was a principal cause of the taste for the exotic in Russian eighteenth-century garden building.

The impact of the work of the British in Russia is not likely to have been so significant, however, had the ideas they introduced not been developed by Russian architects. The native development of ideas that had arisen in Britain is the third aspect of the link between the two architectural cultures. The seeds sown by the British in Russia bore original fruit there, original both in its abundance and in its aesthetic nature. Drawings in British publications of buildings in the Chinese or neo-gothic style stimulated the creation of a wide variety of structures. The fashion for the oriental and the fascination with the medieval were developed with a scope and originality in Russia that it would not have been possible to predict from looking at the first chinoiserie summerhouses or at the knight's pavilions in the imperial parks near St Petersburg. The impact of early romantic fantasies on Russian estates at the end of the eighteenth and beginning of the nineteenth centuries was truly astonishing and led to the creation of new buildings seemingly far removed from their initial evocations. This was true not only for the neo-gothic and Chinese styles, but also for neo-Palladian classicism. Behind the British ideas which stimulated the first signs of change in the architectural culture of Russia from the 1760s to the 1780s lies a larger process, however. It is quite wrong to discuss these particular Anglo-Russian contacts out of context. On one hand they must be seen within the general progress of architectural links between the two countries, and on the other within the overall European development of architecture in this period.

The relationship between the British and Russian cultures in the eighteenth century has long attracted the attention of scholars. At the end of the nineteenth century books were written about the British community in Russia,[36] but research has concentrated mainly on the field of literature.[37] Only Anthony Cross, in his fundamental research into the human movements and interconnections of this period, has looked at the cultural relationship as a whole.[38]

The history of European architecture has undervalued the significance of Anglo-Russian connections. This has been the case for a century and a half. Many works dedicated to Russian classical architecture have maintained that the inspiration for the style came from French theory and practice.[39] This view has been so frequently postulated that even well-known evidence of the Russian use of the achievements of British architecture have been misrepresented. One clear example of this is the attitude to Charles Cameron, whose sympathies for the antique have long been greatly over-emphasised at the expense of his connection with the British neo-Palladian tradition.[40]

The links between Russian and French art in the eighteenth and early nineteenth centuries cannot be denied. The work of architects Vallin de la Mothe and Thomas de Tomon in St Petersburg, the fact that the major masters of Russian classicism,

Bazhenov and Starov, studied with Charles de Wailly, as did Zakharov with Chalgrin, the popularity of the Empire style in Russia – all bear witness to a French orientation in Russian classicism. The dramatist Griboyedov's aphorism about the combination of 'French with the Nizhny Novgorod accent' is true in the field of architecture.[41]

While I do not seek to deny a role for French ideas in Russia, it is my view that they were little more than a fashion. The essence of Russian architecture in the eighteenth century developed along a path quite different from that of French architecture. The latter is characterised by a peaceful, measured development of classicism. The seventeenth century in France had formed a powerful frontier between the remainders of the French medieval tradition, which had persisted in the sixteenth century, and the architectural projects of the reigns of Louis XV and Louis XVI, of the Revolution and the Empire. At this time in France there was neither a serious fusion nor a counterposing of the baroque and the classical.

A completely different situation developed in Russia. The architecture of the late Middle Ages was not only close to the Russian architecture of the seventeenth century, but it was still alive for at least three-quarters of that century. The stylistic chaos of Peter the Great's time, when traditional Russian and various European traditions were interwoven, found fruit in the synthetic character of the Russian baroque, which succeeded in uniting all the characteristics of Russian architecture of the modern age. In the 1750s baroque triumphed in Russia, and was certainly showing no signs of stylistic exhaustion. Numerous examples demonstrate how it came splendidly to life in combination with the traditional Russian style as, for instance, in the city buildings of Moscow or Kiev. It was a demonstration of that tendency for a synthesis of different stylistic forms which is incompatible with the uncompromising nature of the renaissance. The long Russian renaissance, which began with Italianisms in church and fortress architecture in the fifteenth and sixteenth centuries, continued to emerge in odd places in the eighteenth century but never became a flood that could cut across the path of medieval traditions. Only the Russian neo-classicism of the late eighteenth and early nineteenth centuries managed fully to achieve this. Even this, however, did not become a Russian 'renaissance'. Indeed, everything was against this: the general European context, the evolution of the relationship with the antique at that time and, more significantly, the cultural assimilation of renaissance forms in architecture. A long 'hidden renaissance' in Russia (not a rebirth of the antique but a transition from the architecture of the Middle Ages to that of modern times) was crowned in the eighteenth century by the absorption of neo-renaissance influences, above all of Palladian neo-classicism of the British type.

Another important point must be made. In many of the classicist works of Bazhenov, Velten and Neyelov, the baroque and rococo traditions manifest themselves explicitly in buildings adopting British ideas of chinoiserie and neo-gothic.

Thus, it appears that the Russian brand of classicism in architecture is marked by its highly significant neo-renaissance characteristics as well as by a general complexity of stylistic composition. This is what mainly distinguishes it from French classicism and what, in my opinion, brings it close to the neo-classicism of Britain.

It was on British soil that neo-classicism displayed both a very strong Palladian character and features of understated baroque and rococo, while still fitting into an aesthetic environment where medieval traditions continued to predominate. The role of neo-Palladianism, and of neo-renaissance characteristics in general, has long been acknowledged by architectural historians. It has also not infrequently been said that the exotic styles born in Britain had close links with the rococo. Thus drawings by British classicists such as the Adam brothers, made before they became familiar with the original antique monuments, show the use of baroque motifs at an early stage in the development of British neo-classicism.

To understand the significance of Anglo-Russian architectural links, the typological proximity of British and Russian neo-classicism is essential. It explains how the ideas of the British masters became, as Nikolai Lansere described them, a 'link in the entire chain' of Russian architecture.[42] The aim of this book is to provide for the first time a detailed study of the emergence and development of this link.

From these introductory remarks about the general character of the connections between Russian and British architecture, let us turn to specific buildings and ensembles, created in the 'Golden Age' of Anglo-Russian architectural associations, the era of neo-classicism. We shall look first at the work of Charles Cameron, then at the contemporaneous phenomena of neo-gothic and orientalism and, finally, at the somewhat later work of Cameron's pupils.

Chapter One

CHARLES CAMERON

3 Alexander Orlovsky, *Charles Cameron*, 1809.

THE STORY OF CHARLES CAMERON (pl. 3), the builder of the imperial residence at Pavlovsk and of the Roman baths in Tsarskoye Selo, and the Chief Architect to the Russian Admiralty, is an unusual one.

It was many years ago that one famous scholar of this period declared, 'The incognito of Charles Cameron, which he himself created and which time has so jealously preserved, must eventually be exposed.'[1] Nothing surprises the historian of the age of Cagliostro and Casanova. But among all the disguises and concealments of identity that we encounter in eighteenth-century Russia – a count with an invented name who turns out to be the emperor himself; a grandee possessing the gift of evoking shadows of the past who is exposed as a charlatan; a darkly dressed traveller delayed by chance at a post-station who is revealed as the grand-master of a mysterious order – the incognito of Charles Cameron was among the boldest and most successful. It outlived its creator by more than two centuries, and it has only recently been uncovered. It was so solidly established that even today there is pressure for its preservation. Our investigation into this intrigue will probe not one but two, possibly three, lives: those of Charles Cameron and his namesakes.

Cameron's career is not only interesting, it forms an important page in the history of Russian art. It would be hard to overestimate this architect's significance. Since the nineteenth century his name has stood as one of the ten great masters of Russian classicism. The Cameron Gallery at Tsarskoye Selo is the only imperial construction in Russia to bear the name of its creator.

The admiration his work continues to evoke echoes the view of his contemporaries: 'I am captivated by Cameron the architect, by birth a Jacobite, educated in Rome, he is known thanks to his work on ancient baths, he has a wonderful mind, afire with inspiration.'[2] These lines from a letter sent by Catherine the Great to Voltaire in the summer of 1781 give the elements of Cameron's life history as he presented it when introducing himself to the empress. From the same source we learn that the architect told his Russian acquaintances that he had in Rome been at 'the home of the Pretender'[3] and that he was 'Miss Jenny's nephew'.[4] This was enough – he had a precise social and political pedigree.

Jenny Cameron had became famous during the 1745–6 uprising of the Scots on behalf of the Stuarts. According to legend, she had brought to the Jacobite camp two hundred and fifty soldiers and a herd of cattle. She was then presented to the Pretender's elder son and won his heart.[5] It was told how she had accompanied her lover at the head of the division of soldiers. A pamphlet 'published by the decision of Parliament' in 1746, intended as an attack upon her, nevertheless described her as 'the Amazon of the North', who bore all hardships for the sake of love. Her memoirs, which appeared in London,[6] were eventually revealed as forgeries, but, published in several languages, they spread Miss Jenny's fame throughout Europe, and word of her reached St Petersburg. It was this lady whom the architect named as his aunt when he arrived in Russia and presented himself to Catherine the Great. The empress informed her correspondents with joy that a representative of this famous Scottish family had joined her service.

Jenny Cameron certainly had a relative called Charles Cameron. He was the son of her cousin, Donald Cameron, known as 'Gentle Lochiel',[7] who had played an important role in the 1745–6 uprising, commanding the rebel troops at Culloden in April 1746. After their defeat, the Jacobite forces had broken up. With his wife and his sons Donald Cameron had fled to France where his status among the emigrés was high, and he was welcomed at Versailles. After the deaths of his father and brothers, Charles Cameron of Lochiel became the head of the clan and returned to his native land.

According to the architect himself, he was an aristocrat, a representative of an ancient family who had suffered for his devotion to the old dynasty. As Charles Edward Stuart, the Pretender to the British throne, had lived in Rome for a long time, it would have been natural for Cameron to spend time there. He studied the antiquities and met Winckelmann, Piranesi, Hubert Robert and Clérisseau (some of the latter's drawings, coincidentally, have ended up in Russia). The association with Miss Jenny gave Cameron a romantic aura. At the Russian court he was certainly accorded different treatment from that usually shown to ordinary craftsmen. And the architect's behaviour towards Russian officials corresponded to what might be expected from one of aristocratic status: he totally ignored them. Some scholars have actually cited this as evidence of the architect's high birth. The image of Cameron as the architect-aristocrat has been consolidated by numerous works on the history of Russian art, in studies by Igor Grabar, Nikolai Lansere and Vladimir Taleporovsky, and in encyclopedias and textbooks.[8]

On close scrutiny, however, contradictions appear in the details of Cameron's biography. A London address appears on the title-page of his book *The Baths of the Romans*,[9] which was published in 1772. Charles Cameron of Lochiel, however, would have been in exile in that year. Moreover, it is strange that the head of the clan could not draw the Cameron of Lochiel arms accurately in his drawing album.[10] Documents preserved in British archives disclose that there existed at this time an architect bearing the same name.[11] There is much to suggest that it is in fact he who carried out the famous building work on the imperial residences in Russia, rather than the aristocratic emigré.

The origins of this second Charles Cameron were far from exalted. He was the son of Walter Cameron, a London building contractor with an average-sized business who also occupied himself with land speculation. How can it be proved that this, rather than the aristocratic Cameron, was the architect to Catherine the Great? Documents discovered by Isobel Rae offer a vital piece of evidence: they show that Charles Cameron's father, Walter, regularly paid land rent for a house in White Horse Street in London beside Lord Egremont's estate. This is the address given on the title-page of *The Baths of the Romans*. The romantic origins of Charles Cameron, the empress's architect, suddenly collapse. It is evident that the son of a member of the Carpenters' Company represented himself as an aristocrat and a rebel, and deceived the empress. He managed to maintain this fiction for thirty years, throughout his career in Russia.

But how did he come to be so familiar with the details of the life of his famous namesake? Why did he decide to put himself forward as a representative of the Cameron clan?

The full story of the fate of Charles Cameron of Lochiel is unclear. Biographical dictionaries record that in the mid-1770s he returned to Britain from exile and attempted to establish a normal relationship with the ruling dynasty. To this end a military company of members of the clan was formed, and it was proposed that this company should serve the Crown. However, when Cameron fell ill, his soldiers were recruited by the French. He hurried to Glasgow to dissuade them from this course of action, but then disappeared. It must be remembered that the situation was dangerous for him: he could, after all, have been accused of having formed a rebel army. A rumour circulated that he had died.[12]

In 1785, after the Jacobites had been granted an amnesty, a book was published in Rome called *Memori per le Belle Arti*.[13] It was signed by a Charles Cameron. Only a few copies of this publication have survived, and there is only one in Russia. Nevertheless, interest in the work of Charles Cameron the architect was always great, and attention was therefore paid to the *Memori*. However, it seems curious that the creator of Russian palaces should write of Italy but give no information about the buildings at Pavlovsk or Tsarskoye Selo. In spite of this, the book has routinely been included in the list of works by the architect, and the enigma surrounding its authorship was for a long time forgotten. That was unfortunate, for it is this book that reveals one of the most original pages in the life story we are pursuing.

If the *Memori* is read carefully, it becomes clear that the architect who worked in Russia could not have written it. It would have been quite impossible to have followed trivial events in the life of Rome, to have met Italian poets, to have visited Dante's grave in Ravenna and, at the same time, to have been involved continuously in construction work a thousand miles away. Who then was the author of the book?

Despite the book's genre – it is, after all, a set of memoirs – it contains few autobiographical details. It can be concluded only that the author was distinguished and British, with a broad education, well acquainted with Italian culture and familiar with a circle of experts in Roman antiquities, of prelates and artists. He was deeply imbued with the spirit of Italian art, as befitted one who was educated and had lived for a long time in Rome. Among the very few British names in the *Memori* is that of James Byres. Byres, a Scottish laird, was a Jacobite who had emigrated young in 1746 and was close to the court of the Pretender. He was interested in art and was an architect and draughtsman.[14] He was also a great expert in Roman antiquities, which he showed to foreign visitors, among whom was Princess Dashkova,[15] president of the St Petersburg Academy of Sciences.

It seems that the author of the *Memori* knew of the existence of his namesake, the architect Charles Cameron.[16] He speaks of him very respectfully in connection with his work on the study of baths. The paths of these two men could have crossed in Rome in 1768, when they were both living there; they certainly had similar interests – the *Memori* includes a special section on the excavations of the baths of Diocletian, Caracalla, Titus and others.

Recently, with the kind help of Sir Donald Cameron of Lochiel, new documents relating to the early years of Charles Cameron the architect have come to light (through references found by Mrs M. Smith). These documents add even more strikingly to the details already known of this complex story.

In a letter of 30 May 1753, written by Charles Rainsford, Deputy Lieutenant of the Tower of London, to Lord Cornwallis, it is stated that, on the evening before his execution, the famous rebel Dr Archibald Cameron (who had attended upon the Pretender during the rebellion of 1745–6) had made a last wish, to see a friend. This friend was admitted to the prisoner's cell, and he was, according to Rainsford, Walter Cameron, 'a carpenter, a house-keeper in Piccadilly'[17] – in other words, the father of the architect Charles Cameron. Dr Cameron apparently asked Walter to take care of his wife and youngest son (called, it seems, Charles, as were the sons of so many supporters of Charles Edward Stuart). Charles Cameron, the future architect, would also have been a young boy at this period, so it is possible that the two boys spent some time together in the house in Piccadilly.

The later life of Dr Archibald Cameron's youngest son is not easy to reconstruct, although he seems to have spent some of it in France – where he published in 1760 his book *Histoire de Jean de Calais* – and some of it in Italy. It is most probable that he was in fact the author of the *Memori per le belle arti*, discussed above, and this would explain why Charles Cameron the architect is mentioned in its pages. The relationship between these two men adds yet another dimension to the convoluted tale of family origins and personal biography as told by the architect to Catherine the Great.

What then do we know of the architect? What were his life and work really like before he travelled to Russia? He was born in the mid-1740s into a family with an average income. At first his life was fortunate and unexceptional. It was intended that he should inherit his father's building business, and accordingly, in 1760, his father prepared the necessary documents at the Carpenters' Company, formalising their relationship as master and pupil.[18] Everything was proceeding as expected, but then something caused Charles Cameron to set his life on a different course. He dropped his studies and never became a member of the Carpenters' Company. We do not know enough about him to attribute the change in direction to specific experiences, but there is one document that sheds some light on his mood and spirit.

This is an album of drawings which has been preserved from 1764 (pls 4–15).[19] In it are collected the first of Cameron's known works, somewhat over a hundred of them, and they are highly unusual for a pupil of the Carpenters' Company. There is a clear contrast between the everyday life of a building contractor's son and the intense images of the drawings which immerse the viewer into the artistic worlds evoked by their author. Here he is not an architect, but a master of applied art.

The large-format album is bound in leather and decorated with gold lettering. Some pages carry depictions of bowls, vases and lamps in baroque, rococo and classical forms. On one there is a goblet. It takes the form of a demon's head or perhaps that of a bad-tempered ancient god, one of those not marked by beauty, such as Silvanus or Pan. The misshapen face has crooked features: angry eyebrows, eyes squinting in rage, teeth bared. At the ends of the dishevelled beard are various berries and grasses. On the head

4   Charles Cameron, vase. Drawing from the 1764 album.

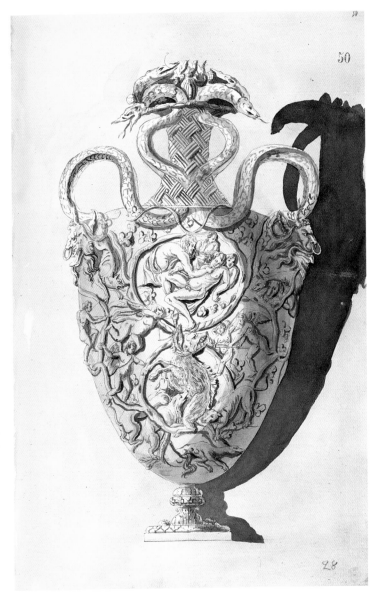

5 (above left) Charles Cameron, goblet. Drawing from the 1764 album.

6 (above right) Charles Cameron, vase. Drawing from the 1764 album.

is a helmet decorated with dancing devils and running hounds. All this overflows into a faded rainbow of colours close to earth tones. It seems like some strange flight of fantasy by a baroque sculptor or a carver of later antiquity. Cameron has given great life to these figures and satiated his imagination with demonic shapes.

On other pages we can see a bowl in the form of a cupid carrying a huge shell (a curly-haired little boy with small wings), different lamps with handles entwined with snakes, or a vase in the shape of a boot which, instead of a buckle, has a funny head with plaits. On one page is a tripod fixed on a massive pedestal with curved consoles. It is supporting a flat bowl. Winding around it is an unpleasantly realistic snake and some kinds of animals, 'devilish' squirrels or lizards with supple bodies and long tails, are clambering inside. There is an inscription just legible on the pedestal below which exclaims, 'Oh, poor Sterne'.

The last pages show pilasters with arabesques; these are more classical as their definite form imposes restraint. Over a vase surrounded by foliage an owl is opening its wings, and above that is a many-sided ancient mirror, some intertwined bodies of dragons, a rectangular frame and, beyond, little figures dancing among fine, curved branches.

7 (above left) Charles Cameron, part of a dish. Drawing from the 1764 album.

8 (above right) Charles Cameron, pitcher. Drawing from the 1764 album.

These pages also reveal a rich ornamental play that is less gloomy than that on the vases or the candelabras.

This play is connected with the culture of the romantic grotesque which, in the period of the Enlightenment, was a form of expression for a subjective, deeply individual sense of the world. The romantic freedom of his creative imagination was what was supposed to distinguish the artist attracted by this ornamental play. In Cameron's drawings it takes on characteristics of irony. It is as if laughter sounds through his work, but it is not mirthful laughter. These works are marked by a gloominess of mood, bearing witness to a troubled perception of the world. It is easy to assume that Cameron was experiencing some alienation from the life around him at this transitional stage of his life. He was looking more deeply into himself, into the world of artistic logic he had created, and he was at the same time keenly aware of his isolation. The pre-romantic grotesque in Cameron's work turns into the phenomenon that the Russian philosopher Mikhail Bakhtin called 'a carnival experienced alone'.[20]

16

9 Charles Cameron, part of a dish. Drawing from the 1764 album.

This definition precisely conveys Cameron's mood at the time of executing these drawings. He was not satisfied with his studies at the Carpenters' Company. The young man aspired towards artistic work, but he was, as it were, alone.

It seems that his work pleased the architect Isaac Ware, with whom Charles became associated, although he was officially apprenticed to his father. At that time many buildings designed by Ware had been erected: St George's Hospital in London (1733), the Clifton Hill estate in Bristol (1746–50), Lord Chesterfield's house in London (1748–9) and the town hall in Oxford (1751–2) among others. Occupying a high and influential position in the Office of Royal Works, Ware could probably have furthered his protégé's architectural career. But Ware had something else in mind for Cameron. He wanted to republish Andrea Palladio's measurements of the Roman baths.

This undertaking was of great importance for the development of the architecture of European neo-classicism. The study of ancient monuments would be directed along the path marked by the great sixteenth-century master from Vicenza, and the two ideals that ruled the minds of eighteenth-century architects would be joined together: those of ancient Rome and the Renaissance. The revival of antiquity would be fused with the revival of the Renaissance.

This project forged a direct link between three generations of Palladians: Lord Burlington, Isaac Ware and Charles Cameron. In 1730 Lord Burlington had first published the measurements of the baths in his work *Fabriche Antiche di Andrea Palladio*. But this work was not complete and, moreover, had been printed in a very small edition. It is known that Ware was close to Burlington. In 1738 he wrote in the preface to Palladio's *Four Books on Architecture*:

> My Lord, Your giving me free access to your study, wherein many of the original drawings of Palladio, besides those which compose this work, are preserved, and taking upon you the trouble of revising the translation, and correcting it with your own hands, are such instances of your friendship to me, that I cannot too publickly return your Lordship thanks for favours that surpass all acknowledgment.

10 (above left)   Charles Cameron, vase in a land-scape. Drawing from the 1764 album.

11 (above right)   Charles Cameron, lamp. Drawing from the 1764 album.

It is possible that it was Burlington himself who suggested that Ware should publish the material about the baths, but work was begun only after Burlington's death. Ware, himself no longer young, involved Cameron in the project as a draftsman, indicating that Cameron himself understood the value of the work. He wrote:

Some copies from the studies of Palladio relating to these Baths were engraved and published under the direction of the late Lord Burlington; but that valuable work becoming very scarce, Isaac Ware, Esquire, Secretary of the Board of Works, formed a plan of reprinting it: Mr. Charles Cameron (who studied under him for some time) made it his business . . . to complete the designs Mr. Ware left imperfect at his death . . . He proposes giving [the designs] to the public, verified, and corrected; with their measures from his own observations; adding the antique ceilings, paintings, and other ornaments belonging to the Thermae. He likewise proposes to

12 (above left) Charles Cameron, tripod. Drawing from the 1764 album.

13 (above right) Charles Cameron, tripod. Drawing from the 1764 album.

accompany this work with views, elevations, and sections, from accurate drawings taken on the spot, representing the present state of these buildings, and showing the authorities upon which the restorations of Palladio are founded.[22]

After Ware's death in 1766, the young man decided to carry on working on this publication and, in this way, to gain entry to the profession of architect. Indeed, he already felt himself to be one, for when he wrote his name in the fifth volume of *Vitruvius Britannicus* he added after it the word 'architect'.[23]

In 1768 Cameron set off for Italy. His reasons are given in *The Baths of the Romans*: he considered that the measurements of the baths by Palladio, 'never having received his last corrections, appear under a very imperfect form. What is now offered to the public is intended to correct this deficiency: the buildings he described have again been measured, and the errors which have escaped him, corrected.'[24] It is hard to know

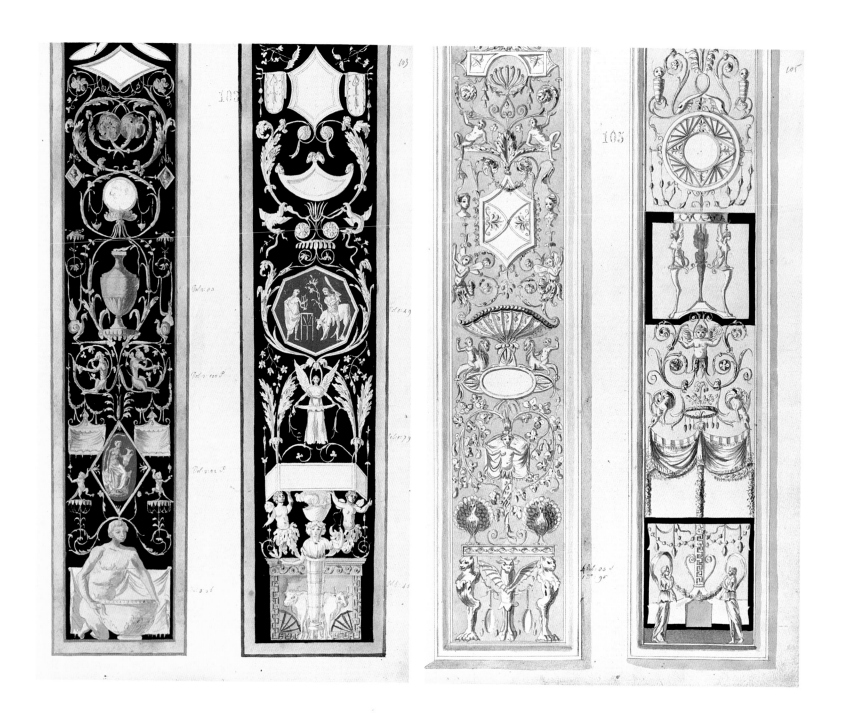

14 (above left) Charles Cameron, design for a pilaster. Drawing from the 1764 album.

15 (above right) Charles Cameron, design for a pilaster. Drawing from the 1764 album.

exactly how Cameron carried out his intentions: no information about his travels has survived, apart from the fruits of his journey, his book. In it the architect says hardly anything about himself. He merely recalls that,

> the lower floors of the bath buildings were so filled in with earth that, without special work, it would have been impossible even with difficulty to look at their construction. Having received permission from the late Pope Clement XIII to carry out excavations in such places as might assist me in my design of illustrating the Baths . . . I chose for my chief researches those of Titus in preference to the rest, as being situated on the declivity of a hill and, consequently, more easy of access.[25]

Striving to understand fully the details as well as the composition of ancient monuments, young Cameron caught that special mood that affected all those living in the artistic atmosphere of Rome at the end of the eighteenth century. Thus Goethe, who arrived in Italy a few years after Cameron, wrote:

> It must be recognised that it is a hard and sad occupation excavating ancient Rome from under the new Rome; but it must be done, hoping for eventual complete satisfaction. Remains of such splendour and of such devastation are uncovered as go beyond our understanding. What the barbarians did not touch has been destroyed by the builders of modern Rome . . . This mass is quite calmly influencing us as we hastily run hither and thither.

Rome gave Cameron a new direction for his interests, a new line for his thought, as it did for many other artists of that era (pls 16, 17). The basis was created on which his relationship to the classical would grow. 'Dearer than anything is that which I carry in my soul and which, constantly growing, can constantly be filled up,' wrote Goethe on leaving Italy.

On his return to London, Cameron, fired with hopes, finished *The Baths of the Romans*, which was published in 1772 by the London publishing house of George Scott. The complete title was: *The Baths of the Romans explained and illustrated with the restorations of Palladio corrected and improved. To which is prefixed, an introductory preface, pointing out the nature of the work, and a dissertation upon the state of the arts during the different periods of the Roman Empire*. It was a large-format volume (40 × 55 cm) of excellent quality, with 100 illustrations from engravings on copper. The text occupied 140 pages. It was printed with parallel texts in English and French with quotations in Italian, Latin and Greek. The book contained also a second group of images, both pictorial and literary, created by Cameron himself. These give a completely different impression from the intense and gloomy images of his 1764 album. *The Baths of the Romans* is permeated with a feeling of clarity and wholeness, even enlightenment. An extract from the first chapter could serve as an epigraph to the entire work: 'everywhere you encounter so much elegance and beauty. In the fine words of Pindar: "Beginning, remember: the face of creation/Must be made light." '[26]

Cameron's book is divided into three unequal parts: the preface in which the author discusses his position with regard to artistic theory, a separate essay on his ideas on the artistic history of Rome and a section dedicated to the baths themselves. In the first instance he gives his views as an architectural theorist, in the second he is an historian and to some extent a moralist, and in the third he speaks as an archaeologist and

16 (below left) Charles-Louis Clérisseau, (?)*Paestum*. From the Italian sketches of the 1760s.

17 (below right) Charles-Louis Clérisseau, *Baths in Rome*, 1760s. From the series *Views of Italy*.

architect. As this book is the closest we come to a documentation of Cameron's architectural understanding at this date, it deserves more detailed scrutiny.

Cameron's The Baths of the Romans

The main thrust of the book's introduction is an insistence on rigorous adherence to the classical ideal, and on the notion that the creative urge must be followed only when 'governed by art's pure and original models'. Cameron sharply criticises the baroque, its 'wild and fantastic inventions which are to be met with, in the greatest number, in those places where the arts have flourished most, in Rome'. The masters of the later baroque he calls 'a tribe of imitators, who, struck by the praise unmerited in this point at least, which their masters had acquired, reduced architecture . . . to so confused and corrupt a state, as hardly to be exceeded by that Gothic barbarian which they themselves held in the utmost contempt.'[27] However, among his contemporaries, he saw 'men of discernment' who have established 'the old and true method of building by unanimously giving to Palladio the first place among the modern architects.' It is apparent that Cameron's fixed and unshakeable professional position stands behind these words.

The essay on 'The history, and progress, of architecture among the Romans, following the order of time from the era of the commencement of their luxury, to that of their fall' is daring. In his argument the young architect moves a long way from his own profession. He informs his readers that in the age of the Republic – that 'noble state structure' with 'sound rules of administration'[28] – the distinguishing characteristics of the Romans were their 'simplicity of manner and purity of morals unknown to future ages'.[29] Then, with a passion worthy of Cato, whose attack on the luxury prevalent among the Quirites he quotes by the page, he considers Roman law and the way in which it was directed against excess. He connects the appearance of different types of buildings with changing needs, provides details about the fall of Rome and rushes through the Middle Ages up to the Renaissance.

The essay is attractively written and gives many details that suggest that its author must have been remarkably well read for someone of his background. He was familiar with Cicero's letters to Atticus and Tertulian's treatise 'On Sights', with Seneca's epistles and the writings of St Jerome. He had also read Livy, Tacitus, Strabo and Sallust and he quotes from Theodore and St Augustine. The essay continues:

> Whatever ideas our imagination may have formed from what has been above recited, they can by no means be adequate to the grandeur and magnificence of the ancient city of Rome, which . . . is still considered . . . worthy of the admiration of all nations.[30]

This was written in a spirit close to that of the treatises of the Italian humanists. Cameron's work undoubtedly tends to a stylisation in traditions reminiscent in some degree of those in which Palladio was brought up. Cameron continued Palladio's undertaking, perpetuating and reflecting his refined feeling for form. For Cameron, Palladio was inevitably a model to imitate in his architectural work; he also strove to share his view of the world. Nor was this unusual within English Palladian circles. Universalism, as a certain continuity in respect of the Italian academies of the sixteenth century, was seized on by Burlington and those close to him, possibly not without influence from the works of Shaftesbury. The classicism of the early eighteenth century had been formed against the background of these ideas. In the 1770s Cameron was stating his principles in broadly the same context, and this is one of the most attractive aspects of his architectural philosophy.

The third part of the book is the largest and that most concerned with architecture. Here Cameron describes the purposes of the numerous bath buildings. Well-chosen quotations from Homer's *Odyssey*, from Ovid's *Art of Love* and from Lucian's treatise 'Hippius, or the Baths' reveal everyday details and give the reader the feeling of being there with the Romans visiting the baths. There is even a description of the typical pattern of a day in ancient Rome:

18 Charles Cameron, *View of the Baths of Constantine*. From *The Baths of the Romans*, 1772.

19 Charles Cameron, *Exedra of the Baths of Agrippa*. From *The Baths of the Romans*, 1772.

23

Роспись в банях Константина.

20 Charles Cameron, after a wall painting in the Baths of Constantine. From *The Baths of the Romans*, 1772.

The time from six o'clock to eight o'clock (by current calculations) was spent on visiting. From eight to ten, lawyers carried out their business. The hours from ten to twelve were spent on various activities. They slept from twelve to two . . . before going to the baths. At three they had dinner and at four, Martial tells us, he sat down to work at the same time as the person he was writing to was sitting with a bottle.[31]

The last line of Martial, to which Cameron refers, reads: 'You are always busy offering Ambrosian delicacies.' Cameron was clearly turning to all manner of sources to achieve an authentic picture of Roman daily life.

The engravings based on Palladio's reconstructions accompany the text and occupy a separate section of the book. Illustrations within the text show views of monuments in Rome and various small baths elsewhere, in Pompei, Paris and Bologna.

The author's personal enthusiasms are revealed in a series of his own etchings which Cameron places immediately after Palladio's reconstructions. Most of these show fragments of decorations from the Constantine and Titus baths. Cameron's drawings are light and his sheets are rich in free space. He chooses to depict human figures framed by foliage of a comparably large size. This method of mixing scales creates an unusual impression and was subsequently used quite frequently by Cameron in his own interiors.

Together with his drawings of decorations from the baths, Cameron also published a number of etchings that had no connection with the baths: ceilings from the Palace of Augustus, from Hadrian's Villa at Tivoli and even from the Villa Madama. These pages are effectively part of the sketch diary that he brought home from Rome. From these drawings it is possible with some degree of confidence to know what the architect was studying and in what he was interested during his stay in Italy. Compared with his vases in the 1764 album, these works show Cameron adopting a stricter style. This change corresponds to the other transition in his work, from decorative and applied art to architecture.

One essential question remains unanswered. Was *The Baths of the Romans* created by Charles Cameron independently, or did the young artist simply finish Ware's work? He himself wrote that his work 'in Rome was to complete those of I. Ware's projects which were unfinished at the time of his death'. However, this applies only to the plans, façades and cross-sections of the baths. Apparently, several of the copper-plates were ready at the time of his departure for Italy, as his additions were made on insets which were attached to the pages of the book. The text, the illustrations and the set of etchings were all done by Cameron alone. We can, moreover, sense his interest in decorative detail: from the vases of his student years he has moved to fragments of ancient murals. In conclusion, it has become clear that, although the book could hardly have appeared had Burlington not found Palladio's sketches in Vicenza and published them, or had Ware not begun work on their republication, the general design and final appearance of the treatise are attributable to the young architect, who even then had what he himself expressed as the desire to 'take everything to its true completion'.

Work on the book provided Cameron with an education. For five years he was employed on it on his own. These years systematised his views, giving them an order and teaching him a great deal. They offered a school of classical drawing, whereby the architect reproduced figures that he had seen on pieces of relief or during the excavations of the Baths of Titus. It was in this process that he absorbed the architectural logic of ancient constructions. He went deep into the secrets of classical decoration and worked on a method for creating decorative compositions that had the utmost clarity of structure and yet were densely packed. He would always have before him the image of antiquity that he had found in his study of ancient authors and their commentators, in excavations and measurements, in long observation and his own imagination. In short, Cameron's concept of classical architecture had been conceived, and it was to be realised in the buildings that he would create in Russia.

The book was sold in London and Paris. Cameron exhibited his drawings of the Antonine baths at the Society of Arts in London to coincide with the publication of the book, and this attracted additional attention. It was reprinted in 1774 and again in 1775. Cameron lived in his father's house surrounded by pictures and books, of which he had accumulated a considerable number. An inventory of his property listed '10 book-cases, 20 busts, 20 pictures, 20 portraits, 500 books with copper engravings, 500 books with other illustrations, 300 more books and 1,000 engravings'.[32] His career, it would seem, was set on course for success, and he began to take part in his father's business, making drawings for the redecoration of a house in Hanover Square, London.

The hopes which seemed to open out in front of him, however, more than once evaporated, either through his own fault or as a result of events beyond his control. In 1775 his life was overturned by his father's bankruptcy,[33] and something very strange occurred: he brought a legal action against his father, demanding the return of his pictures and books. It is impossible to say with certainty whether this was an agreement between father and son whereby the architect would try to save some of his property, or whether relations within the family had become so bad that recourse to the courts was the only option. It is certain, however, that this situation would have some kind of permanent psychological effect. Everything that his life had consisted of had collapsed by the mid-1770s. He experienced poverty, family dishonour, the shame of his own law suit, which would still be talked about by London builders in 1791, and an unhappy love affair with Ware's daughter.[34] He was not succeeding in obtaining either commissions or a position. He applied for a job as a district surveyor in Middlesex but was unsuccessful.[35] It is not known on what he lived.

At the same time he was increasingly aware of his own capabilities and recognition of his talent was slowly growing, although he may not have known of this. The Italian architect Ottavio Bertotti Scamozzi, who had carefully studied *The Baths of the Romans*, wrote in 1775: 'I read the book with indescribable avidity, hoping to find in it the magic thread which would lead me to the true path through the complex labyrinth of the bath buidlings.'[36]

When in 1779 the Empress of Russia, Catherine the Great, conceived a plan for her palace at Tsarskoye Selo, to create 'an ancient house with all its decor', where everything would be authentically arranged and where Roman dishes would be served and Roman clothes would be worn,[37] it was not surprising that she should turn to Charles Cameron to help realise this idea. His book had earned him a reputation as a 'great expert on antiquity', with whom, according to Catherine, it would be interesting to 'craft baths with a hanging garden and a gallery for walks'.[38]

To Russia

So it was that Cameron's life underwent a decisive change of scene. In August 1779 he left London on an English ship bound for the port of Elsinore in Denmark. From there he sailed to Kronstadt, and finally to St Petersburg, the young Russian capital, then just seventy-five years old. The huge city was at that time built entirely in the baroque style. The powerful River Neva with its numerous tributaries, the canals, the islands, the broad regular gardens of the luxury mansions on the banks of the rivers, all gave St Petersburg a magnificent appearance. The imperial palaces, the monasteries and the churches created by Bartolomeo Rastrelli and Savva Chevakinsky with their rich decor, their abundance of gilded detail, their bright colouring usually in turquoise or dark red, looked like enormous jewels set in mounts formed by the residential districts. These were strictly regular and controlled in their architecture. They were built in accordance with specific model designs, whose use was obligatory. Neo-classicism was still only just taking up its starting position for the attack on the baroque. Very few buildings had been erected in the new style: Yury Velten had built the large Hermitage; de la Mothe, the small Hermitage and the Academy of Arts; and Rinaldi had designed the Marble Palace. Cameron was to play a clear and very significant role in establishing neo-classicism in Russia. He had landed in most original surroundings and very special tasks lay ahead of him.

For many years Cameron was to live removed from the everyday life of Russia, with its problems, its attempts to develop its economy, its difficult wars and its peasant rebellions. His task was to provide a brilliant backdrop against which the performance of court life could take place. This was particularly lavish during Catherine's reign. Whole showers of jewels or estates with thousands of peasants were bestowed on her favourites and her military leaders. The halls in which announcements would be made about her gifts of entire towns or counties had to be correspondingly luxurious, and the parks surrounding her palaces had to resemble the Garden of Eden, places where one would meet monuments to her victories at every step. It was Cameron who was assigned to create this fantasy world.

Cameron was presented to the empress and charmed her. He became Catherine's personal architect. This was a matter of great pride to him. Throughout his life he signed his sketches: 'AIM' – the Architect of Her Imperial Majesty.

The history of Cameron's work in Russia is such that he was effectively the architect of two of its most famous ensembles: Tsarskoye Selo, an imperial estate about twenty miles from St Petersburg, and Pavlovsk, the residence of the heir to the throne, Grand Duke Paul, and his wife, Maria. From 1780 to 1795 he was involved, in differing degrees of intensity, in rebuilding existing constructions and in designing and erecting new ones. Only towards the end of his life did the nature of his work change. Unlike Quarenghi, Starov, Lvov and Bazhenov, he did not undertake private commissions. Not until the first years of the nineteenth century was he given any work in the capital or any provincial town. Cameron's creativity was completely concentrated on constructions of an exceptional character; he built the most luxurious of buildings and grandiose residences, and he used unusual materials – valuable stones and china, glass and lacquer.

His fortunes shifted with political events, and his career progressed at a very uneven pace. For the first five years of his life in Russia (up to 1785) he was burdened to the limit, at Tsarskoye Selo and Pavlovsk. During that time he created the designs for almost all his constructions: the Agate Pavilion, the galleries, the Tsarskoye Selo apartments in which he created the famous Arabesque, Lyons and Chinese Halls, the Bedchamber and the Green Dining Room. Moreover, in these years he also built several pavilions in the Tsarskoye Selo park, the pyramid and two Chinese bridges.

All this work was completed by 1787. The designing of the town of Sofiya, which was to be included in the Tsarskoye Selo ensemble, was actively undertaken from 1780 to 1785, although the implementation of Cameron's ideas was not only prolonged but also incomplete.

At Pavlovsk he began work on the palace in 1781, had built most of it by 1783 and had finished it by 1787 (excluding the interiors).[39] The Temple of Friendship, the Apollo Colonnade, the Aviary and the Obelisk had been erected by 1783, and in 1786 the Memorial to Parents was built. In the course of the next twenty years Cameron would build yet more pavilions for this ensemble.

At Tsarskoye Selo he would do various pieces of finishing work. The construction

21   Charles Cameron, design for the central hall of the Agate Pavilion, Tsarskoye Selo. Detail of pl. 47.

of the Chinese Village was endlessly drawn out; it had been begun long before Cameron arrived and was in fact never completed. At the beginning of the 1790s he developed the bath complex: he created a *pente-douce* leading to the Agate Pavilion, and then in 1792 planned the Temple of Memory,[40] dedicated to the Turkish wars, which was to precede the *pente-douce* and to meet the movement from the Gatchina Gates with a triumphal arch.[41] In 1795 the architect created a design for a tiny domestic chapel behind the Agate Pavilion; this was subsequently built by Ilya Neyelov who made considerable changes to Cameron's design.

These were Cameron's major works in the eighteenth century. There was, in addition, a small number of unfulfilled projects: four park pavilions and orangeries.[42] Attention, however, must also be paid to work of quite a different character: in 1803–5 Cameron served as the architect to the Admiralty.

From the biographical point of view a complex picture arises. The unusually active, feverish activity of Cameron's first five years contrasts strongly with the almost empty years of the following decade, when long periods seemed to be taken up with trivial finishing work, and when in general nothing of any significance was done. Nothing similar is encountered in the careers of the majority of other great masters working in Russia in the last quarter of the eighteenth century. Quarenghi, for example, was constantly complaining in his letters about the inhuman burden of his work, and his activity both as an architect and as a draughtsman is remarkable. Neither can it be said of Lvov with his various 'projects'; he was attracted one minute by the idea of erecting buildings from earth and the next by the theory of pyrostatics (ventilation), and was constantly planning estate buildings to be constructed in different regions. Velten, Kazakov and Starov were all also more productive than Cameron. Bazhenov, even when he was out of favour, built much more than Cameron – for private commissions.

A clear contradiction can be noted between what Cameron's contemporaries called his 'extreme haste' and his desire 'not to do anything slowly' which marked the beginning of his professional life in Russia, and the subsequent onset of a deep apathy apparently dictated by the destruction of his hopes, which once again overtook the illusion of broad perspectives and the rapture he had been experiencing in his work. I shall try to unravel what happened and to understand the events that caused such disillusionment in the master architect.

Cameron was accepted for service on 25 October 1779, and on 17 August 1780 he was given an edict signed by the empress: 'In charge of all the building in Tsarskoye Selo in producing work according to the highest approved plans, will be the architect, Cameron, who was sent for from England.'[43] Such a task could turn the head of the most cold-blooded person, let alone that of an architect who had not built a single building before the age of thirty-six. For the first time in his life Cameron was being given the opportunity to realise his ideas. He began to build with feverish determination and with unshakeable independence, taking no notice of established procedures or order of work and paying no heed to construction officials. A description of Cameron's attitude to work in his first years in Russia has been preserved:

> He did not inform anyone that he was preparing for work . . . and then he hastened to try to break things down and then to start building, meanwhile looking for various types of craftsmen . . . [coming to] arrangements with some of them about which he would inform one construction department but about other jobs he would give no information at all until the work was already finished . . . He always wanted money or materials to be given to him immediately . . . If everything was not immediately done as he demanded . . . then he would often simply send in the bill.[44]

Thus it was with such passionate haste that he created the halls of the Tsarskoye Selo palace and the Agate Pavilion.

At Pavlovsk Cameron behaved rather differently, but no less decisively. He was aware of the bad relations between Catherine and her son, Paul. Taking his cue from the mood of the empress, the architect refused to stand on ceremony either with officials or with the august owners of the estate. The Grand Duchess Maria wrote to her steward, Kuchelbecker: 'You know well from your own experience that it is impossible to influence Cameron with gentleness but tell him . . . that he is unbearable and that he should be careful.'[45] She would insist that 'Cameron must be put in his place',[46] that she was 'impatiently waiting for an answer from him'.[47] Or she would say: 'Ask Cameron for God's sake to do something in good taste',[48] or demand that 'he should stop all these large projects, marble which has to come from Carrara'.[49] Misunderstandings were constantly arising: 'I have just sent for Cameron – he was not at home and they think there that he will not be returning until tomorrow. This is insupportable.'[50] Nevertheless, Cameron created such remarkable buildings and parks that it was impossible not to acknowledge him: 'I request you to ask Cameron to finish my waterfall. Tell him that I am extremely pleased with his cutting down [in the park]. This creates a splendid effect and I am full of hopes that he will build something very fine.'[51] And again: 'Cameron's visit to Pavlovsk afforded me great pleasure. Tell him in my name that I am convinced that his work has considerably embellished Pavlovsk.'[52]

It must not be forgotten that in his first years in Russia Cameron created works of the highest artistic quality, which would earn him a reputation in the history of architecture as one of the most refined masters of the eighteenth century. Cameron's interiors and the baths at Tsarskoye Selo evoked admiration from his patroness, Catherine the Great: 'We are building with him here a garden in the form of a terrace with baths below and galleries above. Here there will be so much beauty, so much beauty.'[53] And from his contemporaries: 'He has a mind which inspires . . . the apartments will be exceptional [although] nothing is yet finished except for two rooms . . . no one here has seen anything comparable.'[54] 'People are excited because he has found materials which light the torch of imagination.'[55] 'Quarenghi said that these rooms are as magnificent as they are unique and that anyone who has not seen them cannot have any idea of what they are really like.'[56]

Despite such praise from Catherine, conditions of work seem to have been difficult for Cameron. Even in those years, when he was creating bright, joyful compositions which strikingly combined the simplicity of harmonious proportions with a luxurious use of materials and detailed craftsmanship, his mood was at times heavy. He was easily hurt, and his attitude to life was poisoned by the problems he encountered. He had probably put so much into his ideas and nurtured so many hopes that creative prospects would await him in a Russia unhampered by persecution and malevolence, that any unpleasantness irritated him and threw him into despair. On 5 October 1783 he wrote:

> I had the ambition to receive praise and if it is possible I shall tear myself from the mouth of hatred . . . it is better to submit to the dangers of upsetting one's mood and health than to pander to people in their ignorance . . . I want to believe in the justice and carefulness of my actions, announcing that I cannot be responsible for my constructions . . . if they are altered by ignorant contractors . . . I have always carried out my work with joy . . . but it is quite beyond my strength to explain . . . the labour and the trouble it is to bring each job to its true conclusion with people whose main characteristic is their . . . deceptiveness . . . it will be easier for you to imagine than it is for me to describe how I feel.[57]

He asked the empress's personal secretary, Count Alexander Bezborodko, to help him carry out his work, so that he 'might be happier than at this moment'.[58]

After several misunderstandings with contractors, the architect took a number of measures to improve his situation. He was strict in his relationship with builders: 'Work is not moving but Mr Cameron will not allow anyone to do any work until he himself has looked at all the architecture.'[59] Then he took a risky step. On 21 January 1784 an announcement appeared in an Edinburgh journal with an invitation in the name of the Russian empress:

> Wanted: two clerks who have been employed by an Architect or a very considerable builder, who can draw well . . . Two Master Masons, Two Master Bricklayers, A Master Smith.[60]

Applicants were promised not only a substantial wage but also that they would be given 'a pice [sic] of Ground'.[61]

Approximately seventy experienced workers replied to this invitation.[62] In May of the same year they set off for St Petersburg on the ship *Betsey and Brothers*. One of them wrote home:

> Our first landing in Rusia was at Cronstade . . . and Mr Cameron . . . came on all haste himself and his wife . . . They were very glade to see us and gave us a grand treat at a teavron [tavern] . . . We was ordered to want for nothing but call for whatever we wanted . . . It is out of Mr Cameron's own poket that we are subsisted till the end of the quarter.[63]

The letter reveals many of the illusions which the workers were under, but it is possible to reconstruct to some degree what the architect had promised them. It is important to note that Cameron had invited the workers at his own risk, without the consent of the authorities, hoping to organise a colony of craftsmen who could carry out the work necessary for the erection of his buildings. It is true that he had asked Bezborodko to help him in this undertaking, but he set things in motion before he had received permission. As a result there were long discussions about taking on the workers. A scandal broke out. The British craftsmen were very upset: 'We are most upset by Cameron and Forester [sic] who contracted us in Britain . . . We know that we are in a foreign country and have no one to defend us.'[64]

Cameron's position was now even more difficult. He could not support seventy workers and their families, the official institutions took a long time with paperwork and numerous confusions arose. Eventually, however, the Scottish craftsmen were taken into service and proved useful. Many of them remained in Russia: among these were William Hastie and Adam Menelaws who would later become well-known architects in their own right. Although Cameron's behaviour in this incident, despite the obstacles he met, was crowned with success, his official position not only did not improve, it became critical.

Throughout the five years of his most active work at Tsarskoye Selo, Cameron, insofar as one can judge from documentary evidence, paid no attention to financial considerations. He paid the contractors what they asked for, or sometimes did not pay at all; he demanded expensive materials; he sent for furniture from abroad and various decorations for the palace halls and then would not accept parts of his orders; he required the highest quality and insisted on some jobs being done several times over; and so on. He aspired only to 'bring a job to its true completion' and never thought about how money could be saved. This did not please Catherine, and the result was another blow to his illusions.

Catherine, on 19 October 'of this year [1784] has ordered Privy Counsellor Strekalov to investigate . . . the construction work at Tsarskoye Selo done by the architect, Cameron'[65] and 'to check all that has been built and done, to have experts testify as to its solidity and to look at the correspondence between the condition of things there and the prices charged.'[66] In other words a special commission was ordered to investigate Cameron's work. Its members were first and foremost interested in 'how much each item had cost', and they immediately made an accusation: 'It is not unknown that many of the things which he has bought or sent for on various occasions are not to be found in the rooms . . . [it is unknown] whether they have been returned to their previous owners.'[67]

The investigation was to continue for several years, during which time Cameron was given hardly any new commissions. All this was extremely unpleasant for him. At first he tried to ignore the investigation. The commission could not start work because Cameron 'despite having received the order to give his account . . . disappeared to St Petersburg without giving any information and has been living there for four days.'[68] Major-General Soymanov and Privy Counsellor Strekalov were responsible for check-ing all aspects of the architect's work in his absence. The architects Ivan Starov and Luigi Ruska were required to look at all the constructions and give their conclusions. It was reported that 'they are meticulously built . . . there is nothing that suggests they are not solidly constructed'.[69]

However, there was a serious shortfall on various items and deficiencies in the finishing of certain rooms. The architect was felt to be mainly to blame for this, and had to locate or account for missing items. For many months he was forced to answer endless questions, often necessarily trivial ones, because of the confusion in the Tsarskoye Selo construction office or because of the empress's forgetfulness about gifts she had made. Cameron wrote in irritation: 'With my own hands I intend to give to whomsoever is ordered to accept them any objects belonging to Her Imperial Majesty and now in my living-quarters such as, for instance, the candelabra, the basins and so on.'[70]

A special report had to be written about a 'missing' chest of drawers by Denois which Catherine had in fact presented to Prince Potemkin and then forgotten. Cameron had lost the note that proved this, and witnesses had to be sought. Naturally they could give evidence only at second hand, and the direct participants in the 'gift of the chest of drawers' could obviously not be approached.[71]

A farcical incident took place over a matter of eight copper pillars which were to have embellished the doors of the Chinese Hall. Cameron had ordered them to be fixed horizontally, but Strekalov and Soymanov searched through all the rooms for them for a long time, assuming that they would be standing vertically.

As a result of all this not only was Cameron tormented for a long period but the officials themselves suffered a great deal of unpleasantness. Taking advantage of Cameron's apathy and reluctance to get down to work, they attempted to get rid of him by handing in the following report: 'We have [here] the architect, Cameron, who is not now carrying out any work at Tsarskoye Selo and yet is receiving a salary of 3,000 roubles',[72] and he was also, they added, claiming extra expenses for papers, pencils, a translator and the like.

Although the commission did not in the end find any particular misdemeanours, and although nothing of significance was blamed on him except carelessness, Cameron had lost his former passion and enthusiasm for work.

He was to stay mainly in Tsarskoye Selo in the late 1780s and early 1790s, despite being given very little to do. In August 1791, however, he went to England, 'having received temporary leave with the intention of returning to his construction' and with a letter of recommendation in which Bezborodko reminded Count S.R. Vorontsov, the Russian Ambassador in London: 'Your Excellency knows him and so I am willingly despatching him to you.'[73]

The architectural society of his homeland met Cameron with hostility, although it was admitted that he had attained 'high office in a foreign country'.[74] His application for membership of the architectural club then being set up in London was rejected, and unpleasant rumours were circulating about his past.[75] Cameron once again left England. Back in Russia his absence had, in fact, strengthened his position as court architect. Perhaps fears had arisen that he might one day leave and not return. At Tsarskoye Selo he was soon given the order to construct a second gallery, the Temple of Memory and the domestic chapel, developing the bath complex that he had created before his visit to England. He spent another four years on these projects. Once again, however, the Tsarskoye Selo building office put a number of obstacles in his way. The letter that Cameron wrote enumerating the materials necessary for the construction of the second gallery was supposedly lost, and building work was delayed for almost a year.[76] It is difficult to believe that such occurrences would motivate any architect to produce inspired work.

A Gentleman Abroad

It seems extraordinary that Cameron should have produced work of such high quality, and so soon after his arrival, transplanted as he was into a strange new world in Catherine the Great's Russia. The circumstances of his life, his environment and his interests provide some insight into how this was achieved. Immediately on arrival in Russia, Cameron was accommodated in a wing attached to the Tsarskoye Selo Orangery. Tsarskoye Selo means literally Tsar's Village, and the Orangery stood, and still stands, on the village's Sadovaya (Garden) Street, quite close to the Large Palace. Only one side of this street was built on, the other being open to the park. Three windows of the wing looked on to the park.

The architect's flat was spacious. A separate entrance led into the vestibule from which there was access on the right to Cameron's private rooms and on the left to several adjoining rooms stretching along the walls of the Orangery and providing his studio. On the ground floor of the wing were four large living rooms with a staircase, square in plan, leading to the entresol.[77] The architect redesigned and rebuilt all the accommodation.[78] He created a unique 'suite of rooms in a ring', so that each room could be separated off in such a way that it did not hinder access to the others. The most ceremonial of the rooms was the large dining room, with its three broad windows. Its walls had three semicircular niches where statues perhaps stood, and a low colonnade of the Tuscan order. For this room Cameron requested marble tiles from the building office. It was easy to pass from the flat to the Orangery, where over a hundred orange trees stood in tubs.[79]

Probably of not least importance for the lonely architect was the fact that at the other end of the building in a symmetrically placed wing lived the English gardener John Bush, who was the creator of the Tsarskoye Selo parks. A visitor to St Petersburg in 1781 visited the Bushes and wrote in her diary: 'Had a good English dinner. Mrs Bush and her four daughters [are] agreeable people.'[80] She also mentioned the enormous salary that the gardener received and the various culinary tricks of his wife. In May 1784 Cameron proposed to Bush's daughter Catherine and married her.[81] At that time he was surrounded by pupils. Although these frequently changed, the architect was nevertheless constantly working with several young people. Among these were the future architects and builders Ivan Rostovtsev, Pavel Lukin, Alexsander Shmidt, Fedor Utkin and Nikolai Rogachev.[82] It would appear that loneliness and hardship had gone from his life. However, we must remember that Cameron married two months before the commission to investigate his work was instituted. His peace was again to be shortlived.

In Cameron's home there was much to reflect its occupier's habits and tastes. While still in England he had become a bibliophile and had begun to collect engravings and pictures. He had apparently lost all his collection when his father's property was sold. In Russia he once again indulged these enthusiasms and assembled an enormous library, the catalogue of which filled two hundred pages.[83] His reading tastes characterised him as a typical 'intellectual' of the era of the Enlightenment, with encyclopaedically broad interests.

As far as can be judged from the contents of his library, Cameron was interested in accounts of conspiracies, rebellions and coups. On his shelves could be found volumes of du Tertre's *Selected History of Investigations, Conspiracies and Revolutions*, books about political coups in ancient Rome and eighteenth-century Poland, France and Spain, and works describing the events that established Catherine the Great in power in 1762. He read about such other 'engrossing subjects' fashionable at that time as an essay 'on the theory of somnambulism and magnetism', the rise and fall of the Order of Malta, and the lives of Peter the Great and the Duke of Marlborough. He had a copy of the book of poems by Frederick the Great that Voltaire had mocked so caustically.

The architect's interests included other precise sciences: among his books can be found works on practical chemistry and physics, an introduction to mathematics as well as *The Art of Throwing Bombs*. Nor were the *belles-lettres* neglected. Cameron possessed works by Rousseau and Voltaire, Mably and Molière, although of the latter's plays only *Tartuffe* can be found in the catalogue, which speaks for itself. He was especially attracted by antiquity: he read Sophocles and Aeschylus, Polybius and Pliny, Apuleius's *Golden Ass* and Longus's *Daphnis and Chloe*, Cicero's Catiline speeches and Demosthenes's *Philippics*. His attention was attracted by numerous works on geography, history, philosophy and the religions of ancient Greece and Rome.

Architectural publications were represented by the works of architects from different countries: there were books by Fischer von Erlach, Guarini, Perrault, Boullée, Scamozzi and Soufflot. He owned several English treatises: works by William Kent and Isaac Ware, dedicated to Inigo Jones, William Chambers's *Designs of Chinese Buildings, Furniture, Dresses, Machines and Utensils* and the essays of Batty Langley and James Paine. He also had the Frenchman G.L. Le Rouge's publication *Détails des Nouveaux Jardins à la Mode*.

Charles Cameron spent seventeen years in the rebuilt wing attached to the Tsarskoye Selo Orangery, of which twelve were after his marriage. Here he worked with his assistants and established his library and collections. He was not, however, to live out the whole of his life in this home.

A New Regime

In December 1796 Catherine the Great died in the Winter Palace in St Petersburg. The heir to the throne, who had been in disfavour for a long time, was at his Gatchina estate some forty miles from the capital. A courier hastened to him, but Grand Duke Paul already knew of his mother's death. The courier met him at Tsarskoye Selo at the Post Station which Cameron had built. Changing horses the new emperor hurried to St Petersburg.

Paul's coronation meant a change of personnel surrounding the monarch, including the court architects. Several days after Catherine's death, Cameron was dismissed. 'His Imperial Majesty has commanded that the architect Cameron should not live at Tsarskoye Selo and that his assistants and pupils living on a state salary should be taken away from him.'[84] It would seem that the architect had not been warned in vain during the endless problems with the work on Pavlovsk. When he had insisted on having his own way, he had been told not to 'annoy Paul Petrovich, it may end badly'.

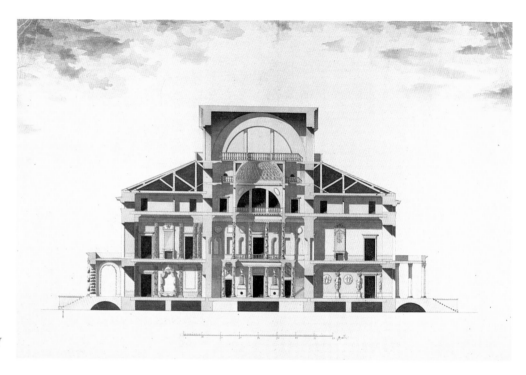

22 Charles Cameron, project for a palace, possibly Baturin, late eighteenth century.

Cameron was out of favour for three years. He turned to private commissions but did not find many of these: he designed a pavilion for an estate near Moscow and he worked on designs for the Baturin Palace for the Razumovskys, one of the richest families in Russia (pl. 22). However, it would seem that Cameron's role in the creation of this palace was not as great as has previously been supposed: the attribution is based on little more than the building's neo-classical style.[85] A letter has been preserved declaring that an Englishman worked at Baturin,[86] and there is a copy of a plan on which Cameron's name is mentioned.[87] However, this is not enough to establish his authorship. I shall deal further with questions of this attribution later, in the discussion of Adam Menelaws (see Chapter Six).

Rewards and punishments quickly succeeded each other in Paul's four-year rule. His anger against Cameron lasted longer than in many other cases, but in August 1800 the architect was again accepted into state service. He was offered accommodation in the same Orangery but in the other half, in rooms that had previously been part of the Bushes' apartment. He was given work at Pavlovsk, but none at Tsarskoye Selo where nothing was built in this period. Indeed, quite the reverse: Cameron's last contribution to the ensemble, his nearly completed Temple of Memory, was dismantled. He did, however, create the famous Three Graces Pavilion and the Elizabeth Pavilion in Pavlovsk park.

Soon the circumstances of his life would again change dramatically. Paul I was murdered in December 1801, in the recently built Mikhailovsky Castle in the middle of St Petersburg. The conspirators penetrated this palace-fortress which was surrounded by moats and had been designed by Cameron's longstanding rival, Vincenzo Brenna. The heir to the throne, the Grand Duke Alexander, knowing of the conspiracy, made the famous statement to the assembled guards officers: 'The Emperor Paul has died of an apoplectic fit. Under my rule everything shall be as it was under my grandmother.'

Catherine the Great's exiled grandees soon returned to St Petersburg. Officials whom Paul had dismissed were recalled to their former service or were given new posts. Cameron, too, was offered a responsible position: in 1803 he was appointed Admiralty architect on the recommendation of Admiral Nikolai Mordvinov, whose wife was English and who favoured everything British. Now Cameron left Tsarskoye Selo for ever and settled in the capital.

This was St Petersburg in the first years of the nineteenth century. As yet it lacked the architecture of Karl Rossi – the magnificent buildings of the Senate and the Synod, the Palace Square, the theatre and the street leading to it which would later be given Rossi's name. The mass of August Montferrand's St Isaac's cathedral had not yet risen above the city. The old brick Admiralty with its earthen rampart had not yet received its monumental attire; building had only just begun on the avenue beside it, and it seemed somehow empty. The banks of the Moyka were just beginning to be strengthened with stone, and iron bridges built to cross it. On the tip of Vasilevsky Island a vast Stock Exchange adorned by columns and with a jetty and embankments around it was under construction. The Kazan cathedral (pl. 23), with what the contemporary writer F.F. Vigel described as its 'glade of columns', was just raising its head. Throughout the city residential areas were being built or completed. To contemporaries it seemed as if they were growing not by the day but by the hour. Interior decorations were *à l'antique*: there were vases carved with mythological depictions, tables and chairs resting on eagles, gryphons or sphinxes. Mahogany had come into fashion, decorated with lyres, the heads of Medusas, lions and rams. Walls were no longer covered with silk: drapes were hung over them and around columns.

In the suburbs, too, things had changed. For a time Tsarskoye Selo and Pavlovsk were visited less frequently, but the islands near the northern part of the mouth of the Neva were being built over with *dachas*. 'You can imagine', wrote Vigel, 'the amount of building work that was going on then all over St Petersburg.'[88] As he wrote in his memoirs, 'Four architects were then well known: two Russians, Zakharov and Voronikhin, an Italian, Quarenghi, and the French, Thomon . . . There was one other . . . architect, who was, of course, much higher than the comrades in art who had come to us . . . This was the Cameron who built the Tsarskoye Selo colonnade and who was alive and well and living in St Petersburg.'[89]

23 Charles Cameron, project for Kazan cathedral, St Petersburg, *c*.1800.

The post of Admiralty architect brought very many responsibilities. In Cameron's charge were not only the martitime buildings of St Petersburg, but also constructions in all Russian ports and in many factories producing items for the ship-building industry. It was essential to build and repair lighthouses and hospitals, sheds for galleys, warehouses for timber, coach-houses, powder cellars and provenance magazines. The Admiralty architect was also given major town-building projects. Cameron had to 'examine and certify' plans for the ports of Riga, Reval, Nikolaev, Kherson and Archangel.[90] In St Petersburg the rebuilding of the largest and most important structures was imminent: the Galley Harbour on Vasilevsky Island with its dozens of buildings, the maritime hospital and, in addition, the building of the main Admiralty itself which had been designed by Ivan Korobov. Cameron was faced with numerous tasks, many of which he completed.

For Cameron a period was beginning which would be full of toil and petty administrative matters. He was obliged to think about such things as the maintenance of buildings where coal was stored, the repair of forges on the wharves, or improving the stores where meat was salted. This could hardly have satisfied a craftsman who was used to building fine constructions in the imperial parks. However, there were also occasionally grander projects, and these met with varied success.

In 1804 Cameron made a design for St Andrew's cathedral in Kronstadt, the main church of the Russian Navy.[91] This turned out to be too expensive, and the architect drew up another, more modest, plan which was accepted by Alexander I.[92] Work started on the cathedral in accordance with Cameron's plan in 1805, but a year later Andreyan Zakharov altered its architectural design.[93]

One of Cameron's most significant works at the beginning of the nineteenth century was the maritime hospital in Oranienbaum (pl. 24).[94] This consisted of twelve identical blocks and numerous service buildings. Cameron found an interesting solution in his plan for the hospital. He gave it the character of a small, ideal settlement. The patients' buildings were divided into two by a wide green boulevard where convalescents could promenade. There were eight blocks on one side of the boulevard and four on the other, placed in pairs at each end of the road. There was thus a broad gap between buildings. Thanks to this the four central buildings and the middle part of the boulevard had a magnificent view. The hospital stood on a hill. Below could be seen the large lake of the Oranienbaum park. Beyond that there stretched a panorama with the palace ensemble.

24 (below left) Charles Cameron, the hospital at Oranienbaum: copy of the plan by Cameron, 1806.

25 (below right) Charles Cameron, project for galley sheds, 1806.

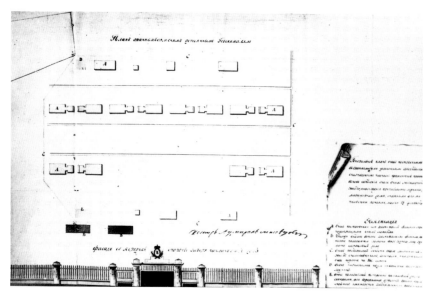

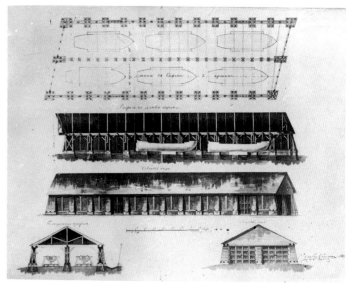

Cameron's hospital was also fated not to remain as the architect had planned it. The complex was spoilt by the building of one monotonous block which stretched the whole length of the boulevard. In addition, Cameron's wings were dismantled.[95]

No more fortunate than the Oranienbaum maritime hospital was the fate of Cameron's design for the lighthouse on the island of Seskar near Kronstadt. It, too, was revised by Zakharov so that nothing remained of Cameron's concept.

Cameron worked out a major design for the Admiralty stables which has not been preserved. Almost everything we know of them is derived from a brief description by Cameron himself in a letter to Admiral Chichagov, a colleague of the Navy Minister, on 29 April 1805: 'I have the honour to present for Your Excellency's examination my design for a stone stable for the Admiralty to hold 100 horses with the necessary living quarters for them, coach-houses, a smithy, barns.'[96]

One of Cameron's most sophisticated works from the time of his Admiralty employment was his design for 'galley sheds for the port's rowing fleet' (pl. 25).[97] This work belongs to that rare group of preserved sketches that were undoubtedly drawn entirely by the architect himself. He skilfully used simple constructive elements to create a unique proportional structure and style for the walls. The blind walls of a small building, the slanting edging of pylons standing on a very low pedestal and thus seeming to emerge from the ground itself, the brownish-green colour of the plan, the shade of withered grass, all this gave it a natural and chamber-like quality that evoked the park pavilions in the style of rustic cabins which were erected by many architects – including Cameron at Pavlovsk – in accordance with the fashion of the late eighteenth century.

With his position as Admiralty architect Cameron was provided with an apartment specially arranged for him in the Mikhailovsky Castle (pl. 26).[98] Tsar Alexander had left the castle on the day of his father's death and never appeared there again. The court also avoided this building with its terrible associations, and a most unusual use was made of it. It was transformed into a large hostel, where different halls and apartments were given over to various officials from the Engineering Ministry. The building thus became known as the Engineers' Castle. F. Vigel wrote of it:

> You can imagine my amazement when I entered the former throne room of Paul I . . . there were rows of windows and on the splendidly painted ceiling were depicted Jupiter the Thunderer and all his Olympus . . . The place where the throne

26 Giacomo Quarenghi, *View of Mikhailovsky Castle in St Petersburg*, 1800s.

27 Alexander Orlovsky, group portrait of Cameron (second from the left), Poshman and the Sukhtelen brothers, 1809.

had been was discernible by the preserved carved figures under it and the huge mirror . . . was among the forgotten or abandoned decorations. But the walls of the hall were bare, not even covered by paint: along them up to half their height were densely packed painted wooden book-cases without glass or curtains. Their shelves, moreover, held treasures that any bibliophile would envy.[99]

It was the bibliophile P.K. Sukhtelen who had placed his rare editions in the throne room. Charles Cameron, moved perhaps by the same passion for books, had met him and had seen his study-library. Thanks to Sukhtelen, the architect gained entrance to the friendly circle of St Petersburg engineers, builders and artists.

In 1809 the popular St Petersburg artist Alexander Orlovsky drew a group portrait of four men conversing in domestic surroundings (pl. 27). One of them is even wearing a dressing-gown and slippers. Those depicted are Alexander Poshman, Charles Cameron, Peter Sukhtelen and his brother, Ruff Sukhtelen. Alexander Poshman was an engineer, who in 1809 became a state counsellor and dealt with 'improving the salt business'.[100] He was elected an active member of the Free Economic Society and wrote books on agronomy.[101] Peter Sukhtelen, as described in the 1808 list of members of the Engineers Department, 'was at this time Engineer General, Quartermaster General for all the engineering departments and pioneer regiments, inspector from the Military Committee for the military colleges and member of the department of water communications, and so on.'[102] He was a major military engineer in his time, building dozens of fortresses, ports and other defence structures. His brother Ruff was likewise a bibliophile and one of the first custodians of the St Petersburg Public Library. As far as can be judged from a whole series of caricatures produced by Orlovsky, among the Sukhtelens' constant guests were the engineers Spengler, Garting and Betankur, usually accompanied by Vigel, the artist Reykhel, the Mikhailovsky Castle warden, Bryzgalov, and the architect Giacomo Quarenghi. Probably many of them were linked by their membership of the Freemasons, and it certainly seems likely that Cameron was a member of a masonic lodge. Another group portrait has also been preserved, in which Cameron appears with Poshman and Orlovsky above the attributes of 'arts and sciences', as well as the symbols of freemasonry.[103]

The architect, who had lived for a long time in Tsarskoye Selo, on his own or within his family circle, made many new acquaintances in his last years and joined in the life of the St Petersburg intelligentsia. Thus something common can be found between the beginning and the end of Cameron's life. In the early 1760s in London he had lived successfully among the people who surrounded Isaac Ware – people who were interested in Palladio, the Roman baths, the recently excavated ancient sculptures, people who had the general desire to achieve the classical ideal in architecture. In the middle of the first decade of the eighteenth century he was again in the company of cultured, cosmopolitan people who, as far as can be judged from individual reminiscences, shared his aspirations and valued his talent.[104] Moreover, at this time he lived comparatively peacefully, particularly after his official retirement on 25 May 1805.[105]

Forty years of his life lay between these two periods; these were years filled with creativity, but they were far from being free of disillusionment, hardship and unpleasantness. Cameron died in St Petersburg at the end of 1811, not long before the start of the war with Napoleon. He seems to belong in that part of the nineteenth century that still had one foot in the eighteenth century and was as yet unaffected by the changes that the war would bring.

Such are the events that form the biography of Charles Cameron, his activities and their consequences. To some degree they convey his rough and passionate character and the unique nature of his personality; they lay some foundations for an understanding of the architect's work and of his role as a major link between British architecture and the development of a more Europeanised cultural and architectural environment in the court circles of Russia.

Chapter Two

THE ARTISTIC WORLDS OF
TSARSKOYE SELO

The court of Catherine the Great spent a large part of the summer at Tsarskoye Selo, a huge estate twenty-two miles from St Petersburg (pl. 28). On one July evening in the mid-1780s, in the Hermitage Pavilion deep in the park, the courtiers were playing the old game of *burim* (*beaux-rimes*). Each had to write a phrase on a piece of paper and pass it to the next person to add another. One of the grandees wrote: 'My castles in the air.' Catherine took the paper from him and added: 'They are not in the air and I add something to them every day.'[1]

This story can be interpreted in different ways, but it reveals the artistic uniqueness of Tsarskoye Selo in a particularly telling fashion. The 'castles in the air' of Russian thought in the age of the Enlightenment were embodied here in the constructions of architects. Tsarskoye Selo was the unique locus and laboratory of new ideas in Russian eighteenth-century architecture: we can see here, with great clarity, the various stages, types and varieties of building reflecting the relationship between Russian and British architecture at this time. It is highly significant that this relationship was realised precisely in that place where for two centuries the country's best architectural talents were concentrated.

No other ensemble of palaces and parks has such importance for Russian culture as Tsarskoye Selo. It is not just that each architectural style of the eighteenth and nineteenth centuries has left its splendid monuments here: the visual beauty so impressive in all the buildings of Rastrelli and Cameron exerts an unusual spiritual fascination at Tsarskoye Selo, where the whole ensemble developed its own architectural poetry. Its landscapes, and the buildings erected in the parks, were immortalised in the unforgettable images of the eighteenth-century poets Mikhail Lomonosov, Gavril Derzhavin and Ippolit Bogdanovich, and in those of such nineteenth- and twentieth-century poets as Lev Mey, Innokenti Annensky, Nikolai Gumilev and Anna Akhmatova. Neither in the depths of Siberian exile nor in the busy life of the capital on the banks of the Neva did those who had been at school with young Alexander Pushkin at the Tsarskoye Selo *lycée* forget the nurturing place of their youth, their friendships and their young hopes. Pushkin's own words encapsulate the special impact of this imperial village, inherited from Catherine, on generations of intellectuals:

> We are all the same: the whole world is foreign to us
> Our fatherland is Tsarskoye Selo.

Tsarskoye Selo is a whole constellation of artistic worlds brought to life by the different nuances of aesthetic thought in the eighteenth century. The architectural ensembles that were developed here included not only gardens and palaces but also model villages, an ideal town and different kinds of *fermes ornées*. Each comprised its own special world. A massive chinoiserie complex was created to suggest an

28 Charles Cameron, *View from Catherine the Great's Apartments towards the Hanging Garden, the Agate Pavilion and the Cameron Gallery*, 1790s.

29 Tsarskoye Selo: view of the Catherine Palace from the Old Garden.

exotic 'oriental game'. The programme of another garden was designed to evoke a 'world of political dreams', where the latest political events and points of view were represented by monuments, pavilions or allegorical landscapes. In addition, a large area surrounding the park formed the 'world of enlightened well-being'. This included a town, several villages, farms and estates, all designed to promote the impression of the existence of prosperity among Catherine's subjects. At the centre of these 'worlds', the nucleus to which all roads led, was Catherine's new, neo-classical palace, devoted in both its design and decoration to the ideal of the antique world. Thus an architectural articulation of the antique was placed at the geographical and ideological centre of many different allegorical worlds, offering a potent symbol for the empress and her court.

However, before turning to the British motifs for the Tsarskoye Selo architecture, let us briefly examine the development of the estate in the first half of the eighteenth century. At the turn of the century, after his first victories in the northern wars and after he had won for Russia the northern shores of the Gulf of Finland, Peter the Great (1672–1725) gave the old Swedish farm to his favourite, A.D. Menshikov. But then as often happened, in 1710 he returned it to his wife, Catherine I. From this time Tsarskoye Selo became the favourite imperial residence. In turn the court architects Braunstein, Schlutter, Trezini, Zemtsov and Chevakinsky built the palace and enlarged the regular gardens. Tsarskoye Selo became particularly magnificent during the flowering of Russian baroque in the mid-eighteenth century, when Bartolomeo Rastrelli was working there.

> If fine buildings twinkle like stars,
> Then Tsarskoye Selo is clearly worthy
> To be called a constellation.

These lines by the eighteenth-century poet Mikhail Lomonosov evoke the image of Rastrelli's ensemble: lavish, shining and bright, like the geometric proof of some remarkably harmonious theorem. The luxurious palace (pls 29–32), completed in the mid-1750s, glowed with shining decorations and paint: white columns and gilded details against a background of bright turquoise walls and roofs painted silver. It was like a magnificent piece of jewellery on a monumental scale. The huge park, developed along an axis perpendicular to the palace, consisted of square and rectangular spinneys musically melodious in their proportions and intersected by paths spreading out in star formation. Their design was both strict and unusually varied: in it the radial avenues

30 Tsarskoye Selo: view of the Catherine Palace from the Old Garden.

43

31 Rastrelli, the Catherine Palace, Tsarskoye Selo: enfilade.

at one point crowded together as though trying to merge, and the next relaxed into a diamond shape; and then again they would flow together in several lines towards one point.

Standing among the *parterres* of the mid-eighteenth-century Old Garden a viewer could take in the entire three-hundred-metre length of the palace. Today it is easy to imagine courtiers walking among the tidy spinneys, or the procession of the imperial suite, constrained by etiquette, attired in gold-embroidered uniforms and ceremonial dresses, and bedecked with jewels; while on the other side of the palace, a carriage drawn by twelve horses slowly turns in the courtyard, which is surrounded by the low semicircular buildings of the circumference linked by wrought-iron railings. This was Tsarskoye Selo in the 1750s.

Time passed and fashions changed, leaving buildings that had lost their lustre and planting that was overgrown. Yet regardless of the efforts of the architects who worked here in the ensuing decades, Rastrelli's palace remained the basis of the ensemble. The first to confront it with further innovations was Charles Cameron, whose work for Catherine the Great during the 1780s created a new neo-classical image for Tsarskoye Selo.

The first of the Tsarskoye Selo worlds we shall try to enter is the antique ensemble created by Cameron, whose ideas signalled a turning-point in Russian classicism. During the 1760s and 1770s classicism in Russia had been understood as an academic system of compositional principles and modes, using the orders to create a feeling of restraint and peace that contrasted with the dynamism of the baroque. Such a concept was upheld by the French architects who had come to Russia and by the Russians who had studied in Paris, notably Vallin de la Mothe, Ivan Starov and Vasily Bazhenov (the latter two, pupils of Charles de Wailly). Catherine the Great was not pleased by this: 'We have Frenchmen who know too much and build ridiculous houses which are no good inside or out and all because they know too much.'[2] From a letter to Baron Grimm, her greatest confidant, it appears that she wanted to invite to her court 'two Italians'. She succeeded in finding them: Giacomo Trombara and Giacomo Quarenghi; a third architect invited at the same time was Cameron.

Cameron took up the reinterpretation of classicism with greater determination than did the Italians. He was one of the first architects in Russia to see antiquity not as an

32 Giacomo Quarenghi, *View of Tsarskoye Selo*. Rastrelli's Catherine Palace and parts of Sadovaya Street are shown, with the Orangery on the left.

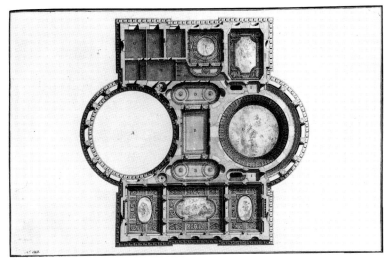

33 and 34   Charles de Wailly, project for the Pavilion of Arts and Sciences, 1772. Left: plan; right: elevation.

35   Charles-Louis Clérisseau, House of Antiquity for Tsarskoye Selo, 1773.

abstraction or a scheme but as an immortal ideal capable of being constantly reinterpreted in a contemporary work of art.

Catherine's plan in the 1770s was to build 'a Graeco-Roman rhapsody in my Tsarskoye Selo garden'.

> One or more artists are wanted . . . who will research Greek or Roman antiquity to find a building there with a complete setting . . . It would be appropriate to summarise the age of the Caesars, the Augustuses, the Ciceros and such patrons as Maecenus and to create a building where it would be possible to find all these people in one . . . if some of these sheets of drawings were to please the empress enough that she should wish to see them realised then . . . they would be united in some way in a single building and all necessary means would be provided for execution of the designs within the garden.[3]

Thus ran the invitation to create such an edifice, which was sent out to the French Academy of Architecture at the beginning of the decade. In response to this request came designs for the Pavilion of Arts and Sciences by Charles de Wailly[4] and a House of Antiquity by Charles-Louis Clérisseau (pls 33–5). Clérisseau attempted to find a building in which it would have been possible to find several of the famous Roman figures together at one and the same time. He decided that they might have met in the baths. Clérisseau's House of Antiquity, based on the composition of the Baths of Diocletian, would have been larger than Rastrelli's entire Tsarskoye Selo palace and so was totally unsuitable. He was, however, the first to come to the conclusion that the baths were the archetypal building of ancient Rome and could be used to stage a reconstruction of antique life in the way the empress desired. This suggests a motive for Catherine the Great's invitation to Charles Cameron, whom she knew 'for his book on ancient baths'. Moreover, when the architect arrived in Russia he was immediately asked his opinion of Clérisseau, to which he replied that he felt great admiration for the French master.[5]

The Baths and the Cameron Gallery

The baths at Tsarskoye Selo were the first work that Cameron created in Russia. Indeed, they were his first big practical architectural work anywhere. It was this work, and the gallery on the same site, that brought their creator lasting fame. 'The gallery . . . still bears Cameron's name – the only building in Russia which has, by the will of fate, preserved the name of its creator', wrote the Russian art historian, Igor Grabar in 1903.[6] There was something remarkable in the fascination exercised by the gallery and the baths that has caused them always to be singled out from among all the magnificent Tsarskoye Selo buildings. To contemporaries of Cameron it seemed that in these works an ancient, Olympian and divine beauty had been reborn. The great Russian eighteenth-century poet Gavril Derzhavin called Cameron's gallery 'a temple where the graces dance to the sound of the harp'.[7] Another famous poet, Ippolit Bogdanovich, declared that 'it is only possible for the Gods to have created' such halls.[8] Alexander Pushkin also gave this structure its due, calling it 'the temple of the Minerva of Rus'.[9]

There are few buildings in Russia which have been considered worthy haunts for the muses or Minerva by a whole constellation of poets. A more potent dynamic stimulated these poetic images than the conventional use of mythological subjects. In his construction Cameron succeeded in achieving something that can still be felt today, something that is striking in the sensuality of its classicism. He managed to suggest the presence of the antique world by means of those visual forms which still dominate our conceptions of ideal ancient beauty. Although a relatively small building, it has a power that derives above all from the emotional impact of the composition. It has neither the blinding splendour of the model works of the eighteenth-century French architects, nor the balanced rationalism displayed by the quiet Palladians such as Quarenghi. And yet the baths at Tsarskoye Selo represent the very flesh of classicism: they are the realisation of the deepest, intimate, personal belief of Cameron in the ancient ideal. This is what struck the viewer then, as it does now.

Cameron worked on the baths from 1779 to 1792, and it is instructive to follow the development of his idea. His plan was for a small, refined building to be erected close to Rastrelli's palace, next to the wing that had recently been built by Yury Velten (pl. 36). (Subsequently, in the 1790s when Catherine's last favourite, Platon Zubov, settled in its ground floor, this became known as the Zubovsky wing.) Together these buildings would mark the boundary between the regular garden and the new picturesque garden.

In his first design (pl. 37) Cameron counterposed the lower floor to the upper one, allowing each to convey quite a different image. The ground floor was heavy, monumental, weighty in the mass of its masonry. The architect covered it with coarsely worked, porous stone which looked as if it had been eaten away by wind and rain. This was a kind of 'pedestal of time'. It gave the whole building a feeling of antiquity, creating the illusion of a genuine ancient monument. The first floor, in contrast, was light and airy (pls 38–43, 47). As described in the 1920s by art historian Gollerbakh, its architecture was 'exceptionally fine for its exquisite simplicity: the stucco walls were coloured in a gentle yellow shade against which the red Pompeian niches stood out and the white Ionic columns gleamed in a graceful row.'[10]

On three sides the pavilion seemed to be separated from the surrounding space by its precise edges. Looking at the façade that faced the Old Garden one was struck by the integral flatness of the wall which halted the development of movement of the space of the regular park. No order was applied here. The flat niches around the windows, the balustrades of the false balconies gently curved with a fine line, the cornice with its slight projection and, above all, the single rhythm emphasised the flat planes and the graphic nature of the design of the façade.

In this composition there was a particularly attractive contrast between the broad but very shallow niches around the windows and the narrow, elongated dark embrasures, as a result of which each window was given a special weight. Moreover, the large flat window-frames concentrated the viewer's attention on the few strongly indented parts

36 Ground-floor plan of Cameron's baths at Tsarskoye Selo: the Cold Baths.

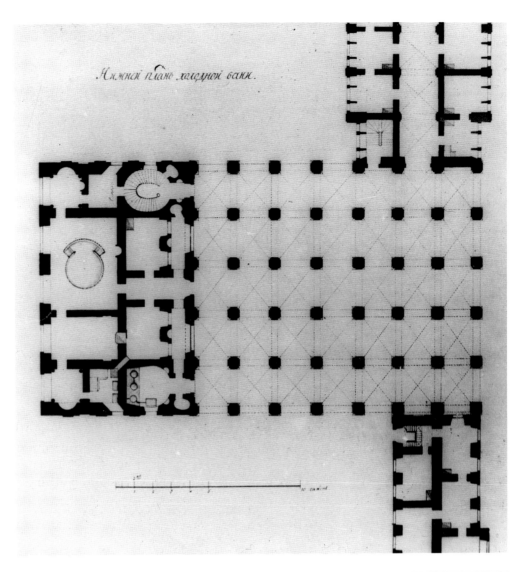

Нижней план холодной бани.

37 Charles Cameron, initial design for the Cold Baths at Tsarskoye Selo (freestanding building): elevation, 1779.

38 (following page top) Charles Cameron, section through the baths, Tsarskoye Selo, early 1780s.

39 (following page bottom) section through the Relaxation Room in the Cold Baths, Tsarskoye Selo: alternative proposal, early 1780s.

1 743 ... N.º 11047.

1 743 ... N.º 10987.

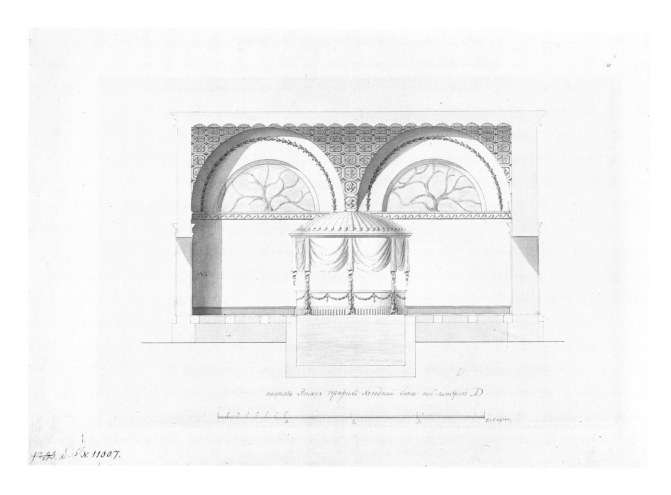

нижняго Этажа профиль холодной бани под литерою D

44 (right) View of the Cold Baths at Tsarskoye Selo, with the arcades of the Cameron Gallery. Drawing of the 1780s.

45 (above) Charles Cameron, the baths, Tsarskoye Selo: elevation of the Agate Pavilion.

42 (facing page top) Charles Cameron, section through the baths, Tsarskoye Selo, early 1780s.

43 (facing page bottom) Charles Cameron, design for a hall in the Agate Pavilion, Tsarskoye Selo, early 1780s.

46 (right) Charles Cameron, the baths, Tsarskoye Selo: detail of the elevation facing the New Garden.

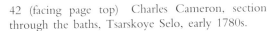

40 (page 49 top) Charles Cameron, section through the Relaxation Room in the Cold Baths, Tsarskoye Selo, early 1780s.

41 (page 49 bottom) Charles Cameron, design for the Relaxation Room in the Cold Baths, Tsarskoye Selo, early 1780s.

of the composition – the red niches with statues of naiads placed in the piers (pl. 45). Over this musical harmony of niches and embrasures soared large round medallions, the work of the French sculptor Jean Rachet. Here, in allegories of prosperity, victory and well-being, Flora, entwined with garlands, was gathering a basket of flowers, river and sea nymphs were circling in a dance, Cupid was carrying sheaves of corn and the goddess of Glory with a laurel wreath was burning the enemy's weapons on a victory bonfire.[11]

On the side facing the new picturesque garden Cameron used a different composition. The ground floor again served only as the monumental foundation for the building (pl. 44), while the first floor was distinguished by the complex structure of its volumes, by the lavishness of its decor, by the abundance of its sculpture. On three sides the building was closed and turned inwards, but here it opened out, drinking in the landscape to become welcoming and exultant.

In the centre was placed a rotunda with a cupola (pl. 46). This was supported by light Ionic columns. The projecting semi-circular portico attracted the visitor into the shade of the rotunda, where in the broad and squat niches it was possible to discern a bronze Mercury and a Vesta. The end columns of the portico unexpectedly split into two and the colonnade became a plane running along the wall, turning into corner pilasters, then appearing on protrusions which projected forwards. In the niches dark bronze statues stood on marble pedestals, allegories of Water and Fire, Earth and Air. Among the representations of the four elements stood images of Cupid and Psyche created by the French sculptor L. Adam. A poetry of mythological forms was alive among the refined Roman architecture. Cameron sharpened the viewer's feelings and transported his mind to ideal ancient dreams.

However perfect the external architecture of Cameron's baths, it was the interiors finished in precious stones that struck his contemporaries. In addition to marble, bronze, porcelain and gilt, red jasper and green, and green with red veins, of crimson agate and eastern mountain crystal were used. The building, legendary even in its creator's lifetime, became known as the Agate Pavilion (in Russian literally the Agate Rooms). Derzhavin called it a 'chamber worthy of Olympus', where gems shone like 'the beams of stars'.[12]

The interiors of the baths were not only famous for their expensive finish. They were a very rare example, the only one in Russia, of a place where the ancient model was followed not just in its artistic forms but also in its functional construction. Cameron was trying to resurrect here the Roman culture of bathing.

In these rooms Cameron reconstructed the ceremonial chambers of the private baths of ancient Rome, such as those of Petronius or Seneca. An expert in antiquity, he naturally did not base his work on public baths. Their scale would have been too grandiose. He turned to a model that was more appropriate in type and character. However, he made use of artistic methods and decorative motifs characteristic of imperial Roman buildings. Thus, he combined an intimate scale of construction with monumental decoration. This was one of the most striking features of all Cameron's work.

According to his description in *The Baths of the Romans*, in ancient times,

in the most finished and the most refined baths there was the following accommodation: an apoditory or place for undressing, an unctuary or place for keeping oils, a spheristery or large room for exercises . . . a hot bath, a laconic or hot room for sweating, a tepidary or warm room with heated water and, finally, a frigidary or cold bath. There were also other rooms there for banquets and meetings.

The order of use of the Roman baths was, in Cameron's opinion, as follows:

Having undressed the visitor went into the unctuary where he anointed his body with simple cheap oil before doing some exercises. Kept here also were the best fragrant oils which were used after coming out of the baths . . . Having annointed themselves, bathers would pass directly into the spheristery . . . for all sorts of exercises . . . These completed [they] moved to the adjacent warm baths where they sat and washed . . . They sat in the baths lower than the level of the water . . . after washing they returned along a different route from that by which they had come.

47   Charles Cameron, design for the central hall of the Agate Pavilion, Tsarskoye Selo, early 1780s.

From the hot bath they went straight into the tepidary and . . . they spent some time there so that their bodies did not have to adjust too quickly to the temperature of the frigidary.[13]

In the Tsarskoye Selo baths the entrance was on the ground floor and led into a corridor, on either side of which were the service rooms. The bather then turned into a hall with a bath, the frigidary. Where were they supposed to undress? Apparently here. Cameron paid particular attention to this question in his book: 'However there was not always an apoditory [place for undressing] in the baths; from what Lucianus says it is clear that the cold bath was also used for this purpose.'[14] In this room, according to Cameron's design, the floor should be covered in white marble brought from Greece and the ceiling decorated with carving and paintings.[15] In the centre of the hall he wanted to build a bath of white marble with a canopy over it supported by eight white and gold porcelain pillars. A bronze seat covered with polished gold was to be found under the water. The bather could see large sculpted compositions beneath

49 (facing page)   Charles Cameron, Agate Pavilion, Tsarskoye Selo: central hall.

the arches, all dedicated to mythological episodes connected with the seas or rivers. There was Pan following a nymph who was half hidden in reeds by a river bank. The centaur Nessus was transporting Hercules' wife on his back across the water. The blood of the dying Acis, the shepherd who loved Galatea, was turned into a stream.[16]

When one had undressed and bathed in this hall it was possible to turn left, first into a room with a warm water bath and then into one with a hot bath. This did not follow the Roman pattern, but was typical of the Russian steam bath. There on the latticed vault of a stove were piled two hundred and fifty red-hot cannon balls. Water was poured over them, making steam.[17] The bather's return journey submitted to the Roman practice of making a gradual transition to the low temperature area. Once again the bather was in a hall with a bath from which it was possible to pass into a room for resting, a small square vaulted room almost wholly occupied by a most luxurious ancient couch. This was shielded by round medallions on the sails of its canopy dedicated to the myths of love: Cupid and Psyche, Aphrodite and the handsome Adonis, Selene the moon goddess and the exquisite Endymion.

Even more lavish were the rooms on the first floor, which formed the Agate Pavilion itself (pls 48–50). The central hall dominated here. The architect made the other rooms small so that the hall could be spacious. It seemed unexpectedly large and high considering the far from grandiose size of the bath building as a whole. The visitor's eye moved immediately from the lower to the upper part of the hall, to take in the peaceful decoration of the walls. The very broad spacing of the Corinthian columns, the even rhythm of the lofty French windows, the simple rectangular outlines of the niches, the large round medallions with their bas-reliefs placed over the embrasures, all this gave an impression of balance. Looking up, the ceiling (pls 51, 53)

48   Charles Cameron, executed variant for the decoration of the central hall of the Agate Pavilion, Tsarskoye Selo, early 1780s.

50 (above left) Charles Cameron, Agate Pavilion, Tsarskoye Selo: central hall.

51 (above right) Charles Cameron, Agate Pavilion, Tsarskoye Selo: ceiling of the central hall.

52 Charles Cameron, Agate Pavilion, Tsarskoye Selo: fireplace in the central hall.

53 Charles Cameron, Agate Pavilion, Tsarskoye Selo: ceiling of the central hall.

was covered with the densely luxuriant form of the multi-faceted canopy. The complex vault comprised an intertwined pattern of carved and gilded polyhedrons in all imaginable forms and proportions. It seemed that a feeling of ceremony and magnificence permeated the very air, filling the space.

The three-branched candelabras reminiscent of a tree with luxuriant foliage were, in Cameron's design, to be held in the hands of sculpted women in ancient dress (pl. 52). The sculptures came to life through their contrast with the strict architectural forms. This impression was strengthened by the lamplight playing on the marble.

Cameron liked to juxtapose rooms to give contrasting impressions, and he did this with the small spaces to the side of the central hall. Here his principal tools of contrast were the materials. To the right of the main hall was the Agate Study (pl. 56), where a deep reddish-brown stone covered the bases of the walls, which were divided into large panels, each edged by strips of green jasper. This jasper was used also for friezes, plinths, door panels (pl. 54) and window frames. The cross-vault crowning this high oval room was painted dark green (pl. 55). Numerous bronze decorations glowed dimly against the stone. The decoration of the vault was a fantastic composition in a

54 Charles Cameron, project for doors
in the Agate Study, Agate Pavilion,
Tsarskoye Selo, early 1780s.

55 Charles Cameron, Agate Study,
Agate Pavilion, Tsarskoye Selo: ceiling.
Photo of the 1930s.

56 (facing page) Charles Cameron,
Agate Study, Agate Pavilion, Tsarskoye
Selo.

57   Charles Cameron, Jasper Study, Agate Pavilion, Tsarskoye Selo.

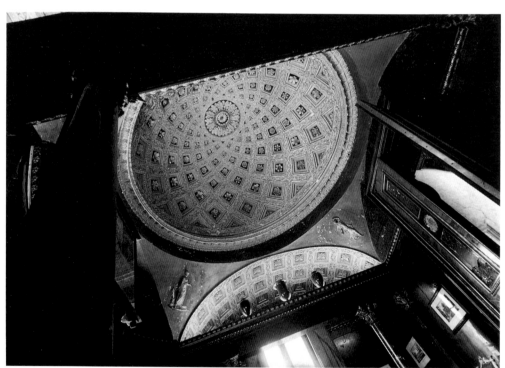

58   Charles Cameron, Jasper Study, Agate Pavilion, Tsarskoye Selo: ceiling.

Roman grotesque style: five allegorical paintings in rectangular frames were surrounded by figures of gryphons with pointed wings, their claws touching the tripods.

On the other side of the main hall the most luxurious room was the Jasper Study, sited symmetrically opposite the Agate Study and even more lavish (pls 57, 58). A massive gilded dome rested on the heavy circle of its foundation. From its dark-cream sides projected bas-relief figures of dancing nymphs. Further, in the depths of the room segments of cylindrical vaults were divided by the measured lines of rectangular articulations. These too were fully gilded. Below them ran the entablature and the frieze, of dark red and green stone with golden profiles.

In January 1784, when work on finishing the Agate Pavilion was still in progress, Cameron submitted for the empress's approval plans and a model for a new part of the baths complex. This was a long, two-storeyed promenade gallery which would subsequently take the architect's name. His proposal was that the gallery should be linked to the palace and the Agate Pavilion by a covered walkway, which would create direct access from Catherine the Great's own rooms. It was proposed that in fine weather she could walk in the colonnade and on bad days she could use the central part which would be enclosed by glass.

If the baths were designed to help 'live an ancient life', then the gallery served to create the emotional mood necessary to promote aspiration to the ancient ideal. Beneath the colonnade one felt distanced from the present moment, from the hurly-burly of ordinary life. Everything predisposed one to contemplation and calm, recalling the promenading of ancient philosophers in the gardens of the Athens Academy or under the porticos of Roman villas. The gallery, which was erected in 1787, struck its contemporaries by its 'magnificent silence'.

The architecture of the Cameron Gallery used ideas established during the first stage of development of the baths complex. The ground floor again served as an intentionally archaicised foundation for the first floor, which was light and refined. Above, Cameron used the same Ionic order with capitals derived from the Erechtheon. All this strengthened the integral connection between the two structures.

From the park could be seen the dark dense mass of the ground floor and above it the white colonnade with two porticos projecting forwards. If one stood right beside the façade, it seemed as if the first floor was flying upwards. It was outlined against the sky like part of an ideal celestial world. Not for nothing did Pushkin refer to the gallery as 'a mansion rushing to the clouds'. However, the poet was also impressed by the lower part of the building, with its heavy power and tense monumental strength. The viewer's glance took in the bold and coarse rustication covering the wall of the ground floor. Pilasters projected from this highly plastic mass and between them were arches with deliberately coarse key-stones. At the cornice the coarseness of the covering disappeared, as if the passing of the centuries had smoothed the stones to leave a smooth wall above. The simple capitals of the columns here provided a gentle transition from the severity of the ground floor to the sparkling elegance of the first floor (pl. 59).

The end wall of the gallery recalled an ancient temple. The oval ceremonial staircase gave the composition a sense of ascent from the earth up into a world of perfect ancient harmony that seemed by some miracle to have survived the centuries (pls 60–2). As soon as a visitor approached the steps, enclosed by pedestals of gigantic statues of Hercules and Flora, he was protected by them from the surrounding park. The staircase seemed to embrace him in its flights and to lead him upwards. Ascending he would see in different perspectives the pediment, the columns, the capitals, all of whose strict lines created a refinement of great simplicity.

At last, on the first floor the visitor found himself between unusually widely spaced columns giving an unaccustomed sense of spaciousness. The entire park could be seen from here (pl. 63): the lake on which there was an island, the greenery overhanging the water, the neo-gothic admiralty, with its towers recalling a small castle, the Rostral Column in the distance and nearby a grotto from Rastrelli's time, turquoise with gilded details. There were boats, swans and the light ripple of waves disturbing the smoothness of the water, as well as ladies and their escorts in beautiful court dress. It was a truly charmed island in the world of the eighteenth century, a place where ancient heroes could have lived. Of this scene the poet Derzhavin wrote:

59 Charles Cameron, Agate Pavilion, Tsarskoye Selo: detail of capitals.

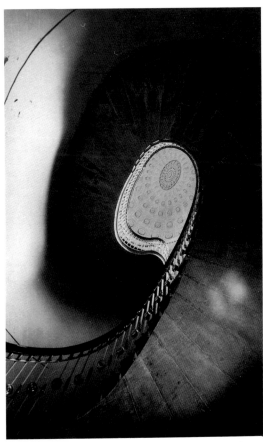

60 Charles Cameron, Agate Pavilion, Tsarskoye Selo: staircase.

61 Charles Cameron, Agate
Pavilion, Tsarskoye Selo: staircase.

62 (facing page) Charles Cameron,
design for the staircase in the Agate
Pavilion, Tsarskoye Selo, early
1780s.

63 M. Vorob'ev, *The Cameron Buildings at Tsar-skoye Selo from the Lake*, 1820s.

Here idols were preserved,
And altars smoked with sacrifices.[18]

Further, beyond the park's trees, which were not then very tall, was a sight still more surprising: an entire town, called Sofiya, which had been specially constructed by Cameron to embellish the views from the park. I shall discuss this settlement later, for the moment it is important only as one of the most curious elements in the panorama visible from Cameron's Gallery. Beyond the town was rural land, fields in which 'wheat is sown and glades lie close beside'. Catherine the Great wrote to Voltaire that she could see for about 100 *versts* (about 100 miles) from here.[19]

The feeling of space was undoubtedly the strongest sensation that Cameron's work here created. Contemporaries ascending into the gallery could not stop themselves from exclaiming, 'What views! What a lot of air!'[20] This feeling was to a significant degree created by a device that Cameron used with considerable boldness, and which has often been remarked upon by students of his work. As we have already noted, he positioned the columns much further apart than was permissible under classical rules, so that the large spaces between the supports exquisitely framed the views of the park. Why did Cameron, the convinced devotee of classicism, do this with such delightful freedom? What was the derivation for this composition, which had such a striking effect?

It is usually accounted for as merely an eccentricity, but the source emerges if we move in under the canopy of the gallery. The columns support a classic entablature in the Ionic order. The building is divided into three aisles: two open to the air and one behind glass intended for walks in inclement weather. Neither scholars nor visitors have paid much attention to the inner walls dividing the first floor of the building into its parts. But it was here that Cameron made use of an unexpected device once he had established the canonicity of the order. On the inner wall he put a small second order, of Tuscan columns supporting the entablature. If this is overlaid upon the large order of the gallery, the full logical and canonical system of orders results.

It is well known that Cameron did make a design like this (pl. 64). Moreover, there is reason to believe that he had seen a sketch of Palladio's, depicting a gallery with a similar order system. In the collection of Lord Burlington, whose links with the architect and his mentor, Ware, have already been discussed, there was a drawing (now

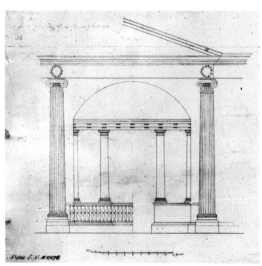

64 Charles Cameron, design for the Cameron Gallery, Tsarskoye Selo, early 1780s.

in the RIBA) bought by Burlington in Italy. Palladio, working on the design for his famous Basilica had, in one of his variations, proposed constructing a two-storey building with arches cut out below, covered with rustication which also extended on to the Tuscan pilasters. The upper floor would have broadly spaced Ionic columns with arched windows between them. The windows would have small supports with Tuscan capitals. In creating his gallery, Cameron deliberately split Palladio's scheme into two parts and shifted its components around. Such boldness is as characteristic of his work as his concern for the emotional appeal of his buildings.

Sun, air, light and shade, heat and cold, greenery below and sculpture on the colonnade were all taken into account and used to create a particular atmosphere. Catherine wrote: 'This colonnade is particularly pleasant in that, in the cold weather, it always has one side where the cold is felt less. The middle of my colonnade is glass, below and round about there is a flower garden, the ground floor of the colonnade is busy with ladies of my acquaintance who are there like nymphs among the flowers, and on the colonnade stand busts of great people of antiquity – Homer, Demosthenes, Plato and others' (pls 66, 67).[22]

These busts were one of the attractions of the gallery. It was populated with the shadows of antique military leaders and emperors, writers and philosophers, and even those of contemporaries. 'So if you are curious to know who these honoured people

65   Tsarskoye Selo: Cameron Gallery and the Private Garden.

66 Tsarskoye Selo: Cameron Gallery: elevation towards the New Garden.

are, here is a list which I have made for you as you walk,'[23] wrote Catherine the Great to Baron Grimm. The majority were Roman emperors, from Julius Caesar to Vespasian, from Antonius Pius to Septimus Severus. Beside the portrait of Hadrian was to be placed a depiction of his favourite, Antinous, who was deified after his death which he had welcomed for Caesar's sake. In the choice of heroes for the sculpted decoration of the Cameron Gallery we see the empress's enthusiasm for imperial Rome on the one hand, together with a desire not to forget the historical and mythological figures who were popular in this, the age of Enlightenment. Therefore, here could be found Socrates and Plato, Heraclitus and Ovid as well as Apollo, Minerva, Bacchus, Ariadne and Hercules. The busts were made of bronze from Italian plaster casts of the ancient originals. Catherine's secretary Khrapovitsky recalled: 'Because of my knowledge I was charged with choosing the best ancient busts from the Tsarskoye Selo grotto for casting in copper and placing on the colonnade. There were enquiries about the bust of Plato which had not been seen for a long time and which it was hoped I would find.'[24]

The two contemporary busts in the gallery were of the famous poet and scholar of the Russian Enlightenment, Mikhail Lomonosov, and the leader of the opposition in the British Parliament, Charles James Fox. It was Catherine who decided to give Fox this honoured place. Khrapovitsky reported her as saying: 'Fox's bust was brought and I ordered that it be placed in the Hermitage and that a bronze should be made for placing on the colonnade in Tsarskoye Selo between Demosthenes and Cicero.'[25] He continued: 'Before dining everyone was taken to the colonnade and shown how the bronze bust of Charles Fox had been placed between Cicero and Demosthenes.'[26] The immortalisation of Lomonosov made a strong impression on the courtiers at that time. It had not been expected that such a distinction would be accorded to the late academic, and several considered themselves equally deserving of such an honour. Thus the poet Gavril Derzhavin addressed a request to Catherine:

67 Tsarskoye Selo: Cameron Gallery: colonnade.

66

68 Tsarskoye Selo: Cameron Gallery: south elevation.

To vex those who envy me
Place me among the famous men .
In your splendid colonnade.[27]

But his wish was never granted.

The rows of bronze busts in Cameron's gallery setting brought the colonnade to life.[28] They gave a special literary quality to the impression of antiquity that lay behind the construction of the whole complex. Moreover, walks in the gallery were made more entertaining, even edifying.

At the beginning of the 1790s the narrow passage linking all parts of the baths was made into the Hanging Garden. A terrace on arches was built, and on this, in front of the Agate Pavilion, was made a flower garden. Contemporaries could not but recall the gardens of Semiramis. The Hanging Garden was linked to the park by a gentle slope, or *pente-douce* (pl. 68). Walking up the *pente-douce* one was met by eight bronze statues of the Muses, depictions of Venus, Mercury and Flora[29] and gigantic vases in the antique style (pls 69–73). These gave the ascent to the Agate Pavilion a special feeling,

69 The Cameron buildings at Tsarskoye Selo. Drawing of the 1790s.

and the architecture here combined to produce a powerful impression. The gently sloping arches of coarse stone, rising one after the other out of the ground, the squat columns at the sides, the vaulting below, the huge fantastic antique masks on the key stones, all created a romantic image. It seemed as if antiquity itself had reappeared on earth, gradually to materialise on the soil of Tsarskoye Selo.

It was precisely at this stage that the two worlds of Cameron's ensemble became clearly crystallised. The lower one was permeated by a mysterious, gloomy, romantic feeling. The upper one was light, sunny, joyous and carefree, magically evoking a sense of the ideal, ancient life, and it was one of the most striking exponents of this spirit in Russian and world classicism. At the beginning of the twentieth century the Russian art critic Erich Gollerbakh put it thus:

> The columns shine white and distinct in the twilight, after the sun has set, when amber reflections from sweeping clouds glow and fade. Lilac shadows fall and are

70 Giacomo Quarenghi, *View of the Cameron Gallery*, 1790s.

71 Tsarskoye Selo: *pente-douce*.

72 (below left) Tsarskoye Selo: *pente-douce*.

73 (above right) Tsarskoye Selo: *pente-douce*.

extinguished. The last late swallows return to their nests. The sky grows dark, the rustle quietens, the mirror of the lake loses its lustre . . . At such an hour the irreproachable beauty of the Cameron Gallery is especially captivating and its lines engrave themselves . . . unforgettably on your memory.[30]

Cameron's bath designs in Tsarskoye Selo span many years, but I have described them together here to preserve the unity of the account. Turning back to the 1780s, we shall now examine the interiors which Cameron created for Rastrelli's Catherine Palace.

★   ★   ★

The halls of the Catherine Palace are among Charles Cameron's finest works. His contributions in the field of architectural interiors have long been valued. Even in the 1780s the opinion was that the rooms created by Cameron were 'so splendid and so unique that if one has not seen them one can have no idea of what they are like.'[31] This characterisation is perhaps truer than many pronouncements from later scholars, who frequently tried to measure Cameron in accordance with the standard criteria of classicism, attempting to explain the beauty of his creations by their 'faithfulness to the spirit of ancient art'.[32] Such commentators emphasised that his 'magnificent ensembles of interior decoration are filled with knowledge of the ancient classics'.[33] They considered that 'Cameron's decorative motifs sent one's thoughts to the architecture of the distant times of antiquity . . . to the art of the times when the Roman and Pompeian baths were constructed, to places where Cameron and a whole constellation of his brilliant contemporaries had opened most valuable pages of a genuine, true and stirring art.'[34] In his interiors they saw adherence to a definite system of Roman decoration manifesting itself in the 'completely unmodified' application of a number of rules with regard both to the overall composition of the halls and to individual details of the vaults, the domes, the doors and so on. They even went so far as to maintain that 'deviations from these rules were not permitted by Cameron himself but only by his restorers.'[35] As a result, historians have portrayed him as a rather doctrinaire bore. But this was not his character at all.

Cameron's interiors were above all original—far richer and more significant than dogmatic neo-classicism. Cameron introduced into his creations much that did not exist in the buildings of antiquity: porcelain and Chinese lacquer, Russian gems and stained glass, inlaid wood parquet and silk wallpaper. He could convey the symmetry obligatory to classicism by a mere hint. He created walls and doors of glass in order to move space. Without hesitating, he placed his Chinese Hall in the middle of apartments decorated in the antique style. He 'grew' an entire forest of tin-plate in his Palm Room. He converted Pompeian paintings and depictions on Chinese lacquer into three-dimensional architecture. He would use some motif that he had noticed in a Roman interior in such a way that it became appropriate and irreplaceable in surroundings that were quite different in purpose, scale and character. Cameron worked with total freedom, unhampered by any stylistic restrictions or rules.

This freedom was acquired through a thorough study of the Roman baths and other ancient structures. He had the ability to create endlessly varied ceiling designs and arabesques, vaults and ornaments. His creativity began not with some art-historical idea nor with a sketch, but with his view of an entire architectural concept.[36] That is why his compositions are so various. He was not striving to make the composition of the halls of the Catherine Palace stylistically integrated; on the contrary, they were all completely different and his aim was that people should be struck by their variety, rather than be impressed 'by the abundance and lavishness' of one and the same style, as was the case with baroque interiors.

Cameron created two suites of apartments in the Catherine Palace. First were the rooms of the heir to the throne, Grand Duke Paul Petrovich and his wife Grand Duchess Maria Fedorovna. This suite comprised the Green Dining Room, the Serving Room, the Blue Drawing Room, the Chinese Blue Drawing Room, the Bedchamber and a studio for painting and ivory carving. It was completed in 1782. Simultaneously he began work on the public and private rooms of Catherine the Great: the Arabesque Hall, the Lyons Hall, the Chinese Hall, the Domed Dining Room, the Silver Study, the Bedchamber, a boudoir (the so-called Snuff-Box Room) and the Palm Room (later the Mirror Room). This work took eight years, from 1780 to 1788. I shall begin this

74 Tsarskoye Selo: Cameron Gallery.

account with the earliest rooms, those belonging to the Grand Duke. Although both suites were virtually destroyed during the Second World War, the Grand Duke's apartments can be seen today, thanks to a major Soviet reconstruction programme, whereas Catherine's still await restoration.

The Green Dining Room is outstanding (pls 75–6, 78). The first impression is one of colour. On the light green walls, with their small, precise, pale pink porphyritic crystals, stand out reliefs which are blinding in their whiteness. The room seems light in any weather, as if there were always a clear sky, sunshine and greenery beyond the window. Next, one is struck by the relationships of scale, inevitably comparing oneself with the caryatids that decorate the walls and seem unexpectedly large. On first entering the room these figures, dressed in ancient costume, seem to move towards one, stepping away from the walls. This impression is created by the deep projection of the reliefs. The eye then finds other images, small figures on medallions. A complexity of scalar structure gives each type of decorated element its own ornamental

75 (above) Charles Cameron, design for the Green Dining Room, the Catherine Palace, Tsarskoye Selo, early 1780s.

76 (right) Charles Cameron, variant design for the decoration of the Green Dining Room, the Catherine Palace, Tsarskoye Selo, early 1780s.

77 (facing page top) Charles Cameron, Green Dining Room, the Catherine Palace, Tsarskoye Selo: detail of the decoration.

78 (facing page bottom) Charles Cameron, Green Dining Room, the Catherine Palace, Tsarskoye Selo.

life. The large figures become static and balanced. The small figures on the medallions with their numerous 'characters', on the other hand, seem to reveal some ancient stage where distinctive events are occurring and in which the viewer becomes a participant.

The large figures and the medallions are linked by a network design composed of remarkable intertwinings of branches, zigzags of vines, unusual vases and high canopies. The different motifs appear to be in a state of constant transformation. The vases grow one out of the other, to create a columnar support (pls 77, 79). Enormous tendrils of vines seem to give birth to monumental figures from which branches again stretch upwards, as fine as the ornamentation below (pl. 80). The depictions of plants in their precision and symmetry becomes similar to the architectural details and the vases turn out to be formed from flower petals and beautifully cut leaves. The sharp quality of the delineation is one source of the overall refinement. In front of us is the world of the Roman grotesque enlarged many times and made three-dimensional. It is attractive and it is hard to resist the temptation to luxuriate in its images. They intrigue the viewer with a visual invitation to look into the ancient scenes with their small figures, to understand how the column-supports are composed, to see how the plant designs emerge from the wall. After long scrutiny, they come to life with intangible movement through a correspondence of proportion, a harmony of individual motifs, a breach and a rebirth of compositional themes and, no less important, through an enjoyment of perfection in the detail.

Almost every individual motif adheres to the ancient spirit and yet the Green Dining Room as a whole is not subordinated to such archaism. Here we can clearly see Cameron's ability to use the alphabet of classical art in order to express the feelings aroused in him both by his work on the innumerable forms of vases and funeral urns, candelabras and chalices in the early years of his youth, and by his study of the finishing of the Roman baths. The cold Olympianism and ungovernability of his own tempera–ment emerge in his compositions, and characterise the Green Dining Room as quintessential Cameron.

In each of the other rooms in Paul Petrovich and Maria Fedorovna's apartments the architect used an original decorative style. Taleporovsky describes how, 'In . . . the former painting studio all the ornamentation was painted whereas in the ivory carving studio everything was sculpted'.[37] Cameron built the staircase leading to the Grand Ducal reception rooms and from the landing it was possible to pass through the Chinese Blue Drawing Room (pl. 82) and thence to the Blue Drawing Room (pls 83, 84). These halls were decorated with relative simplicity. In both the walls were covered with silk – in the latter room this had a blue pattern, in the former it was painted in

79 (facing page) and 80   Charles Cameron, Green Dining Room, the Catherine Palace, Tsarskoye Selo: details of the decoration.

81　Charles Cameron, design for a ceiling, 1780s.

82 (facing page)　Charles Cameron, Chinese Blue Drawing Room, the Catherine Palace, Tsarskoye Selo.

the Chinese style. In the general composition of these rooms the fabric served as a homogeneous but decoratively packed background, neutral in comparison to the very rich parquet floor made from numerous different woods, and the brilliant and lavish painting of the ceiling which formed a very complex vault.

In the Grand Ducal Bedchamber Cameron used a different method of his own devising for 'bringing antiquity to life' (pls 85–8). Here he made a real-life reconstruction of a room like those depicted in Pompeian perspective murals. He translated into architecture, in a most unusual way, the image of a painted interior. This gave birth to a hall of a kind that had not existed in Roman architecture but that had been depicted by ancient artists. He tried to transport the visitor to an artistic world which would have seemed fantastic to Roman masters too, effectively bringing to life the dreams of those who created the Pompeian villas.

Here we find unusual order and striking proportions. Refined porcelain columns stand along the walls, one minute far apart, the next close together. Similar columns project forwards into the space of the room, supporting a canopy which rises up in a pyramid. It seems that from floor to ceiling many threads are connected together. This

83 Charles Cameron,
Blue Drawing Room,
the Catherine Palace,
Tsarskoye Selo.

84 Charles Cameron, Blue Drawing Room, the Catherine Palace, Tsarskoye Selo.

impression is strengthened by the columns themselves, white with gold, twisted below, then somehow rolled out of leaves, smooth at the top and wound around by garlands.[38] They support the white cornice stretching the length of the room. According to Cameron's drawing preserved in the Academy of Arts,[39] this was to be decorated by a chain of little medallions with gold heads on them. The design is so light and shining that the ceiling appears to retreat, to rise higher. On the ceiling painting can be seen female figures circling, playing with ribbons in a joyful dance.

The apartments that Cameron created for Catherine the Great consisted of a sequence of rooms (pls 89–93): first the halls, then the Dining Room and last Catherine's private rooms. The Arabesque Hall reflected the freedom with which Cameron used compositional themes and separate motifs of the classical interior.[40] He surrounded the room with emphatically graphic Corinthian columns with unusual capitals and a cornice covered with ornamentation and a simple one-panel pedestal.

This order gave the hall a monumental quality, and it was also rendered luxurious and intricate by the ornamental arabesques which gave it its name. Cameron used these

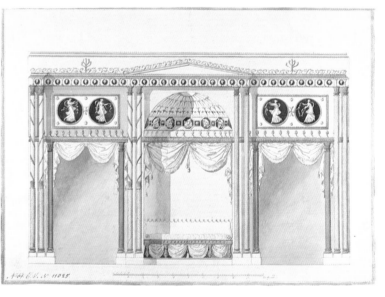

85 (facing page top) Charles Cameron, Grand Ducal Bedroom, the Catherine Palace, Tsarskoye Selo.

86 (facing page bottom left) Charles Cameron, design for the Grand Ducal Bedroom, the Catherine Palace, Tsarskoye Selo, early 1780s.

87 (facing page bottom right) Charles Cameron, design for the Grand Ducal Bedroom, the Catherine Palace, Tsarskoye Selo, early 1780s.

88 (right) Charles Cameron, Grand Ducal Bedroom, the Catherine Palace, Tsarskoye Selo.

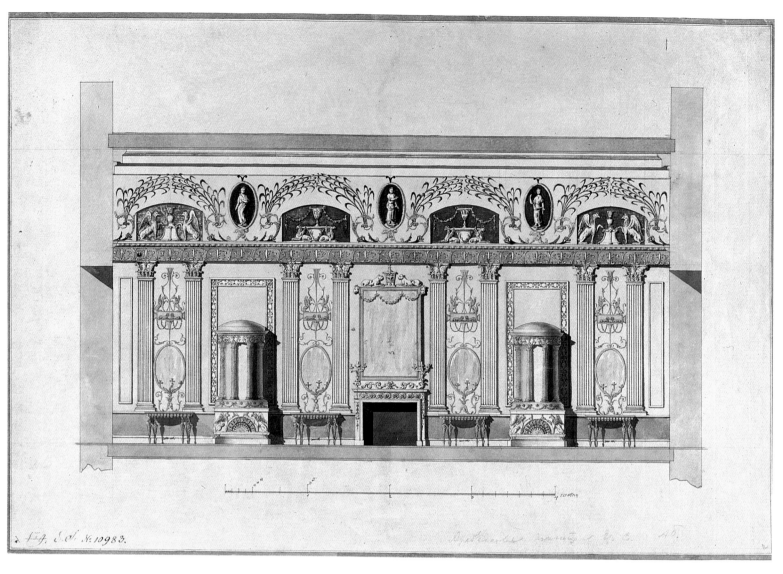

89 (above) Charles Cameron, design for the Arabesque Hall, the Catherine Palace, Tsarskoye Selo,
early 1780s.

90 Charles Cameron, design for a ceiling in the
Arabesque Hall, the Catherine Palace, Tsarskoye Selo,
1780s.

91 Charles Cameron, Arabesque Hall,
the Catherine Palace, Tsarskoye Selo.
Photo of the 1920s. The room no longer
exists.

92 Charles Cameron, Arabesque Hall,
the Catherine Palace, Tsarskoye Selo.
Photo of the 1920s.

94 Charles Cameron, design for a stove in the Arabesque Hall, the Catherine Palace, Tsarskoye Selo, 1780s.

in endlessly varied ways, in contrasting scales and in unexpected combinations with especially selected furniture. From them he created multi-coloured pictures enclosed in gilded frames. Very complex·compositions were the result, but these were inevitably symmetrical; in some the parallel branches of a spiralling pattern of plants included first the figures of ancient divinities, then the bodies of mythological monsters, then medallions in all possible forms. On these were depicted priests at sacrificial altars, Roman matrons, the graces dancing, the flight of cupids and much else. Beside these arabesque panels he placed huge gilded arabesques and under them mirrors, beneath which were tables with carved fringes and curved legs made in the same style. The arabesques somehow descended into the room, becoming real objects, while the candlesticks and the tables changed, in the opposite way, to become part of the decor. One of the most remarkable details of the Arabesque Hall was the use of stoves in the form of rotundas with spiralling columns, flat domes and square pedestals on which were portrayed gryphons with fan-shaped rosettes (pl. 94).[41]

From the Arabesque Hall one passed into the Lyons Hall (pls 95, 96). Cameron's sketches usually associated with the Lyons Hall demonstrate how long and intensely he laboured on finishing the Catherine Palace.[42] He produced at least three variations for the finishing of this room. In one the composition was purely ornamental.[43] Fine Pompeian columns, pilasters inscribed with a grotesque pattern of flowers, winged infants and so on, with medallions in place of capitals, rose into the slender cornice. Over this was a narrow strip where fairytale squirrels with curly tails played with infants. Between the pilasters were complex designs totally lacking the usual figures of people and animals. All this emphasised the ornamental and graphic nature of the decoration. Here the most important element was the line, which at one point stood out as a broad edging and then in an improbable and complex way curled into a fine pattern.

Other drawings presented a different appearance for the Lyons Hall.[44] In these the composition consisted of juxtaposing decorative surfaces which were packed to the extreme. Below, there were lapis lazuli panels; above, the walls were covered with tapestries of Lyons silk. The hall was crowned by two cornices and between them were paintings of scenes from the Old Testament executed in the Pompeian style. The parquet in the Lyons Hall was luxurious, employing twelve different species of non-native timber, including olive, rosewood and blackwood.[45] When he had finished the room Cameron apparently decided that it was not sufficiently refined. He managed to have decorations of mother of pearl inserted into the parquet, and the door panels encrusted with pearl shells and with mother of pearl. All the carved details were covered with pure gold leaf.[46]

The nature of Cameron's exotic interior style is revealed in the large Chinese Hall (pl. 97), with its two tiers of windows, in the middle of the Zubovsky wing. This could be reached through the Lyons Hall, and was surrounded by a low colonnade supporting the cornice-shelf, above which stood Chinese porcelain vases.[47] Higher still were panels covered with lacquer paintings of black, red and green flowers. The furniture was in the Chinese style and the chandeliers were in the form of copper lanterns.[48] This magnificent room no longer exists, and we depend on drawings and other records for our knowledge of it.

Cameron's Chinese Hall was quite different from the rococo interiors created by Knobelsdorff at Potsdam or Rinaldi at Oranienbaum. He rejected a decor that would embrace the space of the hall, and the composition was unexpectedly severe. Cameron was striving to overcome the rococo elements in chinoiserie. He created a definite rhythm along the horizontal and the vertical. Like the rococo architects, however, he made considerable use of Chinese porcelain but, as if in a museum, he 'displayed' the Chinese vases on shelves and 'framed' the Chinese paintings. Cameron did for chin-

93 (facing page) Charles Cameron, Arabesque Hall, the Catherine Palace, Tsarskoye Selo. Photo of the 1920s.

95 (above) Charles Cameron, variant design for the Lyons Hall, the Catherine Palace, Tsarskoye Selo, early 1780s.

96 Charles Cameron, project for the decoration of the Lyons Hall, the Catherine Palace, Tsarskoye Selo, early 1780s.

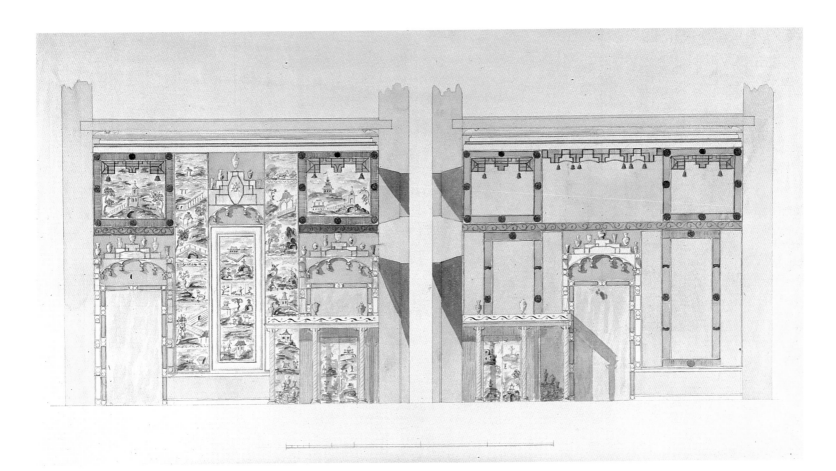

97 (above) Charles Cameron, design for the Chinese Hall, the Catherine Palace, Tsarskoye Selo, early 1780s.

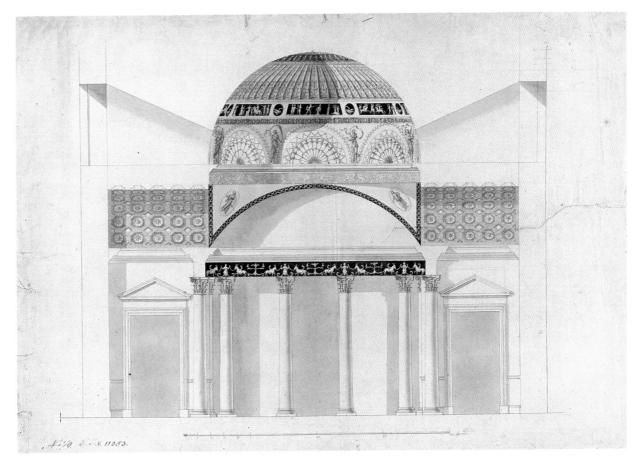

98 Charles Cameron, design for the Domed Dining Room, the Catherine Palace, Tsarskoye Selo, early 1780s.

99 Charles Cameron, Domed Dining Room, the Catherine Palace, Tsarskoye Selo. Photo of the 1930s. The room no longer exists.

100 (facing page top) Charles Cameron, Domed Dining Room, the Catherine Palace, Tsarskoye Selo. Photo of the 1930s.

101 (facing page bottom) Charles Cameron, designs for stoves.

oiserie in his interiors what Chambers had done in his Chinese park pavilions in England. He tried to convey an impression of worthiness, of using precise motifs, he attempted to work out a way of 'classicising the Chinese style'. His use of chinoiserie should be seen in the context of the general fashion for orientalism, which is the subject of a later chapter.

To the right of the Chinese Hall was the Domed Dining Room (pl. 98), where a strongly contrasting impression was created.[49] Here the antique character of the interior was particularly evident (pls 99–100, 102). The hall was planned to resemble part of a Roman house. A high dome was erected over the central square area, which was surrounded by a Corinthian colonnade. Abutting on to this were cylindrical arches decorated by a strict geometrical design. They covered the rooms to the side which were finished in a severe style.

The middle of the room, the 'banqueting hall' itself, was extraordinarily lavish. The surrounding columns were finished, as one description had it, in 'something resembling porphyry lacquered and burnished'.[50] A brightly painted frieze was proposed. China

stoves with gilded doors were made (pl. 101). There were gold and silver lamps in the form of eagles. The dome was painted to appear unusually high.

The peculiarity of the room lay in the fact that its most important area was a long way from the windows. Cameron divided off a space in the centre that was protected from all outside influences. In this way, wrote Taleporovsky, he tried to create the illusion that 'this antique hall . . . would seem to be under a southern sky,'[51] and he succeeded spectacularly.

In a letter to Baron Grimm, Catherine wrote:

I am writing to you from a little room made of solid silver embossed with a pattern of red leaves. Four columns with the same pattern are supporting the mirror which serves as a canopy to a divan upholstered in red-green material with silver, Moscow-made; the walls are of mirrors framed by silver pillars with the same red leaf pattern on them. A balcony goes out into the garden and it has mirror doors which are such that they always appear open even when they are closed . . . this little room is very luxurious, brilliant and cheerful, it is not burdened with heavy decorations and is very pleasant.[52]

102 Charles Cameron, Domed Dining Room, the Catherine Palace, Tsarskoye Selo: dome. Photo of the 1930s.

Her description relates to the room on the other side of the Chinese Hall from the Domed Dining Room, known appropriately as the Silver (or Red) Study (pl. 103).

Beyond this little *cabinet*, where the silver was covered with a red pattern and reflected crystal in its gleam, there was a light white Bedchamber with dark lilac pillars and the dull glow of massive bronze details (pls 104, 105). In this intimate room, also now lost, Cameron tried to create an impression of the utmost unity and integration. He used different paths to this end. In the manner typical of Robert Adam in England, the decorative patterns of the ceiling and floor were of almost identical design. Above, all was light, with curving bands and fine radials converging at the centre enclosed in a circle, and then in a square, all precisely mirrored in the dark decorative parquet below. The walls of frosted glass overlaid on white flannel[53] reflected a milky white light and were lined by fine rustication. In this room Cameron affected people not by the density of his decor or the abundance of his motifs, but by a technique depending

90

103 The Silver Study, the Catherine Palace, Tsarskoye Selo. Created by Charles Cameron and redesigned by Giacomo Quarenghi.

on the revelation of each detail. In this softly shining, light environment he made every element of the composition sound independently in the larger harmony. A particular role was played by the round blue-and-white medallions dedicated to celebrations of Apollo, Bacchus and the Muses which were specially made by Wedgwood to drawings by Flaxman.

The room was refined, luxurious and severe. Its decor encouraged concentration rather than entertainment and was created by Cameron for solitude. He did not have in mind the intrigues of court life. It seems that he was also not very concerned with the tastes of the lady who was commissioning his work, as he created halls one after the other, each time generating different sensations. His interiors provided an ideally fine living environment permeated by constant changes of mood and by unusually subtle

104 Charles Cameron, model for the Bedchamber of Catherine the Great, the Catherine Palace, Tsarskoye Selo, early 1780s.

105 (facing page) Charles Cameron, Bedchamber of Catherine the Great, the Catherine Palace, Tsarskoye Selo.

promptings to awareness of an inner refreshment. One moment he was bringing ancient images to life with all the precision of an archaeologist; the next he was transported to 'the real China', trying to convey the original style of the East; the next again, he was making a luxurious salon upholstered in Lyons silk according to the latest French fashion; then he moved in the world of antique fantasy, into a 'Rome of Caesars and Patrons of the Arts' such as had never existed and which he created in the reflections of milky-white and dark-lilac glass among mirrors and coloured porcelain. At one moment he could make a person who had just entered one of his rooms feel vast, and at another that he had become strangely small and had found himself in a valuable snuff-box, made by some brilliant jeweller. Indeed, Catherine herself used just that phrase.

To quote again the owner of the apartments: 'I have another little room in which, as on a snuff-box, white and blue are linked with bronze, there is white and blue glass and the design is all arabesques' (pls 106–8). This room was very small: there was room

106 (right) Charles Cameron, Snuff-Box Room, the Catherine Palace, Tsarskoye Selo. Photo of the 1930s. The room no longer exists.

107a (facing page top left) Charles Cameron, Snuff-Box Room, the Catherine Palace, Tsarskoye Selo. Photo of the 1930s.

107b (facing page top right) E.P. Hau, *The Snuff-Box Room, c.*1860.

108 (facing page bottom) Charles Cameron, Snuff-Box Room, the Catherine Palace, Tsarskoye Selo.

only for a sofa 'covered in blue material' which stretched from one wall to the other. The integral and luxurious nature of its interior was taken to the extreme. All parts of the decor were indivisibly linked to a single expanse of ornamentation executed in unusual materials and covering the entire study. The walls and ceiling were covered in milky-white glass and all the decor was made of blue glass on a lining of foil. Ornaments and bas-reliefs were of bronze which was light and, according to eye-witnesses, 'incomparable in its design'.

Beyond this miniature space lay the last of Cameron's creations in this part of the Zubovsky wing. This was a room with mirrored walls and majolica pillars and frieze. In the first half of the 1780s this was the Palm Room, one of the most exotic interiors created by Cameron (pl. 109).[55] its four walls were covered 'by twenty-eight palms of white tin', equally spaced around the room so that their thick tin crowns joined together. The architect demanded that 'palm leaves should be added so that in this chamber the seams should be covered'.[56] The branches stretched to the centre of the room, where stood 'one large tree'.[57] The walls, moreover, were covered in mirrors which led this 'palm grove' away into the distance. Here Cameron used a method that was completely theatrical. With some artistic courage the tin trees were designed in such a way as to give an almost naturalistic impression of a forest of metal palms!

The Palm Room, later replaced by the Mirror Room, crowned the rooms created

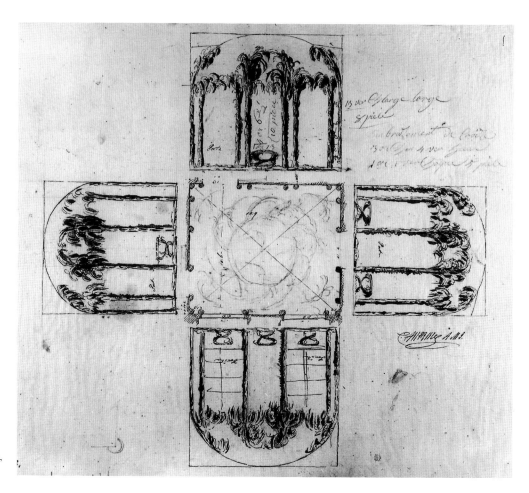

109 Charles Cameron, design for the Palm Room, the Catherine Palace, Tsarskoye Selo, early 1780s.

by Cameron in this part of the Catherine Palace. The colonnade of the Cameron Gallery could be seen in perspective in the doors of this room, which formed an ante-room to the Hanging Garden and the exterior complex beyond.

Contemporaries experienced the halls of the Zubovsky wing and the baths complex together, feeling their movement and the views they successively revealed. Thus one of the ladies-in-waiting at the court, Vera Golovina, remembered how the appearance of the palace changed in the 1780s:

> The first hall of this new construction was decorated with paintings, then there was another one whose ceilings and walls were decorated in lapis lazuli and whose floor was parquet, half of mahogany and half of mother-of-pearl. Then . . . there was a hall finished in Chinese lacquer. Then there was a bedroom, very small but very beautiful and a *cabinet* of mirrors . . . [which] served as an entrance to the colonnade that could be seen in the distance from the doors. On the terrace . . . [the Mirror Loggia] stood a divan and a table upholstered with green morocco leather . . . All this structure . . . was alongside a small wall which projected forward, going round it you met on your left a splendid flower-bed planted with most beautiful and most fragrant flowers. On this side the terrace ended in luxurious halls [the Agate Pavilion] . . . [further ahead] was the colonnade which consisted of a glass gallery with a marble floor, around which . . . was another open gallery with columns supporting the roof from which there was a broad view in all directions.[58]

Thus the movement leads again to the baths and gallery complex, already discussed, and from the latter to the park, which could the surveyed so expansively from the Cameron Gallery.

96

The Park

From the eighteenth century onwards a picturesque or landscape garden was known in Russia as an 'English garden', and the first such park in Russia was created at Tsarskoye Selo. From here ideas of imitating nature spread to thousands of estates throughout the country.

The magnificent regular park (pl. 110) that existed at Tsarskoye Selo in the mid-eighteenth century had ceased to satisfy the tastes of the court even before the new English fashion appeared. At the end of the 1750s, when more and more rococo elements began appearing in Russian baroque, new features appeared in park ensembles bearing a promise of different games and impressions. Here at Tsarskoye Selo a large lake was dug out beside the carefully mown lawns, the Great Pond, on which it was possible to go boating. On a hill above the lake a colossal sledge-run three hundred metres long was created. From a tower a *pente-douce* led down via several 'humps', small

110 Plan of Tsarskoye Selo in the 1790s. 1: New Garden. 2: Chinese Village. 3: Catherine Palace. 4: baths, Cameron Gallery and *pente-douce*. 5: Menagerie. 6: Temple of Memory. 7: town of Sofiya. 8: church of St Sophia. 9: road to St Petersburg. 10: Bablovsky Park. 11: Otdelnyi Park. 12: fields.

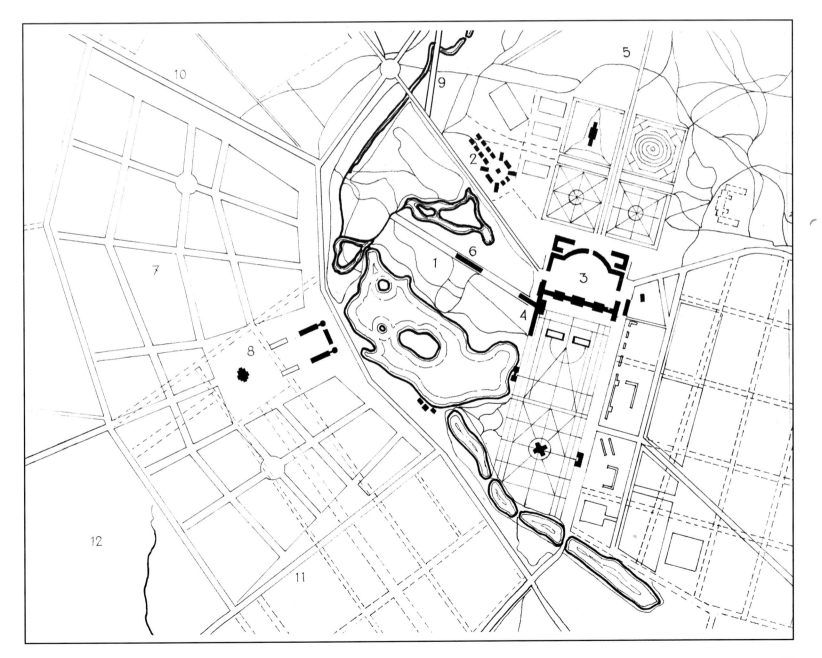

111 Tsarskoye Selo: Cameron Gallery: view from the Old Garden.

112 (facing page) Tsarskoye Selo: view of the Siberian Bridge, designed by Vasily Neyelov in the 1770s and built on the model of the Palladian bridge at Wilton.

rises quickly followed by a renewed descent. In winter people descended by sledges and in summer, by special carriages created by Nartov, the famous mechanical engineer and member of the Academy of Sciences. The speeds achieved were spectacular. Ladies were terrified and even some of the court gentlemen took part in such amusements with no great pleasure.

By the 1770s these recently invented amusements had lost their appeal. Catherine, as a leader of fashion, was absorbed in something new:

I adore English gardens, with their curved lines, *pente-douces*, ponds like lakes (archipelagos on dry land); and I despise deeply straight lines and identical *allées*. I hate fountains that torture water into running contrary to its nature . . . in a word, anglomania is more important to me than 'plantomania'.[59]

These words from a letter from Catherine the Great to Voltaire were written in 1772 and convey the mood in which the Russian landscape garden was born.

Considerable preparation was carried out for the making of a new garden at Tsarskoye Selo. John Bush, well known as an experienced English gardener, was invited over from England and when he returned home his son, Joseph, continued his work. John Bush was born 'Busch' in Hanover but had lived in England since the 1740s, owning a nursery garden in Hackney, to the east of the city of London, which he sold when he left for Russia in about 1771.[60] To the august owner of Tsarskoye Selo it did not seem enough to send the gardener her invitation merely in writing, and so she sent Vasily Neyelov, one of the architects who had worked on the estate since Rastrelli's day. He was accompanied by his son Peter, who was also an architect. Very little is known about the Neyelovs' stay in England. Vasily did not spend long on English soil, probably only six months in all,[61] but it is probable that Peter Neyelov was there for much longer. A.G. Cross believes that they could have visited Kew, Syon House, Osterley Park, Alexander Pope's villa in Twickenham, Hampton Court and Windsor.[62] Unfortunately none of their sketches has been preserved. (Drawings done by Peter Neyelov on other journeys, to the Crimea for instance, can still be seen in the Hermitage.) From their English visit have remained only sketches copied from architectural books, mostly of buildings at Stowe. This park attracted Russian architects because of its numerous pavilions.[63]

At the same time in Russia people were anxious to acquire different books and treatises revealing new ideas about gardening. It is certain that the following publications were being used in Russia in the 1770s: William Chambers's *Designs of Chinese Buildings, Furniture, Dresses, Machines and Utensils* of 1757, and his *Plans, Elevations, Sections and Perspective Views of the Gardens and Buildings at Kew in Surrey* of 1763; Charles Over's *Ornamental Architecture in the Gothic, Chinese and Modern Taste* of 1758, P. Decker's *Chinese Architecture* of 1759, and J. and W. Halfpenny's *Chinese . . . Architecture Properly Ornamented* of 1752. These were studied not only by Vasily Neyelov and his sons Peter and Ilya, but also by Yury Velten, Antonio Rinaldi and all those who took part in creating the park at Tsarskoye Selo. Indeed, each seems to have had his favourite source. Judging from their designs,[64] Rinaldi preferred Decker, whereas the Neyelovs liked Chambers and Halfpenny[65] and Velten liked Over. Anyway, preparation for creating the first English park in Russia was intensive.

The location did not favour the construction of a picturesque park. Around Tsarskoye Selo stretched a smooth, gloomy plain covered by stunted forest, and there was insufficient water, but this did not stop the architects and gardeners. Powerful hydraulic structures were erected. Canals, which in some places ran underground through vaulted galleries, were miracles of technology for their time and brought water from twenty miles away. Numerous lakes were dug out linking the channels. With the help of a waterfall they were connected to the Great Pond, whose banks were constructed so as to have headlands and bays. Artifical hills were created. Finally, attractive groups of trees were planted.

It must be realised that this first Russian attempt at the landscape style was a long way from the parks that would soon be created in the environs of St Petersburg by Cameron and later by Pietro Gonzago. This first garden was something of a plaything. It did not show the passionate, unbounded admiration for nature that is experienced in the works of Kent and Brown. Thus far the Russian garden communicated only the desire not to be left behind the rest of Europe. Moreover, the pavilions were constructed in accordance with particular models. The Siberian Bridge crossing one of the channels was an exact copy of the Palladian bridge at Wilton built by Roger Morris in 1737.[67] The Admiralty and the kitchen attached to the Hermitage Pavilion and built by the Neyelovs carried traces of the English neo-gothic in the style of Kent. Similarly, they erected a pyramid in the form of that existing at Kew, meant to recall the pyramidal tomb of Sestius in Rome.[68]

100

113 Tsarskoye Selo: the lake in the New Garden. In the distance is the Chinese Village.

The Tsarskoye Selo pavilion was dedicated to sentimental memories. Behind it were buried three of Catherine the Great's favourite English greyhounds and on the tombstone was engraved an inscription by the French Ambassador, Count Ségur: 'Here lies Zemira and the mourning graces ought to throw flowers on her grave. Like Tom, her forefather, and Lady, her mother, she was constant in her loyalties and had only one failing, she was a little short-tempered . . . The gods, witnesses of her faithfulness, should have rewarded here for her loyalty with immortality.'[69]

The Tsarskoye Selo pyramid erected by Vasily Neyelov in 1771 for Cameron's arrival had fallen into decay. The architect rebuilt it to its former style, slightly changing the proportions.[70] All the pavilions revealed their purpose with inscriptions, so that this new Tsarskoye Selo picturesque garden adjoining the regular garden became densely packed with literary offerings.

All these small architectural events were to have momentous consequences. The aristocrats began to imitate the empress's garden and were followed in their turn by the provincial landowners. Seeds of the idea of a landscape garden and the neo-gothic

114 Charles Cameron, project for the Triumphal Arch of the Temple of Memory, 1792.

emerged from Tsarskoye Selo in the 1770s to bear rich fruit elsewhere in Russian soil. These will be discussed later in the chapter on neo-gothic taste in Russia. My concern here is with the features that would soon appear in the Tsarskoye Selo garden, and turned this once modest park into one of the most interesting ensembles of the age of Enlightenment.

Part of the park was laid out to represent a model of Catherine the Great's political dreams on the international front. This was the time of the Russo-Turkish wars in which Rumyantsev, Radishchev, Suvorov, Ushakov and Greig won brilliant victories. The empress wrote:

> While this war continues, my garden at Tsarskoye Selo becomes like a toy, after each glorious military action a suitable monument is erected in it. The Battle of Kagul . . . resulted in an obelisk with an inscription . . . the Sea Battle of Chesme produced a Rostral Column in the Great Pond . . . moreover, I have had the idea of having a Temple of Memory built in the little forest, the approach to which would be through Triumphal Gates where all the previous actions in this current war will be represented on medallions [pl. 114].[71]

Thus grew up a developed system of allegories, expressed in symbolic panoramas, buildings recalling this or that historical event and monuments. The landscape was dotted with columns and obelisks on pedestals bearing edifying inscriptions, like that on the Rumyantsev Monument: 'In memory of the victory on the River Kagul in Moldavia, 21 July 1770, under the leadership of General Count Rumyantsev, 17,000 Russian troops made the Turkish Vizier, Hamil-Bey, flee along the Danube with his force of 150,000 men.'[72] Such structures gave the feeling of serenity and celebration. This was straight classicism without breaking the canons and with a traditional treatment of order.

In 1771 Yury Velten erected the Ruined Tower in honour of the Russian taking of the Turkish Ochakov fortress (pls 115, 116). This was perceived in quite a different way. It took the form of part of a gigantic ruin buried under the earth. The capital of a Doric column and an arch reared up in front of the viewer, who was struck by the cyclopean forms. Up on the square created by the colossal abacus was a summerhouse with arched embrasures, made in a conventional Turkish style. The allegory symbolising the mighty power of Greece with its ancient past slumbering under Ottoman rule was conveyed by the grotesque and hyperbolic architectural form.

115 (below left) Yury Velten, Ruined Tower, Tsarskoye Selo: variant design.

116 (below right) Giacomo Quarenghi, *The Park at Tsarskoye Selo*, 1790s. Left to right: Velten's Ruined Tower, Cameron's postal station in Sofiya and Rinaldi's Orlovsky (Triumphal) Gates.

117 Tsarskoye Selo: the Great Pond with the Chesme Column, designed by Antonio Rinaldi.

In the same year, 1771, as Catherine's letter describes, Rinaldi created designs for Triumphal Gates and a Rostral Column (pl. 117) in the centre of the Great Pond to commemorate the sea victory of Russian sailors led by Alexei Orlov, the brother of Catherine's first favourite, and Captain Greig, a native of the small Scottish town of Inverkeithing, who had entered Russian service to fight against the Turkish fleet.

All these structures were erected on quite deliberately selected sites. However, it is not easy to elucidate the precise significance of the eighteenth-century park allegories, and it is quite impossible without the key that unlocks the content of any given composition. In this case, fortunately the notes of Khrapovitsky, the private secretary of Catherine the Great, are of great assistance in reconstructing the empress's intentions. He recorded his conversation with Catherine when awaiting the arrival of Potemkin, her former favourite. It must be remembered that all this happened in the context of constantly erupting wars with Turkey.

In 1791 Catherine lamented the fact that to honour many military leaders she had ordered the construction of 'Triumphal Gates but had completely forgotten Prince Grigory Alexandrovich Potemkin-Tavrichesky'. 'Your Majesty,' said Khrapovitsky, 'you know him so well that you have not honoured him.' 'Yes, that is true. However, he is also a man and perhaps he would also like some honour', replied the empress. Then Khrapovitsky continued, 'So it was ordered that in Tsarskoye Selo the Triumphal Gates should be illuminated and decorated with naval and army armatures and a banner should be inscribed with verses selected from Petrov's *Ode to Ochakov*: "You enter with splashing waves into Sophia's Temple".'[73]

This held the literary key to the allegory represented by the views of the Tsarskoye Selo park, which was begun as early as the 1770s. The significant phrase was: 'You enter with splashing waves into Sophia's Temple'. Sophia's temple, of course, was Hagia Sophia, the famous symbol of the city of Constantinople. In the course of the Turkish wars the idea of sending troops by sea to the capital of the Ottoman Empire to occupy it had been frequently proposed. It was supported by, for instance, General Suvorov and Admiral Ushakov. Catherine the Great was attracted by this idea, or at least she wanted to give that impression. The banner fixed to the Triumphal Gates also hinted at such a military-political perspective, and that was revealed further in a whole set of park views.

The initial inscription on the Triumphal Gates was as follows: 'Orlov has saved Moscow from the plague', in reference to Orlov's having set off for Moscow when he learnt that a bad epidemic of the plague had broken out there and that there had been a popular revolt brought about by panic. However, Orlov soon ceased to be the empress's favourite and the inscription on the gates changed accordingly. Immediately after passing through the Triumphal Gates the visitor was met by Velten's Ruined Tower, dedicated to the Victory of Ochakov and, further on, by the bank of a stream, he could see the Turkish Pavilion (pl. 118), a copy of a building standing on the banks of the Bosphorus. In order to ensure the copy was precise, a special ship had been sent to scrutinise the model in Constantinople.[74] The same stream was adorned by the Red or Turkish Cascade, with a little tower on each side of it reminiscent of the Orient. The construction of this is attributed to Cameron.[75]

These structures were intended to attune the visitor to a Turkish mood. Beyond them began that part of the park that provided the allegory of political dreams. In front of the viewer stood a long Ionic colonnade, raised on a small base and decorated by

118 Giacomo Quarenghi, *View of the Turkish Pavilion*, 1790s.

numerous statues and bas-reliefs.[76] Attached to this was another Triumphal Arch.[77] Cameron's famous design for the Triumphal Arch shows an arch embellished with round medallions showing battle scenes.[78] These are those very medallions representing 'all the previous actions in this current war' of which Catherine had written.

There can be no doubt that Cameron was precisely following the empress's intention here in erecting a Temple of Memory which was indeed the apotheosis of the theme of victory in the Russo-Turkish wars. (Unfortunately, in 1797, the building was demolished on Paul I's command). As it stood in a raised position in the park, above the lake, it was probably from this point that it was possible to see, through the broadly spaced colonnade, the whole panorama, its allegorical significance proclaimed by a banner fixed at the beginning of the Triumphal Path.

On the lake stood Rinaldi's Rostral Column and across the smooth water, in the distance, could be seen the dome of a cathedral. This provided the most interesting part of the composition. The cathedral was built to the south of the Tsarskoye Selo park, beyond the Great Pond, and bore the name of Saint Sophia. It was constructed by Cameron, and it was generally believed that the architect had built a copy of Hagia Sophia in Constantinople.[79] In fact this building had little in common with its famous namesake, but the resemblance that people in the eighteenth century saw between the two structures will be discussed below. Here it suffices to stress that the unusual dome of Cameron's cathedral was *considered* to be related to the church in Constantinople. The symbol of sea victories was combined with the symbol of the re-establishment of an Orthodox Byzantium, while the lake represented the Black Sea, which opened the route to the capital of the Turkish Empire.

The Triumphal Path around the park continued beyond the Temple of Memory. The Temple stood two hundred metres from the baths, along the axis of the *pente-douce* of the Cameron Gallery, and on leaving the Temple it was possible to see the formal sculpture on the *pente-douce*. Approaching it a ceremonial procession could ascend into the splendid world of ancient harmony which Cameron had created as a reward for victories and martial feats, and could enter those 'mansions which it is only proper for the gods to create'. Contemporary heros acquired immortality because of this association with the eternal antique ideal, which had been rendered visible by Cameron in his baths and gallery. Bringing antiquity to life here took on a concrete meaning. The whole concept of the park, and the composition of its elements formed a triumphal procession towards this aim. Soon the poets put this into verse, as here in the words of Ivan Bogdanovich.

> Monuments of famous Russian deeds have appeared.
> There in their glory antiquity
> Has raised a temple for herself.[80]

In the extensive legacy of poetry devoted to the park at Tsarskoye Selo, the glory of the ancient ideal is consistently fused with the glory of Russian deeds.

It is not, of course, a matter of whether the proposed triumph of Potemkin did or did not take place, or of whether it was for some other celebration that these structures were erected. The significance lies rather in the fact that a considerable part of the Tsarskoye Selo park had been turned into an allegory and conveyed the impression of a continual victory celebration. It was as if permanent decorations had been erected, among which a triumphal festivity could take place at any moment.

Overall, a unifying system of stylistic and symbolic relationships had been created between the different parts of the ensemble, to which Cameron gave a classical precision. The baths, the Cameron Gallery, the *pente-douce* and the Temple of Memory formed a powerful antique nucleus for the ensemble, providing its main organising element. To one side was the grandiose and fantastic Chinese ensemble with its own integrated spatial structure. This will be discussed in a later chapter on orientalism. Beside the avenue that led from the Triumphal Gates to the baths, on the other side of the classical nucleus, was the section of the ensemble devoted to the victory theme. Beyond the lake was another part of Tsarskoye Selo, the town of Sofiya, which was created entirely by Cameron.

Of course, it is not only the allegories but also the architectural works and the sculptures which give the ensemble of the park its charm, as they dissolve in the quietness of winding paths, the rustling of leaves, the ripple of streams, the lapping of the waters of the lake. The charms of this man-made environment made the 'silent hymns' of the victory monuments sound all the more loudly and made the fantastic fairytales of the oriental structures even more attractive. As the following passage from Pushkin shows, this atmosphere readily gripped the visitor's imagination:

> On the following day early in the morning Maria Ivanovna woke up, dressed and went quietly out into the garden. The morning was magnificent, the sun was lighting the tops of the lime trees which had already turned yellow with the fresh breath of autumn. The broad lake shone motionless. The awakening swans swam majestically from under the bushes overhanging the banks. Maria Ivanovna was walking near a fine meadow where a monument had just been erected to the recent victories of Count Peter Alexandrovich Rumyantsev. Suddenly a white dog of some English breed started barking and ran towards her. Maria Ivanovna was afraid and stopped. At the same moment a pleasant woman's voice called out: 'Don't be afraid, she won't bite.' And Maria Ivanovna saw an elegant lady sitting on a bench opposite the monument. She sat at the other end of the bench. The lady stared at her and Maria Ivanovna for her part cast a few sideways glances and was able to look her over from top to toe. She was in a white morning dress, a night cap and a sleeveless jacket. She seemed about forty. Her face, round and rosy, expressed majesty and calm and her blue eyes and light smile had an inexplicable charm. The lady was the first to break the silence. 'You are surely not from here?' she said.

Thus wrote Pushkin in *The Captain's Daughter*,[81] placing the meeting of his heroine with Catherine the Great in precisely the Tsarskoye Selo setting described above.

If we follow the heroine of Pushkin's story to the place where she stopped, having come to ask the empress to forgive her fiancé, we arrive at the most interesting and unusual of the Tsarskoye Selo worlds created with Cameron's help, the 'world of enlightened wellbeing', the grandiose setting of the model town of Sofiya.

Sofiya

The town of Sofiya (pl. 119), built by Charles Cameron, is among the least known of the architectural ensembles created by British architects in Russia, indeed it has hardly been studied at all. It was founded by Catherine the Great next to Tsarskoye Selo in 1780.[82] The town has been almost forgotten because it existed for only twenty-eight years. By 1808 it had been abolished as a community and most of its houses had been demolished for their bricks.[83] However, at the end of the eighteenth century it had an important role to play as a district or *uyezd* centre, built to replace the old settlement attached to the Tsarskoye Selo imperial palace. But its significance was not limited to this. It was proposed that Sofiya should become one of the centres of the St Petersburg *guberniya*, or region,[84] and to this end a market place and factories were built there, operated by a specially assembled population of merchants and workmen.[85]

All this was done for the specific purpose of creating the setting for an ideal life, which could be acted out before the eyes of the court. As a result, it was more a model

119 Giacomo Quarenghi, *Central Square in the Town of Sofiya*, 1790s.

town than a real settlement, and from the Cameron Gallery foreign visitors were shown as one of the sights what the Belgian nobleman, the Prince de Ligne, called 'the view of the little town,'[86] which ran in a semi-circle around the Tsarskoye Selo park. There was street lighting in the town (unprecedented in Russia in the 1780s), but the lamps were lit only when Catherine was in residence at Tsarskoye Selo. The Scottish craftsmen invited to Sofiya by Cameron were so impressed that they even wrote about this lighting in their letters home.

Sofiya was the first post station on the road from St Petersburg to Moscow, so naturally many famous travellers spent time there. Among the most important was the well-known Russian Enlightenment figure, Alexander Radishchev, who was persecuted for his attack on serfdom and who dedicated to Sofiya the first part of his highly political book, *A Journey from St Petersburg to Moscow*. Another was the Prince de Ligne, already quoted, who wrote about the town in his memoirs. According to the first guide book for this route, published in 1802, anyone who travelled from the capital along the road towards Moscow was met by the line of 'huge Sofiya houses', the 'outstanding cathedral built in the image of the Constantinople Sofia, the many vast state buildings for the Post Office [pl. 120], the Office Buildings, the Arcade and the residential houses'.[87] All these buildings were constructed by Charles Cameron, who had arranged them in an unusual fashion.

Sofiya's purpose, to provide a pleasant view within a landscape, was unambiguously stressed in the order for the founding of the settlement signed by Catherine the Great:

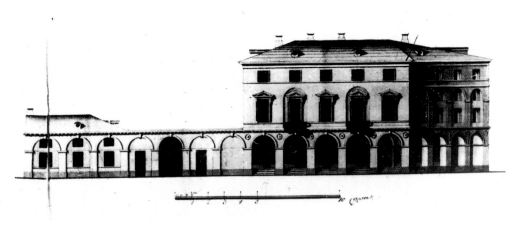

120 Tsarskoye Selo: Post Office in Sofiya. Copy after a drawing by Charles Cameron, 1780s.

'to dispose the streets corresponding to the paths of the neighbouring garden so that they should create a view.'[88] With its fan-shaped plan, the town embraced the whole south side of the park. Seven longitudinal streets led towards the side of the park. Had they continued beyond its boundary they would have converged at a point in the area of Cameron's baths. This is reminiscent of Versailles, but the irregular form of these paths made the plan more picturesque and gave each quarter of the town a unique shape.

That part of Sofiya that faced the imperial residence was intended to be particularly lavish. Documents show that Cameron made sketches not only for individual buildings but for entire street frontages.[89] In effect, he created a design to frame architecturally the Tsarskoye Selo park (pls 121, 122). This was achieved with model houses, which provided a strip of elegant three-storey façades. To these we shall turn later.

All this was highly unusual for a landscape garden. In conventional theory, the boundary of such a park should lose itself amidst the splendour of nature. Here, by contrast, it was proposed that a park be surrounded by architecture. The imitation of nature – winding streams and paths, lakes, picturesque clumps of trees – took on a specific and theatrical character in these conditions, which seemed to underline the fact that they had all been created by man. The theatre of the landscape park was united with the theatre of architecture.

It is significant that the panorama from the Cameron Gallery was not limited to views of the park and the town. Catherine the Great wrote to Voltaire: 'Sitting in the colonnade I can see in front of me Pella [one of the imperial palaces] although it is at least 35 *versts* from here and, besides Pella, I can see for about 100 *versts* around me.' There is doubtless some exaggeration in her words, but they do show with great clarity the scale of the spatial relationships here. The attractiveness of the distant vistas is confirmed by a drawing of the Cameron Gallery (now in the Hermitage) in which a courtier stands in the colonnade looking at the surroundings through a telescope.[91]

A more precise impression of the panorama is given in idyllic form by a contemporary description of Sofiya: 'you can see settlements a long way distant with neat gardens and vegetable patches, you can make out people sowing corn as well as nearby glades.'[92] This idealised picture shows the aspiration of the territorial planning. Trees that were felt to be in inappropriate places were moved.[93] There was concern about the well-being of the forest.[94] Dams and mills were built in the nineteenth century, to 'make a view' for the neighbouring paths.[95]

The territory of Sofiya also adjoined the Pavlovsk estate of Grand Duke Paul Petrovich, the heir to the throne.[96] Thus all three ensembles to which Charles Cameron contributed – Tsarskoye Selo, Sofiya and Pavlovsk – fused into one spatial entity.

Let us turn to the internal layout of Sofiya. In the centre was a square, open to the side of the park. On the square stood three buildings given over to the town's administration. These had been built by Vasily Neyelov a long time before the settlement was founded, and in the 1780s they were rebuilt by Cameron in line with new needs. In the middle was a small building with tall, richly decorated windows. Its portal with a round window above the door and its balustrade running the whole length of the block had a baroque character. The façade of this central block faced the park, and two long identical wings stretched into the park with butt ends embellished by decorative towers.

Behind these buildings stood the city's main landmark, the church of St Sophia (pl. 123). Scholars have disputed the authorship of this building. It is known that Cameron prepared the first design (pl. 124), but this was so luxurious that Catherine refused to accept it. It is true that she valued the model of the temple which Cameron had made

121 Model house 'of the larger type' for Sofiya. Copy after a drawing by Charles Cameron, 1780s.

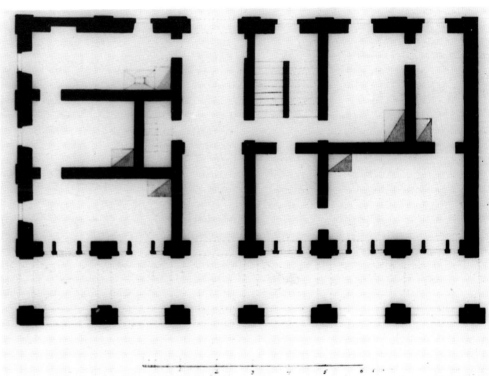

122 Model house 'of the larger type' for Sofiya. Copy after a drawing by Charles Cameron, 1780s.

and her personal secretary wrote to Ivan Betskoy, president of the Academy of Arts, 'that you, dear Sir, are ordered to place it in the Academy.'[97] The idea of building a cathedral was not abandoned, however. Information has been preserved which shows that work on the building was led by the famous Russian architect, Ivan Starov, the creator of the Tauride Palace in St Petersburg,[98] but it has become uncertain who actually designed this large edifice in Sofiya.

123 Charles Cameron, St Sophia, Tsarskoye Selo. Photo of the 1910s.

At the beginning of the twentieth century a silver commemoration plaque was found – a survivor from the ceremonial founding of the church. This depicts Catherine the Great's monogram with an inscription in English, 'Charles Cameron, Architect'.[99] Even this did not satisfy the researchers. There have been many instances when a ceremony has been held, a plaque with an inscription set in place and then long delays have caused the building to be completed according to an entirely different design. Recently, however, I have located a letter from Cameron to Count Bezborodko, Catherine's personal secretary, which explains the whole confused story. Thus Cameron writes:

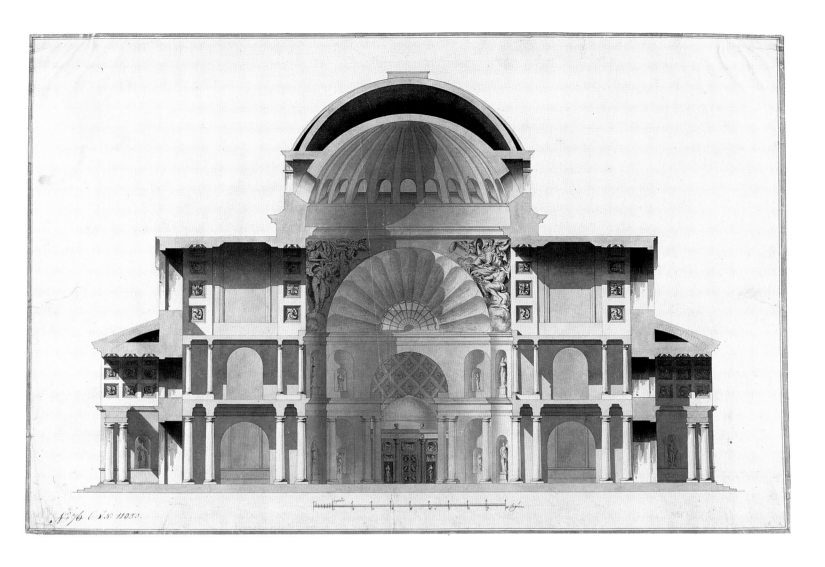

124 Charles Cameron, design for St Sophia, Tsarskoye Selo: first variant, early 1780s.

It has been designated that work should start on the construction of the Sofiya church. I ask Your Excellency that the person who takes on this construction should be a stonemason and a person who is truly an expert in this area and who can be relied on . . . My reason for expressing these thoughts is the following, I do not have here a master stonemason to check the work done at Sofiya and it is almost impossible to defend oneself from the deceptions of contractors without being constantly present during construction work . . . which I am unable to be. The Sofiya church consists of many arches whose construction is very complex . . . If something goes wrong it will be because of bad builders, for I am prepared to answer personally for the plan of this church.[100]

This letter would seem both to prove Cameron's responsibility for the building, and to explain why another architect was invited to supervise the work.

Money for construction work was first issued on 16 August 1783.[101] It was decided to complete the church in four years, and the work was finished on schedule on 29 May 1787, with substantial contributions from Scottish workmen.[102]

The church has a square plan, with strict Doric porticos on all four sides. There are no embellishments, only the flat window recesses. Five domes rise up over this monumental block, one enormous one on a powerful drum, and four small ones. The central dome gives a strange impression. Apart from the usual drum base there is another wider structure below it whose significance is not immediately clear. This

111

125 Charles Cameron, St Sophia, Tsarskoye Selo: interior. Photo of 1910. The interior was destroyed twice, in the 1930s and during the Second World War.

structure, however, holds the key to one of the mysteries that the Sofiya cathedral has presented to scholars.

Eighteenth- and nineteenth-century sources determinedly declare that the cathedral did resemble Hagia Sophia in Constantinople. This was also maintained by Catherine the Great in her letters, in the memoirs of those close to her, and by the authors of old travel guides. However, Cameron's construction is totally classical and from the outside it is impossible to find any resemblance to the Constantinople building. Perhaps there is something in the interior? In its ruined and boarded-up state this has long been difficult to penetrate, but I lately managed it and once inside the confusions disappear.

Internally, the central dome is a double structure (pl. 125), in which the lower dome recalls the dome of Hagia Sophia. The split drum cuts through the windows, which are positioned approximately as they are in Constantinople. The strange construction visible from the outside in fact supports the second casing of the dome. In its entirety Cameron's interior must have created a very powerful effect, with its huge open space and its inner red granite colonnade executed in the Ionic order with Erechtheion capitals like those in the Cameron Gallery. Photographs from the 1930s are our only record of this interior, since the church suffered badly in the Second World War.

The square and that side of the town facing the park was to be developed with houses based on the larger of Cameron's two types, while the rest of Sofiya was to have dwelling houses of his smaller type. Building to model designs was common in eighteenth-century Russia. As early as the founding of St Petersburg, Domenico Trezini had made the first standard designs for residential houses. Later, such model units were designed by Le Blond, Kvasov, Leim and Hastie, but in this field Cameron created an original system. He designed the nucleus of a section of dwelling house with a simple internal plan that could easily be transformed. The façade had three floors; on the ground level was an arcade and above that an elegant first floor, with lavishly framed windows and balconies, and on top of that were low rooms looking outwards with square embrasures.

By joining such nuclei together in series it was possible to create buildings of any length. This was very convenient in Sofiya, with its irregular street arrangements. The design work was carried out from 1781 to 1784,[103] and in 1785 the first house was built on the larger model.[104] Houses of the small type were unpretentious little detached houses with attics. In total more than thirty houses were erected in Sofiya to Cameron's standard designs.

From 1783 to 1785 Cameron built Sofiya's large post station. This was a whole complex of buildings, comprising the post house itself and two stables for fifty horses, a coach-house, storerooms and accommodation for the postmasters. All parts of the post depot were linked by an arcade which merged into the central building as a covered gallery at ground level. The low one-storey outbuildings were linked into two long blocks, perpendicular to each other.

The façade of the Sofiya post station was unusual. The sides of the main building, on the edge of the complex, came together at an obtuse angle and could be seen at the same time, but they were executed in different ways. Although they were of equal height, three storeys looked out on to one street and four on to the other. The façade visible from the park was in a more luxurious style. Its ceremonial first floor was embellished with pedimented windows and corbels and by balconies with wrought iron railings.

The progress of construction was fairly complex. In a letter that I have discovered, Cameron tells Count Bezborodko of the difficulties encountered:

It is quite beyond my strength to describe to Your Excellency the trouble and bother it is to finish any work properly with people whose main characteristic is deceitfulness, an example of which is given by the post station for which, although many instructions were given nothing was done, last year on the 15th of July it was stated that the construction could not stand, I protested at that time about their carelessness, showing where things were bad and advising what needed to be done . . . everything was left as it was or painted over so that it appeared to have been corrected, it will be easier for you to imagine than it is for me to describe . . . how I feel.[105]

Finally, in 1787 the construction was completed.

The Sofiya post station acquired an unexpected popularity in Russian literature, and thanks to this we can evoke a feeling of what life was like there in Cameron's time. Alexander Radishchev wrote in his famous *A Journey from St Petersburg to Moscow*:

The rut, which my wagon had stumbled into, woke me. My wagon had stopped. I raised my head. And I saw . . . a building with three storeys. 'What's that?' I asked my coachman. 'The post station.' 'But where are we?' 'In Sofiya', and he unharnessed the horses. And then he said, 'Master, for vodka?' Although such a collection is not legal everyone is happy to pay . . . Twenty kopecks came in useful

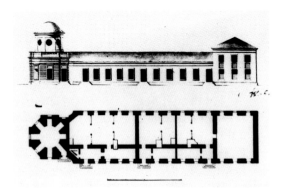

126 Offices and administrative buildings, Sofiya, Tsarskoye Selo, rebuilt by Charles Cameron, 1780s. Copy of drawing of 1810.

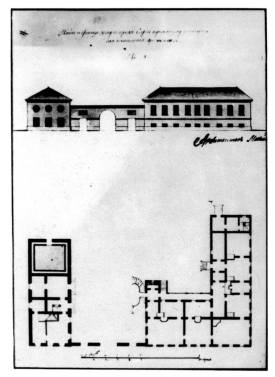

127 Governor's House, Sofiya, Tsarskoye Selo, rebuilt by Charles Cameron, 1780s. Copy of drawing of 1810.

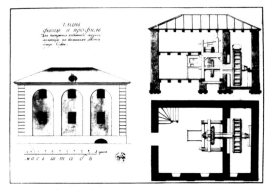

128 Mill, Sofiya, Tsarskoye Selo, rebuilt by Charles Cameron, 1780s. Copy of drawing of 1810.

. . . I found the post commissar snoring; I took him lightly by the shoulder . . . He jumped up hurriedly and, without opening his eyes, asked: 'Who has arrived, not . . .?' But coming to himself and catching sight of me, he said: 'I can see, young man, that you were used to behaving in such a way with former coachmen. They used to be beaten with sticks. But it isn't the old times now.' In a rage Mr Commissar lay down on his bed. I very much wanted to treat him as one did former coachmen when they were caught in deception. But my generosity in giving the town coachman vodka aroused the Sofiya coachmen to prepare my horses as quickly as possible and at the very moment that I was intending to commit a crime on the commissar's back, the bell sounded in the courtyard.[106]

Some travellers, however, entered into much more amicable relationships with the station's inhabitants. Thus in the epilogue to Pushkin's *The Captain's Daughter* we read:

Maria Ivanovna arrived safely in Sofiya . . . She was allotted a little corner behind a screen. The postmaster's wife immediately started chatting to her, informing her that she was the niece of a court boilerman and she initiated her into all the mysteries of court life. She told her at what times the Mistress usually woke up, took coffee, had a walk, and which courtiers were with her at that time, what she had deigned to say at her dinner table the previous day and whom she had received in the evening – in other words, Anna Vasilevna's conversation deserved several pages of historical notes and would have been valuable for posterity. Maria Ivanovna listened to her attentively. They went out into the garden. Anna Vasilevna gave the history of each avenue and each little bridge and, having looked their fill, they returned to the station very pleased with each other.

What did the other inhabitants of Sofiya do, those who did not work at the post station? They were for the most part craftsmen carrying out work at the palace and in the park: stonemasons, painters, smiths and carpenters. Charles Cameron organised a small colony of British craftsmen here, who did most of the work on his buildings. They had a special street. On it the architect built sixteen houses designated for them. Living there were men from Adam Menelaws's business, Andrew Dick's stonemasonry business and John Brown's stone business, the masons Alexander Campbell and Isaac Little, the plasterers William and George Lyon, and others. There were sixty-nine men there and, adding their wives and children, they made a community of about one hundred and forty people.[107]

Apart from the British, there were also Russian workers living in Sofiya. They worked at four factories which were also designed to add to the picture of 'enlightened well-being' reigning in the town. These institutions had an unusual character – they were built as the first industrial schools in eighteenth-century Russia. As a document of the period described it:

To encourage hand-made goods . . . factories in March of this year of 1782 . . . have been instituted in this town. The first is a spinning mill, the second is for linen, the third for cloth of different types of silk. And information was published in the newspapers about these places so that people who wanted to give serfs for training there or free people who wanted to start training there could do so.[108]

This enterprise links the concept behind Sofiya to the enlightened ideas of the 1780s.

All the town's inhabitants would meet at the market, which was held around the church. Catherine the Great attended this herself and made substantial purchases. Ordinary inhabitants used to buy here 'cotton scarves and printed scarves, canvas, silk, spun and not yet spun, scarves and hats made out of wool and mohair . . . beef, mutton, veal, flour, meal . . . and other provisions.'

★ ★ ★

Thus lived the town constructed by Cameron (pls 126–8). Around it it was hoped to create a no less exemplary rural environment. A design has been preserved for the regular replanning of the villages lying close to Tsarskoye Selo,[110] and Quarenghi worked out plans for model schools, churches and a priest's house.[111] This was not the limit of the attention paid to the rural environment. On the space enclosed by the boundaries of Sofiya, Tsarskoye Selo and Pavlovsk was built an agricultural school, a project led by Andrei Samborsky,[112] who was a former priest from the Russian Embassy church in London and a member of the Society of Arts. Innovative agricultural methods were tested on this large territory. Throughout the whole complex of Tsarskoye Selo Samborsky's school played the role of a grandiose, improved farm of the type which was not infrequently found in eighteenth-century parks elsewhere.

The greatest activity in replanning the Tsarskoye Selo lands and in the creation of Sofiya took place in the 1780s (pl. 129). In the ensuing decade official interest in it

129 Project for replanning the land around Tsarskoye Selo. Drawing of the 1780s showing the palace and park complex and, to the south, the town of Sofiya. To the north is the village of Greater Kuzmino, which was intended to be transformed into a model rural settlement. Note the road network.

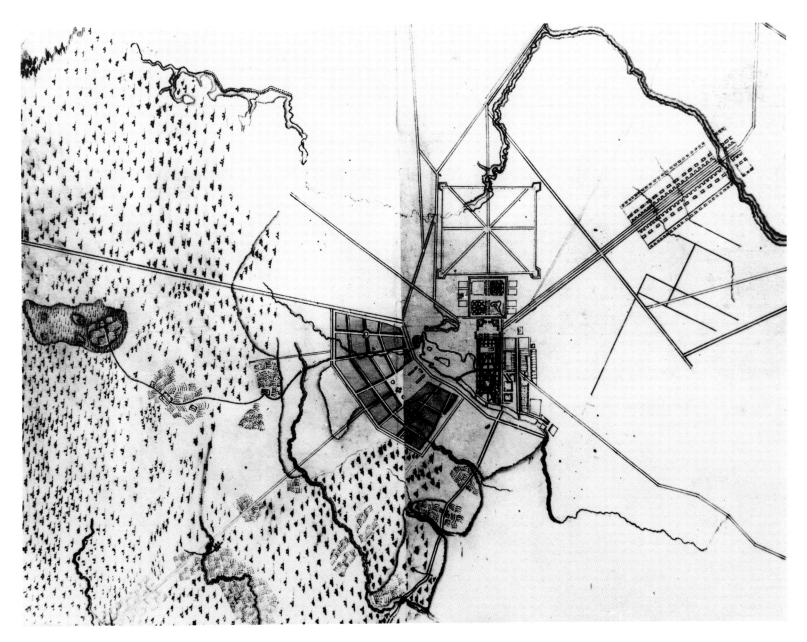

115

substantially diminished. Most probably this was a result of the political changes arising after the French Revolution. Sofiya began to be occupied by grenadier battalions rather than by craftsmen and merchants, and the town was neglected. The triumphal theme which was taking over the Tsarkoye Selo park to an ever greater extent was gradually edging out images of 'enlightened well-being'. The city which was to provide a view for the park's avenues did not have a long life, but its history does provide invaluable evidence of the architectural dimension of the Russian Enlightenment of the 1780s, and of the origins of many features in town planning in nineteenth-century Russia.

All these undertakings in Tsarskoye Selo, Sofiya and the neighbouring lands reflected a definite aesthetic concept whose realisation became increasingly idealised to correspond with the ideas of the Enlightenment. The vocabulary available for expressing this concept grew by the creation of fragments of an idealised environment, be it town, village or landscape, as well as through the pursuit of stylistic solutions appropriate for the treatment of different themes such as war, victory, prosperity or the romantic memory. This is significant not merely for the history of Tsarskoye Selo. Similar undertakings were found in many estate ensembles: on royal estates and in grand houses both in the capital and in the provinces. We have looked at only one example, albeit one of the most brilliant, which characterises what can be conventionally called 'the enlightened conception of the environment'. However, the artistic worlds of Tsarskoye Selo were far from being introspective. From them and to them stretched the threads of influence and imitation whereby these unique complexes of architectural ideas found their reflection in many regions of Russia during the last quarter of the eighteenth century.

Tsarskoye Selo as a whole played a significant role in the development of the architectural links between Britain and Russia. It reflected both specific inspirations and the diversity of elements through which the British influence was transmitted. In Tsarskoye Selo British craftsmen created magnificent works of art, and we have examined the contribution of Cameron. His work was continued in the nineteenth century by his pupils William Hastie and Adam Menelaws. They worked in various Russian towns but their contributions at Tsarskoye Selo were particularly fine, and we shall turn to these in a later chapter.

As well as launching such men as Hastie and Menelaws on their careers, Tsarskoye Selo produced the first of several architectural phenomena that were inspired by the English example. It was here that early neo-gothic constructions were erected in Russia, and here that the first large Chinese ensemble was created. We shall discuss these in the chapters on chinoiserie and neo-gothic. It was here that an archaeologically strict classicism was first introduced into Russia. And it was here that the landscape garden of the English type first appeared. It was from Tsarskoye Selo that all these ideas began to make their way into Russian architecture. It is also true, however, that an important part in this process was played by another famous estate ensemble for which Charles Cameron was once again responsible, Pavlovsk.

Chapter Three

PAVLOVSK

ON THE MORNING OF 25 May 1782 Charles Cameron left his house in the village of Tsarskoye Selo together with several compatriots, among them the empress's gardener John Bush, and got into a carriage. They travelled for about three miles along a bad road and soon saw some picturesque little hills, among which dodged a small stream called the Slavyanka. Five years previously, Catherine the Great had given the lands lying alongside this stream to her son, the Grand Duke Paul Petrovich and his new, second wife, Maria Fedorovna. Land was a traditional gift from wealthy parents to their children on the arrival of the first grandchild, who in this case was the future Tsar Alexander I. The estate had been named Pavlovsk, after its new owner. Now, in May 1782, the British travellers crossed the Slavyanka by a wooden bridge and ascended a hill, whereupon the procession came to a halt. A man speaking French with a pronounced German accent approached. This was the estate manager, Karl Kuchelbecker, who told them everything had been prepared for laying the foundation stone of the palace. Numerous workers were crowding around and at some distance away stood the priest who was to conduct the service that Russian tradition demanded should mark the commencement of work. On simple trestle tables were laid out refreshments for the craftsmen: several buckets of vodka and some barrels of beer.

The ceremony began. 'The first foundation stone was laid. From this time on they have been zealously working on laying the foundations', wrote Kuchelbecker (on whose account I base this description of the day) to the Grand Duchess, Maria Fedorovna, who was in Italy.[1] At that time the heir to the throne and his wife were travelling through Europe under the appropriately assumed titles of Comte and Comtesse du Nord. Cameron was to build their new palace in their absence.

A sympathy towards British culture had manifested itself at Pavlovsk even before Cameron's arrival in the early 1780s. Around the two small houses – the Grand Duke's residence, Marienthal (literally Maria's valley) and his wife's home, Paulust (literally Paul's consolation) – two picturesque little gardens had been built at the end of the 1770s. These included all the pavilions typical of English gardens of that period: a monk's hermitage, a charcoal burner's hut, a trellis, a Chinese summerhouse, a ruin and a mill.[2] The wooden bridges and the umbrella summerhouse were apparently built following the Halfpennys' published designs of 1750 which included sketches for 'rural buildings in the Chinese style'.[3] It is interesting to note that the ideas of the English garden craftsmen had reached Russia not directly but through Germany and, more precisely, through Württemberg, whence the Grand Duchess originated as Princess Sophia Dorothea of Württemberg (she became Maria Fedorovna on joining the Russian Church). The Hermitage Pavilion resembled one from Maria Fedorovna's childhood home, on the Etupes estate near Montbéliard in eastern France, and the Old Chalet, erected at Pavlovsk in the late 1770s, was, at her wish, a copy of the Alte Turme in the Gogenheim Park in Württemberg.

These original structures at Pavlovsk were very simple. The Hermitage was a small square building with a latticed window. Inside it was a hearth, 'in the chimney, an iron kettle on an iron tripod . . . a table of plain pine, a pine bed with a reed mattress, three simple spoons.' The associations of this building compensated for its unpretentiousness. In a similar hut in Etupes Maria Fedorovna's uncle had predicted a very prosaic fate for his niece at the same time as the heir to the Russian imperial throne was offering his hand to her, the daughter of a minor German prince; the contrast between the ordinariness of her uncle's prediction and the extraordinariness of her fate always struck her forcefully.[4] There was also a legend, according to which a hermit had lived a most righteous life in this hut when dense forest still surrounded it. Catherine the Great chanced to hear of him and wanted to come from Tsarskoye Selo to pay a visit. The monk took fright and fled, leaving the vacant hut as a royal plaything.[5] It is piquant to remember that, in the light of the tense relationship between Paul Petrovich and his mother, it used to be said in Pavlovsk that the 'hermit' had fled on the approach of the empress. Many legends grew up around Pavlovsk, mostly relating to the Grand Duchess Maria Fedorovna, whose tastes had a significant effect on the appearance of the estate.

From the standpoint of historical reputation, Cameron's most dangerous rival at Pavlovsk has been not so much Vincenzo Brenna or Pietro Gonzago, who worked here after him, but rather Maria Fedorovna herself. Memoirs-writers and scholars have variously emphasised her role in the creation of the ensemble.[6] The nineteenth-century Russian writer, Count Vladimir Sologub recalled:

> Pavlovsk . . . was in its time the property and personal residence of the empress Maria Fedorovna. It had the appearance of a rich and flourishing oasis where, on all sides, the presence of its royal owner could be felt. She was both a committed and involved estate manager and a hospitable hostess, without, however, stepping down from the dignity of her office. In her time the court observed a strict etiquette and yet at the same time had a hearty cordiality so that it was relaxed and easy at Pavlovsk . . . At the farm and in other rural buildings there stood tables laid with many delicacies and black bread just in case guests felt hungry. We children often treated ourselves.[7]

The celebrations that were held in the pavilions entwined with roses; the milk in blue Chinese cups on white tables with gilded details that stood in thatched cottages; the albums with verses singing the praises of the 'charmingly heavenly way of life'; the august and worldly ladies cultivating flowers or working 'for the poor at special times': these are the characteristics of the 'Pavlovsk style' if it is viewed as being generated by the lifestyle and tastes of Maria Fedorovna.[8]

The cultural contribution made here by Charles Cameron was plainly at a different level. His work was strikingly different from earlier attempts to create a landscape garden on the estate. As an architect who had a deep feeling for the sublimity of the natural landscape, who was a supporter of the strict and serious use of sentimental references and whose soul was filled with 'true enthusiasm', Cameron had to engage in a struggle against what had formerly been done at Pavlovsk. He did not like the trivial pavilions stamped out routinely in accordance with the Halfpennys' works like others all over Europe, and he went so far as to have some of them destroyed.

In Pavlovsk Cameron assiduously tried to achieve his ideal of the grand estate. Although his concept was not fully realised, and although much was reworked or never properly executed according to his wishes, Pavlovsk nevertheless represents a complete and integrated world that was particularly dear to Cameron for the rest of his career. We shall see the determination with which he fought to preserve his ideas, and the sad consequences this had for his career. For him the vision was not confined to architectural plans, it was part of his spiritual life, it was his poetry. As Taleporovsky was later

130   Charles Cameron, Pavlovsk Palace: view from the courtyard.

to describe it, 'everything that was Pavlovsk suddenly came to life with Cameron's arrival. Each work of Cameron's contained a definite idea . . . or a symbol.'[9] Thoughts of antiquity, its art and its myths in the form in which they inhabited the architect's imagination were to permeate everything at Pavlovsk, from the palace halls to each detail of the park.

The Cameron period at Pavlovsk began immediately after the architect's arrival in Russia in 1779 and continued until 1787 when he was replaced as estate architect by the Italian, Vincenzo Brenna, although he continued working on individual projects until 1803. The period we shall now examine is the period of the crucial introduction to Russia of English Palladianism. It begins at the end of 1781, when Cameron was simultaneously charged with building the palace, constructing the park and erecting pavilions within it.

Pavlovsk: The Palladian Villa

Cameron selected for the palace a site on a small hill rising above the Slavyanka river (pl. 131). On the entrance side, two long wings curved round to form a courtyard, modest in their architecture and rising only to a single storey with a mezzanine (pl. 130). Arches with deeply inset windows constituted their decoration (pl. 134). Narrow

119

131 Pavlovsk: the palace, the Centaur Bridge and, in the foreground, the Cold Baths designed by Charles Cameron.

inner passages leading towards the central palace block ran behind a semi-circular Doric colonnade. In the shade of the colonnade could be seen small bays with sculptures in the ancient style (pls 132, 133). Severity and simplicity were combined with lightness and a poetic quality.

The palace itself stood out within this expansive composition on account of its elegance and refinement. The façade was so divided that the ground floor was almost equal in height to the first floor, while the upper floor appeared quite low. Four pairs of powerful double columns with lavish Corinthian capitals were supported by the simple arcade. Above the building rose a flat dome with sixty-four miniature columns around its drum (pls 135, 136). Cameron increased the visibility of the dome by designing a portico without the conventional pediment.

All four façades of the palace were different, a common feature of late eighteenth-century British architecture. This difference was particularly emphasised in that part of the structure that would be seen from the lake. The wings and the gallery retreated, and the central volume dominated (pl. 137). In contrast to the horizontal structure of

132 (above) Pavlovsk Palace: colonnade.

133 Giacomo Quarenghi, *View of the Palace at Pavlovsk*, 1790s, showing the palace as Cameron built it, before later additions and changes.

134 Charles Cameron, Pavlovsk Palace: courtyard elevation.

135 Charles Cameron, Pavlovsk Palace: design for the elevation facing the lake, early 1780s.

the palace façade, here everything was subordinated to development along the vertical. The building rose harmoniously above the hill and the lake, casting its reflection into the water. The peaceful, measured view of the palace obtained while walking on the opposite bank, or while approaching along the Tsarskoye Selo road, was part of the architect's intention (pls 138, 139).

136   Charles Cameron, Pavlovsk Palace: dome.

The portico played a significant role. Only the columns at the extreme ends were left in pairs, while in the middle they were placed singly (pl. 140). The corners of the protruding volumes were strengthened, while the centre was freer. The palace was monumental without being ponderous. Its lightness and its quality of hovering over the landscape were, however, combined with solidity and dignity. Cameron strove to turn the building into an integral part of the landscape composition over which it would rule not by the 'power of might' but by an air of aristocratic 'right of existence'. The dome, visible from afar in different parts of the park, served as a landmark as it rose elegantly, often unexpectedly, among the trees.

This dome was one of Cameron's boldest creations, without any specific precedent in either the ancient or the classical tradition. Sixty-four columns would seem rather too many for the flat dome of a country house, but his composition of many small elements was deliberate. By this architectural prolixity he sought to convey a sense of the richness and complexity of the idea that he had realised in a classically

123

137   Pavlovsk Palace: view from the lake.

140 (facing page) Charles Cameron, Pavlovsk Palace.

138 (below left) Anon., *The Palace at Pavlovsk*, 1790s.

139 (below right) Pavlovsk: the palace and the Centaur Bridge.

finished form. Seen from the park, this light and rich cupola reads as an unusual, enormous round temple, of a kind that had never existed in antiquity, erected over the palace.

These are the compositional themes and elements of the palace, but their significance lies in the cultural milieu their use sought to evoke. The portico over the arcade, with its lavishly framed windows along the sides of the columns and between them, is, of course, an attribute of the Palladian villa on the Venetian terra firma, which became translated into the classical English estate. The dome was a symbol of Beauty inspired by Reason in the imaginings of the innumerable European successors to the Venetian humanists, of those from Bergamo to Weimar who had created neo-classicism and had

141 Charles Cameron, Pavlovsk Palace: window on the north façade.

sensitively reworked its images. Such a dome would signify a temple of antique spirit and thought evoking the whole tradition of Palladio and his English successors.

The side façades of the Pavlovsk palace did not have colonnades, and the viewer's impression changed sharply according to whether the building was seen from the courtyard or from the lake. The windows of the first floor served as the focal point of the composition on both the north and the south sides of the façade. It would have been natural to have a similar solution for the side elevations, and the majority of classicist architects did precisely that. But Cameron always acted differently from others, and in a further expression of the picturesque English tradition, he resolved the design of the side façades in different ways. The north façade was dominated by the flatness of the wall, on which window framings appeared to be 'hung' (pl. 141). The opposite façade stressed the wall's mass by cutting into it a series of deep arches, with richly varied mass and geometry in the pedimented windows placed within them (pl. 142).

Here Cameron demonstrated his love for variety, contrast and a mixture of impressions. Where earlier traditions of classicism in Russia tended, as noted above, to the static, Cameron brought a skill in combining elements that did not combine easily: lyricism, an exalting variety, grandeur.

The architects who worked at Pavlovsk after Cameron did not support his aspirations and altered the concept of the palace. Fortunately the main corpus remained untouched, but the wings were rebuilt by Vincenzo Brenna. At the hands of Brenna, Quarenghi, Voronikhin and Rossi, Cameron's light colonnaded galleries became massive semi-circular blocks. Gonzago painted the lower part of the gallery adjoining the main corpus with a perspective mural that was magnificent but totally alien to Cameron's aesthetic.

The Interior of the Palace: Reconstructing Cameron's Idea

Cameron's vision for the internal decoration of the Pavlovsk palace is among the many mysteries of Russian architectural history (pl. 143). Many scholars have highlighted the

142 Charles Cameron, Pavlovsk Palace: windows on the south façade.

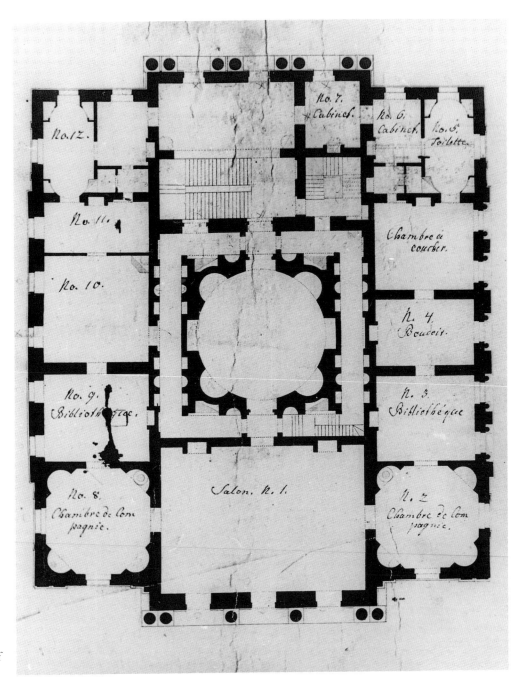

No. 12.

No. 7.
+ Cabinet.

No. 6.
Cabinet.

No. 5.
Toilette.

No. 11.

Chambre à
coucher.

No. 10.

n. 4.
Boudoir.

n. 3.
Bibliothèque

No. 9.
Bibliothèque.

Salon. n. 1.

No. 8.
Chambre de com
pagnie.

n. 2.
Chambre de com
pagnie.

143 Charles Cameron, Pavlovsk Palace: plan of the first floor, early 1780s.

difficulties of ascertaining his intentions here. The problem lies in the fact that as early as the end of the 1780s Brenna began replanning the most important rooms and decorating them in his own fashion. He was attracted by the lavish 'imperial' antiquity which Wölfflin would later call antique baroque, and produced works that were conspicuously luxurious. The preference of Pavlovsk's owners for Brenna over Cameron revealed their taste and has even, in a historical perspective, served to clarify the distinctive nature of Cameron's aesthetic, for the classic and lyrical qualities of Pavlovsk were manifestly due to the influence of his personality and not the result of Maria Fedorovna's attentions. In 1803 Brenna's work was also destroyed by fire. The palace was rebuilt by Andrei Voronikhin, the architect of the famous Kazan cathedral in St Petersburg. Voronikhin's admiration for Cameron is well known, and it can therefore be assumed that he tried to preserve the original qualities of the architect's work here. The history of the Pavlovsk interiors is complex and it is hard to unravel Cameron's intentions, but it is essential to make some attempt at it.

Above all we know that Cameron created the plan for the palace. Along the side façades on the ground and first floors enfiladed suites of rooms ran through the whole building from front to back. Between them on the courtyard side was the vestibule and the main staircase, with a spacious landing hall on the upper floor and beside it a narrow 'black' staircase set into a square. On the park side were large halls stretching one after the other along the façade. All these rooms were grouped around a central square through which a circular hall rose from the first floor to the dome. This hall stood apart from the rest of the building inside a broad internal corridor which was square in its outer plan.

This basic structure has been preserved, and we can learn something about Cameron's further ideas from his letters. Thus in one he wrote:

> The Grand Duchess should not miss the opportunity to acquire some bas-relief figures and ornaments used in finishing the loggia. Casts and moulds should be taken of these and sent here as I can make splendid use of them for finishing Her Highness's house. Moreover if it were possible with the Grand Duchess's cooperation to get some patterns of the finishing of the Medici villa, this could be used with great taste . . . in the finishing of Her Highness's house.[10]

Cameron also wanted to have 'marble from Carrara' for the 'staircase, the facing of the hall and the columns'.[11] Where appropriate, he was happy to buy original antique architectural fragments: 'I have nothing against some of the fireplaces being made from ancient fragments as, when used well, they give a very good effect.'[12] He wanted as many original ancient statues, busts and vases to be acquired as possible, and at another point he insisted on making eight eighteen-foot marble columns as well as some eleven or twelve-foot columns from white marble, or with a covering of Sienese *brocadella* or perhaps jasper.

Let us imagine what a guest might have seen on entering the palace if Cameron's ideas had been realised. In the vestibule the visitor would have found himself in a relatively severe room reminiscent of the palace's external architecture (pl. 144). Its walls, like the façade, were covered with rustication decorated to look like stone and crowned by a cornice with triglyphs.[13] The floor was paved with the same stone tiles as the porch. This emphasised the gentleness of the transition from the courtyard to the interior. Mirrors fitted into the side doors expanded the space. Decorated statues standing on pedestals along the walls and the decorations above them showed images connected with the cult of nature. For the vestibule the sculptor Ivan Prokofyev made allegorical depictions of the 'twelve months'; signs of the zodiac framed by 'rural armature' appeared in medallions. Statues painted to look like bronze stood out against the background of yellow walls. The matt surface of the dark floor gleamed. Light poured in from the windows and sparkled, reflecting in the mirrors. In the central arch could be seen the gently curving staircase.

This was not brightly lit. Cameron had foreseen this and therefore sought to make it especially light and celebratory of arrival. He envisaged an all-white staircase with eleven-foot columns of white marble.[14] The first-floor hall was spacious, with similar statues and the same Doric frieze as on the lower floor.[15]

From this one could see through the open doors to the circular central hall (named the Italian Hall (pl. 145)) which was comparatively small in area but rose to the dome with eight enormous columns. Four deep semi-circular niches, probably containing statues, and four broad open doorways were placed between the columns. The hall would have been brightly lit, but around it ran the darker corridor of which we have already spoken. Visitors are not now shown this corridor and scholars have generally

144   Pavlovsk Palace: vestibule.

ignored it, but its significance is worth pursuing, for in my judgement it is the key compositional element of the palace.

It was totally dark. Not one window illuminated it. It was immersed in gloom but, even so, its walls had twenty-eight niches, which have survived. In these Cameron wanted to place ancient funeral urns, pitchers, busts, cups, pieces of capitals – all those things which he had drawn in his youth when copying the Italian engravings he had seen on his travels to Rome. Here these images appeared not on sketches and not in museum halls and not among excavations and ruins but in his creation, in a house created by his imagination. In this context the compositional intention becomes clear. The visitor was to find himself as if in Roman catacombs or in a passage in some excavated part of those Roman baths that Cameron had penetrated, with the aid of lamps and spades, during his time in Italy. By this means the ancient world would have

145 Pavlovsk Palace: Italian Hall.

come to life in the palace, appearing in precisely the form in which it was understood by the eighteenth century: on the one hand as the shining brilliance of ideal representations and on the other as the twilight of romantic reveries. In the centre of the palace the Olympian gods would again, in Taleporovsky's phrase, 'illuminate the beauty of architecture and life'.[16] Here too, as at Tsarskoye Selo, we see Cameron's special talent for conveying the 'flesh and blood' of antiquity in a real and a sensual way.

There were exits from this corridor in three directions: to the landing of the main staircase, to the room where the ceremonial chamber was to be (now the library in the northern suite of rooms)[17] and to the large drawing room, the famous Grecian Hall. In 1789, when it was completed by Brenna, this last was a 'rectangular hall decorated by sixteen Corinthian columns going round the entire room, standing out from the walls and, thus, forming a kind of temple interior'. With little attempt at modesty, Brenna described the room to Prince Pototsky in Poland:

The columns of green marble, a little less than an elbow in diameter, the proportions of the hall which I found, the decorative richness of the ceilings, the decoration of the walls, the beauty of the ancient ornaments and the ways in which they are used,

146 Charles Cameron, design for the frieze of the Dancing Room, Pavlovsk Palace, 1784.

147 Charles Cameron, design for a capital for the Large Dining Room, Pavlovsk Palace, 1784.

positioned lengthwise along the rooms behind the columns over the niches in which stand statues, not to speak of the magnificence of the furniture which was specially made to my designs – all this makes this room one of the finest in the country.[18]

Cameron's original ideas for this room were more modest. He wanted to face the walls in marble, making two fireplaces decorated with ancient figures. It was important for him that the room, surrounded by its inner colonnade, evoking an Olympian Temple, should be placed right in the centre of the whole palace, under the dome which marked it from outside. Cameron, moreover, had no need to seek a special luxuriousness for the Grecian Hall. Enriched by columns and with the narrow passage-way full of ancient originals, a more restrained composition would probably have been appropriate as giving a feeling of space and consolation. This would have been further enhanced by the fenestration, for on the side directly opposite the entrance from the Italian Hall were three large windows which opened on to the park – and its principal panorama. Here the visitor saw glades on the banks of the Slavyanka flowing into the lake, a yacht, a bridge, on the far bank clumps of trees and beyond them a field; in the middle of it stood the Apollo Colonnade, a memorial erected by Cameron to the god of light and poetry.

It is highly significant here that the British architect turned the whole composition of the palace out towards the landscape of the park, creating a development from one to the other that was wholly English, but wholly original in Russia.

Beside the Grecian Hall Cameron built ceremonial rooms, rich in form, octagonal with deep semi-circular niches. These spacious palace chambers constituted another suite of rooms that turned towards the park. From them, as if going back to the palace façade, ran the private suites of Maria Fedorovna and Paul Petrovich.

Maria Fedorovna's apartments were thus in the southern suite of rooms. If we follow the path of a person wishing to get from the staircase to the living quarters by the shortest route, we notice something rather absurd. One would pass in this order: the Dressing Room, the Bedchamber, the Boudoir, the Study-library, the Small Drawing Room.[19] This was how far a servant might have to go in order to announce that a guest was waiting below. But Cameron was clearly not thinking of practicality or domestic convenience. On the contrary, the intended route through a sequence of rooms of increasing intimacy was exactly opposite to the shortest route. Herein lies the significant point. The normal route would obligatorily have taken the visitor across the central hall, thus traversing the 'corridor of antiquities' twice, on through the Grecian Hall to pass along the suite of rooms moving back towards the palace façade. The important guest was thus certainly intended by Cameron's design to experience the ancient splendour of the palace to its fullest extent. For everyday life there was a back staircase to reach the Boudoir and the Bedchamber, but Cameron as architect of the environment for a cultural milieu produced a celebratory aesthetic sequence in which the soul of the palace would be revealed and the visitor would be struck by the contrasts and the magnificence of the images created in each space: in the vestibule, the staircase, the corridor of antiquities, the round hall and the other halls.

Such was Cameron's notion for the ceremonial first floor of the palace. By contrast, the planning of the ground floor was comparatively simple. The central hall, small with four columns in the middle, did not play any particular aesthetic role. The space around it was divided into four rectangular rooms; these were not large, the biggest of them lying underneath the Grecian Hall. In the years 1784 to 1786 Cameron finished the New and General Studies in the southern suite, the Billiard Room, the Old Drawing Room, the Dancing Room (pl. 146) and the French Drawing Room in the northern suite and the Large Dining Room (pl. 147) under the Grecian Hall. Although his creative freedom was limited here, he managed to find solutions which were perhaps not as brilliant as at Tsarskoye Selo but which had a particular restrained and refined style. Thus Cameron was partially obliged to develop another manner for his decorative works, without vaults, complicated architectural moulding, multi-colouring or unusual materials. Here mirrors, gilding and the colour white reigned. Decorations were distinguished by their severity and by the graphic nature of their design. All the decoration of the halls was emphasised architecturally. The theatrical quality of the rooms characteristic of Tsarskoye Selo's interiors is quite absent at Pavlovsk.

These were the themes that Cameron developed for the internal decoration of Pavlovsk. Unfortunately, the owners of the estate did not give him their support. The Grand Duke and Duchess constrained his aspirations in all sorts of ways, communicating their orders through their steward Kuchelbecker: 'I should warn you in general that all his grandiose ideas about importing marble from Carrara should be rejected', wrote the heir to the throne.[20] In fairness, it must be said that Paul Petrovich and Maria Fedorovna had their own difficulties. They did not have sufficient money for the construction work. They were forced to write letters such as the following: 'We, the undersigned, come running for the favours of our gracious . . . Mother . . . to take sincere cognizance of our extreme financial need . . . [as a result] of maintaining our out-of-town properties and of the necessity of completing work which has been begun.'[21] But the empress's replies were not all that agreeable: 'one must suppose that you are constantly being robbed and are therefore in need although you lack nothing.'[22]

The architect either failed to understand this situation or did not want to understand it. He insisted on his own way. Relationships soured. Soon the utmost irritation sounded in the Grand Duchess's letters: 'Finally, I shall repeat to you that I am confident that you, my dear Kuchelbecker, have done the best that was possible. As far as Cameron is concerned, I shall put aside my judgement of him until you have informed me of the essence of the matter.'[23] And several months later: 'You have already had enough experience to realise that there is absolutely no point in gentleness with Cameron but tell him directly that his behaviour is insupportable and advise him please to be more careful.'[24] The architect did not heed advice of this kind.

Misunderstandings and disagreements concerning the finishing of the halls arose at every turn. Instead of antique fragments, huge marble columns and such like, quite different objects began appearing. The same letter refers to 'a table top of green marble with black specks, . . . three white marble busts (one with the neck broken off). A picture from the same marble – rectangular with a bow and quiver hanging on a bust represented on it' and so on. It was not at all what the architect wanted.

The situation deteriorated with time. The owners of the estate became totally disillusioned with Cameron, and work on the most important rooms was stopped. The plans for the main, first floor were also not realised. He proposed working on the ground floor and his suggestions regarding these rooms were accepted, but without any enthusiasm: 'My husband agrees, albeit unwillingly, that there should be an arch in the bedroom, but on condition that its forms should be as little disagreeable as possible. So ask Cameron in God's name to do something in good taste and especially not something that is decorated in arabesques.'[25] This was already a thrust at Catherine the Great, who particularly liked Cameron's arabesques in her apartments. Serious quarrels took place over trifles. Initially Cameron tried to object but the opposition continued. 'Reprimand Cameron, my dear friend, for the medallions in one and the same colour . . . Cameron did not wish this. For God's sake, my dear friend, ensure this will look reasonable.'[26] Cameron had to submit to Maria Fedorovna's wishes: 'Yesterday evening I sent . . . to Cameron who was as mild as a lamb. He even asked that it should be conveyed to me that he finds the colour blue charming.'[27] We see the architect reconciling himself to the fact that many things in the palace would not be in

132

accordance with his ideas. Even in their partially realised state, however, his designs and the aspirations they demonstrated were highly significant for the development of Russian architecture.

For the Grand Duchess, the palace itself was not her only concern:

> Let us talk of the garden which will be my consolation . . . Is the aviary ready? I entertain myself with the hope that it will be beautiful; for you promised me that, my dear Kuchelbecker. What is the Dairy doing? Will it be under a roof? What shall I find that is new in my garden? Will it be sown with rare flowers? Will the colonnade be finished? Is the flower-garden in front of the aviary ready? Has my forest been cleared? In a word, shall I find much new? I confess to you that it will indeed be a special day for me when I see my dear Pavlovsk again.[28]

Shifting our focus with the Grand Duchess, let us examine the developments in the park from 1780 to 1787.

The Picturesque Park

The park at Pavlovsk is one of the largest in Russia: at the end of the eighteenth century it covered approximately one thousand hectares. The little picturesque gardens and romantic, even whimsical pavilions represented the amateur enthusiams of Maria Fedorovna herself. She was a passionate gardener, and for this she must be given her due. As with the interiors, we have to establish what precisely Cameron did in the park and how he envisaged it, but in this case the answers should be more gratifying, for here he did succeed in bringing his dreams to fruition, in animating the space of the park with them. Thus the distinguished twentieth-century Russian art historian Mikhail Alpatov could write that: 'All of Pavlovsk in its entirety constitutes an enormous and integrated poetic world and not for nothing is one pillar on the edge of the park called 'the end of the world'.[29] And this world was harmonious, calm and caressing. A very specific moral atmosphere reigned there. Again in Alpatov's words, here there was not feeling of 'aching melancholy as in romantic gardens with their ruins and their memories of an irretrievable past, there is neither loss nor loneliness . . . here . . . the buildings have not submitted to cold brilliant perfection'.[30]

Cameron's concept for the landscaping was distinguished by its clarity and its consistency (pl. 148). The large palace became the focal point for the composition of the park. On it converged all the 'lines of development' of the ensemble, which was clearly divided into several areas. A broad avenue of three rows of lime trees led from the palace. To the right and left of the avenue were two picturesque and differing compositions sited on flat, slightly elevated terrain. On the opposite side the palace was skirted by the Slavyanka river. The Slavyanka valley was a magnificent extended composition whose character changed several times as it passed through the landscape. In essence, this was an ensemble within the ensemble of the park. Higher up, on the left bank of the river, was another independent part, the Upper Garden, situated in an open position. Beyond that, on the other side of the Tsarskoye Selo road, a site was created for the village of Pavlovsk, a small regular settlement of ten geometrically precise clusters. Opposite the village, on the right bank of the Slavyanka were the Swiss Hills. In these areas Cameron created an environment where a poeticised landscape worked in co-operation with the architecture.

Apart from these the architect demarcated three other areas, much larger in size, situated round them and stretching right to the boundary of the estate. These were Menagerie (*Zverinets*), Large Star (*Bolshaya zvezda*) and Silver Birch (*Belaya beryoza*). In Cameron's time these were all tracts of dense virgin forest penetrated only by simple

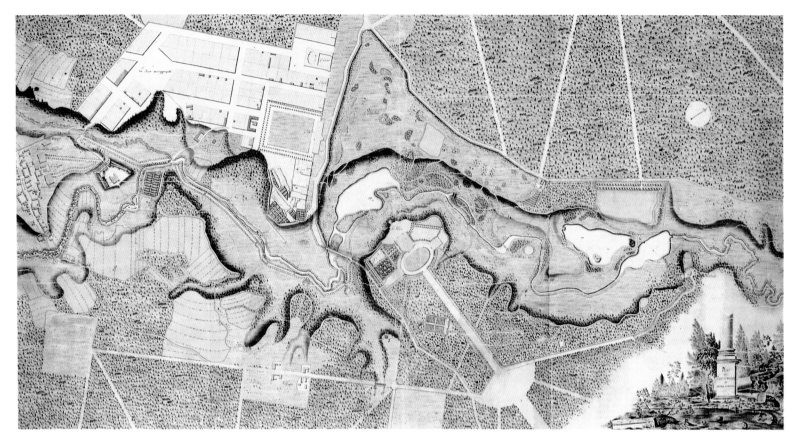

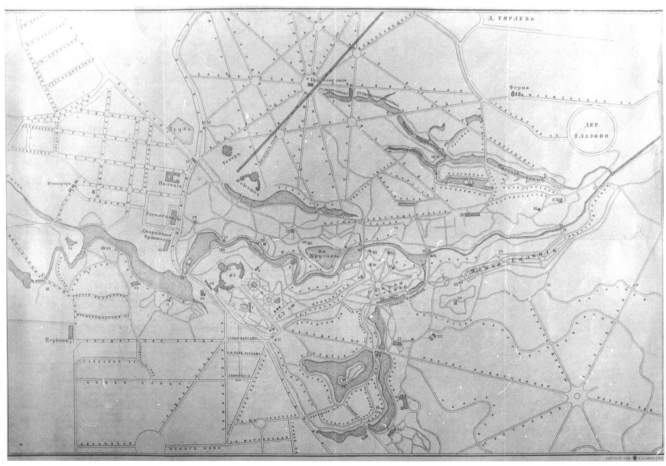

148 (facing page top) Plan of Pavlovsk, 1790s. Photo from the archives of V.A. Tauber.

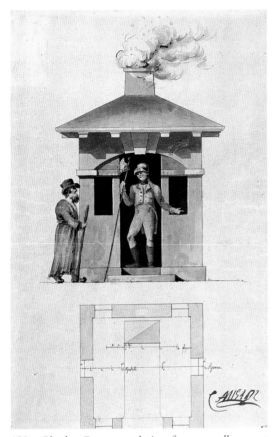

150 Charles Cameron, design for a guardhouse at Pavlovsk, 1780s.

149 (facing page bottom) Plan of Pavlovsk, late 1870s.

cuttings forming a geometrically precise pattern. Here was another kind of park environment from that at the centre of the ensemble, a kind characterised by the strictness, even the severity, of its structure. Here there reigned the utmost clarity and simplicity which emphasised the grandeur of the wild forest in contrast to those glades where 'nymphs gambolled' in the landscaping images of a vaguer sentimentalism. The contrast between the centre of the estate and its periphery was an important element in Cameron's vision.

An interesting composition was developed to the east of the palace, in the region of the triple lime avenue. This 'perspective', as they used to say in the eighteenth century, was and remains very effective. The rows of carefully trimmed trees framing the broad central road and the side pathways created a peaceful rhythm. The avenue emerged on to the Parade Ground. In Cameron's time this was a fan-shaped area where Duke Paul organised inspections of the small guard which was based on the estate. Despite the small size of the guard, its discipline was strict. N. Sablukov, one of Paul's retainers, gives evidence of this:

The reader should not imagine that because all sorts of merriments and festivities were taking place at Pavlovsk that meant an end to the severe disciplinary measures instituted at Gatchina and the capital. On the contrary, there were just as many of them, if not more for, as the daily inspections involved not large corps as on manoeuvres but small divisions, this resulted in any inadequacy becoming much more obvious. Moreover there was at Pavlovsk the so-called citadel or fort, Bip, where offending officers were placed under arrest.[31]

A significant amount of space at Pavlovsk was given over to military exercises. The territory involved stretched from the Bip citadel, which in Paul's reign was included in the number of 'real fortresses of the empire', along Soldatskaya (Soldier) Street to the Parade Ground where inspections took place; and from this along the triple avenue to the palace. It is difficult to imagine that the military elements of the park ensemble were close to Cameron's heart or particularly welcomed by him, but the landscape planning had to take account of Paul Petrovich's passion for parades and troop marches.

The space on either side of the Triple Avenue was subject to Maria Fedorovna's whims. The right-hand side, as one stands facing the palace, was covered by forest. A path meandered whimsically along its edge, along the brow of the bank of the Slavyanka. A thicket hid the Dairy which Cameron had constructed. This was one of the first rustic cabins to be built in a Russian park.

The Dairy (pls 151, 152) was not entirely Cameron's own work. It was reminiscent of 'the dairy of His Highness, the Duke of Württemberg', whose plans had been especially sent to Cameron with the inscription: 'Her Imperial Highness wishes to have something of this kind . . . the most convenient place for . . . the construction is in the upper part of the garden, in the most remote corner on the edge so that the cows could go straight from the milking stall into the forest . . . It is also essential that this building should be hidden . . . so that nobody should have any idea of its existence until they are right upon it.'[33]

Cameron completed a plan for this building at the beginning of March 1782. He imagined a six-windowed hut 'made of broken stone with a high thatched roof and an overhang on the coarsest of trunks.' Inside there was 'a refined hall with a dome and this held white and gold stools with down cushions and covers . . . made of East Indian material with flowers . . . on . . . the windows [were] matching curtains with fringes, scallops and tassels'.[34] The result was a 'many-layered surprise'. First there was dense forest, the thicket. Suddenly a decrepit cottage appeared. On entering the cottage the visitor discovered an interior of refined luxury.

In 1786 Cameron built the Memorial to Sister Frederika, which was subsequently

151 Charles Cameron, Dairy, Pavlovsk, 1782.

152 Charles Cameron, design for the Dairy, Pavlovsk, early 1780s.

renamed the Memorial to Parents (pl. 153). This small temple-niche was near the Dairy but not visible from it, in a melancholy and at that time remote part of the forest. Later a sculpture by Ivan Martos was placed in it which depicted, in the words of an early nineteenth-century guide, 'a mourning wife with a crown on her head; she was supported by a broken piece of tree trunk . . . she is approaching her parents' memorial with the intention of spending several minutes at their grave but, overwhelmed with feeling, she puts down her lamp . . . and overcome by grief she lowers her head conversing in her thoughts with the dead whild a genie is throwing the lids off the funeral urns.'[35]

The rustic backwater, the quiet and the melancholy of the right-hand side of this part of the garden are counter-posed with the self-consciously Roman refinement of

153 Charles Cameron, Memorial to Parents, Pavlovsk, 1786.

the left-hand side. Here the planning brought to life a very complex ornamental game. In 1786 Cameron constructed a maze with an exceptionally confusing design made from hedges of yellow acacia. The intricate patterns composed of flowers and shrubs were illuminated with the antique spirit thanks to the large number of antique sculptures and copies which were placed here. The Duke and Duchess could play bowls under the fixed gaze of Roman busts. And winding towards the Triple Avenue was a long spinney curving like a wave, an arcade of greenery with ornaments made from the specially cut crowns of the trees. Around it were placed about forty Roman vases and funeral urns. The leisure garden was permeated with the spirit of antiquity. It was as if this part of the garden was stamped with the immortality of ancient joy. Cameron conveyed this feeling with greatest strength in the architectural centre of the composition, the *Volière* or Aviary (pls 154–8).

The instructions were clear: 'Her Highness especially turns your attention to the construction and equipping of the *Volière*. She hopes that you will make a pearl out of it. Properly speaking, this subject is presented for your consideration and for you to do everything so that it should be an honour to your taste, spare no pains or labour.'[36] The design was completed by Cameron at the beginning of 1781 (pl. 154) and by the autumn of the following year it had been erected.

Its lightness and elegant simplicity are felt by anyone who sees this building. The architect joined his three pavilions, two small ones at the sides and a central slightly larger one, with a small light drum and a flat dome, with a Doric colonnade. There was a particular charm in the Aviary's interior (pl. 157). Its central part was spacious and covered by the light dome. In the aisles of each pavilion were low colonnades with

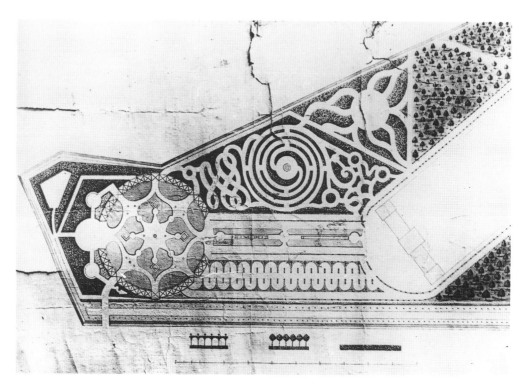

154   Plan of the Aviary area, Pavlovsk, 1790s.

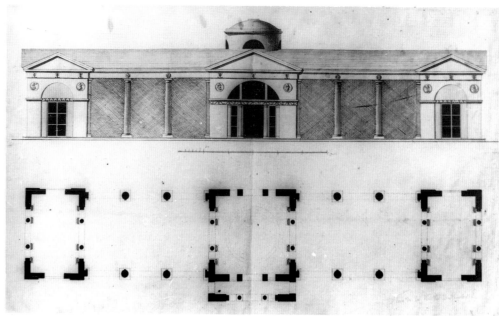

155   Aviary, Pavlovsk: plan and elevation, 1781.

156   (facing page) Charles Cameron, Aviary, Pavlovsk.

157 Anon., *Interior of the Aviary, Pavlovsk,* early nineteenth century.

broad arches thrown across their entablatures. Remarkable perspectives opened out within the building as the spectator looked from one end of it to the other. When the sun was shining, beams of light poured from above through the semi-circular windows, forming stripes on the sides of the dome, the bas-reliefs and the columns and laying a pathway of light on the marble floor. Hung between the columns in the aisles of all three parts of the Aviary was a fine net intertwined with plants. Exotic trees stood in tubs in the galleries and among them flew birds – nightingales, starlings, quail. Contemporaries recalled how birdsong resounded here early in the morning and at dusk. Soft divans upholstered in white material with blue trimming stood in the halls of the pavilions and at the windows hung curtains of white muslin with blue ribbons.

The park in the area of the Triple Avenue was thus very varied. It was synthesis into a purely Pavlovsk style, which united elements different in the character of their planning as well as in their treatment of planting, their architecture and mood.

158 Charles Cameron, Aviary, Pavlovsk.

The Slavyanka Valley

The Slavyanka valley is not simply the most interesting part of the Pavlovsk park; nor is it merely the most perfect of the landscape compositions with which Cameron's name is connected; it has a greater significance yet. It represents one of the greatest achievements of landscape gardening in Russia. It is inevitable that all writers on the history of Russian parks and estate architecture should have devoted close attention to this outstanding example. Moreover, since the early nineteenth century the Slavyanka valley has also frequently been described and discussed by foreign scholars.[37] However, most of those writers who have examined the unique quality of the landscape composition have treated the end product as a totality, rather than distinguishing the developments of different periods – and the aesthetics they reflected – as distinct pieces of creative work. My concern here is, therefore, to evoke the Slavyanka valley as it was originally envisaged by Cameron and as he realised his ideas for it in the years 1781 to 1787.

It is easy to understand the basic concept behind Cameron's plan if you walk along the valley. It is clearly divided into several areas, each of which has been treated in a different way, creating a constant change of impressions. Vasily Zhukovsky, a Russian poet of the early nineteenth century and tutor to the future Alexander I, wrote about it in his elegy, *Slavyanka*:

> I walk through the glade along a meandering path;
> With each step there is a new picture in front of my eyes.

Landscapes which differed totally in their mood opened up before the viewer:

> Then suddenly through dense forest there flashes in front of me
> As if through smoke, a light valley;
> Then suddenly everything has vanished . . . the forest has grown thick
>   round about
> All is wild around me and gloom and silence.[38]

The composition is best understood as a sequence of 'new pictures' created by Cameron. As it entered the territory of Pavlovsk park, the narrowish Slavyanka was about thirty kilometres from its source and approaching an area where its banks were formed by fairly large cliffs. Here it met a mill-pond and further on meandered gently, passing under a simple wooden bridge. On the right-hand side there was a steep bank, at the foot of which, at the point where the stream called the Tyzva joined the Slavyanka, stood Marienthal, the small palace constructed in 1777, before Cameron had begun work here. The house was surrounded by an earth rampart on which stood cannon. The inscription on the gates announced: 'This rampart is the remains of fortifications made by the Swedish General Kroniort in 1702 when he was defeated by General Apraxin and tried to retreat through this place to Dudorova Hill as described in the journal of Peter [the Great].'[39] It was on the site of this house that Vincenzo Brenna later constructed the neo-gothic fortress of Bip for Paul Petrovich (pls 159, 160).

Immediately after the confluence of the Tyzva the steepness of the Slavyanka valley receded, and a path wound along the river bank. Over this rose the Swiss Hills, one of the first park areas created by Cameron.[40] Low hills alternated with beautiful valleys and were covered by forest where the tops of firs and pines, birches, willows and ash could be seen; hawthorn bushes grew lower down, stretching their branches towards the path.[41]

159 (right) I. Chesky, *View of the Fortress of Bip from the Lake*, 1800.

160 (facing page) Vincenzo Brenna, Fortress of Bip, Pavlovsk.

Beside the water stood Holland, which was erected by Cameron.[42] We have no visual record of this building, and know only its name and that inside there was a shed for cotton. In Paul's reign single-masted vessels with a raised stern, called *treshkoty*, sailed on the dammed Slavyanka and their sails could be seen in engravings and in pictures depicting this part of Pavlovsk. Placed on the bank was another maritime attribute or, more accurately, a curiosity: stuck into the ground was a whale rib, a present from Count Orlov to the heir to the throne.

Cameron erected an obelisk in the Swiss Hills commemorating the founding of the estate (pl. 161). On this was the inscription: 'Pavlovsk began to be built in 1777.' The memorial was set up on an artificial crag made of broken stone. A canopy or divan was cut out of this crag from which opened out a view over the left bank of the Slavyanka.

The slope there was more gentle but there was no flat area beside the water and the path was driven upwards. From the obelisk could be seen, beyond the trees and the palace orangeries, the dome of the hospital church built by Quarenghi in 1781–4 and the crenellated walls of the house next to it which had been constructed by Brenna for Count Kutaysov,[43] Paul's valet who was elevated to Count when his master came to the throne. All these structures stood on the territory of what was then the village of Pavlovsk. To their right could be seen the broad Tsarskoye Selo road as it turned towards Pavlovsk palace. Finally a stone bridge built by Cameron closed the perspective of the Slavyanka. This was built in the style of Roman bridges, with a double-spanned arch supported in the centre on an island.

Crossing a little bridge with railings made of boughs, over another small stream, visitors would head towards the palace. This would constantly appear and disappear in front of them among the picturesque clumps of trees scattered on the slope. The further away you stood, the better the view. Close to the palace, when the path veered to the right along the little bays formed by the overflowing Slavyanka, the palace disappeared to reappear again at full height in front of anyone who ascended the last

162 A. Bugreyev, *View of Pavlovsk*, 1803.

spur of the Swiss Hills. At the beginning of the nineteenth century Cameron built an elegant colonnaded pavilion here called The Three Graces, after the sculpture it protected (pl. 163). We shall look at this in detail later.

★ ★ ★

The bridge and the panorama of the palace form the boundary of one part of the Slavyanka valley. Beyond it a new composition unfolded, so that two magnificent compositions had their interface here: the palace with its wings and the landscape that Cameron created around the lake. The palace dominated, elevated on a hill with clumps of trees concealing the galleries receding into the background. The central block strove upwards, crowned by a dome, its severe edges contrasting with the picturesque quality of the features delineated in the landscape. The curving banks of the lake, which had been formed by yet another dam, were followed by the little paths which wound along them emerging right on the water's edge. Others provided a route upwards. On the left bank the upper route, which broadly encircled the lake, allowed one to see the palace from various sides, in differing perspectives. The whole composition was revealed, and could be fully appreciated. It gave that impression of perfection and harmony that characterises Cameron's best work.

On the right bank near the palace the trees approached the water more closely, and beyond them the sloping lawn served as a natural pedestal for the palace. Beside the lake, on a small peninsula, stretched out a 'family glade'. Trees were planted here to mark births, marriages or other events in the imperial household, and amongst them in 1787 Cameron placed an Urn of Fate on a pedestal, a magnificent vase of green jasper.

The upper park above the lake was treated with a delicate touch that gave it a subordinate presence. The broadest part of this composition was revealed towards the entrance from Tsarskoye Selo. Old plans show how the paths freely slipped along the

163 Charles Cameron, Pavilion of the Three Graces, Pavlovsk.

164 A. Bugreyev, *The Valley of the Slavyanka,* 1803.

boundaries and in several places were linked by brief stretches of avenue. Only one of these cut across the middle of a field,[44] avoiding the edge in order to lead to the Apollo Colonnade, which Cameron created here in 1780–83 (pls 165–8, 170).

This double circle of Doric columns with a strict frieze of garlands was the only architectural feature of the upper garden. The palace in the distance provided the

165 Giacomo Quarenghi, *View of the Apollo Colonnade and Cascade, c.*1800.

166 (above left) Charles Cameron, design for the Apollo Colonnade, Pavlovsk.

167 (above right) Giacomo Quarenghi, *View of the Apollo Colonnade and the Hospital at Pavlovsk*, early nineteenth century, showing the colonnade in its original position (later it was moved to the banks of the Great Pond).

168 Charles Cameron, Apollo Colonnade, Pavlovsk.

169 Anon., *The Old Chalet at Pavlovsk*, early nineteenth century.

background for the panorama. Cameron's Hermitage and Old Cottage, or Chalet (pl. 169), were hidden in clumps of trees. The Apollo Colonnade with its statue of the god of light himself in the centre gave a particular significance to the entire composition. It was from this that there began at Pavlovsk a cult of Apollo, a glorification of the god of poetry and the muses, of the images of perfection and harmony in antique art with which the entire ensemble was gradually becoming permeated. Finally, statues of Apollo, the Muses and the Graces appeared in the Old and New Sylvia (or Woods) and in the Private Garden. 'The god of poetry rules the park', wrote the French poet Emile Dupré de Saint-Maure on visiting Pavlovsk.

Beyond the lake the Slavyanka valley became much narrower and the river flowed through a different landscape of close-packed copses of trees (pl. 157). Twice making sharp turns, it meandered and formed a peninsula.[45] The landscape was restricted from the right bank by a slope which retreated into the depths covered by forest densely impenetrable to the eye. Individual bushes and trees which projected slightly created an

170 Charles Cameron, Apollo Colonnade, Pavlovsk.

impression of bas-relief. On the left bank the boundary of the composition was lost in copses and glades which came down to the river. On the peninsula in 1780 Cameron built the Temple of Friendship in the form of an antique temple-rotunda, with a blind external wall with no windows and only one oak door; it was ringed by sixteen fluted Doric columns (pls 171–9). This building was reminiscent of William Chambers's Temple of Pan at Stowe, but in its details bore the distinct signature of Cameron.

Inside, the Temple of Friendship was decorated by alternating rectangular and semicircular niches. These were crowned by arches, the fine archivolts were entwined with grapevines whose young shoots were interwoven with old dry twigs. Facing the entrance stood a statue of Catherine the Great as an ancient goddess, and around the walls were benches with elaborately carved legs.

The symbolic significance of this construction and its details is curious. Originally it was to have been called the Temple of Gratitude to commemorate Catherine's gift of Pavlovsk to her heir and his wife.[46] But in the summer of 1780 Count Falkenstein came to Russia, the disguised Holy Roman Emperor, Joseph II, who at that time was

148

171 The Slavyanka river at Pavlovsk.

an ally of the Russian court. All manner of advances were made to him, including several buildings that were founded with his participation (such as the Joseph cathedral in Mogilev). He was entertained at Pavlovsk. He himself wrote to his mother, Maria Teresa: 'After dinner at the Grand Duke's – or rather the Grand Duchess's – country house, I was made to take part in laying the foundation stone of a temple, dedicated to Friendship. I could not refuse. All this was accompanied by many courtesies and declarations of eternal friendship, at which Panin, Potemkin and various other people were present.'[47] Such was its political significance that laying the foundation stone of the small Temple of Friendship was a far more lavish occasion than laying the first stone for the whole Pavlovsk palace had been.

Below the Temple of Friendship, along the entire right bank of the Slavyanka, projected a chain of small groups of birches, willows, maples, pines and firs. Behind them could be seen a solid wall of forest, 'crowns of firs and the softly defined crowns of birches'.[48] Cameron was working on the creation of the landscape composition in this region in 1785–6. On the left bank the flat part of the Slavyanka valley broadened

172 Charles Cameron, Temple
of Friendship, Pavlovsk.

173 Charles Cameron, Temple
of Friendship, Pavlovsk: detail.

174   Charles Cameron, design for the Temple of Friendship, Pavlovsk, 1779.

175   Charles Cameron, Temple of Friendship, Pavlovsk: detail.

176   Charles Cameron, Temple of Friendship, Pavlovsk: detail.

177 (above) Charles Cameron, section through the Temple of Friendship, Pavlovsk, 1779.

178 G.S. Sergeiev, *The Temple of Friendship on the Banks of the Slavyanka*, 1799.

179 Charles Cameron, design for the kitchen adjoining the the Temple of Friendship, Pavlovsk, 1780s.

and he found it possible to build a supplementary reservoir not far from the river. This Round Lake was separated from the river by a narrow neck of land, but it was decided that this should be cut through by a large waterfall. Maria Fedorovna wrote to Kuchelbecker on 3 April 1789: 'Please ask Cameron to finish my waterfall. Tell him that I am exceptionally pleased with his rock clefts which give a wonderful impression and say that I hope that he will make something charming out of my waterfall.'[49]

In this area of the park Cameron did not introduce any major architectural accent. There are no classical images here. The architect operated only with landscape elements, in particular highlighting the wildness and isolation of this, the last part of Pavlovsk to be created in the 1780s. The waterfall Cameron made comprised only broken stones; it took on a different appearance after Brenna's rebuilding in 1792. But still in the 1780s the area of the Round Lake (pl. 180), the end of the garden and the forest backwoods, was poeticised by Cameron's hand, his park elegy created among the

180 Pavlovsk: the Round Lake.

gently rippling waters of the Slavyanka, the lake and the waterfall. In them is reflected, as Zhukovsky's elegy to Slavyanka put it:

> Now an emerald hill crowned by trees;
> Now a decrepit willow bending its flexible branches
> To its twisting roots
> Bathing its shady head in their waters . . .
> There a swan hiding in bushes by the bank
> Shines motionless in the gloom . . .
> But the day fades . . . in the shade the forest bends to the waters,
> The trees are clothed in evening darkness,
> Only sunset with a crimson stripe
> Washes their quiet tops.[50]

The first seven years of Cameron's work on the Pavlovsk ensemble created a clear and perfectly integrated composition. Its centre, the palace, was crisply defined, monumental and at the same time free in its relationships with the other parts of the whole; it was permeated with the antique theme, steeped, in Cameron's conception, with images of the classical world through which he sought to bring the illumination of Enlightenment culture to the entire ensemble. Each part of the park expressed a laconic idea with seriousness and gravity. Everything around the palace was unified by a single scale; all the compositions situated close to the house were imbued with antique images, each of which was fully realised without interweaving with others or being distracted by anything from the contemporary world. Beyond that area were regions with a different character, scale and rhythm: the Menagerie, the Silver Birch, the Great Star with their cuttings breaking through the forest, but all playing their part in a complete, unbroken, majestic idea. Cameron did not seek to surprise the viewer, he sought simply to allow him to experience feelings aroused by the landscape and structures into which he had poured his talent with considerable persistence and passion. The whimsical images of pre-Cameron Pavlovsk retreated in the face of more sophsticated dreams. Hermits' huts rotted away, dairies where milk had foamed in Sèvres bowls were removed and amusing Chinese summerhouses were dismantled, to be replaced by the antique beauty of Roman mosaic, colonnades and streams flowing à l'anglais among hills and trees.

Much of Cameron's Pavlovsk pleased his contemporaries, but the owners remained disappointed, as was clearly conveyed by their letters. Thus, a rebuilding of the ensemble was ordered, and was conducted primarily during its owner's reign as Paul I. Vincenzo Brenna added a number of regular elements to Cameron's picturesque composition. During this process he created, not far from the palace, the Great Circles and the Great Flight of Steps which led into the valley of the Temple of Friendship. He replanned the areas of the Old and New Sylvia with a complex, shallow design but none the less effective. Numerous statues appeared there. The Slavyanka valley was also changed. By the Marienthal lake he erected a trellis and a flight of steps with marble statues. At the other end of the Slavyanka valley he built the Pil Tower and an amphitheatre, and he added to the height of the waterfall. As Taleporovsky wrote, expressing the ruthlessness with which Brenna marched across Cameron's philosophical subtleties, Brenna 'looked at the Pavlovsk park with quite different eyes from Cameron's and, rejecting sentimentality, tenderness and comfort . . . he even carved the banks of the Slavyanka in front of the Amphitheatre with architectural forms . . . [During Paul I's reign] they succeeded in changing the image of the Pavlovsk park, transforming it into a powerful and ceremonial imperial garden.'[51]

In his own time there, Cameron himself had been forced to make certain changes. In the letter of April 1789 already quoted, Maria Fedorovna was insisting on the Apollo Colonnade being moved. 'Ask Cameron whether he wouldn't like to move the colonnade and to find a better place for it; what does he think about placing it in the position where it was planned to be? But I should merely like something easy, a hipped roof or, in the end, whatever he wants. Let him do you a drawing and you can bring it to me.'[52]

Below the bridge on which Voronikhin placed four centaurs, Cameron built a Cold Bath in the forest, probably following a design which had been published in a German garden journal, and apparently in accordance with the wishes of Maria Fedorovna.

As it extended, the park took in the Red Valley further downstream along the Slavyanka (pl. 183). Here in the first years of the nineteenth century Cameron erected the Elizabeth Pavilion, a strange construction with several porticos (pls 181, 182): one semi-circular, another in the form of a little porch on four columns, the third with other supports of four columns. On top of the building was a belvedere from which

181   A. Bugreyev, *The Elizabeth Pavilion*, 1803.

182   Anon., *The Elizabeth Pavilion*, 1803.

183 (facing page)   The Red Valley, Pavlovsk.

the surroundings of Pavlovsk could be seen. A contemporary recalled: 'The view from the terrace is charming: on one side the roaring waterfall presents itself to your gaze, on the other a spacious valley with exceptionally varied groups of trees with artificial ruins . . . in the distance rural views, a broad road.'[53]

Artifical ruins were also constructed by Cameron nearby in the same Red Valley, apparently inspired by the ruins in the park at Stowe. These consisted of several arches and among them 'hardly noticeable broken pieces of various statues, columns and bas-reliefs'. The overall landscape composition of the Red Valley is ascribed to Gonzago, however, so it would be inappropriate to describe it as the last landscape ensemble at Pavlovsk by Cameron himself.

Cameron's work at Pavlovsk did end on a high note, though, with the splendid composition of the Private Garden (*Sobstvenny sadik*) adjoining the palace (pls 184, 185). It was called a 'continuation of the palace halls', as its planning was based on axes extending from the internal construction of the palace. The main avenue led from

184 Anon., *A Walk to the Private Garden*, *c.*1820.

Maria Fedorovna's boudoir. Rows of accurately trimmed trees branched off from this avenue and pyramidal plane trees grew along the central path. The entire garden was filled with sculpture: on the terrace of the palace stood marble lions with Flora at their centre and parallel rows of busts and vases placed on pedestals stretched from the palace into the depths of the garden. Rare plants and exotic flowers filled the air with their colour and fragrance making even greater impressions on contemporaries than the architecture. Thus the wife of the Grand Duke Nicholas Pavlovich, the future Empress Alexandra, remembered: 'All the court, it seemed, was gathered in the garden, but I could make nothing out; I remember only the splendid roses in full bloom and especially the white ones which comforted and seemed to welcome me.'[55]

The Three Graces Pavilion, which was built to Cameron's design in 1801, completed this garden (pls 186, 187). It took the form of an original little temple – on two sides the portico had six columns and on the other sides it had four. A light ceremonial Ionic order was used, and an elegant pediment was covered in sculptures depicting Minerva and Apollo. In the centre was a marble group, the work of Paolo Triscorni,

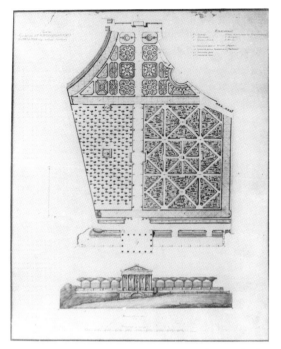

185 (above) Plan of the Private Garden with the Pavilion of the Three Graces, Pavlovsk.

186 Charles Cameron, Pavilion of the Three Graces, Pavlovsk.

187 Giacomo Quarenghi, *The Garden around the Pavilion of the Three Graces*, 1800s.

in which the Three Graces rose up on the pedestal stretching out their arms to a luxurious vase resting on a column. The garden was separated from the Tsarskoye Selo road by a cross-wall made of limestone covered in coarse rustication. The pavilion could be seen from afar – both from the Marienthal lake and from the other side of the Slavyanka – and from near by, from the foot of the palace hill. With this refined work on the ancient theme Cameron completed his work at Pavlovsk and took his leave of the estate.

188   Charles Cameron, design for gates.

Court Life in the 'best English park'

We have to be grateful to John Claudius Loudon for the survival of an illuminating legend about Pavlovsk, since it is recorded only in his *Encyclopaedia of Gardening*, published in London in 1827. Loudon informed his readers that: 'Pavlovsk is the best park in the English style not only in the environs of the [Russian] capital but also anywhere in the Empire.' He then explained that the estate had achieved such perfection because it had been created to a design by Lancelot (Capability) Brown. He claimed that some Englishman, one of Potemkin's gardeners, had sent a description of the area along the Slavyanka to Capability Brown in London and the latter had sent back a design. It seemed to Loudon that there was no other way that such a magnificent picturesque garden could have been created in Russia. The story certainly has no basis in fact, but it bears witness to the faithfulness with which Charles Cameron had transmitted the English ideal into the heart of the Russian empire.[56] Certainly there had been no correspondence with Brown and he had sent no design. There is not the slightest evidence of anything along those lines in the archives. Yet all the same the legend is more than amusingly chauvinist, for it reflects a genuine appreciation of Cameron's work. The inner harmony of Pavlovsk's landscape composition is indeed worthy of comparison with Brown. Without doubt Cameron here showed his mag-

189 K.F. von Kügelchen, *The Palace at Pavlovsk from the Banks of the Slavyanka*, c.1810.

nificent talent as a landscape gardener. He felt the beauty of the Slavyanka landscape and was the first to construct a serious aesthetic response to it. As the English landscape garden philosophy demanded, he preserved the natural charm of the Pavlovsk area while immortalising it as a piece of three-dimensional poetry. The achievement was well appreciated by contemporaries in the arts:

> If it is possible for art to approach nature, to replace it in all its games and appearances, terrible and agreeable, magnificent and simple, then it is, of course, at Pavlovsk that it happens. These sullen cliffs, these roaring waterfalls, these velvet meadows and valleys, these dark, mysterious forests seem to be original creations of graceful nature.[57]

Thus wrote Pavel Svinin, one of the first Russian art historians, as early as 1816.

The unique culture of Pavlovsk developed in its own way as life continued on the estate during the brief four-year reign of Paul Petrovich as Paul I and, after his death, when the place was inhabited by his widow, the Dowager Empress Maria. But if the youthful levity of the early years in Marienthal and Paulust was gone, so equally was any vestige of the sparkling sense of historical continuity with antique Rome, or of geographical continuity with contemporary Enlightenment Europe, to which Cameron had tried by his architecture and landscaping to provide a backdrop, even a catalyst. Admiral Shishkov, a notable scholar of the Russian language and state chancellor of Russia at the time of the Napoleonic invasion, remembered what happened in Pavlovsk during the years 1796 to 1801:

> Our amusements were monotonous and boring . . . after dinner we usually walked about the garden with deliberate and measured steps . . . After our walk, having rested a little, we would gather every day for a pretty tedious conversation. There the Master and Mistress would sit side by side with princes and princesses and would pass the time in desultory talk; and we would sit around the room on chairs as if we were chained statues because we did not dare to chat among ourselves or to get up.[58]

This is what life was like for the courtiers, but for the 'inhabitants' of Pavlovsk, which was declared a town at that time, things were even worse. It was ordered that: 'during the royal presence in the town, there should be no whistling, shouting or idle conversation'. Despite all these severities the 'deliberate and measured' walks were disrupted by various unexpected happenings which struck the feverish imagination of the suspicious tsar. Many contemporaries remembered the famous 'alarm at Pavlovsk'. General Nikolai Sablukov recalled:

One evening (it was the 2nd of August), when [the usual walk was over] the sound of a drum was suddenly heard and everyone took heed because it was still too early for the last post . . . yet the sound of the drum was already resounding everywhere. 'But that's the alarm!' cried Paul and quickly returned to the palace . . . Approaching [it] they discovered that one of the roads leading there had been occupied by a guards division and, moreover, from all sides and with all haste, both cavalry and infantry were thronging towards the palace. They asked where they should go but, on the road, which was not broad enough for the accumulation of troops, there were cavalry, the fire brigade, military vehicles – they were making their way through with terrible cries . . . several ladies . . . were obliged to jump over a fence in order to avoid being crushed. . . . Such an unnecessary crowd of troops, which had such a reputation of being excitable as did the guards, could only alarm someone with the suspicious and untrusting nature of the emperor . . . After long investigations it was discovered that the entire turmoil had been caused by a pipe which someone had been playing in the cavalry guards barracks . . . a day later, almost at the same hour . . . in another part of the garden adjacent to the main road, the sound of a pipe was suddenly heard and several cavalrymen came galloping at full speed up to a path beside the main road . . . in a fury the emperor threw himself at them with a raised stick.[59]

This episode magnificently conveys the atmosphere of that restless, troubled life at Pavlovsk in the years leading up to the murder of Paul I by conspirators in 1801.

At this same time Maria Fedorovna was occupied by much more domestic questions concerning the organisation of the estate, although these issues at time also caused her some worries. The following, to her estate steward, is characteristic:

Your letter has alarmed me terribly but not because of the damage caused by the water which I consider a trifle. But you say that a crevice has been discovered in the mountain? . . . If this crack continues up the hill the house will collapse. I do not understand, my dear Kuchelbecker, how you can be so calm about this nor can I comprehend why you did not immediately inspect the place?[60]

Maria Fedorovna was also worried about more pleasant things: the arrangements for festivities. On 22 July 1787, Paul Petrovich's nameday, illuminations and fireworks were organised.[61] The main element of the illuminated decorations was an ancient temple with an inscription in lights revealing its significance. The Triple Avenue in the middle was to be picked out in little arches of white lights. Each arch had two garlands with different coloured lamps between them. On the other side of the Slavyanka beyond the lake, opposite the garden façade of the palace, an allegorical structure dedicated to 'conjugal love' was erected. On that evening fireworks were let off over the temple, and in front of it on the lake sailed a boat which had cast off from behind the Apollo Colonnade and was covered by boards 'all lit up by illuminations'. In the boat were musicians and singers who performed specially composed musical works, perhaps such as this song from the time of Paul I's reign:

Oh, our gardens, our gardens,
Our most fascinating gardens.
It is our land, our dear land.
You are a happy place.
A place like our own mother to us,
Oh, beloved Pavlovsk![62]

In 1798 at Pavlovsk there took place an unusual festival, following the medieval ceremony of the Burning of Bonfires instituted by the Knights of the Order of Malta. At the time of the crusades this custom signified a liberation from everything worldly and the destruction of earthly thoughts in the 'sacrificial fire' (as these special bonfires were known in the rule of the Maltese knights). In 1797 Paul was elected Grand Master of the order. Along with the appearance of representatives of the order in St Petersburg, some curious phenomena in the poetics of everyday culture arose. A knightly spirit of romanticism was suddenly born.

From the morning of 23 June 1798 guards officers had been arriving in Pavlovsk. The Maltese knights were arriving. They were gathered in the palace. A ceremonial procession carried the regalia of the Grand Master: the seal, the crown, the banner and the sword known as the 'dagger of truth'. Then on the parade ground at the end of the Triple Lime Avenue 'several wagons of timber, brushwood and fir-twigs were brought and then nine bonfires were laid'. The tops of the bonfires were decorated by crowns of flowers and at the sides they were surrounded by fir garlands. To the side was erected a linen tent with black, white and red stripes, for the empress and the ladies of the court.

At about five o'clock in the evening the guards regiments lined up on three sides of the Parade Ground around the bonfires. 'Particularly eye-catching in this formation were the hussars in their so-called 'snow leopards'. Over their shoulders were slung 'snow leopard skins with their heads downwards lined with red cloth with a silver finish and fastenings of the same.'[63] At about eight o'clock in the evening the procession of Maltese knights with Paul at their centre emerged from the palace. The knights marched in pairs carrying lit torches,

ceremonially and slowly . . . in berets with feathers, in red jackets with black mantles thrown over them . . . The knights of the Order of Malta circled all the nine bonfires three times [before the fires were lit]. Clouds of black smoke rose from the burning fir-twigs but when this settled the bonfires started burning with bright flames.[64]

After Paul I's death the Rose Pavilion built by Voronikhin became the traditional place for festivals and spectacles. Plays took place around it using scenery by Pietro Gonzago. The best Russian actors of the period – Samoylov, Semenova, Spiridonova – took part. In July 1814 the final victory of the war with Napoleon was celebrated there. Gonzago's realistic stage sets provided surprises for those who had come to Pavlovsk. As one visitor described it:

I passed the Rose Pavilion and I saw a fine village with a church, a manor house and a village inn. I saw high peasant huts, I saw front rooms with towers, between them I saw various types of fences on the other sides of which there were flower-beds and little gardens. In various places there were piles of straw, haystacks and so on and so forth. The only thing I could not see was people. 'Perhaps,' I thought, 'they're at work.' . . . Convinced of the reality of what I could see I went further and further forward. But suddenly a peculiar change began to happen in front of my eyes: it seemed as if some invisible curtain was lowering on all the objects and was hiding them from my gaze. The closer I approached, the more the fascination vanished . . . another few steps – and I saw the extended canvas on which Gonzago had painted the village; some ten times I stepped back several yards and again saw everything. . . . Eventually I lost my temper with my eyes, my head was spinning in confusion and I hurried away from this place of magic and wonder.[65]

In the 1820s these lavish festivities at Pavlovsk ceased. It had gradually taken on a new image in contemporary eyes. Into the past had gone the era of the estate of the almost-disgraced successor to Catherine the Great who, rumour insisted, might be removed from the throne at any time. During that period, not surprisingly, many courtiers were reluctant to go there. Four years had passed in which Pavlovsk's character was official and ceremonial, the residence of an irrascible and suspicious autocrat. After Paul was gone Pavlovsk began to drift into history, a huge and lavish but patriarchal estate merely living out the rest of its days.

> In bad weather they stay in the palace amusing themselves with various games and with reading and boredom, the constant inhabitant of mansions does not dare to look in here. There are hours when they work for the poor. Supper is at ten in the evening and people disperse – in the outside world it is still very early and very noisy – here it's already late and quiet.[66]

Count Vladimir Sologub, the author of *Tarantass* ('A Carriage'), a popular story in the 1830s, has preserved in his reminiscences some curious details of life at Pavlovsk in that era. The writer's grandmother, E.A. Arkharova, was famous in many memoirs as one of the typical characters from the Pavlovsk 'summer life' of the 1820s. Her *dacha* there

> was spacious . . . The number of people staying in the house was remarkable . . . The old woman did not like [any of the guests] to leave without having dinner . . . I remember these dinners very well. We sat down at the table at five o'clock in order of seniority. The food served was mainly Russian, simple and greasy but abundant. There was a great deal of demand for *kvass* [Russian beer fermented from bread]. The wine, which was of terrible quality, was rarely offered. Grandmother's day inevitably finished with cards.[67]

As Sologub continued, Pavlovsk park in those years would not infrequently see 'a low carriage or gig without springs and with a seat for the driver . . . My father . . . nicknamed this strange gig a "*trufinon*" . . . It used to set off to the glades surrounding Pavlovsk and would stop at nice places. My grandmother would prudently take the reins . . . and the driver Abram would get down from the box and would go for a wander bending down in the clumps of trees. Suddenly he would joyfully exclaim: "A brown mushroom, Your Excellency." "Look for more!" grandmother would cry.'[68]

Such scenes add their own elements to our perception of the estate and the waning Pavlovsk culture.

★　★　★

Despite all the changes in the image of Pavlovsk down through the history of Russian culture, the ensemble always preserved the characteristics that Cameron gave it: the splendour of the architecture and the charm of the landscape compositions, all synthesised into one environmental statement and experience.

Cameron's creation of the house and park at Pavlovsk was one of the great events of eighteenth-century Russian architecture. It is, moreover, hard to overrate its significance in the development of the link between Russian and British architecture. Pavlovsk was an ideal expression of the country-house culture established in Russia in the 1780s, and important not only for the eighteenth but also for the nineteenth century. Cameron's work signified the victory of the neo-Palladian estate – with its outbuildings and picturesque park as developed by British architects and gardeners – over other models of estate construction. French *châteaux* and *maisons de plaisances* were out of favour. In spite of all the difficulties he encountered in building it, Cameron's Pavlovsk played a major role in Russian architecture. The composition of the house, with its central ceremonial block and wings joined by a colonnade, having taken its pedigree from the Venetian Renaissance via English classicism, became established in Russia. It was the ideal to which more modest estates all over Russia would aspire.

Moreover, Pavlovsk demonstrates a freshness in its discovery of classical images that had by that time already faded in the work of the architects of western Europe. They were beginning to look for new sources of inspiration: Gothic and Moorish, Chinese and Turkish. It was not so in Russia. Russian architects in discovering antiquity for themselves were discovering one of the worlds of the modern age. Novelty, enthusiasm, the colossal scale of classicist construction gripping the entire country, in the replanning of hundreds of towns, the building of thousands of estates, stimulated a feeling of immensely strong creative energy and this was a characteristic of the best Russian architects of the next generation.

190 Charles
Cameron, figure on
the Chinese Bridge,
Tsarskoye Selo, 1780s.

Chapter Four

ORIENTALISM IN RUSSIAN
NEO-CLASSICAL ARCHITECTURE

THE CLASSICISM OF TSARSKOYE SELO and Pavlovsk were manifestly part of Catherine the Great's frequently expressed desire to see her land as part of Europe. Perverse as it may initially seem, so too was her pursuit of the Chinese taste, for which Tsarskoye Selo was likewise a test-bed. China might be physically contiguous with Russia, but that boundary was far from St Petersburg, and for a Russian court pursuing Enlightenment modernisation it lay 'in the wrong direction'. As transmitters of culture, European merchants were more intrepid than Russian sailors. Hence chinoiserie came to Russia as a European fashion and it came here, as to much of Europe, through English architectural pattern books.

In the literature on eighteenth-century orientalism in architecture, buildings in England, Sweden, Germany and France have been analysed in some detail.[1] If Russia has been largely ignored by students of chinoiserie, this is mainly because so many of the buildings were shortlived and ill-recorded, so that information on them is predominantly anecdotal. Nevertheless, some of the exotic structures that appeared on the outskirts of Moscow and St Petersburg, and later at some of the estates scattered throughout Russia, have a key place in the general development of eighteenth and early nineteenth-century orientalism worldwide.

The orientalist movement in Russian architecture during the baroque and neo-classical periods is one of the more paradoxical aspects of the relationship between Russian and western European eighteenth-century architecture. The paradox consists primarily in that the 'discovery of the East', which manifested itself in English, French and German architecture before spreading to Russia, was part of Russia's 'discovery of the West'. In opting for Chinese or Moorish styles, Russian architects were trying to keep up with the latest European fashions. Oriental designs came to Russia from the West in spite of the fact that their origins were so much closer, both historically and in contemporary eighteenth-century terms, to Russian than to western European architecture. For many authentic oriental buildings were to be found within the borders of the Russian continent itself, including the Tartar mosques of Kazan, Kasimov and Ochakov; pagodas in the Buddhist monasteries of Buryatia; and the medieval palaces and fortresses of Crimea. We know, too, that Russian architects such as Ivan Starov and Peter Neyelov had of necessity analysed and taken account of these when drawing up plans for urban redevelopment in those parts of the continent.[3]

Nevertheless, the new Russian orientalism was based on very different concepts from those that had inspired the 'originals'. If one factor was a fascination with all the latest European fashions, another even more important one was the desire actually to outdo the Europeans. Of all the European monarchs of the eighteenth century only Peter the Great had deemed it necessary to import a Chinese architect to design the Chinese pavilions for his parks. In 1720 he commanded his envoy Lev Ismailov to organise this;[4] although he failed in this mission, he did arrange for drawings, clothes and vases showing various buildings to be dispatched from China to Russia.

Those Russian architects favouring the 'oriental movement' found themselves in a somewhat ambivalent position within the wider European architectural context. For Russia, eighteenth-century chinoiserie was a Western phenomenon, whereas the French and Germans considered Russian architecture as oriental and drew upon it, along with Chinese, Egyptian and Mauritanian models, for inspiration in their park designs. Late eighteenth-century 'lovers of the unusual' in Europe were offered designs for 'garden houses in Muscovite taste', 'Russian swings' and the like.[5] Well-documented examples are those constructed, for example, on the estate of Prince Montbéliard in Alsace.[6] Even more common was the opinion of western European travellers that the relationship between traditional and neo-classical architecture and planning in Russia offered a close parallel to that between indigenous Indian architecture and that imported by the British Empire. Reginald Heber, a British Archbishop of Calcutta who had previously lived in Russia for some years, wrote: 'Calcutta is a striking place, and so reminiscent of St Petersburg, even if it now seems to me perhaps less splendid than it did before I first saw Russia. The architecture of the principal buildings is the same in both cases.'[7]

This confusing situation was further complicated by the changing European fashions on which Russian exotic architecture modelled itself. In the early days even before Russia's opening up to the West under Peter the Great, it was Dutch interiors, decorated with Chinese lacquers or European substitutes, which had the greatest appeal, so that by the end of the seventeenth century and into the first half of the eighteenth an oriental artistic tradition was already among those established as a standard option for the interior decor of palaces designed by Russian architects. For example, in the second half of the seventeenth century furniture and even some entire rooms 'in Chinese style' were to be found on the Kolomenskoye estate of Peter the Great's father Tsar Alexei Mikhailovich.[8] In Peter the Great's own reign much interest was generated by the large variety of Chinese *objets* adorning the residences of the tsar's favourites, such as Lefort's palace and Menshikov's numerous estates.[9] In a curious passage from an account of the wedding in Danzig of Peter's niece, Catherine Ioannovna, to Prince Karl Leopold of Mecklenburg, a contemporary noted that 'the nuptial bed was placed in a room decorated in Japanese style and filled with Japanese lacquered articles such as are often to be found in Russian houses'.[10]

These were relatively isolated eccentricities, however, and the total number of architectural designs with an 'oriental theme' realised in the whole of the first half of the eighteenth century was not large. They include rooms of the Lefort Palace in Moscow,[11] the Japanese study in Mon Plaisir at Peterhof,[12] and the Japanese pavilion at Menshikov's old Oranienbaum Palace.[13] It is also known that Peter had a design drawn up in France for a Chinese summerhouse.[14] Even so, we can hardly speak of a consistent oriental theme running through these examples; rather, they demonstrate that same ability to synthesise eclectically from a varied range of artistic elements, which was also a feature of English and central European baroque.

As Russian architects and their clients gradually emerged from their passion for Dutch interiors crammed with Japanese *objets*, they turned their attention to a German chinoiserie steeped in the spirit of rococo such as emerged in some buildings designed in the mid-eighteenth century for Elizabeth I's heir, Emperor Peter III. The elaborately rococo chinoiserie which characterised these edifices was soon to be replaced by an oriental building on the English model. It was through these constructions, designed by Antonio Rinaldi, that the 'oriental style' was introduced into Russian architecture as a properly formulated aesthetic concept.

★   ★   ★

The oriental style made its first appearance in the construction of Peter III's palace at Oranienbaum (1758–62), which was followed immediately by Catherine the Great's Chinese Palace (1762–74) in the same ensemble.[15] As we have seen, at this time neo-classicism was born and the baroque disappeared from Russian architecture, and it was during this period of change that chinoiserie increased in importance. 'Chinese taste' became an integral part of the burgeoning style, in which rococo features jostled with the early classicism and elements derived from the first manifestations of interest in 'Anglo-Chinese' gardens which at that time was becoming widespread in Europe. Rinaldi based his designs for the façades of both Oranienbaum palaces on the principles of early classicism, but the layout of the surrounding park was of typical 'Anglo-Chinese' design, combining straight features with curved, pseudo-natural elements. This sinophilia was continued in many of the exotic pavilions as well as in the interiors, whose chinoiserie resembled the rococo style in which the halls of the palace were decorated. The Large and Small Chinese Studies (pl. 191) and the Chinese Bedchamber were perhaps more exotic and interesting than many orientalist interiors designed in the rococo period in Germany and France. The visitor to these rooms was intended to encounter a totally unfamiliar environment.

His 'imaginary China', so vividly evoked in these works, reflected the desperate yearning among contemporary artists for new ideas and impressions. The rococo concept of 'artistic play' dominated Oranienbaum. Rinaldi had no educational pretensions for his chinoiserie nor any ambition to play a part in the creation of a national style associated with a particular region. In this respect he differed from William Chambers and his followers. Rinaldi's exotica were transformed into the grotesque and fantastical; his Chinese Rooms served as powerful decorative stimuli to the observer's imagination rather than as museums conveying an impression of a faraway land. His purpose was to awaken the play of imagination, to intensify the emotions rather than to enrich the mind. The exotica of Oranienbaum seized the soul of the visitor, just as his heart missed a beat at the lightning-quick ups and downs of the *Katalnaya Gorka* (artificial hills, switch-backs and, in winter, ice-hills) in the Oranienbaum park. Incidentally, this example of oriental play at Oranienbaum was never given a specific name by contemporaries, in contrast to its equivalent at Tsarskoye Selo, where part of the park was known as the Chinese 'Caprice'.

Rinaldi had not acquired his taste for architectural exotica during his period of study in Naples or during his collaborations with Luigi Vanvitelli. The Palace of Caserta, on which Rinaldi had worked as a young man,[16] is a typical product of the Italian classicising process of later baroque, and none of the rooms is decorated in an oriental manner. Indeed, at the time of Rinaldi's departure for Russia there was no chinoiserie in Italy. It was to make its first appearance only in 1757 in the kingdom of Naples, when Ferdinand IV commissioned D. Patricola to build a country mansion in the Chinese taste[17] – the Villa Favorita near Palermo. The chinoiserie that in fact developed in Italy after Rinaldi's departure from Naples was radically different from his Russian work in the Chinese taste. His work at Oranienbaum is undoubtedly based on models admired by his clients, Peter III and Catherine the Great, in the latter's case most particularly those to be found in the English garden literature.

Interestingly enough, Rinaldi spent some time in England before his arrival in Russia.[18] The purpose of this visit is unknown; quite possibly, however, he wished to acquaint himself with the special features and architecture of the English garden. At any rate, his stay coincided with the rise in popularity of the 'Anglo-Chinese' style in park design and the appearance of the Halfpennys' first architectural manuals, which were brought to Russia almost immediately after their publication.

191 Antonio Rinaldi, Large Chinese Study, Oranienbaum Palace.

In the 1770s, as chinoiserie took off in Russia, it was the English version of Chinese taste that became well established, supplanting Dutch, German and French models. In fact the process was directly based on those British treatises whose influence was felt in all European exotic architecture of the middle and late eighteenth century. The key works for Russian architects, as for their Western colleagues, had been published in London during the decade and a half after 1750. Most important among them were William Chambers's *Designs of Chinese Buildings* of 1751, the Halfpennys' *Rural Archi-*

192 (above) Antonio Rinaldi, Bugle Room, Oranienbaum Palace.

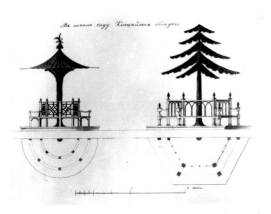

193 Ilya Neyelov after the Halfpennys, design for the Chinese Pavilion, Tsarskoye Selo, 1770s.

tecture in Chinese Taste of the same year (pl. 193), Charles Over's *Ornamental Architecture . . . in Chinese Taste* of 1757 and William Wright's *Grotesque Architecture* of ten years later.[19] Chambers's volume was translated into Russian on the personal orders of Catherine the Great.[20] Of great influence here was the Russian writer Andrei Bolotov, who as publisher of Russia's first magazine with a gardening and landscaping emphasis called *Selskaya Zhizn* (literally 'Country Life', but more accurately 'The Country Gentleman'), played a role akin to that of John Claudius Loudon in England as a disseminator of the new ideas. Bolotov published passages from Hirschfeld on 'Anglo-Chinese' gardens,[21] while Yuri Velten, Peter Neyelov and other architects copied 'Chinese' drawings from English manuals.[22]

In the 1770s the principal arena for fresh orientalist ideas in Russian architecture was Tsarskoye Selo where, as we have seen, even before Cameron's arrival a new and specific aesthetic theme had begun to find expression. In sharp contrast to the allegorical and edifying seriousness of didactic architecture, its purpose was the evocation of a completely exotic 'oriental dream-world'. One section of the park was to 'capture by caprice'. A complex of buildings in the Chinese style was planned, partly realised at the time, and later completed by Cameron at the end of the eighteenth century. This ensemble included the fifteen-odd buildings of the Chinese Village, as well as a theatre, several bridges, a Little Chinatown and the Small and Large Caprices. These Caprices were two man-made hills cut through with arches and studded with strangely planted trees and Chinese pavilions.

The twofold use of the word 'caprice' here was highly typical, and reveals the essence of the entire oriental ensemble. Various stories about the origin of the term have come down to us. One claims: 'The description of the hills as caprices came about when Catherine was examining the estimates for gardening work at Tsarskoye Selo. At first she hesitated but then agreed to the expenditure with the words: "So be it – it is my caprice!"'[23] Another, more interesting explanation is as follows: a guard-post and barrier were situated just at the point where residents of the palace would leave the park when they went for walks; and this was the spot at which they would decide, *po minutnomu kaprizu* (on the spur of the moment), which direction to take.[24] Such Tsarskoye Selo anecdotes are intriguing vignettes which throw light on contemporary reactions to the various styles of the day and also help us to understand the concept of the ensemble. At Tsarskoye Selo a separate world of caprice grew up, devoid of serious purpose, a land of fairytale where buildings, groves and lakes could appear at a wave of the conjuror's wand.

The Chinese Village at Tsarskoye Selo

The original concept for the Chinese ensemble at Tsarskoye Selo was produced by Rinaldi in the 1770s. He proposed to build a Chinese village, theatre and pavilion over the canal in the Menagerie. None of these plans came to fruition in the form envisaged by Rinaldi himself, but his surviving drawings combine a classical clarity of volume with a decorative scheme for the surfaces of the buildings similar to that of the exotic rococo interiors. On the drawings the external walls appear to be conceived to give an impression of being upholstered in Chinese silks depicting dragons, exotic flower bouquets and trees. Here, as at Oranienbaum, classicism manifests itself in 'Chinese' works that retain strong elements of rococo.

This is most clearly seen in the design for a little-known building, dating from the same period as Rinaldi's drawings and marked on a 1778 plan of Tsarskoye Selo with the unambiguous description Little Chinatown (*Kitaisky gorodok*). The 'town' consisted of a number of houses facing each other[26] (twenty-four according to a count of the façades, though in fact somewhat fewer) (pls 194, 195). They were all small, quite toy-like, with one or two windows, but most boasting several storeys. Some possessed tiny porticos, others were decorated with straight lines, while yet others had a balustrade with miniature vases on the roof. The windows, arranged at various heights, were of various shapes: round, square, rectangular, squeezed into narrow slits, some with, others without surrounds and decorated window-sills.

194 The Chinese Town, Tsarskoye Selo. Drawing of the 1770s.

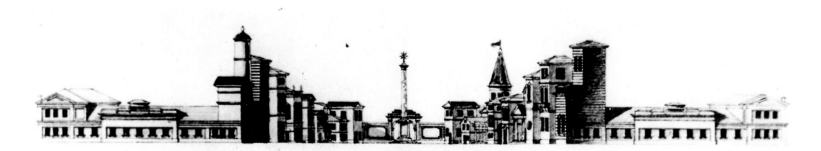

195 The Chinese Town, Tsarskoye Selo. Drawing of the 1770s.

The unmistakably playful character of the town, with its funny little houses, is further enhanced by the almost theatrical use of perspective; all this places it close to the principles of rococo. Elements of chinoiserie were also present, possibly intended as part of the permanent staging for festivities and celebrations. In 1777 a monument to commemorate the annexation of the Crimea was erected in the centre of the Little Chinatown which, in one of the ceremonies, was supposed to symbolise Bakhchiseray, the capital of the Crimean *khans*.[27] This adaptability to various kinds of 'artistic games' was characteristic. Swedish specialists in chinoiserie noted a similar flexibility of purpose at Drottningholm, the country residence of the Swedish monarchs: 'When the king wished to dine *à la Chine* and to spend the day in this way . . . an ace of hearts was pinned to the doors of the audience chamber . . . [but for a conventional dinner] a king of spades was affixed to the doors.'[28]

In the 1770s chinoiserie of a different kind appeared in the work of Yuri Velten and Ivan (Ioghan) Gerard at Tsarskoye Selo.[29] Velten was of a German family, but born in St Petersburg, where he practised as an architect in a style that has been described as 'early classicism'. Gerard was a German engineer who went to Russia at the beginning of the 1770s and was responsible for many important projects – connected mostly with the water supply – particularly in Moscow in the latter part of the century. The kind of Chinese grotesque style created by these two men has been described by Eleanore von Erdberg thus: 'Space is filled with a large number of objects, strange and striking enough to satisfy all possible expectations of the so-called Chinese style.'[30]

The drawings of Velten and Gerard for Tsarskoye Selo are imbued with an atmosphere of abandonment, of remoteness from the rest of civilisation; they are rich in isolated little summerhouses, almost unrecognisably overgrown ruins of ancient Chinese or antique buildings, and structures consisting solely of fragments of rock. The particular view of nature here expressed was as significant as the architecture itself. Velten and Gerard created a milieu where people felt 'different'; they jettisoned the conventional approach to landscape, which now acquired a stark, broken and unfamiliar character. This was a kind of 'caprice of the universe', creating a deliberate impression of neglect and pristine mystery among the piles of overgrown boulders that closely parallels its source in the Anglo-Chinese garden. The oriental pavilions Velten and Gerard proposed to place in this artificial wilderness were also undoubtedly English in inspiration. Little Chinese pavilions, bridges and benches, together with tiny Turkish 'mosques', recalled the pages of the Halfpennys' and Over's pattern books (pls 196–9).

196 (above left) Yuri Velten, design in the Chinese style.

197 (above right) Yuri Velten, design in the Chinese style.

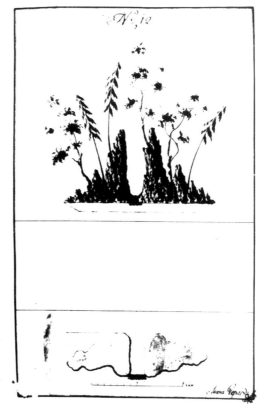

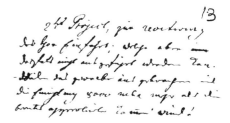

198 (right) Ivan Gerard, project for an artificial rock in the Chinese style, 1770s.

199 (far right) Ivan Gerard, project for the Chinese Bridge, Tsarskoye Selo, 1770s.

The motifs present in Velten's drawings and Gerard's album were only partly realised in the Tsarskoye Selo ensemble, notably in a long cascade of broken stone laid along the edge of the park, and in the artificial hills of the Large and Small Caprices. The Chinese Village was placed between these two hills, creating the impression of a more complex relief than was the case in reality. The visitor from St Petersburg arriving at Tsarskoye Selo first passed the arch of the Large Caprice; then he encountered the 'rocky mountain' with a gate cut through, above which hung trees and bushes planted in unexpected places and pruned into unusual shapes. At the top of the 'mountain' was a Chinese summerhouse with a typical Chinese roof supported by marble columns. He then went through a short, dark tunnel; as he emerged, he saw on his left the Chinese Village, its colourful houses bristling with frightful dragons and sea-creatures. In front, his gaze met the Small Chinese Caprice; to the right lay the park, dotted about with picturesque lakes and islets, and Velten's Creaking Pavilion (*Skripuchaya Besedka*). This was basically an oval tower to which were attached two small wings cut through with arches; above, twelve slender columns supported a curved Chinese roof with a tracer-ied turret and a large weather-vane. The overall intention was that visitors to the imperial summer residence should pass throught this extraordinary world of exotic structures – the world of caprice – before arriving at the palace. At that time this was the main entrance to the Tsarskoye Selo complex, and it was conceived as important for the psychology of a visitor to the imperial residence to create an atmosphere that prepared him for the unusual, that conveyed the impression of a relaxation of conven-tions, a psychological preparation for a world that did not operate by ordinary habits and ceremonies.

The Chinese Village itself consisted of a short street and an octagonal square with a pagoda at its centre (pls 200–4). The history of its construction is complicated and confused. The original idea is ascribed to Rinaldi.[31] His work was continued by the architects Vasily and Ilya Neyelov, father and son, who were the surveyors of the buildings at Tsarskoye Selo. They had acquired a first-hand familiarity with the Chinese pavilions in English parks, during their visit to England of 1771. A model of Chambers's famous pagoda at Kew was specially commissioned by the Russian ambas-sador to the Court of St James.[32] In 1780 all work in Chinese style was entrusted to Charles Cameron, who substituted a new decorative scheme for the pagoda.[33] The original design by Rinaldi's team had been close to that of the Trianon de Porcelain at Versailles. Cameron had the faïence tiles which covered the walls removed, and the freshly plastered surfaces were 'filled with colourful frescoes in the Chinese taste'.[34] In

200   The Chinese Village, Tsarskoye Selo: model. Photo of the 1930s. The village was destroyed in the Second World War.

201 The Chinese Village, Tsarskoye Selo. Drawing of the 1790s.

1785 it was decided to erect an eight-storey tower, to be called the Pagoda. Work on the village continued until 1796, and Cameron gave it an extraordinarily sumptuous decorative character, proposing to place 'on each building various Chinese figures, ornaments to crown every roof, palms fashioned from tin-plate, sixty-eight dragons, also of tin-plate, forty ornamental water-pipes for the guttering . . . eight dolphins.'[35] The central building was to boast 'on the upper roof various Chinese ornaments, eight dragons and palms of tin-plate; and on the middle roof a further eight dragons and palms; and on the lower roof, eight dragons, eight ornamental water-pipes, four palms of tin-plate, thirty-two copper bells with chains around the roof, twenty-four water-pipes with ornaments . . . cornices and ornaments *à la greque*'.[36] Unlike Rinaldi's design,

202 The Chinese Village, Tsarskoye Selo. Photo of the 1930s.

in which the exterior had been 'upholstered with Chinese cloth', Cameron's typical feeling for three-dimensionality created a living and sculptural chinoiserie.

Cameron unified all the constituent parts of the Chinese ensemble by means of four

203 and 204   The Chinese Village, Tsarskoye Selo.
Photos of the 1930s.

exotic bridges (pl. 207), placed in such a way as to enable the visitor to take a long walk from the palace and back, during which he would have met with fantastic buildings in an oriental style.

Opposite the gates of Rastrelli's Great (later Catherine) Palace the canal was spanned by a low stone bridge, with railings made up of elegant vases linked by an elaborate red grille which perfectly simulated coral. Chinese figures holding lanterns were placed on four pedestals of pink granite (pls 190, 205). The path taken by a visitor continued along the central alley of the park, past a so-called Mount Parnassus and across another bridge designed by Cameron and decorated with fantastic dragons. In front lay the Menagerie, housing animals destined for the hunt. To the left was the Chinese Theatre (pl. 206), designed by the Neyelovs (an adaptation of Rinaldi's original project). Further to the left a broad alley led to the Chinese Village and the Large Caprice. The alley was intersected by the canal, over which Cameron threw two 'iron bridges', decorated at each end by porticos, supported by four columns, with ornate tripartite roofs crowned by bouquets, fashioned from tin-plate. The roofs were painted 'like gilded fish-scales' and decorated with twelve gilded tin-plate weather-vanes; the bridges

205 Charles Cameron, figure on the Chinese Bridge, Tsarskoye Selo, 1780s.

178

206 The Chinese Theatre, Tsarskoye Selo. Photo of the 1940s. The building is today in ruins.

207 Charles Cameron, Chinese Bridge, Tsarskoye Selo, 1780s.

themselves were adorned by columns painted with garlands. 'The ceilings, railings . . . façades and all else was decorated in Chinese style.'[37] The bridges were a stone's throw from the Chinese Village.

The Large Caprice towered above the village (pl. 208): a little path led up to the pavilion, which offered a panorama of the western side of the park, dedicated to amusements, fairs and fantasies.

As Derzhavin described it:

> Here is a theatre, there a swing,
> Beyond, an Eastern pleasure-dome.
> Hark how the Muses on Parnassus sing
> While creatures fated for the hunt do roam.

The path descended on the other side of the Large Caprice, past Velten's Creaking Pavilion, and thence back to the Palace.

All these oriental grotesques – the Chinese figures, tin-plate dolphins and dragons, garlands of outlandish flowers bright with colour and gold leaf adorning the bridges and house-roofs, together with bells, burning lanterns and weather-vanes spinning in gusts of wind – seem very far removed from the natural leanings of Cameron the classicist. What they have in common is his great talent for creating a theatrical environment of maximum impact to produce an atmosphere of exotic, artistic play.

A typical feature of eighteenth-century ensembles in the Chinese style was the metamorphosis of some everyday aspect of life into the extraordinary and unusual, where all the elements – for example dining room, bedroom and garden – remained in place but were transmuted into the exotic by a wholly unexpected appearance. At the same time the inhabitants went about their business as usual: guards kept watch and aides-de-camp remained aides-de-camp, but all imbued with the surreality of conducting these habitual actions through the unfamiliar forms of an entirely other world.

179

The internationality of this strange theatrical charade is reflected by the perfect applicability to Tsarskoye Selo of the following eighteenth-century description from the Chinese Palace in the Swedish royal residence of Drottningholm:

> I was so struck by the sight of this unexpected wonderland . . . the Chinese pavilion, the most beautiful thing in the world. The bodyguards were in Chinese uniforms. The aides-de-camp looked like military mandarins . . . My son was waiting at the entrance to the pavilion, dressed as a Chinese prince . . . he handed me the keys to the pavilion, whose interior was even more impressive than the view from outside.[38]

Visitors to Tsarskoye Selo and its park would have experienced an 'artistic transformation' almost identical to that Swedish experience. Whether they arrived on foot or by carriage, they were forced to pass through an unfamiliar world of exotic structures, the 'world of caprice' where everything was different from ordinary life; and then, with a carefully planned suddenness, they would come face-to-face with the Great Palace. It could be said that the route from St Petersburg to the imperial residence led through 'China'. This was a development of the idea of exotic play which had first appeared at Oranienbaum; at Tsarskoye Selo, however, a much clearer contrast was set up with the more solemn, antique theme developed in Cameron's rich complex of bath-houses and galleries. The earnest classical mood was in direct opposition to the playful, the faery, the exotic and fantastical East. We may say that the chinoiserie of Tsarskoye Selo reconciled the rococo motifs of play with the didactic rationalism of Enlightenment classicism.

Orientalism in its British guise soon spread from Tsarskoye Selo to other parts of Russia. A late eighteenth-century memoir records how guests at the Kuskovo estate near Moscow could watch boating on a lake with an island and, moored near by, a Chinese summerhouse on a Chinese craft designed by the architect Alexei Mironov. This project, like so many others, was probably based on a drawing published by

208 The Large Caprice, Tsarskoye Selo.

209 Giacomo Quarenghi, *The Violin Pavilion and the Chinese Village*, 1790s.

210 Yuri Velten, project for a mosque pavilion.

William Chambers.[39] Sailors in unusual 'oriental' costume crewed the yacht. At the Yaropolets estate of Count Chernyshev[40] a miniature mosque with two minarets, to a design taken from William Wright's pattern book, commemorated the participation of Count Zakhar in the Turkish war (pl. 210). For the Chereshenky estate Count Peter Rumyantsev commissioned several buildings specifically for a faery festival, though whether it took place is not known. In any case the estate accounts for 1787 inform us that the 'Chinese [building] was restored to a better condition than ever before',[41] and numerous records also survive of other estates with various Chinese or oriental buildings.

Buildings and interiors in the Russian version of oriental taste made a powerful impression in their time. The famous nineteenth-century writer Sergei Aksakov recalled the Chufarovo estate, on the border of the Kazan province, which he visited as a child: 'I did not hesitate to accept the invitation, and followed Yevseich [an old servant] to a large room . . . [where] I could properly examine the wall-paintings, done, no doubt, by the estate decorator, who also painted barber-shop signs. At that time, however, I admired the Chinamen, American Indians, palm-trees, animals and exotic birds. Compared to any house I had ever visited, the Churassovs' home seemed like Scheherezade's palace.'[42]

The First Step towards Romantic Eclecticism

Unfortunately, most of our information about oriental buildings and parks on Russian estates has to be gleaned from the scanty, usually barely factual, statements contained in the occasional building inventories of the great country houses. Drawings of exotic pavilions erected in the eighteenth century in the provinces certainly existed, but virtually nothing has survived. The only material we have is that from the imperial residences of Oranienbaum and Tsarskoye Selo. At Oranienbaum Rinaldi's twenty-four Chinese pavilions have disappeared, and chinoiserie survives solely in the interiors of the palace itself. Tsarskoye Selo, alone, has preserved its oriental works relatively intact.

Nevertheless chinoiserie and turquerie in Russian architecture of the second half of the eighteenth century retain considerable interest as examples of the permeation of Russian architecture by English influences. The style was at its most widespread in precisely those years when Palladian classicism was also at its most popular, but avoided being entirely absorbed by it. In Russia as in Europe, the relationship of exotic architecture to the mainstream of stylistic development is one of the keys to a full understanding of the period, for chinoiserie co-existed with and adapted itself to several successive major styles.

In baroque, for example, with its ability to unify and synthesise various traditions, exotic elements survived as elements of the larger stylistic vocabulary. Thus, Egyptian obelisks became an integral part of Bernini's Rome, and Chinese roofs accentuated the baroque character of the Palace of Pilnitz, the country residence of the Electors of Saxony. Oriental objects filled the interiors of baroque palaces in Europe and Russia. The rococo period increased the importance of oriental decorative and applied arts, and park pavilions were transformed into grotesquely exaggerated 'porcelain junkshops', reminiscent of the tea-house of Sans Souci or Rinaldi's pavilions at Oranienbaum. Hence arose the notion of an exotic theatricality in which architectural motifs, whether inspired by the imagination or derived from oriental images on lacquered articles or porcelain, became part of the relaxed and uncomplicated rococo artistic 'game'.

It was, of course, a common feature of Enlightenment thought to seek for shared foundations across the boundaries of different cultures. Eighteenth-century classicism, inspired by archaeology, could accept no ideal or model but the antique. William Chambers's contribution was to try to demonstrate theoretically the equal worth of the antique and ancient Chinese traditions. This aroused great interest in Russia, with translations of his treatise circulating freely among both aristocrats and architects. Cameron trod the same path as Chambers in his desire to recreate oriental buildings with the same great accuracy as he recreated antique ones. Here he followed the example of the pagoda at Kew.

At the same time, in numerous pattern books published in English, French, German or even Russian, architects proposed various designs for garden pavilions in every possible 'taste', including Chinese, Indian, Turkish, Moorish, Russian, even Tahitian. They created a complete system of minor styles quite opposed in spirit to that of antiquity. Such styles could co-exist with classicism in the open and independent atmosphere of a landscaped park.

This movement of various interwoven exotic styles bore the seeds of eclecticism. 'Oriental' buildings were less resistant than the classical to such trends because they lacked the support of a strong and continuous European tradition such as the antique provided for classicism. We may trace the origins of eclecticism precisely to such exotic compilations. This search, for unusual and striking sources of inspiration bore witness to the growing complexity of stylistic development in eighteenth-century architecture and the trend towards the disintegration of a unified architectural style.

It must be admitted that the causes of the rise of chinoiserie and turquerie in French and British art were almost entirely absent in eighteenth-century Russian culture. Russian architecture had little enough time to adopt the various versions of the classical heritage known in Europe. There was insufficient time for baroque, rococo or even classicism to be exploited to the full in Russia.

The relative superficiality of this short-lived fashion was well conveyed by the distinguished Russian art historian Igor Grabar when he called Russian chinoiserie 'a pretty toy, created in the days of rococo and similar in its brilliance'.[43] Indeed, in the context of the European tradition, the architecture of Russian eighteenth-century chinoiserie belongs to rococo. Charles Cameron himself did not escape this influence. Even buildings inspired by William Chambers acquired, in Russia, a distinctly playful character, partly because the transformation of Russian architecture, from monumental baroque to high classicism, was achieved suddenly and without a rococo phase. Perhaps this is why the rococo spirit, while rare in Russian architecture, was preserved by, and perhaps found its fullest expression in, Russian chinoiserie.

Thus one effect of the English Chinese taste was essentially to produce a kind of concealed rococo within the classical architecture of the Russian Enlightenment. Its other and more widespread effect was to produce a first fracturing of the classical orthodoxy that in the two generations since Peter the Great had already become the accepted language of statist order in the Russian empire. Chinoiserie broke that mould just enough for gothic to follow it from Europe. By arousing an interest in medievalism, the English neo-gothic led Russians back to a positive view of their own quite different medieval cultural and architectural traditions, which Peter had introduced classical architecture precisely to suppress.

Chapter Five

RUSSIAN NEO-GOTHIC
IN THE AGE OF CLASSICISM

CATHERINE THE GREAT COULD HARDLY have foreseen the consequences of her instructions to Vasily Neyelov in the early 1770s to gather information about English gothic
architecture and to begin similar work in the imperial gardens; after all, at that time she
simply hankered after the 'chivalrous' effect, the spirit of gothic pageantry so fashionable in Britain and much of Europe.[1] Court architecture evidenced a passion for such
'play' and the quasi-theatrical animation of the historical images which buildings could
evoke, and so, as we have seen, construction proceeded apace with the erection of the
two great Chinese ensembles at Oranienbaum and Tsarskoye Selo. There was also talk
of constructing an antique building, with appointments to match, where the shades of
Caesar, Cicero and Maecenas would take their place among the empress's retainers.
(Such a building, in the form of bath-houses had, as we have seen, already been
envisaged by Cameron.)

This was the apparently innocent context in which Russian neo-gothic was born.
However, the appearance of English castles, lodges and towers in eighteenth-century
Russia had unexpected consequences; Catherine might never have initiated her gothic
pageant had she known what undercurrents of Russian culture, some of them very
unwelcome to the government, were subsequently to come to the surface of Russian
social and political life.

By the 1770s less than ten years had passed since classicism had gained approval as
the official architectural style for government and other public buildings, as well as for
general urban reconstruction. A passionate, sometimes bitter conflict was to be waged
between, on the one hand the picturesque, medieval approach to architectural space,
and on the other the merciless regularity of the designs decreed by the state. By the
1830s this battle would have effected radical changes to the urban environment in
favour of classicism. In the 1770s, however, the process was still at a very early stage.
With the exception of St Petersburg, most new Russian building (including that in
Moscow) continued the durable traditional mixture as before. This consisted partly of
the medieval vernacular and partly of the baroque, which had entered Russia in the
seventeenth and eighteenth centuries. The combination was to characterise much of
the country's architecture for nearly a century to come. The medieval tradition was
always under threat from these Europeanised imports, but remained resilient, borne up
by centuries-old custom and an ability to adapt to the national life and consciousness
which obstructed the onward march of the imported and abstract antique ideal.

The English approach to the renewal of local medieval traditions through the gothic,
which was brought to Catherine by Neyelov and others and through reading, would
somewhat perversely serve as inspiration and reinforcement to those, around Moscow
particularly, who yearned to preserve and reinvigorate Russia's own medieval
traditions.

211 (?)Vasily Bazhenov, *Fantasy on a Gothic Theme.*

The Neo-Gothic as Courtly Fashion in St Petersburg

The phenomenon of 'gothic play' has caused intense controversy among Russian art historians: to this day there is no agreed version of the development of Russian gothic architecture.[2] Rather than prolong this debate, let us consider the details and chronology of the movement itself.

Although the origins of Russian neo-gothic architecture in the late eighteenth and early nineteenth centuries are to be found in Britain, very specific individual characteristics are evident in the Russian version. Often it is difficult to discern any gothic elements at all in the buildings around St Petersburg and Moscow of that period, even though they were considered neo-gothic by the Russians. Rather, the British Gothic Revival was used as the inspiration for a revival – spearheaded by Catherine the Great, her architects and several Russian aristocrats – of traditional national architectural styles. As a result, a building might be classified as neo-gothic, even though it was built in the late medieval Russian style with the merest hint of gothic influence, such as pointed arches.

The first neo-gothic buildings in Russia appeared at the imperial palace of Tsarskoye Selo. These were the Admiralty pavilions and the Hermitage Kitchen, designed by Vasily Neyelov (pl. 212). Construction began in the spring of 1772.[3] This is significant in itself, for the architect had returned from his English travels only in the summer of the previous year.[4] Clearly, he completed his design almost immediately on his return to Russia. He must have worked with remarkable speed, for these few months also included his acceptance – however eagerly – of the commission. His dispatch was surely the result of Catherine's personal intervention. Neyelov was probably granted an audience as soon as he reappeared at Tsarskoye Selo, where he lived and worked, for we know that the empress spent the summer of 1771 on this, her favourite estate. No records of the discussion have survived, but the rush of ensuing orders concerning the construction of several buildings gives us an idea of what Neyelov proposed to the empress. He must have described Palladian buildings he had seen, as well as the Chinese and gothic tastes which were influencing British park-pavilion design – for the

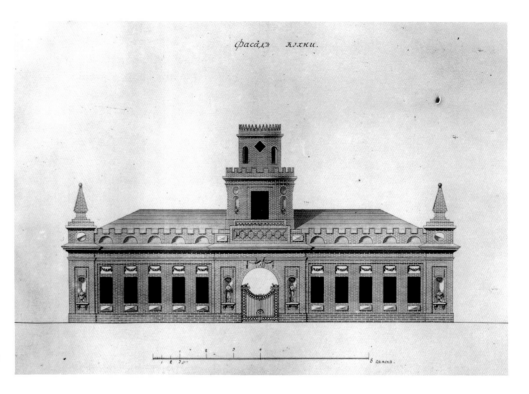

212 Vasily Neyelov, design for a kitchen in the Hermitage Pavilion, Tsarskoye Selo, 1772.

empress was eager to keep abreast of English garden fashions. However, while chinoiserie and palladianism were familiar to Russian architecture, not a single building invoking the 'spirit of chivalry' existed in the imperial gardens.

The Hermitage pavilion, a favourite spot for intimate evening gatherings of the court, was situated deep in the old classical garden at Tsarskoye Selo. It now acquired a neighbour, a new building bristling with battlements and turrets, but somewhat puzzlingly named the Kitchen. Its purpose was apparently practical, and dinners were certainly prepared there for guests attending receptions at the Hermitage, but its artistic intention was in no way associated with its function. It was sited at the edge of the park with, in front, a moat spanned by a bridge leading to the park gates, over which rose a two-tiered round tower. The Kitchen had the appearance of a medieval fortress guarding access to the estate. It was intended to be seen as part of a gothic castle and suggested the presence, behind it, of other buildings from the age of chivalry.

Neyelov's neo-gothic was stylish, decorative and quite devoid of the romantic melancholy of later neo-medieval architecture. The effect was rather playful and welcoming. The battlements and turrets were accompanied by classical niches with antique vases and lush bouquets carved in white stone. The mood of the Kitchen was one of courtly jest which eschewed the true grandeur of the medieval spirit. It was to some extent typical of the rococo follies in the antique, Chinese and gothic styles that were to be found in Russian parts of the time. Against a background of early Russian classicism this rococo-like spirit manifested itself in Neyelov as a combination of baroque, rococo and neo-classicism. The overall composition was strictly symmetrical and classically regular, but what fascinated contemporaries was the symbolism in the medieval decoration. It is in the decoration that the true significance of these first Russian neo-gothic buildings is to be found.

The Admiralty was erected on the shore of the Great Pond at about the same time as the Kitchen (1772–5). It consisted of three buildings: a central two-storeyed block, with lancet windows and stepped attic, to which were attached two towers with battlements and embrasures; and two somewhat larger towers, placed apart and symmetrically on either side of the main pavilion. All were of red brick with white decorative detail. They lacked any sense of medieval austerity; indeed, they gave a more pleasantly decorative impression than comparable buildings in European parks, and continued the theme of light-hearted diversion typical of early Russian neo-gothic.

Curiously, the Admiralty has traditionally been considered to be an imitation of the Dutch architectural style.[5] In fact Neyelov never visited Holland, where neo-gothic was in any case unknown at the time. The building has been attributed to Dutch rather than English influence on anecdotal grounds: it is claimed that, because boat-sheds were usually called Hollands in eighteenth-century Russia (although not at Tsarskoye Selo) Neyelov must have based his design on Dutch rather than English gothic.[6] This reasoning is surely spurious.[7] These first neo-gothic buildings by Neyelov were undoubtedly the result of his observations in Britain. Be that as it may, Tsarskoye Selo was the cradle of the Russian neo-gothic style which was soon to emerge in a rich variety of forms.

In 1773, a few months after work had begun on these neo-gothic pavilions of the Kitchen and the Admiralty at Tsarskoye Selo, Catherine the Great commissioned the architect Yuri Velten to design the first 'medieval castle' (with matching interior), on the route between Tsarskoye Selo and St Petersburg.[8] The spot where the castle stood had been known in Finnish, since before the days of Peter the Great, as *Kekerekekshi*, or the Marsh of Frogs. A kind of local legend about a green frog was invented and transposed into an ironic coat of arms, the 'Green Frog', and the castle was initially called *La Grenouillère* (the House of Frogs) (pls 213, 214).[9] It was later renamed Chesmensky. Velten designed a simple triangular building, with round towers crowned

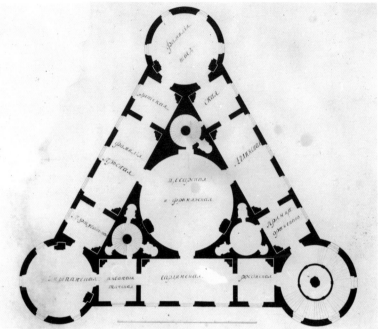

213 (above left) Yuri Velten, design variant for Chesmensky Castle, 1770s.

214 (above right) Yuri Velten, design variant for Chesmensky Castle: plan, 1770s.

by watch-turrets at the corners. A cupola at the centre supported a drum, also in the form of a tower. The overall impression was one of massiveness, wholeness and economy, qualities no doubt intended to evoke the atmosphere of a fortress; and the walls, towers and turrets were studded with lancet windows further to reinforce the medieval image. These features were undoubtedly gothic, but the division of the wall into a rough squat lower section and a smooth, raised mezzanine; the classical cornice above each tower; and the overall symmetry of the façades, combined to give the estate a distinctly Palladian air.

Velten's castle, therefore, was a mixture of gothic and Palladian motifs which separately, and even more in combination, demonstrated the British sympathies of both the architect and his imperial client. Some scholars, seeking a precise model for this castle in eighteenth-century British architecture, have identified as a strong candidate Inverary Castle,[10] begun by Roger Morris and continued in the 1760s by Robert Milne and James Adam. True, at Inverary one experiences a similar 'strange combination of the gothic and Palladian manner',[11] but its layout recalls a conventional Palladian estate very different from Velten's castle with its concentric triangular design.

It cannot seriously be maintained that Velten created an Inverary Castle on the outskirts of St Petersburg. The truth was rather more complex. Velten made use of many different sources, particularly the British architectural pattern books. He relied above all on *The Modern Builder's Assistant* (published in London in 1757) which featured drawings by William Halfpenny of triangular compositions similar to Velten's.[12] Details may also have been suggested by other gothic albums of the Halfpennys.[13] Velten is far more likely to have referred to these widely available pattern books than to illustrations of the Scottish castle, which he could have obtained only with great difficulty.

The courtly medieval pageantry embodied by the castle was based on the overriding importance ascribed by the age of chivalry to the concept of noble birth. For the interior, the sculptor Fedot Shubin created a portrait gallery of grand dukes and Russian tsars from Ryurik to Catherine the Great, the castle's owner, who thereby attempted to demonstrate the legitimacy of her own royal pedigree. In addition there was a collection of portraits of all the European monarchs in the 1770s, intended to be

215   Yuri Velten, Chesmensky church.

seen as a fellowship of knights. There was an implicit contrast between these portraits of ancient and modern rulers and the political concept of the legitimacy of Catherine's rule; such significant undertones, expressed in an attractive and interesting form, would not be lost on her contemporaries.

Having opted for the British version of gothic, Catherine also wished all the furnishings to be executed according to the latest English fashion. In 1773, while Velten was still at work on the design, Josiah Wedgwood was commissioned to create a magnificent dinner service for the castle with the device of the green frog.[14] It consisted of 952 pieces bearing some hundreds of views of British parks, landscapes, ruins and country estates. With the exterior appearance of the gothic castle corresponding to the illustrations on the china service, the design process had come full circle.

This was not the final chapter in the history of Russia's first neo-gothic ensemble. In 1777 construction of a church, also designed by Velten, was begun close by, in memory of the Russian fleet's victory over the Turks in 1770 at the Bay of Chesma in the Aegean. At this time the castle was completed and renamed Chesmensky.

The church, too, was neo-gothic. Here as in the palace the gothic elements strongly distinguished the building as a novelty in its context (pl. 215), but were so far removed from any real sense of gothic architecture's structural principles as to be a mere surface stylisation. Indeed, even that stylisation, with its strange vertical reeding, was a highly abstracted and free reading of real gothic motifs. This distinctive little building perfectly

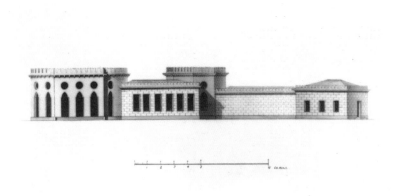

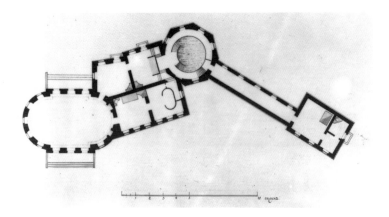

216 (above left) Ilya Neyelov, castle for Prince Potemkin at Bablovo, 1770s.

217 (above right) Ilya Neyelov, castle for Prince Potemkin at Bablovo: plan, 1770s.

demonstrated the importance attached at that time to the mood of a building, and the influence of that mood on the choice of architectural forms. The church had no knightly themes and thus no hint of the grim, fortress-like massiveness of the neighbouring castle. It was bright (red and white), light, festive, rich in decor, and its layout consisted of four 'petals', each completed by an elegant tower crowned with sharply-pointed turrets. Slender white stripes enhanced the walls. The base was covered with horizontal ornament; the upper contour was a kind of gothic filigree. Above the main entrance the wall rose up into an oval like a ship's prow riding a wave. Was this, perhaps, another reference to the victory in the Bay of Chesma? We cannot be certain, but this first Russian neo-gothic ensemble was undoubtedly based on a complex and unified symbolic programme. The architectural forms expressed allegories of contemporary military heroism and imperial power, as well as chivalrous romance, in the spirit of a gothic diversion which was gradually acquiring more serious overtones.

The Chesmensky ensemble demonstrated the two distinct aspects of Russian neo-gothic architecture represented by the St Petersburg and Moscow schools. New chivalric buildings based on English models soon began to appear on the outskirts of the northern city, St Petersburg, notably Potemkin's castle at Bablovo (1782–5) designed by Ilya Neyelov (pls 216–18).[15] Bablovo's picturesque composition, asymme-

218 Remains of Prince Potemkin's castle at Bablovo.

219 and 220   Yuri Velten, church on the Krasnoye estate, 1790.

try of layout and towers with gothic turrets recalled Horace Walpole's Strawberry Hill in Twickenham although it contained only a limited variety of medieval architectural detail. In this it was similar to two castles built for Potemkin by Ivan Starov at Ozerki and Ostrovski.[16] Other members of Catherine's court commissioned buildings in 'St Petersburg gothic' for their estates; for example, Alexander Lanskoi copied the Chesmensky church on his estate near Pskov,[17] as did Mikhail Poltoratsky on his Krasnoye estate near the town of Staritsa (pls 219, 220).[18]

Such St Petersburg-inspired buildings were in sharp contrast to those of the Moscow school. Whereas those around St Petersburg were little more than formal stylistic exercises in the new fashion, Moscow neo-gothic seized upon that deeper potential for evocation of specific mood and for allegorical reference that was also present in embryo in the Chesmensky ensemble.

The Neo-Gothic as National Politics in Moscow

On 10 July 1774 the war with Turkey was brought to a victorious conclusion with the Treaty of Kyuchuk-Kainardzhi, whereby Russia won access to the Black Sea. A great celebration of this event was planned in Moscow. Catherine's deliberate choice of Russia's old capital (in preference to the 'European' St Petersburg) emphasised the point that the struggle with the nomads who had been encroaching on Russian soil for centuries was now at an end. She was also urgently trying to obliterate her image as a foreigner upon the Russian throne which she had usurped without the benefit of any blood relationship with the ancient line of the tsars. In the 1770s, therefore, she was eager to demonstrate her love of Russia by her veneration for Russian history and especially for Moscow, which had already witnessed magnificent festivals whose purpose was to restore the city to its former glory.

In 1772, amid scenes of extraordinary pomp and splendour, work had begun in the Kremlin on a breathtakingly grandiose palace designed by Vasily Bazhenov. This palace was intended to embrace the entire existing ensemble, to occupy the whole of the Kremlin hill and to become the new heart of the city.[19] Fortunately Bazhenov's vision proved too expensive and the Kremlin retained its ancient appearance and character, which was later strongly to influence the development of Moscow neo-gothic in its own right.

The triumph over the Turks was celebrated at three locations. At the southern edge of Moscow, fourteen obelisks in honour of the fourteen principal victories were erected along the route where Field Marshal Rumyantsev's troops were to parade. The obelisks were adorned with paintings of the battles themselves.[20] Thence the troops were to march through two triumphal arches towards the city centre and the main celebration taking place on the ancient Kremlin Square. One eye-witness to this event was Andrei Bolotov, who was also responsible for the spread in popularity of the concept of the English garden, through articles in his journals such as *Economic Magazine* and *The Country Gentleman*. He described the ceremony in these words:

> Every street in the Kremlin was filled with soldiers . . . the whole area [of Cathedral Square] . . . from the Red Porch [the grand entrance to the ancient castle of the Russian tsars] to the Uspensky [Dormition] cathedral was a great dais . . . draped in red cloth, and all the walls of the cathedrals and other buildings were lined with rows of tiered seats to create a vast amphitheatre . . . accommodating a huge number of noble and distinguished spectators . . . But nothing can compare with the magnificent sight which greeted us with the procession of the empress down from the Red Porch, in full imperial uniform and resplendent in power and glory. Her entire court, decked out in gorgeous dress, followed in her train . . . as the ground beneath us shook with the sound and thunder of a great number of bells from the belfry of Ivan the Great. The sound of the great bell was so tremendous that it seemed the Ivan Tower itself trembled, and many of us feared it would collapse. The whole scene was . . . of such splendour and beauty that . . . we were utterly entranced.[21]

This ceremony, played out amid the medieval cathedrals and castles of the Kremlin, set the tone for the ensuing festivities.

The appeal to Russian history, and especially the association of recent victories with its age-old glory symbolised by the ancient edifices of the Kremlin, provided the theme for a large number of architectural allegories expressed by a great range of neo-gothic structures. They were erected for a festival arranged for the common people on the Khodynskoye Field, on the north-west edge of the city and represented Russian, Ukrainian, Tartar and Turkish towns (pls 222–4). The empress ordered the construction of a kind of gigantic 'map' of the northern Black Sea coast (pl. 221). All classical ideas associated with temples dedicated to ancient gods were rigorously excluded. The allegories were to be more specific and recognisable. Their style was as important as the object of their dedication. International but not classical, neo-gothic was considered the perfect vehicle for the purpose.

Catherine wrote to Baron Grimm that:

> the plan drawn up for the celebrations was as dreadful as ever. They wanted a temple to Janus, another to Bacchus, another to God knows what devil, idiotic, ghastly allegorical fantasies, and enormous to boot . . . They made me so angry that one fine morning I sent for my architect Bazhenov and told him: 'My dear Bazhenov, there

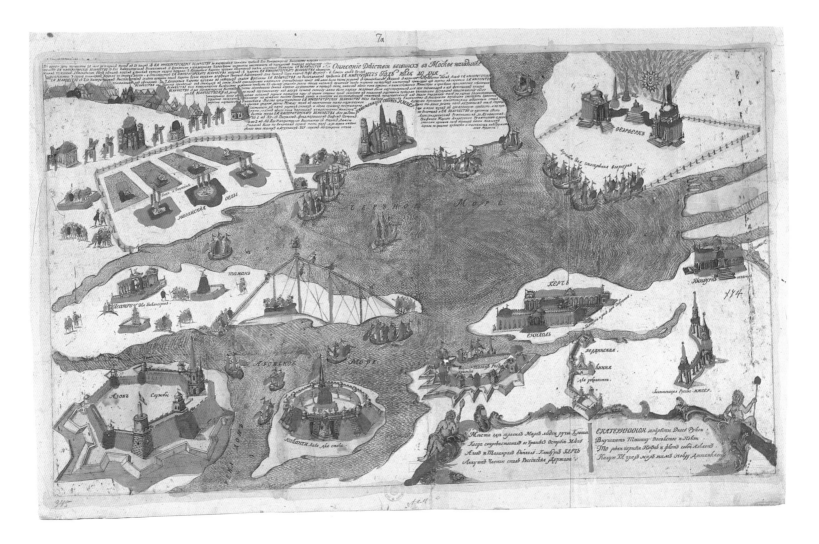

221   Plan of the temporary buildings erected for triumphal celebrations on the Khodynskoye Field, Moscow, 1775.

is a meadow three *versts* [a little over three miles] from the city. Imagine that the meadow is the Black Sea and there are two roads leading from the city. Now, one of them is to be the Tanaïs [the Greek name for the River Don] and the other the Borisfen [the Dnieper]; on the estuary of the former you will build a refectory, to be named Azov [after a Russian fortress] and on the estuary of the latter, a theatre to be called Kinburn [after a fortress which had frequently fallen in and out of Russian hands]. Construct the Crimean Peninsula out of sand and put Kerch and Enikale [Crimean cities] on it to serve as ballrooms. Opposite Crimea I want illuminations which will represent the joy of both states [Russia and Turkey] at the onset of peace . . . Boats and ships, to be illuminated by you, will be scattered over the area of the Black Sea'.[22]

She continued to Grimm: 'You are a natural critic, but tell me honestly – is this an awful idea? . . . at least no worse, surely, than the absurd pagan temples which upset me so.'[23]

There could hardly have been a more favourable set of circumstances for the exploration of neo-gothic themes and ideas. The chivalrous pageantry which had its origins in the dying days of rococo was here realised on a grand scale, but with that new quality of seriousness and moral edification characteristic of the Enlightenment. Allegorically expressed ideas were to be recognisable, therefore Bazhenov's Russian fortresses were designed in consciously Russian style, with the twin-horned citadel-like battlements, multi-tiered towers with tent-roofed turrets and rows of ornamentation

193

commonly found in medieval Russian architecture. In other structures, for example those entitled 'Illuminations of the Russian Empire', Bazhenov evoked the notion of conquest by combining elements of Moscow architecture with motifs of true gothic he had seen in France. Here the decor was a mélange of detail and techniques typical of the Middle Ages in western Europe, Russia and the Orient. Buttresses and pointed gothic arches were juxtaposed with Turkish minarets and tents, yurts (tents) of the nomadic *Noqaitsi* tribe and the tent-roofs and spiral columns of seventeenth-century Russian churches.

Thus a new idiom of architectural symbols, conceived specifically to express complex political and spatial allegories, was developed within this celebratory ensemble

222 Matvei Kazakov, temporary buildings by Vasily Bazhenov on the Khodynskoye Field, Moscow, 1775.

223 Matvei Kazakov, temporary buildings by Vasily Bazhenov on the Khodynskoye Field, Moscow, 1775.

at Khodynskoye. They were based on eighteenth-century British neo-gothic ideas which were in themselves quite rational. The layout of each individual building, precise and strictly regular, was classical. Within these highly conventional plans, however, burgeoned utterly fantastic compositions intended to stimulate the imagination of the public. Medievalism provided an opportunity to explore new forms of expression at a time when there was no tried, tested and generally accepted model to which contemporaries could refer. A new freedom was born, namely the freedom to choose a model for oneself. As the classical norms evaporated, anything and everything was permitted in the atmosphere of legend engendered by Khodynskoye. All this intoxicated not only the public, who came to gaze with wonder on this extraordinary event, but also those who had had a hand in creating it.

Dressing buildings in various medieval guises provided a measure of freedom to architects trained in the classical tradition, and Khodynskoye opened the way for a broad development of Russian neo-gothic. The grandiose sweep of the ensemble was itself in strong contrast to the rococo spirit of the earliest intimate medieval pavilions built in Russia. The light-hearted rococo atmosphere was replaced by other non-classical models usually described as 'early romantic'.[24]

The question of romanticism is a complex one, and much has already been written on the subject. Suffice it to say here that at the end of the eighteenth century Russia, influenced by the French Revolution, experienced a powerful upsurge of new social and political thinking, so that romanticism in the normal sense of the word was hardly to be expected. What did arise was something different and impossible to define in conventional stylistic terms. British neo-gothic stimulated those opposed to classicism in Russian architecture (and perhaps in Russian culture as a whole). This wave of anti-classicism, however was motivated more by a conviction that the medieval represented a still-unfinished past than by the call to an uncharted future which was to be sounded through neo-gothic in the 1820s.[25]

The festivities at Khodynskoye made a great impression on Russians of the time, many of whom left memoirs of the event.[26] Among other unforgettable details they described long lines of carriages with postilions 'dressed as Turks, Albanians, Serbs,

224 Matvei Kazakov, temporary buildings by Vasily Bazhenov on the Khodynskoye Field, Moscow, 1775.

Circassians, Hussars and "genuine negro servants" in crimson turbans'.[27] Magnificent firework displays featured 'a great number of Catherine wheels, stars, suns and fountains of fire exploding into countless brilliant points of light'.[28] The free fare included 'roast ox . . . and fountains flowing with wine'.[29] Above all, their imagination was caught by the pavilions, recalling ancient palaces and richly decorated in the style of the Moscow Kremlin.

Eventually, however, the last fireworks exploded and the gorgeously bedecked buildings lost their lustre. It was decided that the decorations which so vividly celebrated the glory of victories past and present should become permanent.

Tsaritsyno

Only a few months later, in the winter of 1775, Bazhenov completed the first drawings for a neo-gothic palace that, according to a contemporary, 'derives its power from the forms of the past'.[30] This great ensemble, later called Tsaritsyno, was to be built to the south-west of Moscow on the Chernaya Gryaz (Black Mud) estate which had been bought by the Crown from the Kantemir family, descendants of a Moldavian prince who had emigrated to Russia during the reign of Peter the Great. The site was indeed well chosen. It was a broad, flat eminence bounded on two sides by deep ravines. A stream ran through one of them and thence, via a weir, into a lake. This promontory, surrounded by water and steep slopes, became the centrepiece of the new imperial estate of Tsaritsyno.

225   Vasily Bazhenov, design for the Grape Gates, Tsaritsyno, 1776.

226 Vasily Bazhenov, Grape Gates, Tsaritsyno.

The design was itself unusual and unexpected in the age of classicism. It was certainly not a regular one. Two identical palaces – one for Catherine, the other for the heir apparent, Grand Duke Paul Petrovich – and a large staff mansion to accommodate

227 Vasily Bazhenov, Bread Gates, Tsaritsyno.

228 Vasily Bazhenov, Bread Gates, Tsaritsyno: detail.

court officials made up a triangle, round which numerous pavilions of many different sizes, shapes and purposes were laid out to picturesque effect. Other buildings followed the natural curve of one ravine: the huge *Khlebny Dom* (literally, 'Bread House', the domestic centre of the estate and larger than the palaces themselves), the residence of the estate steward, accommodation for servants, and an old church. Another mansion for courtiers completed the curve, with yet more buildings stretching away from it on the other side of the lake in the following order: two small pavilions with a decorative bridge and gate, a pavilion (close to Catherine's palace) for the ladies-in-waiting, the empress's *Maly* (Small) Palace, intended for private receptions and finally the opera house by the *Vinogradnye* (Grape) Gates (pls 225–6).

198

229 Anon., *View of Tsaritsyno*, late eighteenth century.

This kind of picturesque composition was not without antecedents in Russia. It was to some extent prefigured in the old estates of the seventeenth-century Russian tsars,[32] or in the more recent Moscow ensemble of Lefortovo dating from the baroque period.[33] More important, however, was the fact that Tsaritsyno was envisaged as a panoramic sweep to be appreciated from afar. This was the very same approach to the architectural organisation of space which had obtained at Khodynska, where each building simultaneously expressed an individual idea, and was deliberately integrated into a system of local compositions whose totality communicated a larger one. Bazhenov applied this principle to Tsaritsyno. It was a courageous step for this architect educated in Paris on classical models, even granted that picturesque English landscaped gardens were becoming increasingly popular at the time – and, indeed, such a garden was planned around the Tsaritsyno pavilions.

In Bazhenov's final design of 1776 the panorama of the ensemble unfolded to striking effect (pls 230, 231). Small pavilions, their layout precise, simple and logical, stood by the lake at the foot of a steep bank cut through by deep gullies. Their walls were pierced by high lancet windows while buttresses, slender turrets, elaborate battlements and

199

230 Anon., panoramic view of a proposal for Tsaritsyno, 1776.

cornices carved in a gothic style enriched their contours. Between them were two large and ornate bridges decorated with fantastical variations on medieval castle themes, with towers, embrasures, galleries supported by slim gothic columns and lancet arches. This, the foreground of the ensemble, accounted for only the lower structures. Beyond stood higher buildings, including the palaces and, in the distance, largest of all, the Bread House. For the centre of the ensemble Bazhenov proposed a high tower rising to a sharp point. From a distance the whole design resolved itself into a rich and multi-tiered fantasy, creating a total architectural landscape spread out over a vast area. Bazhenov aimed to surpass all the eighteenth-century neo-gothic palaces and castles of Europe. Tsaritsyno was intended to be the mightiest among them, and it was actually constructed as such; but its later history was so complex and dramatic that it overshadowed the architectural significance of this grandiose gothic ensemble.

Before describing Tsaritsyno's ultimate fate it is essential to identify the specific innovations of Bazhenov's architectural language in order to understand how contemporaries, and especially Catherine herself, saw the palace.

This gothic language was built on a conscious system of internal contradictions. In essence Bazhenov remained a classicist who built in a gothic style, for the individual buildings are of regular and rational design; their sense of rhythm, proportion and division are distinctly classical. There remains a distinctive system of architectural orders proportioned according to the accepted modes, in the conventional correlation between the base of the buildings and the walls, and so on. Yet rationality and obedience to the classical norm, never absent from Bazhenov's gothic, were deliberately opposed by qualities of freedom and imagination. Moreover, as in the overall

231 Anon., detail of pl. 230.

200

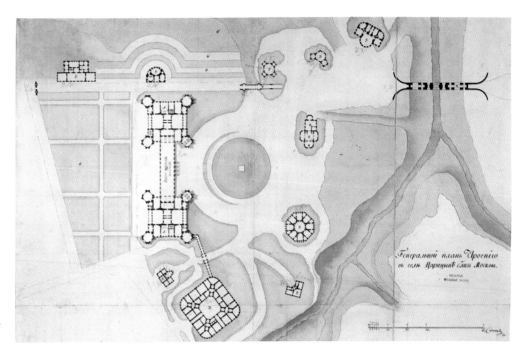

232 Matvei Kazakov, general plan for the palace and estate at Tsaritsyno.

233 Matvei Kazakov, project for the palace at Tsaritsyno.

concept and the smallest detail of the composition, so also in the choice of forms and images Bazhenov turned for inspiration to motifs from Russian medieval architecture to recent baroque structures, European gothic, and finally the orientalist styles typical of pavilions in landscaped parks.

It should be emphasised that, in themselves, these motifs had no independent significance; separately they are not strongly perceptible. Here Bazhenov typically exploited every stylistic recourse known to the architects of the time, using gothic, classical, oriental and fantastic elements simultaneously. The language he created was encyclopaedic, and in this he was a typical product of the Enlightenment. He wished to develop a national style inspired by the patriotic ideals of medieval Russia. However, with the breadth of vision characteristic of the Enlightenment he did not confine himself within narrowly national limits but made use of many elements of the world's

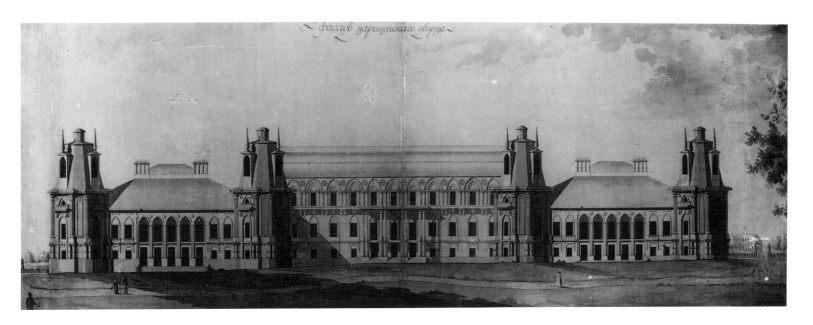

234 Matvei Kazakov, Tsaritsyno Palace.

architectural heritage. The open-minded and impressionable nature of Russian archi-tecture at the end of the eighteenth century is attested by the way British neo-gothic ideas, as interpreted by Bazhenov, served as the spur to the creation of this architectural language.

Its essential elements, therefore, were rationalism and creative freedom, an encyclopaedic range of sources and the emergence of new, non-classical models. This is an important phenomenon in the history of Russian architecture. Bazhenov proposed an approach distinguished, in the age of classicism, by the qualities of synthesis and tolerance to be found in baroque, and his buildings covertly preserved these most significant features of that rejected style. Nevertheless, his work was not entirely rooted in the past; it was also innovatory, and amounted to a strenuous search for a new idiom.

Tsaritsyno itself represents a curious equilibrium at the borders of the Age of Enlightenment and romanticism, although the romantic view of life and art had not yet taken hold. Tsaritsyno may be seen as the creation of an enlightened man dissatisfied with the Enlightenment. He desired more than a mere broadening of architectural knowledge and an increasingly sophisticated application of that knowledge. A new content was required.

That succinct phrase of Ledoux, 'architecture parlante', applies well to neo-gothic and particularly to Tsaritsyno, successor to the elaborate allegories of Khodynskoye which had been expressed by the same stylistic methods.

What message, however, did Tsaritsyno hold for Bazhenov's contemporaries? An official report to the empress from the Governor-General of Moscow, Yakov Bryus, observed: 'I went to Tsaritsyno, where the building has been marvellously done . . . the first view of Tsaritsyno is so fine, so pleasant, so splendid . . . truly I have seen nothing to compare with it.'[34] It must indeed have seemed a great triumph. Work commenced in May 1776,[35] and nine years later, in early 1785, the whole magnificent ensemble had been completed. Two English gardeners, Francis Reed and John Munro, began work on the park.[36] The empress was awaited.

Catherine arrived in Moscow in the spring of 1785. She paid her visit to Tsaritsyno and unexpectedly erupted in fury at the castle: 'The empress returned to her carriage in a rage and ordered . . . the castle [the palace] razed to the ground.'[37] What could have caused so violent a reaction? Catherine herself, in a letter to Baron Grimm, blamed the narrow staircases, the gloomy rooms and heavy vaulting.[38] This explanation is no more convincing than the story (still current) that on the way to Tsaritsyno she had a vision of an open burial vault which she attempted to drive from her mind by destroying the palace.

Catherine was neither excessively superstitious nor mystically inclined – the events of 1762 alone are proof of that – but she was not without fear. She herself had come to power through a coup d'état and was nervous of conspiracies. Most likely it was indeed a plot, rather than a 'vault' which the empress thought she discerned at Tsaritsyno.

There were some grounds for this belief. Bazhenov belonged to a Moscow masonic lodge called Devkalion Second Class.[39] The Moscow masons, very active in the 1770s and 1780s, were led by Nikolai Novikov, a close friend of Bazhenov's. Novikov, as well as being a member of several Moscow lodges, was also busy propagating the ideas of freemasons throughout the rest of Russia.[40] This activity resulted in the formation of the Typographical Company, which became one of the most progressive publishing houses in the country, producing, at Novikov's initiative, a vast number of books covering many subjects, including architecture, Russian and translated works on art, as well as a good number of essays on mystical themes.[41] Magazines of a similar tendency also appeared at this time; clearly the Moscow masons were becoming a significant influence on Russian intellectual life. This was a development that intensely displeased Catherine, as Novikov and his friends were well aware.

The masons sought the patronage of Grand Duke Paul Petrovich; this was particularly unwelcome to the empress, especially as the question was then being asked in

235 Matvei Kazakov, Tsaritsyno Palace.

236 Matvei Kazakov, Tsaritsyno Palace.

society whether he, rather than Catherine, should have inherited the throne from Peter III. The relationship between mother and son became more strained, although it is difficult to tell how well-founded her suspicions may have been as to the existence of a masonic conspiracy, let alone whether Paul was privy to it. What is certain, however, is that government persecution of the masons always coincided precisely with their attempts to forge contacts with the Grand Duke.[42]

Novkov exploited the architect of Tsaritsyno for this purpose. Bazhenov visited Grand Duke Paul Petrovich three times, on the pretence of offering him his professional services; each occasion was followed by repression. Moreover, when the Moscow masonic organisation was forcibly disbanded the members were punished according to the degree of their 'involvement with a certain personage' (i.e. Paul).[43]

237   Matvei Kazakov, Tsaritsyno Palace.

Bazhenov's first visit to the Grand Duke – and the first persecution of Novikov and his fellows – took place in 1785,[44] the year Catherine ordered the destruction of Tsaritsyno. Her anger was undoubtedly connected with the threat of a masonic conspiracy and the possibility of Bazhenov's participation.

At this distance in time we can hardly be sure exactly which aspects of the disposition of the estate or arrangement of the buildings seemed ominous to the empress. Most likely she read Bazhenov's 'language' and perceived therein masonic ideas of some kind. He had, indeed, had the impertinence to incorporate masonic symbols into the decor of the castles and the pavilions. For example, the visitor approaching the castle through the Grape Gates could not avoid remarking on a huge pair of compasses hanging from the arch – the masonic symbol for the 'measurement of virtue'; and we ourselves can still see, on one wall of the Bread House, a large, strange sign whose meaning remains unexplained to this day.

Novikov and his circle played an important role in Russian culture, primarily because they were responsible for a whole new concept of its development and strove to spread their views by means of education. Although their views on architecture have not come down to us, we do know that they had strong opinions on the subject;[45] in addition, the Moscow masons were greatly concerned with medieval literary monuments, so we may be sure that neo-gothic architecture would have attracted their interest. Presumably Bazhenov, as a close confident of Novikov, gave expression to these ideas in his Tsaritsyno 'language'.[46]

In the end, Tsaritsyno was not entirely destroyed. In 1786 Bazhenov was dismissed[47] and Matvei Kazakov appointed in his place. Kazakov erected one new palace on the site of the two previously intended for Paul and Catherine. Bazhenov's many other buildings on the estate remained intact. Indeed the palace itself was designed in a gothic style: two square blocks with faceted towers at the corners were connected by a high rectangular building which housed grand, formal rooms. The red-brick mass of the palace, relieved by columns of white stone and lancet windows, was crowned by a lofty copper roof. Although the great neo-gothic structure was totally rebuilt, the interior was never completed. Catherine's death in 1797 signalled an end to the project, so that Europe's mightiest neo-gothic palace remained uninhabited for ever.

Nevertheless, its importance for Russian architecture was enormous. The grandiose complex found a response throughout the country, with the result that quasi-British, medieval-style buildings became an obligatory element of all the great estates. The masonic connection was manifest again here in this building work carried out in the countryside, outside immediate court circles, and particularly among the Slavophile aristocracy. These people were intimately connected by the ties of the masonic system, and the image conveyed to them – and about them – by the gothic style is suggested by the common Russian belief, at that time, in freemasonry as a phenomenon of English origin. During the 1780s many of these people became the victims of Catherine's repressive government, as it reflected her own increasing fear of masonic influence. So direct was the association that, in Moscow and the surrounding provinces, the neo-gothic came to be seen by many as 'masonic architecture', and by the end of the century the very presence of a building or monument in a neo-gothic style on a country estate could itself signify that the owner was a mason.

The Neo-Gothic and the Medieval Russian Revival

While the affair of Catherine's rejection of Tsaritsyno, the largest neo-gothic palace in eighteenth-century Europe, remains mysterious to this day, the complexity of the story is not just the result of historical distance. The issue of gothic was complex at the time. Thus even such a very different section of the population as the Old Believers, those followers of an ancient spiritual tradition opposed to the official Orthodox Church, also gave their blessing to the new style; they built a neo-gothic church at their centre in the Preobrazhensky Cemetery in Moscow.[48]

In other contexts, and from other architects, Catherine herself found gothic work

238 Matvei Kazakov, project for Petrovsky Castle,
Moscow, 1770s.

239 Matvei Kazakov, Petrovsky Castle, Moscow.

quite acceptable in her own building programme. In the mid-1770s, while building at
Tsaritsyno was proceeding, a number of other large imperial palaces had been planned
(pls 238–41). In 1775 Kazakov began work on the Petrovsky Castle, at a site near
Moscow on the road from St Petersburg (not far, perhaps significantly, from the
Khodynskoye Field). Intended as the empress's last stopping-point when she travelled
from the new capital to the old, it was envisaged as the architectural symbol of Moscow
and the artistic 'gateway' to its medieval monuments.

The design of Petrovsky was quite different from that of Tsaritsyno. Its parts made
up a compact, tightly controlled whole. The main building, at the centre, was square
in shape with its rooms disposed symmetrically. The axis was a large hall, with a domed
ceiling, from which other rooms opened like the arms of a cross. This kind of logical

240 Matvei Kazakov, *View of Petrovsky Castle, Moscow.*

layout, derived, like Pavlovsk, from the Palladian country house, was strangely at odds with normal associations of the gothic, as the service buildings and a network of courtyards surrounding it were arranged in a classically clear and rational mood. The visitor's first view was of low, semi-circular blocks which straightened to form a rectangular space in front of the main house. Behind lay yet another large courtyard flanked by two identical smaller courtyards. The overall layout was hardly less strict than in contemporary classical country mansions.

All the same, Petrovsky was in some respects far from classical. Now usually called Petrovsky Palace, it fully deserved its original description as a castle. Outbuildings and a perimeter wall – with large, faceted towers on several tiers, rounded turrets and battlements above a cornice – girding the entire complex resembled the fantastic walls of a medieval fortress, an impression strengthened by the tightness and economy of the whole composition. The main building was even more unusual in appearance, with numerous details derived from seventeenth-century Moscow architecture. The lower floor, studded with lancet windows, was decorated with short, thick, columns rather like enormous pears. A projecting portico had similar columns connected by arches, each of which accommodated two further small arches, covered in vegetative decor, with a motif called *girka* (from *girya*, a weight) in white stone running between them.

241 Matvei Kazakov, *View of Petrovsky Castle, Moscow.*

The mezzanine was even more richly decorative, with window-surrounds of a highly elaborate design common in late medieval Russian architecture. The mansard roof featured a great number of large and small baroque-like pediments. The whole palace was crowned by a dome on a tall drum with richly finished windows. The dome resembled a gigantic and luxurious goblet which might have graced the tables of the ancient Moscow tsars.

This highly eclectic work by Kazakov laid the foundation for a distinctive Moscow-inspired neo-gothic style. It combined a strictly classical compositional base, inclined towards order, symmetry and proportion, with a fascination for the specifically Russian heritage that was quite different from Bazhenov's interest in European aspects of medievalism. By its incorporation of Russian medieval elements, Petrovsky is the predecessor of the Russian style which was to evolve throughout the nineteenth century and into the twentieth.

The intention in the early 1780s, evidently, was to create a belt of imperial estates in the medieval style to the west and south of Moscow. Two other palaces were planned for sites between Tsaritsyno and Petrovsky Castle, namely at Konkovo and Bulatnkovo.[49] Bazhenov's original designs for these were amended, after his dismissal, by Kazakov. The palace at Konkovo was of particular interest (pls 242, 243); it was begun as a vast pentagonal castle with towers at each corner and wings in the form of large, squat round towers. The belt of new developments was also to include huge imperial stable complexes to accommodate hundreds of horses. As may be seen in one of Kazakov's albums,[50] they too resembled a medieval fortress. Though work continued for several decades, not one of these projects was completed.[51] Altogether, these buildings, dating from the 1770s to the 1790s, demonstrated a range of neo-gothic styles unprecedented in Russia and comparable to similar architectural ventures which flourished in some European capitals almost a century later. In St Petersburg court circles the neo-gothic reappeared under various kinds of British influence during the first half of the nineteenth century, but Moscow was never again to witness neo-gothic

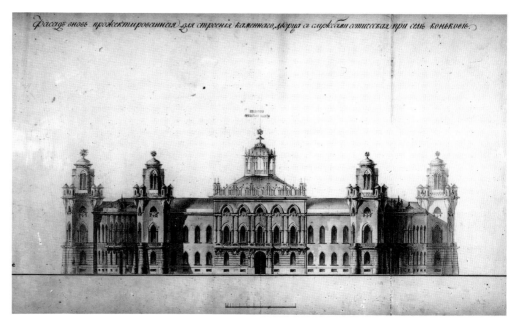

242 Matvei Kazakov, project for Konkovo Palace, 1780s.

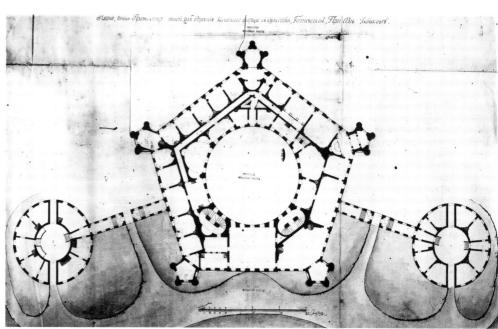

243 Matvei Kazakov, project for Konkovo Palace: plan, 1780s.

construction on such a grand scale, and after the 1830s it was generally displaced by the Russian style for public and official buildings.

At the end of the eighteenth century, therefore, neo-gothic was co-existent and largely interchangeable with the Russian style, in a broad movement of neo-medievalism, but the specifics of this architecture differed between town and country. Country estates inclined more towards European models, whereas urban design (especially in Moscow) tended to feature more elements derived from historical Russian architecture.

The Neo-Gothic on Country Estates

Whatever their associations may have been for Catherine, the neo-gothic buildings on Russian country estates deserve examination as architectural phenomena in their own right. The early heyday of country neo-gothic occurred in the last quarter of the eighteenth century, with only a few individual examples cropping up in the nineteenth.

At first gothic buildings on Russian estates were rather rare, and erected for some special occasion, generally, as had been the case with Catherine, to commemorate some honour or military victory associated with the owner. Thus, some of the earliest neo-gothic buildings appeared on the estates of Field-Marshal Rumyantsev, the conqueror of the Turks, whose military feats were celebrated by the state at Khodynskoye Field. A house in a gothic style, built on his estate of Troitskoye-Kainardzhi (named after the peace treaty), was a compact, classically laid-out mansion adorned with towers and battlements at the corners, decorated with various details in 'fortress' style (with embrasures, etc.) and curling ornamentation.[52]

In 1787 a more interesting palace was erected, again for Rumyantsev, at his estate in Vishenki (Little Cherries) in the Ukraine.[53] Its three buildings consisted of many tower-shaped forms; semi-circular galleries connected the wings with the main block. The clear baroque influence recalls Bazhenov rather than Kazakov's more classical approach.[54]

Gothic motifs became a common feature of fortress architecture and most Russian neo-gothic country houses contained fortress-like elements. This was fully in accordance with the wishes of their owners, who were concerned not only to imitate the castles and knights of old but also to reflect their own military glory – and to incorporate memories of real fortresses built or captured – in the outward appearance of their homes.

Such residences include the mansion on the Krasnoye estate near Ryazan,[55] Znamenka near Tambov[56] and – one of the most curious of all – the Saburovo estate of Field-Marshal Mikhail Kamensky near Orel.[57] The Saburov Fortress, as it was known by local folk, covered an area 400 by 450 metres (pl. 244); it was surrounded by real fortress walls of brick, four metres high and with many round towers (up to

244   The Saburov Fortress, 1780s.

fourteen metres high) crowned with hipped roofs made of stone. The household buildings were built on to this monumental wall. These three estates were modelled on medieval, rather than eighteenth-century fortresses. Their gothic detail was meant to imply a connection between a glorious past and the heroic present.

It is often forgotten that their popularity in Russia derived from the fashion for the English country estate, with its Palladian mansion and landscaped garden, both of which were to become key elements in the appearance and atmosphere of the Russian estates. The Palladian mansion was the focal point, but the park created a picturesque milieu which could accommodate 'temples', be they classical pavilions or gothic towers, and other buildings in various styles.

Even where the main house was classical, it was often the neo-gothic face of an estate which first met the visitor's eye. Gates in the form of two towers with battlements were especially popular. Typical examples include the entrance to the Yaropolets estate of the Goncharov family (pl. 245),[58] the Vorontsovo and the Mikhalkovo estates[59] (the latter now absorbed into Moscow). They were symbols protecting the independence of the estate from outside pressures and emphasising the individual way of life being carried on within.

Many domestic and service buildings, particularly stables, were built in neo-gothic style. Their medieval character lent a fairytale quality to these prosaic structures, as if to continue the playful atmosphere of the park greeting the visitor as he entered the grounds. The stables at Krasnoye, for example, displayed many fantastic gothic features,[60] while those of Maryinka, near Bronnitsy, were modelled on an English park pavilion in a style dating from the 'age of chivalry'.[61]

Eighteenth- and early nineteenth-century Russian neo-gothic churches are of particular interest; moreover, they have been the cause of vigorous argument among art historians. Some have considered that the first churches in medieval style were erected before the arrival of British neo-gothic influence in Russia and ascribed the revival of the medieval tendency in Russian architecture to provincial sources.[62] As evidence they

245 The entrance to the Goncharovs' Yaropolets estate, late eighteenth century.

have adduced churches in Starki-Cherkizovo and Znamenka, apparently built several years before the Chesmensky palace and the Khodynskoye ensemble.[63] Other experts have disputed such early dating of these churches[64] and claimed, instead, that they were built at a time when neo-gothic was already widespread throughout the country. The latest archival research has shown that the latter were correct: neo-gothic was indeed the product of the spread of British ideas in Russia.[65]

Eighteenth-century neo-gothic churches are to be found in various places in Russia, including Znamenka, Starki-Cherkizovo, Podzhigorodovo, Bernovo, Krasnoye, Posadnikovo and Grabtsevo. The most outstanding ensemble of this kind, built at Bykovo, near Moscow, in the 1780s,[66] is ascribed, in the absence of exact evidence, either to Bazhenov or to Kazakov (pls 246–9). The church is of complex design. A

246 The church at Bykovo, 1780s.

247 and 248   The church at Bykovo: details.

high bell-tower stands in front of the western façade. The façade itself is two-storeyed, with large lancet embrasures on the upper level between two multi-tiered towers. The church is on two floors. An impressive winding staircase with broad steps leads on two sides to the more formal upper floor. A monumental arch beneath the staircase gives access to the lower church. The visitor first enters a square *trapeznaya* (originally a refectory or meeting place common in Russian rural churches) before proceeding to the spacious church itself. The exterior offers a striking combination of forms created by the massive cube of the *trapeznaya* and the slender oval of the cylinder soaring above the church, which is crowned by a slender dome and a whole 'forest' of pointed spires. Elaborate and elegant 'gothic' porticoes adjoin the sides of the church. At their base, light, slim columns, topped by little canopy-like pedestals, lean against heavy pointed arches. This motif recalls the decoration of certain medieval Italian buildings which Bazhenov is known to have visited in his youth.[67] Motifs from medieval Russia, together with original gothic detail, are also present in the church itself. There is no denying the complexity and drama of the general composition, with its subtle inter-dependence of forms and elaborate weave of decorative elements. The echo of baroque is strong and unmistakable.

214

249 The church at Bykovo: detail.

If neo-gothic country churches were not a product of seventeenth- and early eighteenth-century local monumental architecture, their designers might still have been influenced by baroque, only recently fallen out of favour. The church at Bykovo is one of the clearest examples of concealed baroque sensibilities in Russian neo-gothic architecture of the classical period. Generally speaking, the architectural function of churches in the rich and varied country estates was to evoke the provenance of the present by reference to the past. They reaffirmed the important and continuing vitality of ancient traditions in a new cultural idiom which became more widespread as the yearning for ancient ideals grew.

The Neo-Gothic in the Heart of Moscow

Neo-gothic urban architecture in Russia developed rather differently, although here too ideological pressure was required to dislodge classicism, which was entering, in those same 1780s, the period of its greatest strength and maturity. At first such pressure came from Moscow, whose antiquity and sacred sites held a spiritual value for Russians in the age of the Enlightenment comparable to that of the classical ideal.[68] All the same, classicism did not give up without a fight. In the 1760s and 1770s a truly titanic struggle was waged between the new creations of classicism and the traditional historical environments of the ancient parts of the city, including, most importantly, the Kremlin. Bazhenov proposed a gigantic classical palace and actually succeeded in demolishing the south walls and towers of the Kremlin. It must have seemed that medievalism was in retreat and that a new ensemble incarnating the power and glory of the antique world would dominate the Moscow skyline.

Harsh reality, however, worked against the radically minded 'people of the Enlightenment' whose ideas were embodied in Bazhenov's work. The practical difficulties and expense involved in the project, intended to embrace the whole of the Kremlin, persuaded the authorities and architects to consider an alternative approach to the development of the old city centre. The question was asked, could the artistic integrity

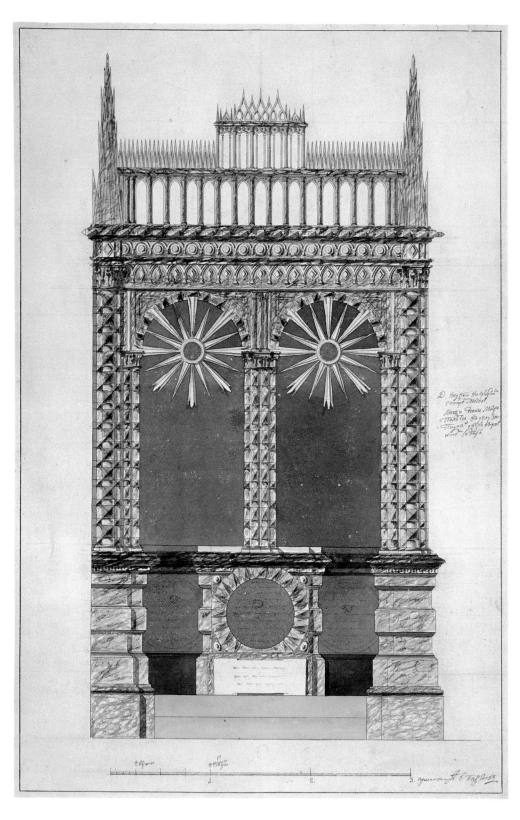

250 Vasily Bazhenov, design for a canopy for the tomb of Metropolitan Iona in the Uspensky cathedral, Kremlin, Moscow, 1773.

of the ancient ensemble be maintained by integrating gothic structures with the classical edifices then in the process of construction? As a result, neo-medieval buildings did take their place alongside the majestic, antique forms of the new Senate.

Bazhenov was involved in the early stages of this venture. In 1773 he was commissioned to design awnings (vestibules) for the tombs of Metropolitans Iona, Philipp and Peter in the Kremlin's Uspensky cathedral (pl. 250) 'in order that antiquity . . . be preserved in all its original appearance'.[69] Bazhenov's response was a decorative gothic superimposed on a classically composed base, recalling the work of William Kent for the choir of Gloucester cathedral.[70]

Voices calling for neo-gothic buildings in the Kremlin were now to be heard more often, and Kazakov completed several projects for churches in a medieval style.[71] In 1775 it was proposed to replace Rastrelli's baroque imperial palace, erected two decades earlier, with a building giving the impression that 'a famous edifice dating from the ancient past had been renovated'.[72] This project was later completed by Nikolai Lvov,[73] who designed *terema* (tower-shaped residences) for the grand dukes and '*terema* in Sytny Dvor';[74] the very word *terem* was a deliberate echo of the sixteenth- and seventeenth-century *terem* palaces in the Kremlin. Lvov substantiated his theoretical interest in Old Russian architecture in an unpublished work entitled 'A study of Russian antiquities in Moscow':[75]

> Those who destroy ancient buildings . . . do not return that which they have stolen. Roaming the sad ruins the lover of antiquity finds not the slightest trace of anything which might tell him where churches or . . . *terema* stood . . . or where the defenders of the Fatherland lived. The grass growing over the ruins conceals . . . the shame of the venerable remains of the past, now lost for ever.[76]

Such attitudes became increasingly widespread and by the beginning of the nineteenth century the patriotic approach to history had finally triumphed over the 'latest fashion' in Kremlin architecture. Extensive works were begun to renovate the surviving monuments, which were to be adorned with neo-gothic additions and detail of every conceivable kind. Attempts were made to render medieval buildings 'more medieval' and romantic. Ivan Yegotov added gothic motifs to the tower of the Borovitsky Gate in the Kremlin and in 1806 proposed a hipped roof for the tower of the Nikolsky Gate.[77] He also drew up plans for the reconstruction of the second ring of Moscow's ancient fortifications abutting the Kremlin, the walls and gates of the area called Kitai-gorod.[78] His design was based on Old Russian fortress architecture, featuring massive forms, a tiered structure and a hipped roof; Yegotov's personal contribution was a whole range of decorative detail such as lancet arches, spires and carved parapets. It was all part of the desire to prettify the medieval past and lend its structures a richer character than they had originally possessed. The aim of these architects was not the preservation of authentic antiquity, but its reconstruction and adornment in the gothic style.

Another example of the addition of romantic features to an original medieval building is Yegotov's reconstruction of the Poteshny Dvorets (Palace of Amusements), standing in the south-west part of the ensemble. He preserved the central section of the building and added rich appointments to the sides in a 'picturesque combination of pointed and semicircular arches . . . decorative parapets, pinnacles, domed towers, panelling and ribbed pilasters'.[79]

Other buildings in a medieval style were erected in the Kremlin and Kitai-gorod, while the walls and towers were being rebuilt. In the Kremlin, for example, during 1809–14, Alexei Bakarev constructed the Catherine Church of the Assumption Monastery to a design by Karl Rossi. Plans were drawn up, but never realised, for the reconstruction of the famous bell-tower of Ivan the Great. Ivan Mironovsky built the printing works for the Synod of the Orthodox Russian Church in 1810–12 on Nikolsky Street in Kitai-gorod (pls 252–5), and to the south of the area Bakarev remodelled the seventeenth-century church of Nikolai Mokrovo (Nicholas the Wet) in the gothic manner.[82]

All the work described above was commissioned by the state; but the community of

251 (right) Design for the Komendantsky Building, Kremlin, Moscow, 1790.

252 Ivan Mironovsky, design for the Synodal
printing works, Moscow, 1810.

the Old Believers, who had no official church of their own and whose relationship
with the authorities was rather strained, also showed their interest in the neo-gothic
approach. Having rejected the innovations introduced into the Orthodox church in the
mid-seventeenth century they were naturally drawn to more ancient styles in architecture, painting, sacred books, religious objects, music and other fields. For many years
the Old Believers were forbidden to construct their own buildings in Moscow, but in
the first, liberal years of the reign of Alexander I they obtained permission to create the
entire ensemble of the Preobrazhensky (Transfiguration) Cemetery. In accordance with

253 Ivan Mironovsky, Synodal printing works, Moscow.

their beliefs they turned for inspiration to the traditional design of the Old Russian monastery.[83] They constructed a high brick wall, with faceted, hipped-roofed towers, to enclose two separate courtyards for men and women. A narrow passage between them led to a richly decorated chapel reminiscent of Bazhenov's neo-gothic work. Strangely enough, a medieval 'romanticism' influenced these buildings of a community which had attempted, for more than a century, to preserve its medieval outlook and way of life.

All these buildings demonstrated the tendency towards the Russian style which

254 Ivan Mironovsky, Synodal printing works, Moscow: detail of exterior decoration.

overtook Moscow neo-gothic at the end of the eighteenth and beginning of the nineteenth centuries. They were a far cry from the archaeologically authentic re-creations of Byzantine and Old Russian architecture that were to appear in the mid-nineteenth century. Even though the Moscow neo-gothic of the day was primarily a decorative cover thrown over buildings of classical and pre-classical design, neo-gothic buildings still played an important part in the formation of the historic city centre. The

255 Ivan Mironovsky, Synodal printing works, Moscow: detail.

ancient Kremlin and Kitai-gorod acquired a more 'romantic' appearance. Kazakov, Lvov and Yegotov wished to create a unique Muscovite world which would revive national historic values. In this they were largely successful, and their work set the pattern for the future development of Moscow architecture, which progressed from a European-influenced neo-gothic approach to one dominated by Russian medievalism.

Early Nineteenth-Century Neo-Gothic around St Petersburg

The picture in St Petersburg was rather different. Neo-gothic buildings in the capital itself, as in the surrounding provinces, betrayed the preference of the *beau-monde* and its architects for a European, and especially an English version of the style. This is well shown in Lvov's Priorat Castle[84] at Gatchina, built for Paul I, and in Andreyan Zakharov's neo-gothic designs for the romantic monastery of St Kharlampia on the same imperial estate, which is about forty-five kilometres south-west of St Petersburg.[85]

Architects themselves were conscious of the differences between the St Petersburg and Moscow neo-gothic schools. For example Karl Rossi, the creator of the famous classical ensembles of St Petersburg, worked in Old Russian forms when fulfilling commissions in Moscow. In 1815 he drew on motifs of European gothic in his projected bell-tower and cathedral for the Nilova *pustyn* (hermitage or monastery) by Lake Seliger, far to the north of Moscow on the borders of the Tver and Petersburg provinces.[86]

In the 1820s Russian neo-gothic once again came under English influence as a result, primarily, of the work of the Scottish architect Adam Menelaws. At Tsarskoye Selo Menelaws created a complete ensemble of gothic buildings in the Alexander Park.[87] The Chapelle (1825–8) (pl. 256) was intended to represent a ruined medieval temple.

256 (above left) Adam Menelaws, the Chapelle, Tsarskoye Selo.

257 (above right) Adam Menelaws, the Arsenal, Tsarskoye Selo.

A gothic arch connected two square towers; one was single-storeyed, the other, with buttresses at the corners, rose to a height of three floors. A narrow staircase led to an open terrace with internal access to a gothic-vaulted chapel. Near the Chapelle Menelaws built a kind of fortress. The eighteenth-century rampart and fosse which had surrounded this part of the park (reserved for hunting) were retained but transformed into the walls of the 'knightly castle', as the architect himself dubbed it. By the walls he placed ruined turreted gates and, at the sides, structures with arched windows and battlements above. A five-storeyed tower at the centre was painted white and hence named the White Tower.

Between 1818 and 1822 Menelaws built a 'farm' at the boundary of the park. It consisted of a two-storeyed house, two low buildings joined by the principal stone wall, and a large cow-shed in the shape of a cross. All were in the style of an English castle of the late Middle Ages. They were of red brick with numerous octagonal turrets and a toothed parapet. Menelaws's other neo-gothic buildings include a llama pavilion (1820–22), the Pensionerskiye Stables (1827–29) and the Arsenal (pl. 257), completed in 1834 after his death.

The total effect of all these buildings lent the Alexander Park a 'knightly gothic' atmosphere. Menelaws's version of neo-gothic returned to the origins of this trend in

England. In his work we find neither the mixture of classical elements, medieval architecture, oriental traditions and Old Russian motifs, nor the intricate weave of sources, models and moods, evident in the work of earlier architects. Menelaws's gothic work, standing at the frontier of classicism and nineteenth-century eclectic historicism, was a precursor of many future developments.

The pavilions of the Alexandria Park, laid out in the 1830s on the seashore by Peterhof, also belong to this group of neo-gothic works.[88] They include more buildings by Menelaws, as well as the well-known chapel commissioned by Nicholas I and designed by Karl Friederick Schinkel (pl. 258).

The development of Russian neo-gothic in the classical period came to a climax in one of the most splendid ensembles of southern Russia, Count Vorontsov's palace at Alupka on the Crimean coast, built in 1832 by Edward Blore,[89] whose work Vorontsov had seen during his period as Ambassador in England. One of its many admirers wrote: 'I simply must mention the mansion being built here by Count Vorontsov . . . Imagine an ancient gothic abbey like those which may still be seen in parts of England. It is entirely of stone and faced with greenstone.'[90]

The palace was sited on a rocky shore high above the sea, with hills in the background. Passing through the main gates, each flanked by a tower, the visitor proceeded via a long, narrow and convoluted path leading between high 'gothic' walls to a courtyard and thence to the main body of the palace. He was greeted by a vista of many towers, Tudor windows, battlements and strange domes. Beyond, sloping upwards stretched a luxuriant romantic garden with dark winding alleys, overgrown southern trees, cairns, waterfalls, streams and superb views of the hills. The effect was as of a stage backdrop placed at the far end of the park. The opposite façade, by no means gothic, was intended to evoke the residences of Eastern potentates, and the terraced park it overlooked recalled the Alhambra gardens. Thus one side of the palace displayed an authentic British medieval architecture, while the other struck a no less convincingly Moorish note.

This deliberate transformation of authentic architectural styles signalled the onset of the new century and a new era. The Enlightenment had finally made way for romanticism. Classicism, yielding to eclecticism, ceased to dominate architecture as it had in the early days of neo-gothic and chinoiserie; and medievalism, no longer obliged to continue its struggle with the antique ideal, lost its dramatic quality. Gothic and antique were now on an equal footing, a development that was only confirmed by Russian architecture in the 1830s. The Anglo-Russian architectural relationship changed in a way that also affected neo-gothic. Whereas in the eighteenth (and the first quarter of the nineteenth) century the 'medieval' style had been very much a British affair, it acquired a more international character when such distinguished men as Schinkel and Viollet-le-Duc took their places next to Blore and also later Sir Charles Barry, whose Houses of Parliament were influential in court circles.[91] For this reason Russian neo-gothic during the classical period, one of the most significant episodes in the Anglo-Russian architectural story, is of particular relevance here. As indicated, however, it would be wrong to see the influence of gothic architecture in Russia as purely a symptom of international interests. Far more fundamental to its appeal was its essential congruence with the long-standing artistic traditions of the Russian town and the Russian estate, both dominated by fifteenth-, sixteenth- and seventeenth-century architecture. Whether consciously or not, Russians of the late eighteenth and early nineteenth centuries understood that neo-gothic could help to preserve the emotional integrity of these indigenous traditions against what to many was the more threatening international import, of classicism. Here too, though, there were British hands at work, as talents among Charles Cameron's craftsmen blossomed into very large-scale work.

258 Karl Friedrich Schinkel, the gothic chapel in Alexandria Park, near Peterhof.

Chapter Six

ADAM MENELAWS
AND WILLIAM HASTIE

IN 1779, WITH TSARITSYNO STILL actively under construction and her interest in gothic still thoroughly alive, Catherine the Great welcomed to St Petersburg Charles Cameron, the architect who would create some of her favourite buildings. Five years later, in 1784, his first designs for her were accepted and building work was begun. On 8 June that year the British ambassador in St Petersburg, Alleyne FitzHerbert, sent an encoded message to the Foreign Office in London, which read:

> I am sorry to inform Your Lordship that there arrived lately on board of some ships from Leith a considerable number of stone masons, brick layers and other artificers of the same class all from Edinburgh and its neighbourhood, who have been sent for by Mr Cameron, a British architect in the service of the empress, in order to complete some extensive building which he is now employed upon at Tsarskoye Selo. Many have likewise brought their wives and families as I am assured of no fewer than 140 persons. They are mostly engaged twelve months and it is to be hoped that when this term shall be expired they will return to their country; however I need not point out to Your Lordship the various ill consequences which must result even from the temporary loss of so many useful subjects [of the British crown] nor how necessary it is to take every possible precaution in order to prevent such emigration in future.[1]

The British ambassador plainly attached great importance to this event although, of course, for reasons very different from those that concern us here. In any case, there is no doubt that the arrival of the Scottish craftsmen in St Petersburg was to have a significance in the history of architectural connections between Britain and Russia that extended far beyond their roles as craftsmen.

Cameron's announcement, published in January 1784 in the name of 'the empress of all the Russias', had invited specialists in various forms of construction to take up employment. It was answered by seventy-three craftsmen, and in discussing Cameron's own work we have seen something of how they and their families, making up FitzHerbert's contingent of '140 people', were received. Documents in Russian archives record that the senior members of the group were the master stonemasons Henry Gordon and Andrew Dick; the master bricklayers John Browne and Isaac Mullender; the master smith James Wilson; the master masons John Cochrane and Adam Menelaws, and the master plasterers Andrew Watson, John Gray and John Hamilton.[2] From the British side, research by A.G. Cross has revealed more detail of the rest of the group accompanying them, showing it to have comprised twenty-seven stonemasons, fifteen bricklayers, fifteen plasterers and five blacksmiths, whom he lists by name.[3] Noteworthy among the junior stonemasons was the 26-year-old David Cunningham, who became Cameron's assistant. Of the whole group, those who would most outstandingly contribute to Russian architecture, in its broadest sense, were the

259   Adam Menelaws, Baturin Palace.

master mason Adam Menelaws, aged 35 on arrival, and the 29-year old junior stonemason William Hastie.

On arrival these craftsmen worked at Tsarskoye Selo, and it was through their efforts that the Cameron Gallery, the Chinese Village and the church of St Sophia in the township of Sofiya were built. The existence of an entire British colony in Sofiya was something of a phenomenon in its time: the street on which the Scottish craftsmen lived was called Angliiskaya Linaya, literally the English Row and, as we noted earlier, Cameron built sixteen houses for his fellow countrymen there.

It would be difficult to paint a rosy picture of the life of this community, for documents show that it was far from easy. On one hand, the British craftsmen frequently had to defend their rights against imperial officials; on the other, conflicts arose with Cameron himself, not noted for his easy-going nature. As a result, most of the Scottish craftsmen did indeed return home, though not as quickly as FitzHerbert had hoped, in the early 1790s.

A small number of them, however, were to spend much of their lives in Russia, and the influence they exerted on Russian architecture is another important dimension of the British contribution. The group that stayed comprised the following: of stone-masons there were John Browne, David Cunningham, David Irvine, Charles Stewart, James and John McVay and Isaac Little; of plasterers there were John Macleod, William and George Lyon, Robert Muir, Shaw Alexander and John Marshall, and of smiths the father and son James and Alexander Wilson.[4] Adam Menelaws and William Hastie, as we have noted, would rise from craftsmen's roles to become notable architects, Menelaws as designer of a number of architecturally and culturally interesting contributions to the imperial estates of Tsarskoye Selo and Peterhof, and Hastie as the most important town planner of early nineteenth-century Russia.

Since these two men had built little before their arrival in Russia they do not feature significantly in foreign architectural literature. At the same time, their work has not hitherto been seriously researched in Russia. In the present account therefore I hope to rectify that omission, following a study of archival material in Russian collections.

Adam Menelaws

Adam Menelaws was the older and more experienced of the two Scots: at thirty-five he was several years older than Hastie (Cross dates his birth to 1748 or 1749),[5] and while Hastie had probably never been more than a junior craftsman, Menelaws had undoubtedly been involved in the construction of some buildings in Scotland, although it has not been possible to identify them. As a result of his experience, Menelaws was not kept at Tsarskoye Selo like the rest, but was almost immediately sent south to the town of Mogilev,[6] between Minsk and Smolensk, to build the cathedral of St Joseph that had been designed by Nikolai Lvov.[7]

This was a highly prestigious and responsible task, for the cathedral was to honour the meeting that had taken place on 30 May 1780 between Catherine the Great and the Holy Roman Emperor, Joseph II. Their negotiations ensured co-operation between Russia and Austria in war with the Turks. The ideological basis for Catherine's eastern policy was the so-called Greek Plan, which we have already encountered in discussing the park at Tsarskoye Selo and the church at Sofiya. A Greek Orthodox empire was to be created, a revival of Byzantium, with the Grand Duke Konstantin Pavlovich at its head. Various buildings were constructed to mark political initiatives in this plan, and those at Tsarskoye Selo and Mogilev were among them. Lvov's design for St Joseph's was reminiscent of Cameron's church of St Sophia. It was square in plan, with a Doric portico and a similar inner dome, again in imitation of

Hagia Sophia in Constantinople. The dedication of the cathedral to the Emperor Joseph's patron saint was an obvious piece of diplomacy.

Thus Lvov entrusted the construction of this ideologically important cathedral to Menelaws, who had doubtless been recommended by his good friend and patron Count Alexander Bezborodko, at that time personal secretary to Catherine the Great. Interestingly, Lvov had been quite explicit that he wanted a British builder to carry out his design: 'Let the British stonemasons teach ours how to build solid, clear and upright buildings,' he said.[8] The work in Mogilev took a very long time, and in 1790 Menelaws travelled to St Petersburg to negotiate a contract for a further term.[9] In 1792 he married Elizabeth Cave in St Petersburg, with Lvov and A. Olenin, the future president of the Academy of the Arts, as his witnesses.[10] He was often away from the job for long periods, but he oversaw the cathedral's construction right through to its completion in 1798.[11]

One of Menelaws's distractions was another job for Lvov, who in 1785 invited him to build the cathedral of St Boris and St Gleb in Torzhok, nearly 1,000 kilometers from Mogilev. Menelaws agreed, although his conditions of work can hardly have been convenient. Lvov is recorded as saying that, 'It is difficult to find anyone less expensive than he [i.e. Menelaws] is at present; his competence and diligence . . . are well known'.[12] This cathedral was finished in 1796, two years before the one in Mogilev.

Thus, throughout Catherine's reign Menelaws was restricted to executing other people's ideas, although he was awarded the title of architect.[13] Admittedly, his subordinate position could be compensated for by the remarkable people with whom he worked. Lvov was, after all, one of the most cultured people in Russia. An architect, engineer, poet and musician, he wrote books on a multitude of subjects ranging from ventilation to a description of Moscow antiquities, from the art of rammed earth construction and Russian songs to 'the science of love' expounded in verse. He was related to and friendly with the great writers Derzhavin and Kapnist, and was close to the most intelligent political minds, such as Bezborodko, who became Chancellor of the Russian Empire at the end of the eighteenth century. Lvov commissioned the great Russian artist Vladimir Borovikovsky to paint the iconostasis in the cathedrals which Menelaws built, and in 1793 in Mogilev Borovikovsky painted a portrait of Menelaws himself.[14]

A very great deal changed in Russia with the death of Catherine the Great in November 1796 and the accession of Paul Petrovich to the throne as Paul I. Menelaws's life also changed. In December 1796 he was appointed to work on the commission that was making arrangements for the new tsar's coronation,[15] for which his main contribution was to build the platforms and bases for the fireworks. After these magnificent celebrations he probably returned to Mogilev, but soon, at the beginning of 1798 and with that job nearly complete, he was summoned to St Petersburg to become involved in the creation of the School of Practical Agriculture,[16] whose formation we have already encountered in connection with Charles Cameron. Menelaws was thus linked with one of the most interesting undertakings in the history of Anglo-Russian architectural contacts.

The School of Practical Agriculture

The school was founded on the initiative of Andrei Samborsky, who had served for a long time as the priest of the church in the Russian embassy in London, and then became the superior priest in the church of St Sophia in Sofiya, and at the same time religious teacher of Paul's son the Grand Duke Alexander Pavlovich. Samborsky had become very interested in English ideas on agriculture, and in London had had close links with the Society for Encouragement of the Arts, Industry and Trade, which also concerned itself with agricultural innovations. He tried to introduce enlightened agriculture to Russia,[17] and in 1780 was given land between Tsarskoye Selo and Pavlovsk, near Cameron's town of Sofiya, to create a model farm as part of that whole panorama of the ideal life which was to be created within sight of the favourite imperial residence.

In addition to the model town of Sofiya, as we have seen, it was decided to construct a model rural area. One purpose for this envisaged by Catherine was as a gigantic 'visual aid' for the education of her grandsons, primarily the Grand Duke Alexander Pavlovich,[18] and it was no accident that the land allocated to Samborsky's venture adjoined the grounds of Alexander's *dacha* (pl. 260), which Catherine had had built by Lvov as a place of education for the future Tsars.[19] Dzhunkovsky wrote a poem in praise of Alexander's *dacha*,[20] and among the illustrations to it is a picture of Samborsky, ploughing the field himself, with his Order of St Vladimir hung over a tree. There is no doubt that the architecture and landscape were intended to be morally improving. In another of her ventures in didactic and symbolic landscape planning, Catherine had the *dacha*'s park laid out to represent the journey of Prince Khlor, in a story written by Catherine herself, through ordeals and temptations to virtue 'on that high hill where the rose without thorns blooms, where virtue blossoms, it captivates my mind and spirit'.[21] A church of 'the Rose without thorns' was depicted on the engraved plan of the School of Practical Agriculture.[22]

For some reason, in contrast to the many undertakings of his mother's that Paul abolished or even destroyed, he not only supported the School of Practical Agriculture but, in 1797–8, turned it into an important state institution, with Samborsky in charge.[23] It was to be a centre for the dissemination of English ideas and methods of land cultivation and farm management. Much attention was devoted to rural architecture, and when Lvov was appointed as head of this section he engaged Menelaws to work with him. Together they designed plans for a model farmyard, model water- and windmills, a smithy, stables, a granary, a dairy and other rural essentials, and began construction of the model buildings. Despite the fact that the Halfpennys' designs had really been intended for park pavilions of slight or insignificant function, all this was done using aesthetic models from their well-known book on rural architecture.

The work was broken off unexpectedly when Samborsky was appointed one of the priests to the Grand Duchess Alexandra Pavlovna[24] and could no longer supervise the school. It seems that Lvov did not want to work with anyone else. He was a man of means as well as a practising architect, and he now built his own school[25] on his estate at Nikolskoye, and then another near Moscow. Lvov clearly persuaded Menelaws also to retire from the Tsarskoye Selo school under the pretext of illness, and then sought by all available means to draw him back into his own employment, eventually succeeding.[26] At Lvov's school Menelaws was concerned with 'teaching students, and the construction of a steam engine'.[27] In 1800 he was sent to England to buy components for this steam engine and all kinds of other machinery.[28] This visit provides evidence for the addition of a significant hypothesis to the established biography of Menelaws.

Projects for Distinguished Patrons

It has long been known that in the early years of the nineteenth century Menelaws began to carry out private commissions for one of Russia's most eminent families, the Razumovskys. Ivan Fomin, for example, featured some of this work in his famous 'Historical Exhibition of Architecture' in 1911.[29] The earliest project for this family

260 The Alexandrov *dacha*, created for Grand Duke Alexander Pavlovich by Nikolai Lvov.

attributed to Menelaws is the vast Gorenki country mansion and landscaped park outside Moscow, where construction of the great house is dated to the 1780s and 1790s.[30] The vast classical porticoed block with long, colonnaded wings is volumetrically simple and stylistically conventional, unlike Menelaws's later independent work, and this may be something of a transitional work, predominantly by Lvov, where Menelaws worked first as executant before taking over the principal role as completion approached.

By the 1820s the Gorenki park was suffiently established to have attracted some attention abroad. The English garden specialist John Claudius Loudon is thought to have visited Russia in about 1814, and in 1827 he described Gorenki with some enthusiasm to a British and international readership in his *Encyclopaedia of Gardening*. He described the estate as

> remarkable for its botanical richness and its huge quantity of grass. The grounds are very extensive, but the surface is level, and the soil is a dry sand. A natural wood consisting of silver birch and wild cherry encloses the park and harmonises with the artificially created views. The house, which was built by an English architect, is highly elegant, and the adjacent pavilions, grottoes and lawn decorated [with flowers] from a magnificent and gay spectacle which is not surpassed in Russia.[31]

The Razumovskys had come from relatively humble stock and owed their family position to one Alexei Razumovsky, whose climb to status and the highest ranks in the empire were due to his handsome face, his magnificent voice and his beautiful nature. When still a boy he had been sent to St Petersburg as a court chorister, and the Grand Duchess Elizabeth Petrovna, daughter of Peter the Great, fell in love with him. After some nasty politicking, Elizabeth eventually ascended the throne as empress in 1741 and Alexei Razumovsky became her favourite. Whether or not she married him secretly, the Razumovsky family spent the twenty years of Elizabeth's reign as the family closest of all to the throne. In the process, they acquired vast lands and effective rulership of the Ukraine, when Alexei's brother Kirill was made *hetman* of the Ukraine by Elizabeth. Foremerly a real local power base, this became an honorary position, but its traditional seat was the town of Baturin. In the 1750s the Razumovskys decided to build a palace on the edge of the town, but it was not until in 1803 that anything was constructed.

From the architectural historian Fedor Gornostaev in 1914 we have a description of the resulting building as it was a century later:

> The graceful, half-ruined forms of the palace give an impression of strict classicism. Feasting your eyes on their inimitable beauty, you positively forget that you are in Russia, that this building is a hundred years old, and you involuntarily view these ruins as a genuine monument of ancient antiquity in Italy, remote and beautiful . . . Through the monumental colonnade you take in the expanse and light of the distant undulating prospects of the Seym, drenched with sunlight. The cloudy-silver shroud of the river, flowing away into the distance, caresses the gaze gently.[32]

Even today, in an even more ruined state, the Baturin Palace evokes similar feelings of repose amid the antique in a superb landscape (pls 259, 261–3). The site where the estate was built is flat, steppe land. Not a hillock or slope is visible anywhere as the River Seym flows between low banks across a broad plain. The palace may have been surrounded by a park, but there are few traces of it now. The overgrown drive, covered with wild grass, leads directly to the palace.

The three-storeyed building presents the visitor with an unusual façade. The ground floor is enclosed by a simple Tuscan colonnade, standing somewhat forward. A central

261 Adam Menelaws, Baturin Palace.

262 A. Belogrud, reconstruction of Baturin Palace:
side elevation.

projection in the middle floor has a small pediment, by conventional standards somewhat out of proportion to the rest of the building, and the composition is completed,
again most unexpectedly, by a large, graduated attic storey. The opposite front, which
faces on to the river, is decorated with a magnificent Ionic colonnade. The plan is
compact and not particularly harmonious, a fact generally attributed to the client's over
involvement in it.

In its time this palace has been attributed to most of the leading architects of the
period. It has been suggested that Antonio Rinaldi was sent for from Italy specially for
the purpose.[33] Giacomo Quarenghi[34] has been suggested, and likewise Nikolai Lvov,
who did in fact visit Baturin.[35] The building has been attributed to Charles Cameron
on the basis of rumours about some drawings he did for the Razumovskys which have
disappeared completely.[36] But Hetman Razumovsky himself wrote of the designs
prepared in Rinaldi's time when the palace was first mooted, that is under Elizabeth in

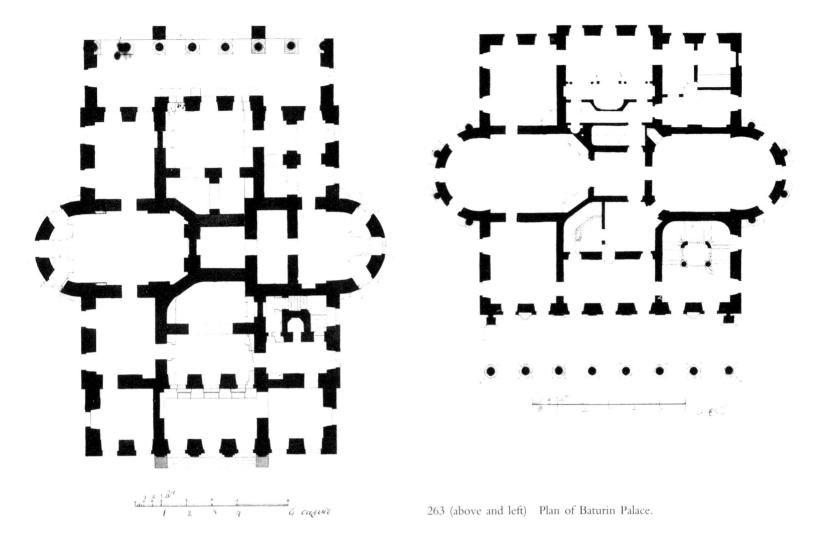

263 (above and left)   Plan of Baturin Palace.

the 1750s, that they would 'remain unrealised' because inadequate money was available from the Treasury,[37] and he was quite frank in admitting that he simply 'did not like' Lvov.[38] The only evidence in favour of Quarenghi is that he built a large number of buildings in southern Russia.

The family archives do, however, contain a letter from Count Alexei Razumovsky that seems to provide the clue. He speaks of Lvov coming to Baturin on 12 March 1800, 'in the absence of the architect, who has gone home to England'.[39] So who was this 'Englishman'?

It is known that Cameron made a trip to England in 1791, when he was working at Tsarskoye Selo,[40] but there is no evidence that he made any other journeys home. Admittedly, after his discharge in 1797 he threatened that he would have to 'earn his living in other countries, where . . . his name was not unknown',[41] but he does not appear to have gone. By 1800 he was re-employed and working in St Petersburg.[42]

As we have seen, however, Menelaws did go home in 1800, to buy components of the steam engine for Lvov's agricultural school. In the circumstances it would be entirely natural for his old friend and colleague to keep an eye on the palace construction job he had in hand at Baturin. This suggests that Menelaws himself may have been the architect of this famous palace.

Menelaws's work must have pleased the Razumovskys, for they commissioned him to build houses and churches on their Ukrainian estates – in Yagotin during 1820–6 and in nearby Teplovka in 1805.[43] Indeed it is possible that it was in order to work on these buildings that Menelaws resigned from state service in 1804.[44]

231

During 1801–3 he built the Razumovskys a vast house on the Gorokhovoy Field in eastern Moscow, which still survives, though in a poor state (pls 264, 265).[45] More expansive than Baturin, with long colonnades curving out from each side of the central block, it shares with Baturin a distinctly unconventional originality. Most notable in this respect is the treatment of the central features of its main front. The central three-storey building is punctuated by semi-circular bays and crowned with a monumental pediment. At each side of the bays are two pairs of Ionic columns on very high pedestals. In the middle of this the colonnade recedes behind a bay and behind it a

264 and 265 Nikolai Lvov and Adam Menelaws, Razumovsky Palace, Moscow.

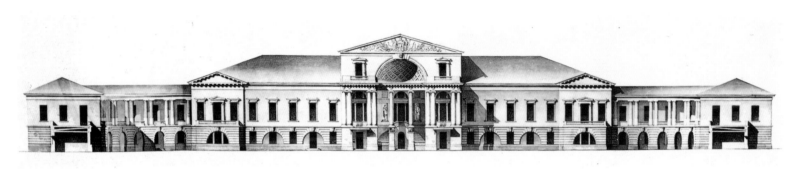

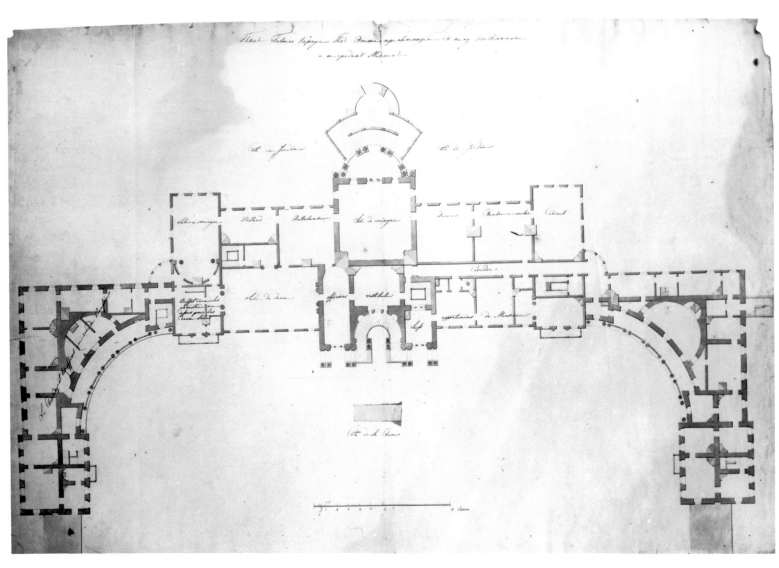

232

266 Adam Menelaws, Egyptian Gate, Tsarskoye Selo, 1820s.

double staircase can be seen, rising on both sides to the first floor. This unusually complex spatial feature creates a rich sequence of architectural events that is characteristic of Menelaws. On the other hand it is very different from the closely integrated, monumental manner of Lvov, to whom the design is sometimes attributed on the grounds that Menelaws had frequently executed projects for him in earlier years.[46]

The years 1806–17 remain something of a mystery in Menelaws's life. The only work we have attributed to him during this period is an orangery and a theatre on the estate of the princes Golitsyn called Pekhra–Yakovlevskoye in the Moscow region, not far from the Razumovskys' Gorenki. This is conventionally dated 1810,[47] but as with so much work of this period nothing conclusive remains in archival or documentary sources to confirm it. Apart from this small work, very little is known about Menelaws's activity in Russia during this period, and it has been suggested that he may have returned to Britain for much of it.[48]

In 1818 a new, very significant period in Menelaws's career began, when he effectively took Cameron's place as personal architect for new developments at the imperial court. He was appointed to the tsar's chancery and designed buildings for Tsarskoye Selo and Peterhof (pl. 266). In Tsarskoye Selo he created the landscaped part of Alexander Park, and the large group of medieval-style buildings within it which we have already examined in the discussion of emergent Russian neo-gothic. Suffice it to emphasise here that these buildings founded a whole stylistic trend in Russian romantic architecture, and were imitated on many country estates.

Later, in 1822, Menelaws drew up a plan for altering yet another well-known estate in the Moscow area, that of Sukhanovo, which belonged to the princes Volkonsky.[49] All this work made his reputation not only as an architect, but also as a landscape gardener. He received commissions from the court to plan the parks for the Mikhailovsky Castle in St Petersburg (pl. 267)[50] and for the Petrovsky Castle in Moscow.[51]

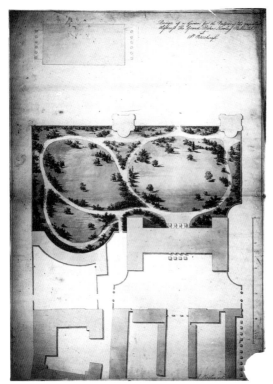

267 Adam Menelaws, project for the garden of the Mikhailovsky Castle, St Petersburg.

In 1825, not long before the November journey to southern Russia on which he died, Tsar Alexander I gave his brother and secret heir, the Grand Duke Nicholas, the land lying idle between the Peterhof and Strelnya estates along the Gulf of Finland. After his accession to the throne, when threats to his position had been quietened by defeat of the Decombrist uprising against him, the new Tsar Nicholas I had a country residence built here. It was to be a palace in the 'rustic style', with a huge park, and would be called Alexandria in honour of his wife, the new empress. All work was entrusted to Menelaws, whose earlier court work had established him as Nicholas's favourite architect.[52]

The park, which ran along the sea shore, was divided naturally into two terraces. The lower terrace ended in the sandy beach, while the upper continued the ridge of hills which ran along the coast. Seven main avenues wound through the park. The three running across it went down to the sea, while the other four, which were longer, ran parallel to it. The view changed at each turn, so that a bright, broad clearing with powerful free-standing oak trees would give way to a dark thicket. Then there might be a dark wooded slope, it would brighten, and after a turn to the right the visitor would see a beautifully sculpted forest edge flooded in sunshine. With great skill and success Menelaws created a truly romantic landscape (pl. 270).

At the boundary of the park, far from Peterhof Palace and the conspicuous glamour of its Versailles-inspired axes and its gilded fountains, Menelaws placed a new palace that was small, comfortable and completely informal. The building was to resemble an English cottage, but here there was none of the 'spirit of chivalry' which had characterised Menelaws's buildings at Tsarskoye Selo. In Alexandria he was playing a different game. The tsar, when he crossed the boundary of the park, wanted to feel himself a private, albeit very sensitive, individual; here, he said, he felt himself to be 'a guest of the mistress of Peterhof'.

This relatively small palace was called the Kottedzh, the Cottage (pls 268, 269). If the evocation elsewhere in 'English'-style work was with the gothic, here it was closer (if anything) to the vernacular medieval than to the ecclesiastical. The building cannot be said to be in any particular style: it is picturesque and flowing, combining features

268 Adam Menelaws, the Cottage Palace, Peterhof.

234

269 Adam Menelaws, the Cottage Palace, Peterhof: detail.

of an Italian villa with echoes of the neo-gothic in a building that is above all domestic: an overgrown suburban villa. The tower is like a graceful belvedere, while the arched intertwinings of medieval patterns on the terraces and cornices are reminiscent of thickets or a winding vine. The lightness and grace of all the details and the house as a whole are emphasised throughout, as it looks northwards to the sea and south from its main elevation over sunny fields. The highly picturesque exterior results, in a typically English-vernacular manner, from the functional amenities of covered terraces, loggias and bow windows which enhance its spatial pleasures and its seaside air.

Externally there is neo-gothic decoration but no trace of gothic gloom. Inside, however, the academic gothic is more obvious. The staircase, the walls, the ceilings, the carving, the furniture, all are exceptionally heavily adorned, almost saturated with decoration. The decor of Menelaws's original project has been preserved. Complete sets of neo-gothic furniture to his designs were specially made by the Gambs furniture factory in St Petersburg. The multitude of objects, cupboards, screens, bookcases, mirrors with lancet doors and frames, clocks in the shape of old French cathedrals, increase the impression that the building is filled to overflowing with decoration in a manner that could itself be more closely related to certain English tastes than to high architecture.

All this creates a world with its own special language – official, yet a domesticated, homely romanticism. As in much of Cameron's work, particularly in installing the English Palladian country house in Russia at Pavlovsk, the cultural ambience here and its associated values were as significant a contribution as any imported architectural language. It was no accident that the founder and leading representative of early romanticism in Russian literature, Vasily Zhukovsky, lived here so congenially during his years as tutor to Nicholas's son, the future Tsar Alexander II. For the man whose main genre was the intimate, meditative elegy, who had earlier won his reputation for translations of Goethe and Schiller but now, from the 1820s, turned increasingly to rendering in Russian the longer poetic works of Byron and Scott, the Kottedzh was a schoolroom that must have reinforced his influence on the young imperial mind.

In 1828 Menelaws proposed for Alexandria 'a farm of ten cows with all necessary services', a two-storey complex of brick walls with Perpendicular-gothic stone window embrasures, all clad in a cosy pitched roof. In 1830 it was completed and started functioning, to be joined later by other agricultural facilities.

Menelaws had made a genuine cultural reincarnation in the visible forms of objects, architecture and the park, that held its own very satisfactorily even with the beautiful chapel-pavilion, the Chapel of Alexander Nevsky, commissioned in 1829 by the tsar from the great German architect Karl Friederick Schinkel. By February 1830 Schinkel had supplied designs, which were approved, for a classic piece of European neo-gothic architecture, rich in stained glass and carving. Menelaws acted as executive architect to Schinkel's project from the start of construction in early 1831 until his death in November the same year.[53]

270   Alley in the Alexandria Park.

Thus Menelaws's career in Russia took him from the post of master stonemason to collaboration with perhaps the greatest European architect of the 1830s, in a series of projects that were always innovative, sometimes specifically the vehicles for an importation of English culture and ideas. In about 1830 or 1831, shortly before his death, he was commissioned to reconstruct a large house on Moscow's main thoroughfare towards St Petersburg, the Tverskaya, as Moscow's so-called 'English Club'.[54] The name derived more from the concept of a gentleman's club than from any specific associations. As a Scottish master mason, Adam Menelaws would not have been an expert on English gentleman's clubs, but the coincidence was appropriate.

William Hastie

William Hastie was born in about 1755. We know nothing of his life in Edinburgh, but at 29-years-old he was in the middle age group of those respondents to Charles Cameron's advertisement who arrived in Russia in 1784. While there is no documentation to illuminate his personality, the evidence of his career indicates a highly intelligent young man, very capable of learning, who repeatedly used his initiative to expand his professional opportunities. The undoubted similarity between Hastie's early work and Cameron's designs suggests that Hastie worked closely with Cameron and may even have been one of his design assistants. For this there is also the indirect evidence that he was taken into Russian state service as an architect's assistant in the imperial chancery in 1792,[55] at precisely the time when Cameron came back into favour with the Empress Catherine and was commissioned to build the Temple of Memory at Tsarskoye Selo.

Hastie's initative manifested itself soon after his entry into imperial service when he compiled an album of his designs and in the summer of 1794 presented it to Catherine. He had drawn a series of elevations for houses and park pavilions, and two neo-gothic country houses[56] that showed the influence of the Adam brothers' work in the medieval style. The empress liked the designs, and on 4 September 1794 wrote to her confidante, Baron Grimm, that Hastie was 'an extremely worthy person, he makes delightful things', and that 'I have taken him on in my service'.[57] Hastie was henceforth called a Master of Architecture. However, he had to be given an architectural rank, a requirement in Russia at that time. He also had to take an examination. Hastie completed the required design for two plans, an elevation and a section of a country house in the classical manner, and the notes of Catherine's chancery secretary Vasily Popov indicate that an examination did indeed take place after the album had been presented.[58]

Country Houses and Public Buildings

In the design for the country house Hastie showed his debt to Cameron, as the scheme clearly imitated the latter's design for Pavlovsk Palace. There is the same square three-storey main block in the centre, with a similar Corinthian portico with paired columns supported by a pedestal covered in rustic stonework and pierced by two open arches; galleries very reminiscent of Pavlovsk were to link the central block to the wings. The designs differ in that Hastie's building does not have Cameron's magnificent dome, the windows at the sides of the portico are disproportionately large, and the wings have an order of their own. Certainly Hastie's design is not enhanced by these differences. The ineffable charm of his teacher's work and the clarity of his spatial design are lost here. The elevation lacks a central focus and the order used in the wings diminishes the significance of the main colonnade. It is very interesting, however, that Hastie placed identical courtyards with two wings each on either side of the palace (four wings were planned altogether). This is not a feature of Pavlovsk, but the same approach can be seen in James Paine's design for Kedleston Hall.[59] It is important to note that Hastie's work, although derivative, was undoubtedly professional. The design also showed that his work fell unequivocally within the English tradition, despite the fact that he had left Britain at a relatively young age.

There is little doubt that Catherine showed the drawings Hastie had made to her latest favourite, Prince Platon Zubov. This was to prove crucial to Hastie's subsequent career. Zubov was almost the only person in Russia who could commission an architect serving in the imperial inner circle for any other task. A whole series of eminent social figures who might have commissioned Cameron in such a way had failed to do so. In this case, however, on 5 July 1795, Zubov having been appointed on Potemkin's death the Governor of Yekaterinoslav and Tavrida, hence effectively Governor of South Russian, won the appointment of Hastie as architect for the provinces under his authority.

Six months earlier, in January 1795, Hastie had married a Scotswoman called Margaret Bruce in St Petersburg.[60] Even after his appointment to work for Zubov, it may have been nearly two years before he actually travelled to these southern provinces to work, as Zubov himself certainly remained in the capital. Hastie may have stayed there with him right through to Catherine the Great's death in November 1796, when the position of Zubov and his retainers naturally changed greatly. Such a situation is indirectly confirmed by the fact that the Hastie designs relating to Zubov's southern provinces date from after Catherine's death. In 1798 Hastie completed another album, this time containing drawings of Crimean sites such as the medieval fortresses of Feodosiya and Kerchi, and views of various towns in that area. It was at this time that he took measurements of the palace of the Crimean khans at Bakhchisaray.[61] These drawings puzzled early twentieth-century researchers such as Lukomsky, who concluded that Hastie had rebuilt the khans' palace, and that Cameron had also been involved.[62] In fact Hastie had merely made measured drawings of the main halls of the ancient khans' residence, as he did of other historic monuments.

In the late 1790s Hastie designed a building for the Treasury and also for the prison in Yekaterinoslav.[63] His design for the hospital in Simferopol dates from the same time.[64] All these designs are significant for showing how Hastie developed an individual style. His interest in large forms, on the civic scale, is obvious, as is his aim to create a composition as clear, precisely geometrical and centred as possible. His hospital has a closed inward-looking form with an unbroken façade turned towards the outer space, and a regularly laid-out garden inside the complex. Already we start to see here the essential style of the future Hastie as town planner.

271 William Hastie, project for a bridge.

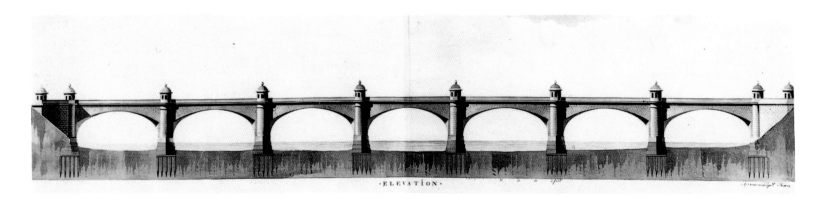

·ELEVATION·

On 3 July 1799 Hastie was discharged from his post under Zubov as provincial architect in Yekaterinoslav.[65] For about two years he was without work, until he entered employment again, probably with the help of James Wilson, an old acquaintance from his period working with Cameron. For a long time Wilson was master smith at Tsarskoye Selo, and at the beginning of the nineteenth century he and his son Alexander became involved in the construction of cast-iron factory buildings in Kolpino, near St Petersburg.[66] The Wilsons had worked very closely with the industrialist Charles Gascoigne, the initiator of this enterprise, who had come to Russia from Britain in 1786. By 1801 Gascoigne already had 'general's rank' in the strict Russian social hierarchy and was a full Russian State Counsellor.[67] Hastie joined the Wilsons to work under him. The nature of his work now changed completely yet again: having begun by designing park pavilions and country houses, and then having spent time on public buildings for the southern provinces, he was now to concern himself with engineering problems.

Hastie worked on the construction of the Kolpino factories for three years, and his collaboration with Gascoigne gave him a whole new education in the technology of cast-iron construction. It is likely that it was Gascoigne who drew Hastie's attention to the designs for metal bridges by the British engineer R. Fulton.[68] Hastie made a proposal for building similar constructions in St Petersburg; his project was approved by Count Rumyantsev, Director of the Imperial Department of Water Transport, and he was taken on in this department.[69] In 1805 he built a model of a bridge in the form of an arch made from separate metal sections bolted together and supported by stone piers.[70] It was tested successfully,[71] and in March 1806 construction began on the first such bridge in St Petersburg, the Politseisky (Police) Bridge, to Hastie's design. The bridge was situated at a crucial place, where Nevsky Prospekt, the main street of the capital, crossed the Moyka river. The decision to build the first such bridge in the very heart of the city close to the imperial palace was indicative of the confidence placed in Hastie, and the prestige he derived from it was certainly justified by its technical novelty in Russia at that time. On 14 November 1806 the bridge was ceremonially opened.[72]

From this good beginning Hastie's professional ascent was rapid. In 1807 he again made use of an approach that had more than once helped him in his career previously. Showing a fine entrepreneurial initiative that today would be called touting for work, he compiled two carefully mounted albums to present to the tsar, who since 1801 had been Alexander I. One of the albums contained drawings of well-known British and French bridges[73] and was the result of painstaking research in large numbers of specialist publications. The other contained Hastie's own designs for the replacement of all the existing bridges over the Moyka with new designs in cast-iron. As a result, during the years 1807–18 Hastie built the Krasny, Siny, Zhelty and Potseluyev (literally Red, Blue, Yellow and Kissing) bridges over the Moyka, to his own designs, as well as the Alexandrov bridge over the Vvedensky canal and another over the outlying Obvodny canal. When Napoleon invaded Russia in 1812 plans for constructing a further four bridges were aborted, and after the victory new designs for these structures were made by the engineer E. Adam.[74]

Hastie was by then engaged in larger work on town planning that also resulted from the Napoleonic episode, as we shall see later. But he continued to put forward his proposals for various other St Petersburg bridges, and in 1819 those known as Teatralny and Koniushenny (Theatre and Stables) were completed.[75] Although by then deeply involved in the imperial town planning programme, it was specifically for this bridge work, as the imperial citation clearly states, that Hastie was awarded a life pension from state funds in 1817.[76] Major contributions at this level by Russian citizens would have been rewarded at that time by the gift of a number of peasants and the income of their equivalent in land, this being before the emancipation of the peasantry from serfdom in 1861. A foreigner could not be given income in this way, but the princely annual stipend of 1,500 roubles awarded to Hastie by this imperial decree, or *ukaz*, was the financial equivalent of some twenty souls annually.

Quite apart from these financial rewards, it was to this work on bridge design that Hastie owed his dramatic advancement in state service. It took him into quite another sphere, where he would leave his mark on the technical and aesthetic quality not just of the capital, but of Russia's whole urban environment.

From Engineering to Town Planning

A further album of his bridge designs attracted the tsar's attention very particularly, and led to Hastie's being 'engaged for the construction of a new town in Tsarskoye Selo', probably in 1808 or 1809.[77] Although the proposed town was very small, the post of architect to it was one of the most prestigious for which an architect working in Russia could hope. For half a century, as we have seen, since the beginning of Catherine the Great's reign, Tsarskoye Selo had been a testing ground for new ideas in architecture. It was here, close to the favourite imperial residences, that models for the organisation of towns and for different types of houses, as well as for styles of decoration, had been tried out. Here Hastie's first master, Cameron, had designed the model town of Sofiya, to the south of the Tsarskoye Selo park, for Catherine. We have already discussed the building of its main square, but beyond that only a small number of the buildings proposed by Cameron were actually erected. Now at the beginning of the nineteenth century the town of Sofiya was in a sorry state. Occasional large buildings alternated with large tracts of wasteland and temporary shacks. Thus in 1808 it was decided that Sofiya should be removed, and a new small town be started on another site to the east of the park. This was plainly also intended to be a model town, but one appropriate to the conditions and requirements of a new era, and the most convincing evidence of this is provided by the subsequent career of its designer, Hastie, as leading imperial town planner. Before examining that later success we shall examine the project which made it possible.

In contrast to Cameron's picturesque design for Sofiya, Hastie's town was strictly regulated. Its general form was rectangular, and all the streets intersected at right angles. The whole territory was divided into blocks of approximately the same size, with each block comprising houses of a standard design. The open space at the centre of the town was literally a square, with the most important buildings – the administrative offices for the town itself, the post office, the treasury, the inn, the civil and religious schools, the market, the workshops and the storehouses – all placed around this central space.

The dominant feature of this design was the total and strict regulation of the architecture and all elements of the municipal services. This applied to the straightness and width of the streets, the height of the houses and to their location only along street frontages in the Western style which Peter the Great had brought to St Petersburg, rather than in the centre of sites in the old Russian manner. It applied to the arrangement of paving, fences and gates, to the organisation of civic amenities such as the water supply, and parks and gardens. Hastie not only designed the façades of the standard houses in strictly classical style, he also fixed the location of each, allotting the precise space for each on the street frontage. In other words, everything in the new Tsarskoye Selo township was to obey a new set of rules, and all the town's sundry requirements had been taken into account with special buildings set aside for administration, education, policing, trade and even for craftsmen to work in.

It has to be said that this strict regulation of life in the town gives it a somewhat monotonous character, or at least that the effect of Hastie's designs for the streets in Tsarskoye Selo is one of overriding uniformity. The post office building resembles the treasury, which is not very different from the inn. Only the municipal administration building is distinguished by two columns in the centre of its façade, otherwise it too is identical to the rest.

Unlike many of Cameron's for Sofiya, these buildings did not remain on the drawing board. The central square was built, with wooden market trading arcades added to the original project.[78] Private houses were also built to Hastie's designs. Some of these have survived, and despite – perhaps because of – the severity and regularity of their architecture, they form a charming group of two-storeyed houses, some of timber some of masonry, sharing the obligatory low columns, the semi-circular Venetian windows in the upper floor and simple pediments.[79]

The emergence of this design at this time, and the construction of such a town with 'modern living comforts', did not happen by chance. Even more than Catherine's Sofiya, it was consciously conceived as a demonstration and laboratory for a larger programme. At this time Alexander I was advancing the idea that improvements of the material aspects of national life, including the regulation of architecture, could change the fate of the people and the country. Extensive replanning of Russian provincial towns, many of them little more than large villages, had taken place under Catherine, but more casually, and largely as an element of the general introduction of local government and better tax-collection networks. Alexander's programme had a more socially interventionist aspiration, though fundamentally a benign one.

In parallel with the programme of civil rebuilding, in which Hastie would play a central role, ran a more limited but aggressively disciplined programme of what became notorious as military towns. These were created during the decade 1808–18. The idea, which was intended to reduce drastically the expenditure on maintenance of the army, consisted in most of the soldiers being settled in the countryside, and being obliged, in their 'time off from war', to work in agriculture. The negative aspects of this programme derived from the insistence that all life in the designated towns would be subject to rigid military organisation and discipline.

The idea was realised on a grandiose scale, with some most unattractive social consequences. Alexander's closest confidant, General Count Alexei Andreevich Arakcheyev, was appointed as the head of the military town project, and he regulated everything, from haircuts and uniforms for each season, to daily routine and the time for different types of work, as well as the distance between houses and the construction of the streets. All these decrees were carried out with extraordinary brutality and applied to the general population as well as the military element. After surviving for some three decades and through some serious uprisings of protest, the military towns were abolished. In Arakcheyev's implementation, the very phrase 'military town' became synonymous in Russia with the fanatical pursuit of order. But this was a vastly exaggerated perversion of an initial conception of Alexander's that was considerably more benign and genuinely sought improved welfare for Russia's burgeoning quasi-urban population through the physical improvement and regularisation of its technically very primitive, still essentially medieval settlements. Thus urban organisation as a whole became much stricter and more rigid at this time. Regularity of planning and uniformity of design were elevated to an unshakeable principle, no freedom or deviation from the laws applying to the entire country was permitted.

It was William Hastie's plan for the little town at Tsarskoye Selo, which had so pleased Alexander, that provided the model of the ideal town to be enacted through a new programme. An imperial decree ordered that 'the architect Hastie' be commissioned 'in the Ministry of Police to examine and alter the town plans of the entire state'. The document itself is no longer extant. Despite extensive archival research I have got no closer than this reference in a slightly later imperial *ukaz*.[80] The date of the original seems to be about 1809.

Standard Designs across the Empire

Hastie's work opened a new chapter in the control of town planning in Russia. A nationwide programme of replanning had begun as early as 1762, on Catherine the Great's accession to the throne. This consisted of replacing their picturesque medieval structure with more formal classical planning. The scope of these undertakings was truly colossal. From 1763 to 1796 the St Petersburg and Moscow Commission on Stone Construction prepared more than three hundred town plans. Once they were approved by the empress, they had the force of law, though even this did not always mean they were carried out. The commission was one of many institutions introduced by Catherine which were abolished by her son Paul during his brief reign from 1796 to 1801. This one was dissolved in 1796, within weeks of his coming to the throne. In 1806, when a new construction committee had been formed within the Ministry of the Interior, Hastie was among the four leading architects appointed to it.[81] Thus in 1808, under Paul's successor, Alexander I, work on replanning Russian towns began to be carried out centrally once again, and Hastie was appointed its director. In the *Book of Drawings and Designs* issued in 1839 as a supplement to the *Code of Laws of the Russian Empire*, all the plans and dates of their approval were published; it shows that more than one hundred town plans were examined, altered or redesigned by Hastie and his office.

Under Hastie's influence Russian town planning as a whole changed significantly. Composition became more regular. A strictly rectilinear system began to predominate, in contrast with the radial, centred structures composed of complex geometrical figures which had been popular under Catherine. The establishment of a firm, rigorous order in planning prevailed completely. But this was not all. Hastie devised a system for regulating civic architecture at all levels. Previously, during the second half of the eighteenth century, a more or less regular plan would be formed and the inhabitants would choose from among a small number of standard house designs (fewer than ten are known), but they more often built as they wished. Now, at the beginning of the nineteenth century, not only were regular plans drawn up, but standard designs for all types of building were introduced, whose use was obligatory. Hastie alone made more than fifty designs for model houses, but more importantly, he created an intermediate link between the standard house and the regular planning of the town as a whole, in the form of a model system for the division of city blocks into individual lots, and for the placing of houses on the sites thus created. He also designed model public squares as focal points within these regular grids.

The designs for model houses were published in 1809, in the *Collection of Façades Approved by His Imperial Majesty for Private Construction in Towns of the Russian Empire*, which comprised designs by Hastie and the St Petersburg architect Luigi Ruska (pls 272a–g).[82] This was followed by another album in 1811, also intended for obligatory application. Under the title *The Division of Urban Quarters into Habitable Sites*, this contained nineteen designs by Hastie for precisely that: the division of urban blocks of every conceivable regular geometrical form into a combination of building lot and public space, with particular emphasis on the treatment of corner sites at street intersections. These were accompanied by seven variants for the treatment of public

272a–g   William Hastie, designs for model houses. From *Collection of Façades Approved by His Imperial Majesty for Private Construction in Towns of the Russian Empire*, 1809.

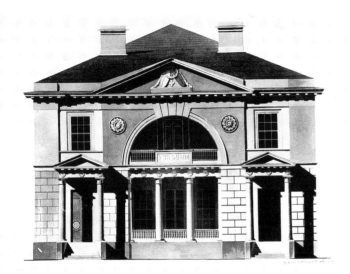

squares.[83] For this body of work Hastie was rewarded with the Order of St Vladimir in the Fourth Degree.[84]

The drawings of the model houses show large numbers of variants for the treatment of the façades. They range from very simple three-windowed, one-storey houses to huge three-storey mansions with side wings. A great deal of inventiveness was required to combine unity of style with variation between the individual designs. In general character, the schemes resemble the houses Hastie designed for Tsarskoye Selo, discussed earlier, though perhaps now reflecting more clearly Hastie's Palladian sympathies, and a continuing faithfulness to the architectural fashions of his British youth. The house designs he prepared were applied in towns across the whole Russian empire, some of the most influential applications, as important regional centres, being in Smolensk, Kaluga, Nizhny Novgorod, Ufa, Staritsa and Saratov.[85]

British ideas can likewise be detected in the designs for model blocks. Hastie designed squares very close in character to the eighteenth-century forms of Red Lion Square and Grosvenor Square in London.[86] It is likely that the squares and groups of Bath and Buxton[87] also had some influence on his work. Elsewhere his designs are particularly reminiscent of the first part of the new town in Edinburgh, which had begun to be constructed to James Craig's plan, with Robert Adam's participation, during Hastie's youth.[88] It is highly probable that Hastie would have seen these designs before he left Scotland for Russia. In any case Hastie's town-planning method can be said to have developed to a large extent parallel to that of his contemporaries in Britain, his drawings of urban blocks and quarters being, for example, very reminiscent of those designed for Edinburgh by William Playfair.

Hastie proposed constructing the urban space of purely geometric forms. Irrespective of whether he was designing a residential quarter or a square, he divided fragments of the town into three-sided, four-sided, circular, five- and six-sided figures of every possible regular shape. As a result any accidents of the relief or the old planning could be included in geometrically precise elements which fitted together like the pieces of a puzzle. Another important point is that Hastie insisted in all cases that development should be confined to the street frontages of the blocks, and regular-shaped gardens be placed in the centre. These gardens were divided into equal-sized private plots. Thus, Hastie's town took on very definite features. Ideally it was a town with construction only around the perimeter of blocks, with a regular distribution of blocks of a similar size, a clear rhythm in the siting of the buildings, which were of similar size, and broad, geometrically shaped open spaces. All accidental elements were eliminated from the planning. Nature was subordinate to the pen and the decision of the architect through a whole new standard typology. Apart from the model houses which the inhabitants were required by law to build, other architects in Hastie's organisation were producing model designs for shops, workshops and storehouses, for small farm buildings and even for fences and gates. In the albums, all were drawn in similar style, to the same scale.[89] Thus all the elements of a regular, classical-style town were defined and it was this model that Hastie strove to put into practice in his extensive town planning work during the two decades from 1810 to 1830. Naturally the reality of the old Russian towns forced modifications to the ideals, and for all Hastie's serious study of the old fabrics there were occasions of direct conflict with local authorities and architects when he insisted on modernisation.

During 1809–11 albums of designs for all these and other types of building were published and sent out to the provinces with a circular on their obligatory status. The principal towns in which Hastie's standard planning models were used were Tomsk, Ufa, Alexandrovsk, Shadrinsk, Petrovsk and Bakhmut.[90] At the end of 1811 Hastie personally produced a plan for the restoration of Podol, a quarter of Kiev which had been destroyed by fire. He also made designs for the reconstruction of the monumental

Contract House, where business transactions were concluded, and of the city council hall and the post office.[91] But in addition to setting up models, he was practical enough to know that in the absence of any previous professional activity of this kind in the provinces, clear instructions must follow as to how the work must be conducted. Thus on 5 December 1811 Hastie presented the Minister of Police with an official memorandum outlining the measures required 'to introduce town plans in the proper order'.[92]

He proposed collecting 'for each province, the plans of the provincial and *uyezd* [district] capitals and of other towns which were previously approved' and adding to them 'quarters for future construction, where it appears necessary'.[93] In addition, it was necessary to obtain geodesic surveys of 'the towns which need to be altered', and then,

> to make plans taking into account the site and other circumstances. When these are approved to make two copies and bind them into a book, and keep one of them in Petersburg and send the other to the Provincial capital to be carried out.

Hastie also insisted on receiving the broadest possible information on the towns for which plans needed to be made, ranging from the properties of the soils to the relief, from the locations of rivers and lakes to the exact placing of existing stone buildings. He also described in detail how this kind of work was to be done. In short, it was a detailed plan for the organisation and most importantly, the implementation, of town planning in Russia.

In January 1812, Hastie was given the rank and status of Court Counsellor. On 19 March 1812 special circulars were sent out to all governors in all parts of Russia. A special drawing office was set up in St Petersburg under Hastie's direction. During 1811 and 1812 the first batch of towns being replanned included Vyatka and Pokrov, in Vyatskaya province, Spassk and Ardatov in Tambov Province, Makaryev in Nizhegorodskaya province, also the provincial capital of Saratov and a large number of *uyezd* centres in Kazan province. Did he but know it, Hastie would soon have to deal with the destruction of urban areas on a far larger scale. The war with Napoleon interrupted town planning work for a time, but at the very beginning of 1813 it brought Hastie a vast and highly demanding commission.

Planning for Moscow

Writing later from the island of St Helena, Napoleon remembered from his exile how the French had taken Moscow and what happened in the ancient Russian capital during their stay:

> Two days after we entered the city the fire began. At first it did not seem dangerous and we thought that it had started because soldiers had lit their fires too close to the houses, which were almost exclusively of wood . . . However, the next morning a strong wind got up, and the fire spread with enormous speed . . . I was prepared for everything except this. Only this had not been foreseen: who would have thought that a people would burn their own capital? . . . I went out to the Emperor Alexander's country palace [the Petrovsky Castle], which lay about one mile from Moscow, and you may imagine the strength of the fire if I tell you that I could hardly touch the wall or the windows on the Moscow side of the palace, which was heated by the fire. It was a sea of fire, the sky and the clouds seemed to blaze, mountains of whirling red flame . . . suddenly they leapt up to the flaming sky and then fell into the fiery ocean.[94]

Eighteenth-century Moscow had disappeared in flames. Of the 9,000 buildings in the city, 6,307 were destroyed – but Napoleon's great army had also collapsed. After

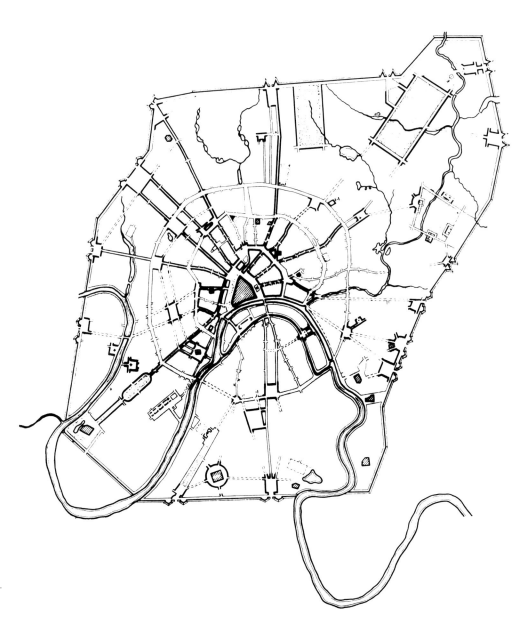

273 William Hastie, proposal for the reconstruction of Moscow, 1813 (according to V. Lavrov).

their retreat and rout the inhabitants began to return to the city, and the great sprawling town had to be rebuilt.

The design of a new plan for Moscow (pl. 273) was entrusted to Hastie, sent specially from St Petersburg. He began work in February 1813, and on 3 July of the same year Count Rastopchin, the Commander-in-Chief of Moscow, reported to A.D. Balashov, the Minister of Police, that Hastie had completed his commission. Unfortunately Hastie's plan for Moscow has not survived, and we can only judge it on the basis of reconstructions, and the large number of written documents which have come down to us.[95] From these we can assemble a general description of his proposal.

Hastie's plan attempted to change the shape of Moscow fundamentally. The city boundaries were simplified, and made more regular. The most important point of restructuring, for Hastie, was the creation of thoroughfares cutting through the city from one end to the other. He tried to turn the main streets into wide, straight avenues and, in a number of cases, to create parallel thoroughfares in order to ease traffic movement. He even proposed creating a new avenue, Novotversky Prospekt, running all the way from the Kremlin to the gate on the St Petersburg Road, alongside what was then Moscow's most famous artery, Tverskaya Street. Hastie devoted particular

246

attention to creating a significant network of public spaces in the city. He advanced the idea of concentric rings of wide boulevards on the site of the ancient fortress walls, circling the city. Thus he wrote:

> The [existing] Boulevard and the Earth Rampart [the line of the present-day Sadovaya or Garden Ring] are a great ornament to the city and, in my opinion, there should be no building upon them except for a few hostelries which might serve the people walking there.[96]

He also proposed increasing considerably the number of squares, creating new ones and regularising the outlines of the old. In his plan there were to be forty-seven squares altogether in Moscow, of which twenty-three would be new.[48] He also wanted to turn twelve of the larger open spaces, known as 'fields', into regularly designed parks. Thus for example, he planned Devichye Field on the city's south-western outskirts as a long, straight vista leading towards the elegant walls and towers of the magnificent Novodevichy Convent.

Hastie's plan has been appositely said by the architectural historian Vitaly Lavrov to have 'marked a new approach to questions of town planning' in Russia.[98] The key elements of this new approach were his view of all the spaces in the city as a single whole, which led to his attempts to create an even distribution of built and open land. Another highly important and novel feature was the perception of this space in terms of the movements through it – hence the prime attention focused on the system of communication in the city. His view of the street as a line of transportation was also new. On a smaller scale, there were numerous innovations in his approach to the arrangement and construction of public squares. In Hastie's plan, elegant areas in front of palaces and churches were no longer purely ceremonial or symbolic, but became the open spaces at transport junctions which on one hand eased the flow of traffic and on the other formed a chain of broader street spaces which created the particular character and role of the various arteries intersecting the city.[99]

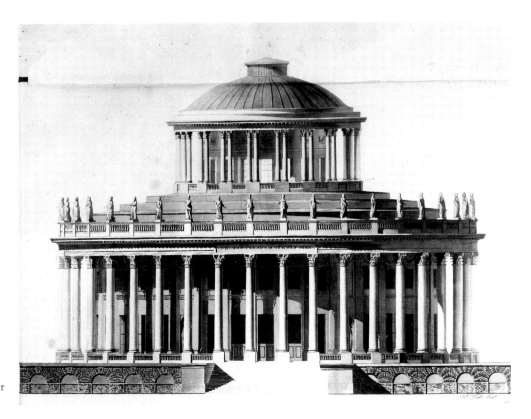

274 William Hastie, project for a hall for meetings.

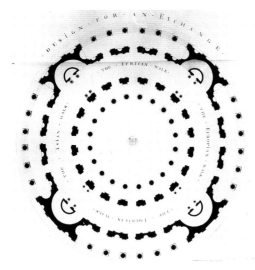

275   William Hastie, project for a stock exchange.

Hastie drew up this plan, which was to change the traditional planning and appearance of the ancient Russian capital, with amazing rapidity. He had it finished in less than six months. But realising such a plan was far less simple. Since the early eighteenth century, in the time of Peter the Great, Moscow had resisted all innovations which would conflict with its centuries-old habits. Moscow contained not only the Kremlin, the medieval monasteries and hundreds of churches, but also a huge inert mass of private properties intersected by a web of narrow streets and alleys. It was primarily this inert mass that ensured the extraordinary resistance of traditionalism in the city fabric. None of the eighteenth-century planners had succeeded in cutting through the tangle of innumerable property-owning interests, land rights and the habitual way of life ingrained in the intricate layout of the blocks. This mass had engulfed the projects begun in the Petrine era; it had defeated Ivan Michurin's ideas for regulation in the 1730s, and also the radical plan of 1775. The same fate awaited Hastie's plan.

The buildings of Moscow had burnt down, but the owners' rights to the land remained. The Building Committee in Moscow produced a critique of Hastie's plan. They calculated that because of the necessity of purchasing land from private individuals, Hastie's squares alone would cost 19,493,921 roubles – a fantastic sum at that time. Building the streets and straightening the alleys would cost even more, being hindered at every turn by the interests of one person or another. In 1817 a new plan was designed for Moscow, principally by the classical architect Osip Bove, who dominated the architectural life of the city after Kazakov's death in 1812, soon after Napoleon's departure. The new plan made more concessions to history and private ownership and fewer to imperial interventionism from St Petersburg.

Nevertheless, Hastie's work had a significant influence on Moscow's development. Many elements of his plan were retained: of the forty-seven squares he had planned, twenty-six were executed; of the twelve proposals for turning 'fields' into parks, six were constructed according to Hastie's idea; the rings of main roads – the Boulevard and Garden Ring – were built as he had suggested, even down to the proposed hostelries. But the most significant points were the planning principles of Hastie's plan, which proposed a new structure for the city. Ultimately Moscow was to develop largely along these lines.

Hastie himself returned to St Petersburg in the middle of 1813, and immediately resumed his usual work. Bridges were still under way, of course, and in the planning field he worked during 1814 on plans for Rodomysl, Skvira, Cherkassy, Chigirin and Vasilkov – all in Kiev province. In 1815 he redesigned the plan of Smolensk and the nearby towns of Gzhatsk, Dukhovshchina and Krasnoy, and he was considering a scheme for Kiev.[100] In 1816 he worked on the plans for Vilno,[101] which he visited in person, as was his habit, in February 1817. His famous plan for Yekaterinoslav (now Dnepropetrovsk), which was carried out in full, was designed in that same year.[102] That December he visited Ufa, and the plan for that town was made during 1819.[103] On 21 August 1819, General Count S.K. Vyazmitinov, who as Minister of Police was the supreme authority for town planning, wrote to Tsar Alexander's office thus:

By special order of His Imperial Majesty, Hastie is concerned with examining all the plans for provincial and *uyezd* capitals presented by provincial governors. For his pains in this sphere he was appointed a Court Counsellor in January 1812, and since then he has continued to concern himself with the examination and alteration of these plans with outstanding zeal. All the plans he has compiled have won the approval of His Imperial Majesty.

In addition, in order to obtain information needed for this matter locally, he was dispatched at the beginning of 1815 to Smolensk, Porechye, Gzhatsk, Krasnoy and Dukhovshchina, and thence to Kiev. In February 1817 he was sent to Vilno. In

276　William Hastie, project for a stock exchange.

December of the same year he went to Ufa, and these tasks, which required sound knowledge and experience in this field, were carried out with distinction, diligence and success, and the plans he created for all of these towns won the approval of His Imperial Majesty.

In describing all these services which Hastie undertakes, and for which he does not receive a special salary, to the Committee of Ministers, I consider it my duty to petition His Most Gracious Majesty to reward Hastie with the Order of St Anna, 2nd degree.[104]

This was a very senior Order, and the regulations in force in Russia stipulated that Orders were to be awarded strictly in order of precedence. To be elevated directly from the Order of St Vladimir, 4th Degree to the Order of St Anna, 2nd Degree would have meant a break with custom. The Committee of Ministers agreed to this for Hastie's sake, but the tsar, who was extremely punctilious on these matters, did not agree, although he also wished to reward the architect. Thus a different mode of honouring Hastie was chosen, and promulgated in the following imperial *ukaz*:

Decree of the Tsar to the Government Senate. In reward for the outstanding labour and diligence in service shown by the architect Court Counsellor Hastie in examining and designing town plans, I most graciously appoint him Collegiate Assessor. Saint Petersburg 17 November 1819.　　　　　　　　　　　　　　　Alexander.[105]

With such rank and his handsome stipendiary pension, William Hastie's contributions to the infrastructure and aesthetics of urban Russia were appropriately rewarded. But he continued to work actively until his death on 4 July 1832. On the engineering front, he returned again to the challenge of bridging with the preparation of a scheme for spanning the wide chanel of the River Neva, which so solidly divided the northern half of St Petersburg from its southern centre. So high was Hastie's reputation in this field that ten years after his death, a special committee was convened to examine the possibilities for constructing such a bridge precisely to his designs, which no later innovations had superseded.[106] On the planning front, he did a great deal of work during the 1820s and very early 1830s on the Siberian centres of Omsk, Tomsk and Krasnoyarsk,[107] and on small towns in the Ukraine and the Volga region.[108] Most of these plans had been approved by 1829.

In all these plans Hastie stuck firmly to his method. He made the boundaries of towns clear and as regular as possible. He devoted much attention to public spaces. In

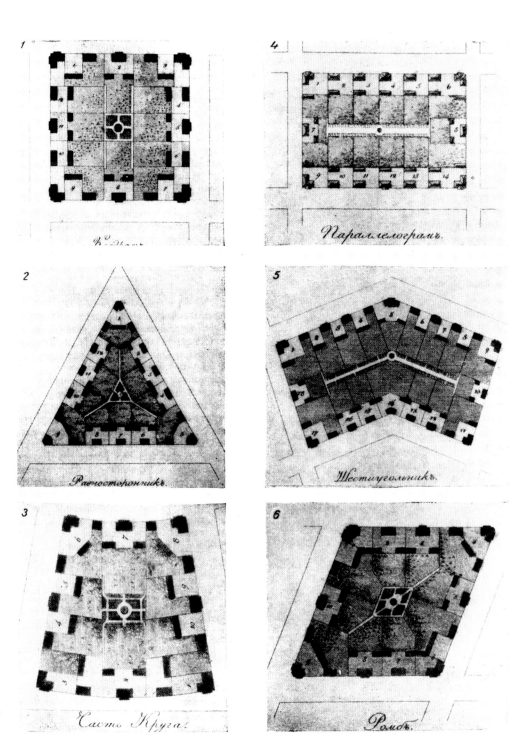

277 William Hastie, model projects for squares and quarters, 1808.

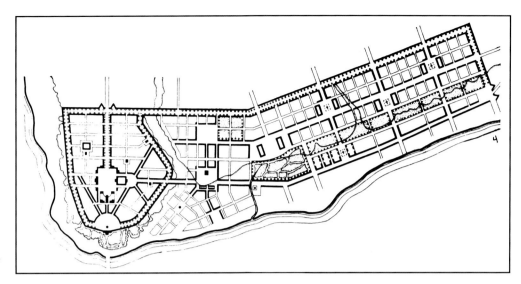

278 William Hastie, project for Yekaterinoslav, 1816.

Yekaterinoslav (Dnepropetrovsk) the avenue he laid out is still one of the main attractions of the city. He tried to create plans based on a regular network, with blocks of various shapes inserted into it (pls 277, 278). Always his work had the characteristic that made his earliest contributions so distinctive: that the ordering and standardisation was not confined to the two extreme scales of overall plan and detailed building type, but recognised the essential role of the intermediary scale, of the planning of the city block and district, in the actual, practical achievement of change. Hastie's huge contribution to the development of Russian towns is indisputable. Many of them still retain features of his planning.

Charles Cameron was clearly right when he took the young stonemason Hastie under his wing in the 1790s and helped him to become an architect. While the pupil did not surpass his teacher in the aesthetic perfection of his designs, he outstripped him by a long way in the physical extent of the impact he made on the built environment of early modern Russia.

ABBREVIATIONS

APDM   Arkhiv Pavlovskogo dvortsa-muzeya (Archive of the Pavlovsk Palace Museum)

GBL OR Gosudarstvennaya biblioteka imeni V.I. Lenina otdel rukopisi (State Lenin Library Department of Manuscripts, now the State Russian Library)

GE OR   Gosudarstvennyi Ermitazh, otdel rukopisi (State Hermitage, Department of Manuscripts)

GIA-SPb Gosudarstvennyi istoricheskii arkhiv Sankt Peterburga (State Historical Archive of St Petersburg)

GIM IZO Gosudarstvennyi istoricheskii muzei otdel isobrazitel'nikh istochnikov (State Historical Museum, Department of Representational Sources)

GIM OPI Gosudarstvennyi istoricheskii muzei otdel pis'mennikh istochnikov (State Historical Museum Department of Written Sources)

GNIMA   Gosudarstvennyi nauchno-issledovatel'skii muzei arkhitektury im. A.V. Shchuseva (Shchusev State Research Museum of Architecture)

GPB OR Gosudarstvennaya publichnaya biblioteka imeni M.E. Saltykova-Shchedrina (State Public Library named for Saltykov-Shchedrin, now the Russian National Library)

IRIO   Imperatorskoe russkoe istoricheskoe obshchestvo (Imperial Russian Historical Society: Collected Papers)

KOGA   Kievskii oblastnoi gosudarstvennyi arkhiv (Kiev Region State Archive)

MIG-SPb Musei istorii goroda Sankt Peterburga (Museum of the History of the City of St Petersburg)

NIMAKh Nauchno-issledovatel'skii muzei Akademii Khudozhestv (Research Museum of the Academy of Arts)

PCZRI   Polnoye sobranie zakonov Rossiiskoi imperii (Complete Collection of Laws of the Russian Empire)

TsGADA Tsentral'nyi gosudarstvennyi arkhiv drevnikh aktov (Russian State Archive of Ancient Documents)

TsGAVMF Tsentral'nyi gosudarstvennyi arkhiv voenno-morskogo flota (Central State Archive of the Navy)

TsGIA   Tsentral'nyi gosudarstvennyi istoricheskii arkhiv (Central State Historical Archive)

TsGIAM Tsentral'nyi gosudarstvennyi istoricheskii arkhiv goroda Moskvy (Central State Historical Archive of the City of Moscow)

TsGVIA Tsentral'nyi gosudarstvennyi voenno-istoricheskii arkhiv (Central State Archive of Military History)

VUA   Voenno-ychetnyi arkhiv (Military Registration Archive)

fond: collection
opis: schedule
ed. khr.: unit of storage

NOTES

INTRODUCTION

1 Pis'ma Yekateriny II k Grimmu. *Sbornik Imperatorskogo russkogo istoricheskogo obshchestva* (Letters of Catherine the Great to Grimm. Collected papers of the Imperial Russian Historical Society), vol. XXIII, St Petersburg, 1878, p. 157.

2 A. Khrapovitsky, *Dnevnik* (Diary), St Petersburg, 1874, p. 343.

3 J. Summerson, *Architecture in Britain, 1530–1830*, Harmondsworth, 1970, p. 396.

4 For greater detail on these buildings see the relevant chapters below.

5 This theme undoubtedly deserves treatment in a separate book.

6 M. Korshunova, *Iuri Fel'ten* (Yuri Velten), Leningrad, 1982, p. 18; Charles Over, *Ornamental Architecture . . . in Chinese Taste*, London, 1757.

7 A. Petrov, *Gorod Pushkin* (The town of Pushkin), Leningrad, 1977, p. 153; W. and J. Halfpenny, *Rural Architecture in Chinese Taste*, London, 1750, p. 1.

8 Compare the depiction of the mosque-pavilion on the country estate of Yaropolets, in Yu. Shamurin, *Podmoskovie* (The environs of Moscow), vol. II, Moscow, 1914, pp. 70–1, and the design for 'a rural mosque' in W. Wright, *Grotesque Architecture or Rural Amusement*, London, 1767, p. 21.

9 IRIO, vol. XXIII, St Petersburg, 1878, p. 207.

10 See drawing by A. Voronikhin.

11 F. Syrkina, *P'etro di Gottardo Gonzago* (Pietro di Gottardo Gonzago), Moscow, 1974, p. 209.

12 F. Vigel', *Zapiski* (Notes), vol. I, Moscow, 1928, p. 183

13 I. Yakovkin, *Opisanie sela Tsarskogo* (Description of the village of Tsarskoye Selo), St Petersburg, 1830; V. Bur'yanov, *Progulki s det'mi po Sankt Peterburgu* (Walks with children around St Petersburg), St Petersburg, 1842, pp. 51, 63, 64, 72; P. Shtorkh, *Putevoditel' po sadu i gorodu Pavlovsku* (Guide to the gardens and town of Pavlovsk), St Petersburg, 1843 *et al.*

14 P. Petrov, 'Znachenie arkhitektora Kamerona' (The significance of the architect Cameron), *Zodchii* (The architect), no. 3–4, 1885, pp. 17–18.

15 Evidence of this are Polovtsev's mansion on Kamenny ostrov (Stone Island) by I. Fomin and the mansion of Kochubey in Tsarskoye Selo by N. Lansere. See G. Ol' and N. Lansere, *N.E. Lansere*, Leningrad, 1986, p. 73.

16 M. Korshunova, 'William Hastie in Russia', *Architectural History,* vol. 17, 1974.

17 V. Tenikhina, *Kottedzh* (The Cottage), Leningrad, 1986.

18 TsGAVMF, fond 131, opis 1, ed. khr. 232.

19 S. Bronshtein, *Arkhitektura goroda Pushkina* (Architecture of the town of Pushkin), Moscow, 1940, pp. 31–6; Peter Hayden, 'Bush', in *Oxford Companion to Gardens*, 1987, p. 85.

20 *Plan des jardins et vue de différens bâtiments de sa majesté impériale à Zarsko Zelo*, engraved by T. Miller.

21 Remarkable notes by Elizabeth Dimsdale have been preserved on her travels in Russia during 1781. Among other interesting facts she records there are descriptions of how the English gardeners lived at Tsarskoye Selo. This material is in the collection of Baron Dimsdale at Royston. I am sincerely indebted to Baron Dimsdale for having allowed me to examine these materials, which have since been published in their entirety by Professor A.G. Cross in *An English Lady at the Court of Catherine the Great: The Journal of Baroness Elizabeth Dimsdale, 1781* (Cambridge, 1989). Additional references to this material may be found in the following exhibition catalogues: T. Talbot Rice, *Charles Cameron*, London, 1967, p. 17; A.G. Cross, *Anglo-Russian Relations in the Eighteenth Century*, Norwich, 1977, p. 34; A.G. Cross, *The 1780s: Russia under Western Eyes*, Norwich, 1981, p. 2.

22 Information on this is preserved in Elizabeth Dimsdale's notes.

23 Precise information on Charles Cameron's marriage to C. Bush in May 1784 was found by A.G. Cross and published in 'The British in Catherine's Russia', *The Eighteenth Century in Russia*, Oxford, 1973, pp. 245–50.

24 J.C. Loudon, *Encyclopaedia of Gardening*, London, 1827, p. 56. Loudon's *Encyclopedia* was first published in 1822. Several later editions followed, notably in 1827, 1834 and the last in 1878, with slightly differing contents. All references in the present work are to the 1827 edition.

25 E. Glezer, *Arkhitekturyi ansambl' Angliiskogo parka* (The architectural ensemble of the English park), Leningrad, 1979, p. 124, *et al.*; TsGIA, opis 399/511, 1789, ed. khr. 251, pp. 1–17; TsGADA, Kabinet, opis 497, ed. khr. 64979.

26 TsGIA, Kabinet, opis 365/1347, 1794, ed. khr. 8, pp. 41–78. The palace was basically completed in 1794, but the finishing of interiors continued later.

27 A. Elkina, *Gatchina*, Leningrad, 1980, pp. 4, 123, *et al.*

28 TsGADA, Dvortsovoe otdelenie (Palace section) opis 449, ed. khr. 62117.

29 TsGADA, Section XIV, opis 1, ed. khr. 51, part 6, pp. 367–8.

30 *Ibid.*, p. 440.

31 J.C. Loudon, *op. cit.*, p. 57.

32 S. Aksakov, *Sobranie sochinenii v 5tt* (Collected works in five volumes), vol. I, Moscow, 1966, pp. 508–9.

33 TsGADA, fond 10, opis 1, ed. khr. 383.

34 A. Bolotov, 'Nechto dlya okhotnikov v angliiskikh sadov' (Something for admirers of English gardens), *Ekonomicheskii magazin* (The economic magazine) (hereafter *EM*), part 21, 1785, pp. 161–6; 'Nekotorie zamechaniya o sadakh v Anglii' (Some observations on gardens in England), *EM*, part 25, 1786, nos 17, 18, 19; 'Opisanie Kevskogo sada v Anglii' (Description of Kew Gardens in England), *EM*, part 36, 1787, pp. 145–53; 'Eshche nekotorie zamechaniya, otnosyashchiesiya do sadov noveishego roda ili . . . angliiskikh' (Certain further notes relating to gardens of the newest . . . or English type), *EM*, part 39, 1788, nos 54–8, 67–74.

35 *O sadakh v Kitai* (On gardens in China), translation of the book by William Chambers, St Petersburg, 1771; *Opyt o raspolozhenii sadov. Perevodeno s angliiskogo yazyka* (Experiment in the layout of gardens. Translated from the English language), St Petersburg, 1778; L. Manza, *Plany dlya raspolozheniya i razdeleniya angliiskikh sadov* (Plans for the layout and subdivision of English gardens), Moscow, 1796; I. Grohman, *Sobranie novykh myslei dlya ukrasheniya sadov i dach vo vkuse Angliiskom, Goticheskom, Kitaiskom, dlya upotrebleniya lyubitelei Angliiskikh sadov* (Collection of new ideas for the decoration of gardens and

dachas in the English, Gothic and Chinese tastes, for the use of lovers of English gardens), Moscow, 1788, *et al.*, ff. 1–26.

36 C.L. Johnstone, *The British Colony in Russia*, London, 1898.

37 M. Alekseyev, *Russko-Angliiskie literaturnye svyazi* (Russo-English literary links), Moscow, 1982; *Epokha Prosveshcheniya: iz istorii mezhdunarodnykh svyazei russkoi literatury* (The epoch of the Enlightenment: From the history of Russian literature's international connections), Leningrad, 1967; *Ot klassitsizma do romatizma: iz istorii mezhdunarodnykh svyazei russkoi literatury* (From classicism to romanticism: From the history of Russian literature's international connections), Leningrad, 1970; *Russkaya kul'tura XVIII veka i zapadno-evropeiskie literatury* (Russian culture of the eighteenth century and western-European literature), Leningrad, 1980.

38 A.G. Cross, *By the Banks of the Thames: Russians in Eighteenth-century Britain*, Newtonville, Mass., 1980; *id.*, 'The British in Catherine's Russia', *The Eighteenth Century in Russia*, Oxford, 1975; *id.*, *Anglo-Russian Relations in the Eighteenth Century*, Norwich, 1977; *id.*, *The 1780s: Russia under Western Eyes*, Norwich, 1981.

39 I. Grabar', *Istoriya russkogo iskusstva* (History of Russian art), Moscow, 1910–14, vol. III; I. Grabar', 'Rannie Aleksandrovskii klassitsizm i ego frantsuzskie istoki' (Early Alexandrine classicism and its French sources), *Starye gody* (The olden days), September 1914; A. Mikhailov, *Bazhenov*, Moscow, 1953; N. Belikhov and A. Petrov, *Ivan Starov*, Moscow, 1951.

40 V.N. Taleporovsky, *Charl'z Kameron*, Moscow, 1939, p. 1.

41 *Rossiya-Frantsiya. Vek Prosveshcheniya* (Russia-France: The age of Enlightenment), Leningrad, 1987.

42 E.F. Gollerbakh and N.E. Lansere, eds., *Charl'z Kameron*, Petrograd, 1924, p. 1.

I CHARLES CAMERON

1 V. Taleporovsky, *Charl'z Kameron*, Moscow, 1939, p. 121.

2 IRIO, vol. XXIII, St Petersburg, 1878, p. 207.

3 *Ibid.*, p. 611.

4 *Ibid.*, p. 196.

5 *Dictionary of National Biography* (hereafter, *DNB*), vol. VIII, London, 1886, p. 289; Isobel Rae, *Charles Cameron*, London, 1971.

6 *Memoirs of Miss Jenny Cameron*, London, 1746.

7 *DNB*, vol. VIII, 1886, p. 289.

8 I. Grabar', *Istoriya russkogo iskusstva* (History of Russian art), Moscow, 1910–14, vol. III; N. Lansere, 'Arkhitektor Charl'z Kameron', in Gollerbakh and Lansere, eds, *Charl'z Kameron*; Taleporovsky, *Charl'z Kameron*; *Istoriya russkogo iskusstva* (History of Russian art), vol. VI, Moscow, 1967, *et al.*

9 Charles Cameron, *The Baths of the Romans*, London, 1772.

10 This album is preserved in the collections of the museum of Pavlovsk Palace. For a discussion of it see T. Talbot Rice, *Charles Cameron*, London, 1968, p. 9.

11 T. Talbot Rice, *op. cit.*, 1968; I. Rae, *op. cit.*, 1971.

12 DNB, vol. VIII, 1886, p. 290.

13 Charles Cameron, *Memori per le belle arti*, Rome, vol. I, 1785; vol. 2, 1786.

14 H. Colvin, *Biographical Dictionary of British Architects*, London, 1978, pp. 178–9.

15 E. Dashkova, *Zapiski* (Notes), Moscow, 1987, pp. 131–3.

16 Charles Cameron, *op. cit.*, 1785, vol. I, p. 212.

17 British Museum, Add. MSS 32731, 525.

18 I. Rae, *op. cit.*, 1971, pp. 17–26, 18.

19 The album is preserved in the collections of the St Petersburg Institute of Railway Transport Engineers (IIZhT).

20 M. Bakhtin, *Tvorchestvo F. Rable i narodnhaya smekhovaya kul'tura* (The work of F. Rable and popular humorous culture), Moscow, 1966, p. 44.

21 A. Palladio, *Four Books on Architecture*, published by I. Ware, London, 1738, p. 1.

22 T. Talbot Rice, *op. cit.*, 1968, p. 11.

23 *Vitruvius Britannicus*, vol. V, London, 1771.

24 Ch. Kameron, *Termy rimlyan* (The Baths of the Romans), Moscow, 1939, p. 2.

25 *Ibid.*, p. 3.

26 *Ibid.*, p. 13.

27 *Ibid.*, p. 2.

28 *Ibid.*, p. 3.

29 *Ibid.*, p. 3.

30 *Ibid.*, p. 11.

31 *Ibid.*, p. 20.

32 I. Rae, *op. cit.*, 1971, p. 35.

33 *Ibid.*, pp. 34–6.

34 D. Stroud, *Henry Holland*, London, 1966, p. 135.

35 T. Talbot Rice, *op. cit.*, 1968, p. 15.

36 Quoted from V. Taleporovsky, Introduction to the 1939 Moscow edition of Ch. Kameron, *Termy rimlyan* (The baths of the Romans), p. XI.

37 GE, Clérisseau collections, 'Explanation to the commission for an Ancient house', p. 1.

38 IRIO, vol. XXIII, St Petersburg, 1896, p. 196.

39 V. Taleporovsky, *op. cit.*, 1939, p. 73.

40 TsGIA, fond 468, opis 37, ed. khr., 344.

41 V. Taleporovsky published in his book drawings of a triumphal arch with medallions with depictions of battles. This was not a free-standing arch, but was proposed to be attached to the gallery of the Temple of Memory. The *Ruchnoi dorozhnik* (Travelling diary) of 1802 contains an extract from a letter of Catherine the Great saying 'I decided to build in a small wooded area a Temple of Memory, where all the deeds in that war would be depicted on medallions'. (*Ruchnoi dorozhnik*, St Petersburg, 1802, p. 11.)

42 In the collections of the State Hermitage, NIMAKh, GNIMA and MIG-SPb.

43 TsGIA, fond 487, opis 13, 1780, ed. khr. 40, p. 1.

44 TsGIA, fond 487, opis 13, 1784, ed. khr. 115, p. 81.

45 From the correspondence of Maria Fedorovna, quoted from Pavlovsk, St Petersburg, 1877, p. 528.

46 *Ibid.*, p. 548.

47 *Ibid.*, p. 520.

48 *Ibid.*, p. 522.

49 Cabinet for the Assistance of Research at Pavlovsk Palace Museum, Correspondence of Maria Fedorovna and Paul with Kuchelbecker; letter of 10 May 1782.

50 *Ibid.*, September 1787.

51 *Ibid.*

52 *Ibid.*

53 From the letter of Catherine the Great to Grimm, quoted from V. Taleporovsky, *op. cit.*, 1939, p. 15.

54 IRIO, vol. XXIII, p. 207.

55 *Ibid.*, p. 196.

56 Quoted from V. Taleporovsky, *op. cit.*, 1939, p. 25.

57 TsGADA, fond 14, opis 1, ed. khr. 52, part 2(5), p. 235.

58 *Ibid.*, p. 237.

59 *Ibid.*, part 2(4), p. 163.

60 *Edinburgh Evening Courant*, January 21 1784.

61 *Ibid.*

62 T. Talbot Rice, *op. cit.*, 1968, p. 8.

63 *Ibid.*; Letter of William and George Lyon to their mother, pp. 19, 21.

64 TsGADA, fond 14, opis 1, ed. khr., 52, part 2(3), p. 229; also pp. 205–30. This question was examined by M.F. Korshunova in her article on William Hastie, 'Arkhitektor V. Geste', *Trudy Gosudarstvennogo Ermitazha* (Proceedings of the State Hermitage), vol. XVIII, 1977.

65 TsGIA, fond 487, opis 13, 1784, ed. khr. 115, p. 1.

66 TsGIA, fond 486, opis 32, ed. khr. 1281, p. 1.

67 TsGIA, fond 487, opis 13, 1784, ed. khr. 115, p. 40.

68 TsGIA, fond 487, opis 13, 1784, ed. khr. 115, p. 7a.

69 *Ibid.*, p. 120.

70 *Ibid.*, p. 83.

71 *Ibid.*, p. 130.

72 TsGADA, fond 14, opis 1, ed. khr. 52, part 3(4), p. 205.

73 Archives of Count Vorontsov, vol. XIII, Moscow, 1875, p. 438; letter of A.A. Bezborodko to S.R. Vorontsov.

74 From the letter of architect Henry Holland to Charles Cockerell, quoted from D. Stroud, *Henry Holland*, p. 135.

75 *Ibid.*

76 V. Taleporovsky, *op. cit.*, 1939, p. 62.

77 These drawings are located in the Hermitage. They were published in V. Taleporovsky, *op. cit.*, 1939, p. 36.

78 TsGIA, fond 487, opis 1, ed. khr. 929, pp. 4, 22.

79 T. Talbot Rice, *op. cit.*, 1968, p. 17.
80 *Ibid.*
81 A.G. Cross, *By the Banks of the Thames*, Newtonville, Mass., 1980, p. 250.
82 Also Alferov, Kushlevsky, Raevsky, Volkov.
83 *Catalogue d'une Bibliothèque . . . de Mr Cameron*, St Petersburg, 1812.
84 Quoted from V. Taleporovsky, *op. cit.*, 1939, p. 25.
85 V. Gornostaev, *Dvortsy i tserkvi Yuga* (Palaces and churches of the South) Moscow, 1914, p. 38.
86 *Starye gody*, March 1914, p. 26.
87 I. Grabar', *op. cit.*, 1910–14, p. 387.
88 F. Vigel', *op. cit.*, 1928, p. 181.
89 *Ibid.*, p. 183.
90 TsGAVMF, fond 215, ed. khr. 174, pp. 30–96.
91 GPB, fond 124, collection of P.L. Vaksel', ed. khr. 1907, pp. 1–2. I have discussed this further in D. Shvidkovsky, 'Cameron discoveries', *Architectural Review*, no. 2, 1982.
92 TsGAVMF, fond 1211, opis 1, ed. khr. 18, p. 11.
93 *Starye gody*, December 1911, p 18.
94 TsGAVMF, fond 215, opis 1, ed. khr. 2, p. 24; ed. khr. 37, pp. 1–11; fond 1211, opis 1, ed. khr. 47, pp. 5–9.
95 TsGAVMF, fond 215, opis 1, ed. khr. 37, p. 24.
96 TsGAVMF, fond 131, opis 1, ed. khr. 2589, p. 1.
97 TsGAVMF, fond 326, opis 1, ed. khr. 8919. The signature on the project is Charles Cameron's.
98 TsGAVMF, fond 215, opis 1, ed. khr. 174, p. 48.
99 F. Vigel', *op. cit.*, 1928, p. 183.
100 *Russkii biograficheskii slovar'* (Russian biographical dictionary), vol. xiv, St Petersburg, 1905, p. 733.
101 A. Khodnev, *Istoriya Volno-Ekonomicheskogo obshchestva* (History of the Voluntary Economic Society), St Petersburg, 1865, pp. 169, 451, 453.
102 A. Savel'ev, *Istoricheskii ocherk inzhenernogo upravleniya v Rossii* (Historical outline of the engineering administration in Russia), part 2, St Petersburg, 1879, p. 317.
103 Published in G.K. Kozmyan, *Charl'z Kameron*, Leningrad, 1987, p. 128.
104 F. Vigel', *op. cit.*, 1928, p. 181.
105 TsGAVMF, fond 215, opis 1, ed. khr. 174, p. 7.

II   TSARSKOYE SELO

1 S. Shubinsky, 'Domashnyi byt Yekateriny II' (The domestic life of Catherine the Great), *Literaturnoe prilozhenie k Nive* (Literary supplement to the journal Niva), no. 2, 1900, p. 118.
2 IRIO, vol. xxiii, St Petersburg, 1878, p. 157.
3 GE OR, Inventory no. 2603, p. 1.
4 *Sharl' de Vaii i russkie arkhitektory* (Charles de Wailly and Russian architects), 1982, p. 7.
5 IRIO, vol. xxiii, St Petersburg, 1878, p. 207.
6 I. Grabar', *Istoriya russkogo iskusstva* (History of Russian art), Moscow, 1910–14, vol. iii, p. 370.
7 Quoted from E. Gollerbakh, 'Kameron v Tsarskom sele' (Cameron at Tsarskoye Selo), in E.F. Gollerbakh and N.E. Lansere, eds, *Charl'z Kameron,* Petrograd, 1924, p. 13.
8 *Tsarskoye selo v poezii* (Tsarskoye Selo in poetry), Petrograd, 1922, p. 4.
9 A. Pushkin, *Polnoe sobranie sochinenii v 10tt* (Complete collected works in ten volumes), vol. i, Moscow and Leningrad, 1949, p. 75.
10 E. Gollerbakh, *op. cit.*, 1924, p. 32.
11 M.G. Voronov and G.D. Khodasevich, *Arkhitekturnyi ansambl' Kamerona v Pushkine* (The architectural ensemble by Cameron at Pushkin), Leningrad, 1982, p. 42.
12 G. Derzhavin, *Sochineniya* (Works), Moscow, 1986, p. 132.
13 Ch. Kameron, *Termy rimlyan* (The Baths of the Romans), Moscow, 1939, p. 13.
14 *Ibid.*
15 TsGADA, fond 14, opis 1, ed. khr. 52, part, 2(5), p. 228.
16 M.G. Voronov and G.D. Khodasevich, *op. cit.*, 1982, pp. 81–7.
17 *Ibid.*, p. 89.
18 G. Derzhavin, *op. cit.*, 1986, p. 130.
19 E. Gollerbakh, *op. cit.*, 1924, p. 40.
20 A. Khrapovitsky, *Dnevnik* (Diary), St Petersburg, 1874, p. 406.
21 RIBA, xvii/22, *Monument historique*, 1975, no. 2, p. 41.
22 E. Gollerbakh, *op. cit.*, 1924, p. 40.
23 M.G. Voronov and G.D. Khodasevich, *op. cit.*, 1982, p. 23.
24 A. Khrapovitsky, *op. cit.*, p. 406.
25 *Ibid.*, p. 373.
26 *Ibid.*, p. 397.
27 G. Derzhavin, *op. cit.*, 1986, p. 92.
28 The scale and character of the busts were indicated by Cameron himself on his perspective of the Gallery. GE OR, Inventory no. 11072; also NIMAKh, Inventory no. A–49.
29 M.G. Voronov and G.D. Khodasevich, *op. cit.*, 1982, p. 93.
30 E. Gollerbakh, *op. cit.*, 1924, p. 36.
31 Quoted from M. Pylyaev, *Zabytòye proshloye okrestnostei Peterburga* (The forgotten past of the environs of St Petersburg), St Petersburg, 1889, p. 462.
32 N.E. Lansere, 'Arkhitektor Charl'z Kameron', in E.F. Gollerbakh and N.E. Lansere, eds, *Charl'z Kameron*, Petrograd, 1924, p. 12.
33 E. Gollerbakh, *op. cit.*, 1924, p. 23.
34 V. Taleporovsky, *Charl'z Kameron*, Moscow, 1939, p. 103.
35 *Ibid.*
36 *Ibid.*
37 *Ibid.*, p. 110.
38 GE OR, inventory no. 11042.
39 NIMAKh, inventory no. A–37.
40 GE OR, inventory no. 11037.
41 GE OR, inventory no. 11087.
42 GE OR, inventory nos 11020, 11041, 11084 *et al.*; NIMAKh, Inventory nos A–39, A–974.
43 GE OR, inventory nos 11020, 11041.
44 GE OR, inventory nos 11084.
45 A.N. Petrov, *Gorod Pushkin* (The town of Pushkin), Leningrad, 1977, p. 68.
46 TsGIA, fond 487, opis 13, 1784, ed. khr. 115, p. 41.
47 GE OR, inventory nos 11036, 11029.
48 TsGIA, fond 487, opis 13, 1784, ed. khr. 115, p. 36.
49 GE OR, inventory nos 11033, 11053.
50 TsGIA, fond 487, opis 13, 1784, ed. khr. 115, p. 44.
51 V. Taleporovsky, *op. cit.*, 1939, p. 115.
52 From a letter of Catherine the Great to Grimm, quoted from M. Pylyaev, *op. cit.*, 1889, p. 462.
53 E. Gollerbakh, *op. cit.*, 1924, p. 31.
54 Quoted from M. Pylyaev, *op. cit.*, p. 463.
55 GE OR, invenory no, 11043.
56 TsGIA, fond 487, opis 13, 1784, ed. khr., 115, p. 40.
57 *Ibid.*
58 V. Golovina, *Zapiski* (Notes), St Petersburg, 1900, p. 31.
59 IRIO, vol. xxiii, St Petersburg, 1878, p. 157.
60 P. Hayden, 'John Bush', in *Oxford Companion to Gardens*, Oxford, 1986, p. 85.
61 A.G. Cross, By the Banks of the Thames, Newtonville, Mass., 1980, p. 220.
62 *Ibid.*
63 This is preserved in the GE OR.
64 His projects for the Chinese Opera and Pavilions at Tsarskoye Selo are evidence of this.
65 The Double Chinese Bridge at Tsarskoye Selo is evidence of this. See the album of work by P. Neyelov in GE OR.
66 See his project for a Mosque (GE OR, inventory no. 8762). Also relevant are the Chugunnge (Cast-iron) gates built near the Ruined Tower at Tsarskoye Selo.
67 On the prototypes for this building see S. Bronshtein, *Arkhitektura goroda Pushkina* (Architecture of the town of Pushkin), Moscow, 1940, p. 3; A. Petrov, *Gorod Pushkin*, p. 125; A.G. Cross, *op. cit.*, 1980, p. 220.
68 G.L. Le Rouge, *Détails des nouveaux jardins à la mode. Deux cahiers de jardins Anglo-Chinois . . .* Paris, 1776, p. 1.
69 E. Gollerbakh, *Detskosel'skie dvortsy, muzei i parki* (Palaces, museums and parks at Detskoye [formerly Tsarskoye] Selo), Petrograd, 1922, p. 85.
70 G. Koz'myan, *Kameron*, Leningrad, 1987, p. 93.
71 *Ruchnoi dorozhnik*, 1802, p. 20.
72 E. Gollerbakh, *op. cit.*, 1922, p. 82.
73 A. Khrapovitsky, *op. cit.*, 1874, pp. 244–5.
74 TsGIA, fond 487, opis 3, 1787, ed. khr. 14.
75 I. Grabar', *Istoriya*, vol. vi.
76 TsGIA, fond 486, opis 37, ed. khr. 344, p. 5.
77 *Ibid.*, p. 5 obverse side.
78 V. Taleporovsky, *op. cit.*, 1939, p. 23.
79 M. Pylyaev, *op. cit.*, 1889, p. 473.

80 *Tsarskoye selo v poezii* (Tsarskoye Selo in poetry), Petrograd, 1922, p. 4.

81 Pushkin, *Polnoe*, vol. VI, pp. 535–6.

82 TsGADA, fond 14, opis 1, ed. khr. 250, part 1, pp. 80–1.

83 TsGIA, fond 1399, opis 1, ed. khr. 704, pp. 1–3.

84 *Ukaz ob obrazovanii pri Tsarskom sele goroda Sofiya* (Decree on the formation of the town of Sofiya in the environs of Tsarskoye Selo), single sheet, dated St Petersburg, 1780. See also PSZRI, vol. XX, article 14358.

85 TsGADA, fond 14, opis 1, ed. khr. 250, part 1, pp. 34–75 *et al.*

86 Sh. de Lin', *Pis'ma* (Letters), Moscow, 1809, p. 108.

87 *Ruchnoi dorozhnik*, 1802, pp. 13, 65.

88 TsGADA, fond 14, opis 1, ed. khr. 250, part 1, p. 6.

89 TsGADA, fond 14, opis 1, ed. khr. 250, part 3(2), p. 158.

90 Quoted from *Charl'z Kameron,* Petrograd, 1924, p. 41.

91 GE OR, ed. khr. 11072; NIMAKh, fond: Cameron, ed. khr. 54.

92 TsGADA, fond 14, opis 1, ed. khr. 250, part 1, p. 82.

93 GIA-SPb, fond 1743, opis 4, ed. khr. 19, p. 29; TsGADA, opis 1, ed. khr. 250, part 1, p. 7.

94 TsGADA, fond 14, opis 1, ed. khr. 250, part 1, p. 351.

95 *Ibid.*, p. 361.

96 TsGIA, fond 485, opis 3, ed. khr. 5, p. 1.

97 TsGIA, fond 789, opis 1, part 1, doc. 854, p. 1.

98 TsGADA, fond 11, opis 1, doc. 956, part IV, pp. 448–9.

99 E. Gollerbakh, *op. cit.*, 1922, p. 41; S. Bronshtein, *Arkhitektura*, p. 38.

100 TsGADA, fond 14, opis 1, ed. khr. 52, part II(5), p. 235.

101 TsGIA, fond 468, opis 37, ed. khr. 366, p. 1.

102 *Ibid.*, p. 6. The silver, gilded and gold objects were made by the jeweller Lund. Works in non-precious metals were by D. Wilson, joinery work by D. Taylor, book bindings by A. Thomas. Wilson and Taylor were among the craftsmen whom Cameron signed up in England (TsGIA, fond 486, opis 37, ed. khr. 336, pp. 3–30).

103 TsGADA, fond 14, opis 1, ed. khr. 250, part 1, p. 7.

104 *Ibid.*, part 2(1), p. 3 105 *Ibid.*, ed. khr. 52, part 2(5), p. 236.

106 A. Radishchev, *Puteshestvie iz Peterburga v Moskvu* (Journey from St Petersburg to Moscow), Moscow, 1980 edn, p. 12.

107 On these see TsGADA, fond 14, opis 1, ed. khr. 25, part 3(4), pp. 187–230.

108 TsGADA, fond 14, opis 1, ed. khr. 250, part 1, p. 87.

109 TsGADA, fond 14, opis 1, ed. khr. 250, part 1, p. 82.

110 TsGADA, fond VUA, opis 1, ed. khr. 22777, p. 1.

111 TsGADA, fond 14, opis 1, ed. khr. 250, part 2(3), p. 148.

112 A.G. Cross, *op. cit.*, 1980, pp. 57–91.

III PAVLOVSK

1 APDM, Correspondence between Grand Duchess Maria Fedorovna and the adminstrator of the Pavlovsk Estate K. Kuchelbecker. Partially published in M. Semevsky, *Pavlovsk: ocherk istorii i opisanie 1777–1877* (Pavlovsk: Notes of history and description, 1777–1877), St Petersburg, 1877. The letter discussing the laying of the palace foundations appears on p. 34.

2 V. Kurbatov, *Pavlovsk khudozhestvenno-istoricheskii ocherk*, St Petersburg, 1911, p. 72.

3 W. and J. Halfpenny, *Rural Architecture in Chinese Taste . . .*, London, 1750.

4 V. Taleporovsky, *Pavlovskii park* (The park of Pavlovsk), Petrograd, 1923, p. 56. For an account of Maria Fedorovna's youthful interest in gardens, of buildings of her father's estate at Etupes near Montbéliard and their influence on Pavlovsk, see P. Hayden, 'Pavlovsk', *The Garden*, June 1982, pp. 219–24.

5 A. Uspensky, *Pavlovskii dvorets i dvortsovyi park* (Pavlovsk Palace and the royal park), Moscow, 1913, p. 27.

6 *Ibid.*, pp. 5, 6, 9 (memoirs of N. Sablukov, S. Glinka *et al.*); V. Taleporovsky, *op. cit.*, 1923, pp. 7, 22 *et al.*; D. Likhachev, *Poesia sadov* (The poetry of gardens), Leningrad, 1982, p. 228; P. Hayden, 'Imperial Culture et Pavlovsk', *Country Life*, vol. CLXXXI, no. 24, 1987, pp. 118–19.

7 V. Sologub, *Vospominaniya* (Memoirs), Moscow, 1931, pp. 188–89.

8 V. Kurbatov, *op. cit.*, 1911, pp. 65–6; A. Uspensky, *op. cit.*, 1913.

9 V. Taleporovsky, *op. cit.*, 1923, p. 6.

10 M. Semevsky, *op. cit.*, 1877, p. 66.

11 Quoted from E. Gollerbakh and N. Lansere, eds, *Charl'z Kameron,* Petrograd, 1924, p. 50.

12 Quoted from M. Semevsky, *op. cit.*, 1877, p. 66.

13 A. Kuchumov, *Pavlovsk*, Leningrad 1976, p. 36.

14 E. Gollerbakh and N. Lansere, eds, *op. cit.,* 1924, p. 50.

15 V. Taleporovsky, *Charl'z Cameron*, Moscow, 1939, p. 108.

16 V. Taleporovsky, 'Kameron v Pavlovske', in E. Gollerbakh and N. Lansere, eds, *op. cit.*, 1924, p. 50.

17 A. Zelenova, *Dvorets v Pavlovske*, Leningrad, 1986, pp. 33, 40–41.

18 V. Shuisky, *Vincenzo Brenna,* Leningrad, 1986, p. 27.

19 See the plan of the palace, published in E. Gollerbakh and N. Lansere, eds, *op. cit.*, 1924, p. 51.

20 *Ibid.*, p. 50.

21 M. Semevsky, *op. cit.*, 1877, p. 15.

22 *Ibid.*, p. 16.

23 *Ibid.*, p. 30.

24 *Ibid.*, p. 54.

25 *Ibid.*, p. 54.

26 *Ibid.*, p. 54.

27 APDM, Correspondence of Maria Fedorovna and Kuchelbecker, letter of Maria Fedorovna dated 14 April 1784.

28 M. Semevsky, *op. cit.*, 1877, p. 30.

29 M.V. Alpatov, *op. cit.*, p. 20.

30 *Ibid.*, p. 17.

31 From the reminiscences of N. Sablukov. Quoted from A. Uspensky, *op. cit.*, 1913, p. 10.

32 *Ibid.*, pp. 10–11.

33 V. Taleporovsky, *op. cit.*, 1923, p. 61.

34 *Ibid.*

35 V. Shtorkh, *Putevoditel' po sadu i gorodu Pavlovsku* (Guide to the gardens and town of Pavlovsk), St Petersburg, 1843, p. 16.

36 V. Taleporovsky, *op. cit.*, 1923, p. 72.

37 From J.C. Loudon, in his *Encyclopaedia of Gardening*, London, 1827, p. 56, to P. Hayden, 'Pavlovsk', *The Garden*, vol. 107, part 6, 1982, pp. 219–25.

38 V. Zhukovsky, *Sobranie sochinenii* (Collected works), Moscow, 1902, P. 100.

39 V. Kurbatov, *op. cit.*, 1911, p. 85.

40 A. Krashchennikov, 'Pavlovsk', in *Pamyatniki arkhitektury prigorodov Leningrada* (Monuments of architecture in the environs of Leningrad), Leningrad, 1983, p. 162.

41 APDM, *Atlas Pavlovskogo dvortsa s sadami, zverintsami i vsemi v nikh imeyushchimisya stroeniyami, ravno goroda i polei* (Map of Pavlovsk Palace with its gardens, menageries and with all the structures found within it, of both town and fields), 1803, published in A. Kuchumov, *op. cit.*, p. 13.

42 V. Kurbatov, *op. cit.*, 1911, p. 86.

43 *Ibid.*

44 APDM, plan of Pavlovsk in 1794, inventory no. 1010.

45 O. Ivanova, *Pavlovskii park*, Leningrad, 1956, p. 20.

46 V. Taleporovsky, *op. cit.*, 1923, p. 70.

47 D. Kobeko, *Tsesarevich Pavel Petrovich*, St Petersburg, 1882, p. 179.

48 O. Ivanova, *op. cit.*, p. 21.

49 APDM, Letter of Maria Fedorovna to Kuchelbecker dated 3 April 1789.

50 V. Zhukovsky, *op. cit.*, 1902, p. 101.

51 V. Taleporovsky, *op. cit.*, 1923, p. 10.

52 APDM, Letter of Maria Fedorovna to Kuchelbecker dated 3 April 1789.

53 *Ukazatel' Pavlovska* (Index to Pavlovsk), St Petersburg, 1843, p. 19.

54 O. Ivanova, *op. cit.*, 1956, p. 28.

55 Quoted from A. Uspensky, *op. cit.*, 1913, p. 16.

56 J.C. Loudon, *op. cit.*, 1827, p. 56.

57 P. Svin'in, *Dostoprinimatel'nosti Sankt-Peterburga i ego okrestnostei* (The Sights of St Petersburg and its environs), St Petersburg, 1816, p. 26.

58 Quoted from A. Uspensky, *op. cit.*, 1913, p. 9.

59 *Ibid.*, p. 12.

60 M. Semevsky, *op. cit.*, 1877, p. 52.

61 *Ibid.*, p. 53.

62 V. Taleporovsky, *op. cit.*, 1923, p. 24.

63 A. Uspensky, *op. cit.*, 1913, p. 13.

64 *Ibid.*

65 F. Glinka, Letter to a friend from Pavlovsk, *Russkii vestnik na 1815g* (Russian Courier for 1815), book 13, p. 26.

66 M. Semevsky, *op. cit.*, 1913, p. 15.

67 V. Sologub, *Vospominaniya* (Memoirs), Moscow, 1931, pp. 198–213.

68 *Ibid.*, pp. 196–7.

IV ORIENTALISM

1 E. Erdberg, *Chinese Influence on European Garden Structures*, Harvard, 1935; O. Siren, *China and Gardens of Europe of the XVIII Century*, New York, 1950; H. Honour, *Chinoiserie: The Vision of Cathay*, London, 1967; O. Impey, *Chinoiserie: The Impact of Oriental Style*, Oxford, 1977; P. Conner, *Oriental Architecture in the West*, London, 1979; N. Beautheac and F.–X. Bouchant *L'Europe exotique*, Paris, 1985.

2 For example N. Beautheac and F.–X. Bouchart, *op. cit.*, 1985, p. 33. Compare with G. Lukomsky, *Russkaya provintsial'naya arkhitektura* (Russian provincial architecture), Part 1, Petrograd, 1915, p. 86.

3 The architect P. Neyelov, for example, drew Turkish-style structures in the South of Russia. Of interest in this connection are the atlases which have depictions of the buildings in Crimean towns, which are preserved in TsGAVMF fond 3, opis 23, ed. khr. 950 *et al*. In the *Atlas ukreplennym liniyam Rossiiskoi imperii* (Atlas of fortifications of the Russian Empire) of 1797, the sheets contain cartouches with depictions of Chinese, Central-Asian and Kazakh buildings. See TsGAVMF fond 3. opis 23, ed. khr. 938.

4 TsGADA, fond 9, opis 2, ed. khr. 45, p. 200.

5 G. Grohman, *Ideemagazin fur Gartenkunst*, Leipzig, bd. 27, 1799, pl. VI. *Ibid.*, bd. 13, 1789, pl. IX.

6 G.Ch. Kraft, *Plans of the Most Beautiful Picturesque Gardens of France, England and Germany*, Paris, 1802, p. 4.

7 R. Heber, *Narrative of a Journey through India*, vol. II, London, 1828, p. 318.

8 M. Gra and B. Zhukomsky, *Kolomenskoe*, Moscow, 1971, p. 120; Z. Popova, 'Rospisnaya mebel' (Decoratively painted furniture), in *Sokrovishcha russkogo narodnogo iskusstva* (Treasures of Russian vernacular art), Moscow, 1967, p. 49.

9 O. Yevangulova, 'Turetskaya seriya zhivopistsa N. Mattarnovi' (The Turkish Series of the painter N. Mattarnovi), in the collection Kul'tura i iskusstvo Petrovskogo vremeni (Culture and art of the Petrine period), Leningrad, 1977, pp. 174–5; Russkaya starina (Russian antiquity), vol. 12, 1875, p. 11.

10 I. Ukhanova, 'G. Burmkorst – peterburgskii master lakovogo dela' (G. Burmkorst: St Petersburg master of lacquer work), in *Kul'tura i iskusstvo Petrovskogo vremeni* (Culture and art of the Petrine period), Leningrad, 1977, pp. 174–5; *Russkaya starina* (Russian antiquity), vol. 12, 1875, p. 11.

11 O. Yevangulova, *op. cit.*, 1977, p. 174.

12 I. Ukhanova, *op. cit.*, 1977, p. 174.

13 A. Raskin, *Gorod Lomonosov* (The Town of Lomonosov [formerly Oranienbaum]), Leningrad, 1979.

14 E. Erdberg, *op. cit.*, 1935, p. 108.

15 The Chinoiserie at Oranienbaum is mentioned in numerous works devoted to the Palace complex as a whole. See for example: V. Kurbatov, *Strel'na i Oranienbaum*, Leningrad, 1928; V. Dakhovich, *Oranienbaum*, Moscow and Leningrad, 1932; S. Zemtsov, *Oranienbaum*, Moscow, 1946; A. Nevstoyeva, 'Ansambl' Rinaldi v gorode Lomonosove' (Rinaldi's ensemble in the town of Lomonosov), *Arkhitekturnoe nasledstvo*, vol. 5, Moscow, 1955; G. Solosin, Z. El'zenger and V. Yeliseyeva, *Gorod Lomonosov* (The town of Lomonosov), Leningrad, 1979; D. Kyuchariants, *Khudozhestvennye sokrovishcha goroda Lomonosova* (Artistic treasures of the town of Lomonosov), Leningrad, 1985.

16 D. Kyucharianc, *Antonio Rinaldi*, Leningrad, 1979, p. 9.

17 E. Erdberg, *op. cit.*, 1935, p. 37.

18 D. Kyucharianc, *op. cit.*, 1979.

19 W. Chambers, *Designs of Chinese Buildings*, London, 1751; W. and J. Halfpenny, *Rural Architecture in Chinese Taste*, London, 1751; Charles Over, *Ornamental Architecture . . . in Chinese Taste*, London, 1757; W. Wright, *Grotesque Architecture . . .*, London, 1767. These were the publications mainly used by Russian architects of the eighteenth century.

20 TsGADA, fond 10, opis 1, ed. khr. 383. See E. Shukina, 'Natural'nyi sad russkoi usadby v kontse XVIII veka' (The natural garden on the Russian country estate of the late eighteenth century), in the collection *XVIII vek* (The eighteenth century), Moscow, 1973, pp. 109–17.

21 C. Hirschfeld, *Theorie de l'art de jardins*, Paris, 1779. Many fragments of this were translated into Russian in A. Bolotov's *Ekonomicheskii magazin*. See also there numerous articles on Eastern gardens, for example —, 1786, part 25, no. 21, pp. 321–5, 337–52; no. 23, pp. 353–75. Also notes on gardens in China, *ibid.*, no. 24, pp. 369–89, and notes on gardens in Turkey, *ibid.*, no. 25, pp. 385–9, as well as some other notes on gardens of Persia and various other nations.

22 In confirming this I came upon the design for a mosque-pavilion by Yuri Velten (State Hermitage Collection, inventory no. 8764, and published in M. Korshunova, *Yuri Felten* (Yuri Velten), Leningrad, 1982, p. 41, cat. 22), which is practically identical to the project published in W. Wright, *Grotesque Architecture or Rural Amusement*, London, 1767, p. 21 ('The Rural Mosque'). This project evokes the pavilion erected in the park at Kew (G.L. Le Rouge, *Détails des nouveaux jardins à la mode. Deux cahiers de jardins Anglo-Chinois*, Paris, 1776, cahier 2, pl. 3).

23 E. Gollerbakh, *Detskoselskie dvortsy, muzei i parki* (Palaces, museums and parks at Detskoye [formerly Tsarskoye] Selo), Petrograd, 1922, p. 83.

24 *Ibid.*, p. 82.

25 GE OR, inventory nos 12983–7, 23303. See D. Kyucharianc, *op. cit.*, 1979, pp. 103–5.

26 GE OR, inventory no. 12882 (Album of work by P. Neyelov).

27 J.C. Loudon, *Encyclopaedia of Gardening*, London, 1827, p. 52.

28 O. Impey, *op. cit.*, 1977, p. 25.

29 On the drawings by Velten, see Korshunova, *Yuri Fel'ten*, cats 16, 19, 21; also the same author's 'Arkhitekturnye chertezhi Yu. Fel'tena' (The architectural drawings of Yu. Velten), *Soobshcheniya Gos. Ermitazha* (Research Papers of the State Hermitage), no. 29, Leningrad, 1968, and 'Graficheskoe nasledie Yu.M. Fel'tena' (The graphic legacy of Yu.M. Velten), *Pamyatniki kul'tury: Novye otkrytiya. Pis'mennost'. Iskusstvo. Arkheologiya (Yezhegodnik)* (Monuments of Culture: New Discoveries. Writings. Art. Archaeology. (Annual)), Moscow, 1976, pp. 302–17. The drawings series totals nineteen sheets, including Hermitage inventory nos 8761, 8762, 8763, 8767, 8768, 8753, 8755 *et al*. Attributions have been made by Korshunova. For the sheets by Gerard, see TsGVIA, fond 418, opis 1, ed. khr. 82, sheets 1–13.

30 E. Erdberg, *op. cit.*, 1935, pp. 12–17, 59–80.

31 A. Petrov, *Gorod Pushkin* (The town of Pushkin), Leningrad, 1977, p. 149.

32 A.G. Cross, *By the Banks of the Thames*, Newtonville, Mass., 1980, p. 22.

33 TsGIA, fond 487, opis 13, 1782, ed. khr. 63; TsGIA, fond 487, opis 13, 1786, ed. khr. 63, p. 1.

34 *Ibid.*, p. 3.

35 TsGIA, fond 470, opis 5, ed. khr. 898, pp. 149–52.

36 Ibid.

37 TsGIA, fond 487, opis 13, 1784, ed. khr. 115, p. 3.

38 O. Impey, *op. cit.*, 1977, p. 29.

39 Yu. Shamurin, *Podmoskovie* (Works in the environs of Moscow), Moscow, 1914, pp. 25–6.

40 *Ibid.*, pp. 70–71.

41 T. Kazhdan, 'Arkhitekturnye pamyatniki v sele Vishenki' (Architectural monuments in the village of Vishenka), *Soobshcheniya instituta istorii iskusstv* (Research papers of the Institute of History of the Arts), Moscow, 1960, p. 85.

42 S. Aksakov, *Sobranie sochinenii v 5 tt* (Collected works in five volumes), vol. 1, Moscow, 1966, p. 442.

43 I. Grabar', *Istoriya russkogo iskusstva* (History of Russian art), Moscow, 1910–14, vol. III, p. 320.

V RUSSIAN NEO-GOTHIC

1 I. Grabar', *Istoriya russkogo iskusstva*, Moscow, 1910–14, vol. III, p. 321.
2 Interest in Russian neo-gothic, which got only passing mention in Russian art-historical works of the late nineteenth and early twentieth centuries, grew dramatically during the 1920s. Publications included the following booklets: N. Kozhin, *Osnovy russkoi psevdogotiki* (Foundations of Russian pseudo-gothic), Leningrad, 1926; *Pamyatniki russkoi psevdogotiki* (Monuments of Russian pseudo-gothic), Leningrad, 1926; *Russkaya provintsial'naya arkhitektura* (Russian provincial architecture), Leningrad, 1927. Kozhin considered that Russia's interest in her own medieval history grew from the deep involvement with Russian medieval architecture. Another study of that period was V. Zgura's *Problemy i pamyatniki, svyazannye s V.I. Bazhenovym* (Problems and monuments connected with V.I. Bazhenov), Moscow, 1928, where neo-gothic was linked above all with reminiscences of the baroque. From the 1930s to the 1970s, a series of important studies on classicist architects accorded serious mention to their works in the gothic taste. Such studies included: N. Belekhov and A. Petrov, *Ivan Starov*, Moscow, 1950; A. Mikhailov, *Bazhenov*, Moscow, 1951; A. Vlasyuk *et al.*, *Kazakov*, Moscow, 1957; M. Budylina *et al.*, *Arkhitektor N.A. L'vov*, Moscow, 1961; A. Glumov, *L'vov*, Moscow, 1980; M. Korshunova, *Yuri Fel'ten*, Leningrad, 1982; and others. However, these studies essentially contain facts, with virtually no stylistic evaluations. In recent years a number of researchers have once more addressed the question of the role of neo-gothic in Russian architectural history of the eighteenth and nineteenth centuries. Examples of this are: Ye. Borisova, 'Russkaya arkhitektura i angliiskaia psevdo-gotika' (Russian architecture and English neo-gothic), in *Vzaimosvyaz' iskusstv v khudozhestvennom razvitii rossii vtoroi poloviny XIX v* (Interrelationships between the arts in Russia's artistic development of second half of the nineteenth century), Moscow, 1982; A. Boris, *Romanticheskaya tema v Moskovskoi arkhitekture kontsa XVIII–nachala XIX vv.* (The romantic theme in Moscow architecture of the late eighteenth and early nineteenth centuries), Moscow, 1988; Ye. Petrova, *Neogotika v arkhitekture Belorossii* (Neo-gothic in the architecture of Byelorussia), Moscow, 1989.
3 A. Petrov, *Gorod Pushkin* (The town of Pushkin), Leningrad, 1977, p. 111.
4 A.G. Cross, *By the Banks of the Thames*, Newtonville, Mass., 1980, p. 220.

5 A. Petrov, *op. cit.*, 1977, p. 112.
6 *Ibid.*
7 This idea of P.N. Petrov arose in the same context as that of the architectural difference between the Siberian Bridge at Tsarskoye Selo and the Palladian Bridge at Wilton, which A.G. Cross refuted in *By the Banks of the Thames*, pp. 220–21.
8 Ye. Tartakovskaya, 'Chesmenskii dvorets' (Chesmensky Palace), *Vremennik IZO* (Bulletin of IZO), Leningrad, 1928.
9 *Ibid.*, article on 'Kekerekekshi dvorets'.
10 M. Korshunova, *op. cit.*, 1982, p. 20.
11 D. Cruickshank, *Georgian Buildings of Britain and Ireland*, London, 1985, p. 217.
12 *The Modern Builder's Assistant*, London, 1751, pl. 31.
13 W. and J. Halfpenny, *Rural Architecture . . .*, London, 1752; *id.*, *A New and Complete System of Architecture in a Variety of Plans and Elevations of Designs of Convenient and Decorated Houses*, London, 1745.
14 G. Williamson, *The Imperial Russian Dinner Service*, London, 1905; A.G. Cross, *Anglo-Russian Relations in the Eighteenth Century*, Norwich, 1977, p. 41.
15 A. Petrov, *op. cit.*, 1977, p. 181.
16 N. Belekhov and A. Petrov, *Ivan Starov*.
17 S. Stankevich, 'Tserkov v Pskovskoi gubernii' (The church in Pskov district), *Zodchii* (The architect), nos 3–4, 1892, pp. 31–2.
18 M. Korshunova, 'Neizvestnaya postroika Yu. Fel'tena v Kalininskoi oblasti' (An unknown building by Yuri Velten in Kalinin county), *Soobshcheniya Gosudarstvennogo Ermitazha* (Research papers of the State Hermitage), no. 34, Leningrad, 1972, pp. 61–4.
19 A. Mikhailov, *Bazhenov*, Moscow, 1951, pp. 49–110.
20 A. Bolotov, *Zhizn' i priklucheniya Andreya Bolotova, opisanye samim im dlya svoikh potomkov* (The life and adventures of Andrey Bolotov, described by himself for his descendents), Moscow and Leningrad, 1931, vol. III, p. 208.
21 *Ibid.*, pp. 212–13.
22 *Russkii arkhiv* (Russian archive), Moscow, 1878, book 3, p. 16.
23 *Ibid.*, p. 17.
24 N. Kozhin, 'V.I. Bazhenov i arkhitektura rannego russkogo romantizma' (V.I. Bazhenov and the architecture of early Russian romanticism), *Akademiya arkhitektury* (Academy of architecture), no. 2, 1957; A. Mikhailov, *op. cit.*, p. 112.
25 In recent years a very convincing case has been developed for the emergence of romanticism in Russia in the 1820s. The case for this as it applies to architecture was made by Ye.A. Borisova in her article 'Russkaya arkhitektura i angliiskaia psevdogotika . . . v russkoi kul'ture serediny XIX veka' (Russian architecture and English pseudo-gothic), in *Vzaimosvyaz' iskusstv v khudozhestvennom razvitii Rossii vtoroi poloviny XIX v* (Interrelationships between the arts in Russia's artistic

development of second half of the nineteenth century), Moscow, 1982, pp. 60–109.
26 A. Bolotov, *op. cit.*, 1931, pp. 207–24; A. Travin, *Zapiski* (Notes), Pskov, 1914, pp. 25–129; G. Vinsky, *Moe vremya* (My time), St Petersburg, 1914, p. 147.
27 S. Liubetsky, 'Tsaritsyno bliz Moskvy' (Tsaritsyno near Moscow), Niva, no. 1, 1870, p. 12.
28 A. Bolotov, *op. cit.*, 1931, p. 222.
29 V. Maikov, *Opisanie uveselitel'nikh ognei, kotorye predstavleny v prodolzhenie mirnogo torzhestva . . . na Khodynke 23 iulia 1,775 g* (Description of the bonfire entertainments in continuation of the celebrations . . . on Khodynskoye Field on 23 July 1775), Moscow, 1775.
30 *Arkhitekturnyi arkhiv*, no. 1, Moscow, 1946, p. 104.
31 A. Rayevskii, 'Okrestnosti Moskvy' (The environs of Moscow), *Syn otechestva* (Son of the fatherland), St Petersburg, 1815, part 25, p. 59.
32 K. Mineyeva, *Tsaritsyno*, Moscow, 1988, p. 33.
33 V. Snegirev, *Arkhitektor V.I. Bazhenov* (Architect V.I. Bazhenov), Moscow, 1937, p. 184.
34 TSGADA, fond 14, ed. khr. 576, p. 145.
35 *Arkhitekturnyi arkhiv*, no. 1, Moscow, 1946, p. 108.
36 TsGADA, dvortovoe otdelenie (Palace department), opis 49, no. 62117.
37 K. Mineyeva, *op. cit.*, 1988, p. 68.
38 A. Mikhailov, *op. cit.*, 1951, p. 156.
39 S. Razgonov, *V.I. Bazhenov*, Moscow, 1987, pp. 107–8, 132–8; *Masonstvo v ego proshlom i nastoyashchem* (Masonry past and present), Moscow, 1914, p. 32.
40 M. Longinov, *Novikov i ego moskovskie martinisty* (Novikov and his Moscow Martinists), Moscow, 1866; A. Zapadov, *Novikow*, Moscow, 1968; N. Novikov, *Izbrannye sochineniya* (Selected works), Moscow and Leningrad, 1951.
41 L. Svetlov, *Izdatel'skaya deyatel'nost' N.I. Novikova* (The publishing activity of N.I. Novikov), 1946.
42 V. Zapadov, 'K istorii pravitel'stvennykh presledovanii N.I. Novikova' (Towards a history of the governmental prosecution of N.I. Novikov), *XVIII veka* (The eighteenth century), Collection 2, Moscow, 1976, p. 47.
43 *Ibid.*, p. 47.
44 *Ibid.*, p. 47.
45 Masonic symbolism contains many signs related to architecture. Construction was fundamental to the masonic concept as they saw its various attributes as models of a well-appointed spiritual world.
46 K. Mineyeva, *op. cit.*, 1988, p. 68.
47 A. Vlasyuk, A. Kaplun and A. Kiparisova, *Kazakov*, Moscow, 1957, p. 200.
48 M. Rusakomvsky, 'Ansambl' za Preo-brazhenskoi zastavoi' (The ensemble outside the Proebrazhensky Gates) in *Pamyatniki*

russkoi arkhitektury (Monuments of Russian architecture), Moscow, 1985, pp. 148–69.

49 A. Mikhailov, *op. cit.* 1951, pp. 162–4; A. Vlasyuk *et al.*, *op. cit.*, 1957, pp. 205–8.

50 A. Vlasyuk *et al.*, *op. cit.*, 1957, p. 205.

51 Construction of the palaces in Konkovo and Bulatnikovo was finally ceased only in 1809, when the uncompleted buildings were sold for demolition.

52 V. Zgura, *Problemy i pamyatniki, svyazannye s V.I. Bazhenovym* (Problems and monuments connected with V.I. Bazhenov), Moscow, 1928, p. 103; A. Nekrasov, 'Problemy tvorchestva Bazhenova' (Issues in the work of Bazhenov), *Akademiya arkhitektury* (Academy of architecture), no. 2, 1937, p. 14; A. Mikhailov, *op. cit.*, 1951, pp. 184–5.

53 T. Kazdan, 'Arkhitekturnye pamyatniki v sele Vishenki' (Architectural monuments in the village of Vishenki), *Soobshcheniya instituta istorii iskusstv* (Research papers of the Institute for the History of the Arts), Moscow, 1960, pp. 80–85; M. Tsapenko, *Po ravninam Desny i Seima* (Around the plains of Desna and Seima), Moscow, 1967, pp. 30–6.

54 The designer of the palace is unknown. It has been suggested that it may have been either V.I. Bazhenov or his pupil who worked in the Ukraine, M. Mostsipanov.

55 N. Kozhin, *Russkaya provintsial'naya arkhitektura* (Russian provincial architecture), Leningrad, 1928, pp. 3–15; N. Kozhin, *Pamyatnik russkoi psevdogotiki XVIII veka v sele Znamenka Tambovskoi gubernii* (A monument of Russian eighteenth century neo-gothic in the village of Znamenka, Tambov district), Leningrad, 1924.

56 N. Kozhin, *Osnovy russkoi psevdogotiki* (The foundations of Russian pseudo-gothic), Leningrad, 1927, p. 5, *et al.*; A. Mikhailov, *op. cit.*, 1951, p. 181.

57 *Orlovskaya oblast'. Katalog pamyatnikov arkhitektury* (Orlov region. Catalogue of architectural monuments), Moscow, 1985, pp. 91–4.

58 *Pamyatniki arkhitektury Moskovskoi oblasti* (Monuments of architecture of Moscow region), vol. I, Moscow, 1975, p. 40.

59 A. Mikhailov, *op. cit.*, 1951, pp. 176–7.

60 *Ibid.*, p. 184.

61 M. Il'in, 'Mar'inka Buturlina', *Trudy etnograficheskogo museia MGU* (Research studies of the Moscow State University Museum of Ethnography), Moscow, 1924; *Pamyatniki arkhitektury Moskovskoi oblasti*, vol. 2, Moscow, 1975, p. 275.

62 V. Zgura, *Problemy i pamyatniki svyazannye c V.I. Bazhenovym*, Moscow, 1928.

63 N. Kozhin, *Pamyatniki russkoi psevdogotiki*, p. 1; *id.*, *Russkaya provintsial'naya arkhitektura*, p. 7.

64 A. Mikhailov, *op. cit.*, 1951, pp. 164–6.

65 Yu. Gerchuk, *Novye svedeniya o neogotikicheskikh postroikakh V.I. Bazhenova. Doklad na konferentii 'Russkii klassitsizm'* (New data on the neo-gothic buildings of

V.I. Bazhenov. Paper to the conference 'Russian Classicism'), Moscow, 1986.

66 A. Nekrasov, 'Novgorodskie motivy v tvorchestve V.I. Bazhenova' (Novgorod motifs in the work of V.I. Bazhenov), *Akademiya arkhitektury* (Academy of architecture), no. 2, 1937, p. 44; A. Mikhailov, *op. cit.*, 1951, pp. 186–7; N. Kozhin, *Pamyatnaki russkoi psevdogotiki*, p. 17, on the project for the church at Bykovo.

67 This was during his study tour to Italy as a Scholar of the Academy of Arts.

68 V. Snegirev, *Zodchii Bazhenov* (The architect Bazhenov), Moscow, 1962, p. 222.

69 TsGADA, fond XVIII, ed. khr. 251, p. 108; A. Mikhailov, *op. cit.*, 1951, p. 168.

70 J. Summerson, *Architecture in Britain, 1530–1830*, Harmondsworth, 1970, p. 397.

71 TsGADA, State Archive, fond XIV, ed. khr. 51, part IV, p. 34; A. Vlasyuk, 'Arkhitektura Arkhangel'skogo sobora' (The architecture of the Archangel Cathedral), Dissertation, Moscow, 1947, p. 236.

72 *Pamyatniki arkhitektury Moskvy* (Monuments of Moscow architecture), Moscow, 1982, pp. 194, 293–4.

73 GIM IZO, inventory no. R–372.

74 A. Boris, 'Romanticheskaya tema v arkhitekture Moskvy XVIII–nach. XIX vekov' (The romantic theme in Moscow architecture of the eighteenth to early nineteenth centuries), Dissertation, Moscow, 1988, p. 54.

75 In the collections of GIM OPI, the album has been attributed by A. Boris and F. Petrov. See A. Boris, *op. cit.*, 1988.

76 GIM OPI, fond 402, opis 1, ed. khr. 109, p. 14.

77 A. Sedov, *Yegotov, M.M.*, 1956, p. 70.

78 TsGIA, fond 1499, opis 2, ed. khr. 789, pp. 1–4; GIM IZO, R–3v48.

79 A. Boris, *op. cit.*, 1988, p. 58.

80 M. Taranovskaya, *Karl Rossi*, Leningrad, 1980, p. 19.

81 TsGIA, fond 797, opis 1, ed. khr. 4009, p. 16 obverse.

82 A. Boris, *op. cit.*, 1988, p. 70.

83 Rusakovsky, 'Ansambl', p. 148.

84 M. Budylina, O. Braitsova and A. Kharlamova, *Arkhitektor N.A. L'vov* (The Architect N.A. Lvov), Moscow, 1961, p. 160.

85 G. Grim, *Arkhitektor Adrian Zakharov* (The architect Adrian Zakharov), Moscow, 1940, ills 3–5.

86 M. Tarkovskaya, *Karl Rossi*, pp. 18–20.

87 A. Petrov, *op. cit.*, 1977, pp. 166–80.

88 V. Tenikhina, *Kottedzh* (The Cottage), Leningrad, 1986.

89 L. Timofeyev and A. Tsarin, *Alupka Simferopol*, 1983, pp. 35–48.

90 N. Vsevolozhsky, *Putevoditel' cherez yuzhnuiu Rossii, Krym i Odessu v Konstantinopol' . . . v 1836 i 1837 godu* (A trip through southern Russia, Crimea and Odessa to Constantinople . . . in 1836 and 1837), vol. I, Moscow, 1838, p. 75.

91 V. Shuisky, 'Arkhitekturnaya grafika Ch. Barri v sobranii NIM AKh SSSR' (Architectural drawings by Charles Barry in the Research Museum of the Academy of Arts of the USSR), *Arkhitektura SSSR* (Architecture USSR), no. 5, 1987, pp. 102–5.

VI ADAM MENELAWS AND WILLIAM HASTIE

1 T. Talbot Rice, *Charles Cameron*, London, 1967, pp. 21–2.

2 TsGADA, fond 14, opis 1, ed. khr. 52, part 3, p. 187.

3 A.G. Cross, 'Charles Cameron's Scottish workmen', *Scottish Slavonic Review*, no. 10, spring 1988, pp. 51–74. This work gives an extremely detailed and well-documented description of the life and activites of the colony of Scottish craftsmen at Tsarskoye Selo (Sofiya). Professor Cross gives a complete list of the craftsmen by name, based on material in TsGADA. Rather than repeat this material here, the reader is refered to Cross's paper.

4 A.G. Cross, *op. cit.*, 1988, pp. 64–5.

5 TsGIA, fond 472, opis 11, ed. khr. 35, p. 1; A.G. Cross, *op. cit.*, 1988, pp. 51–74.

6 TsGIA, fond 472, opis 11, ed. khr. 266, p. 2.

7 M. Budylina *et al. Arkhitektor N. L'vov*, Moscow, 1961, p. 10; N. Nikulina, *Nikolai L'vov*, Moscow, 1972, p. 25.

8 *Chetyre knigi Palladievoi arkhitektury. Kniga 1. Perevod N. L'vova* (The Four Books of Palladian Architecture. Book 1. Translated by N. Lvov), St Petersburg, 1798, p. 2 (written some years before its eventual publication).

9 TsGADA, found XVI, opis 1, ed. khr. 766, part 3, pp. 73–5.

10 A.G. Cross, *op. cit.*, 1988, p. 67.

11 *Arkhiv gosudarstvennogo soveta* (Archive of the State Council), vol. 2, St Petersburg, 1888, pp. 189, 333.

12 TsGADA, found 1235, opis 1, ed. khr. 266, p. 2.

13 *Arkhiv gosudarstvennogo soveta* (Archive of the State Council), p. 333.

14 T.V. Alekseyeva, *B.L. Borovikovskii*, Moscow, 1975, pp. 70, 76.

15 TsGIA, fond 1286, opis 1, ed. khr., 266, p. 2.

16 *Ibid.*

17 A.G. Cross, *By the Banks of the Thames*, Newtonville, Mass., 1980. His chap. 3 thoroughly examines the question of Samborsky's participation in the dissemination of English agricultural attitudes in Russia.

18 N.A. Shilder, *Imperator Aleksandr I*, vol. I, St Petersburg, 1897, p. 228.

19 M. Budylina, *op. cit.*, 1961, pp. 91–4.

20 S. Dzhutivskii, *Aleksandrov uveselitel'nyi sad* (The Alexandrov hanging garden), Kharkov, 1810.

21 G. Derzhavin, *Sochineniya* (Works), Moscow, 1968, p. 83.

22 *Polozhenie prakticheskoi shkoly zemledeliya i sel'skogo khozyaistva* (Statute of the practical school for land management and agriculture), St Petersburg, 1798.

23 *Ibid.*, p. 2; PSZRI, vol. XXIV, no. 18039.

24 A.G. Cross, *op. cit.*, 1980, p. 88.

25 PSZRI, vol. XXIV, p. 688.

26 TSGIA, fond 1286, opis 1, ed. khr. 266, p. 2.

27 *Ibid.*

28 *Ibid.*

29 I. Fomin, *Istoricheskaya vystavka arkhitektury* (A historical exhibition of architecture), exh. cat., St Petersburg, 1911, p. 58.

30 *Pamyatniki arkhitektury Moskovskoi oblasti* (Architectural monuments of the Moscow region), Moscow, 1975, vol. I, pp. 8–10.

31 J.C. Loudon, *Encyclopaedia of Gardening*, London, 1827, p. 51.

32 F. Gornostaev, *Dvortsy i tserkvi iuga* (Palaces and churches of the south), Moscow, 1914, p. 38.

33 F. Gornostaev, 'Stroitel'stvo grafa A. Razumovskogo' (Construction projects of Count A. Razumovsky), *Trudy XIV arkheologicheskogo s'ezda* (Proceedings of the XIV Archaeological Congress), Moscow, 1911, pp. 183–90.

34 I. Grabar', *Istoriya russkogo iskusstva* (History of Russian art), Moscow, 1910–14, vol. III, p. 387.

35 G. Lukomsky, 'Pis'ma grafa A. Razumovskogo k M. Gudovichu' (The letters of Count A. Razumovsky to M. Gudovich), *Starye gody* (The olden days), March 1914.

36 G. Lukomsky, *Baturinskii dvorets* (Baturin palace), St Petersburg, 1812; G. Koz'myan, *Cameron*, Leningrad, 1987, pp. 139–46.

37 *Arkhiv knyazia Vorontsova* (The archive of Count Vorontsov), book 13, Moscow, 1879, p. 438.

38 *Starye gody* (The olden days), March 1914, p. 26.

39 *Ibid.*

40 *Arkhiv knyazia Vorontsova* (The archives of Count Vorontsov), book 13, Moscow, 1879, p. 438.

41 Quoted from G. Koz'myan, *op. cit.*, 1987, p. 140.

42 TsGIA, fond 1286, opis 1, ed. khr. 266, p. 2.

43 I. Fomin, 'Istoricheskaya', p. 58.

44 TsGIA, fond 1286, opis 1, ed. khr. 266, p. 11.

45 M. Il'in, *Moskva*, Moscow, 1970, pp. 207–8.

46 M. Budylina, *op. cit.*, 1961, p. 25.

47 *Pamyatniki arkhitektury Moskovskoi oblasti*, vol. I, p. 14.

48 This is the opinion of M.F. Korshunova.

49 GIM IZO, r–689.

50 GNIMA, r–15912.

51 GIM IZO, r–135.

52 For the Kottedzh and related projects see *Pamyatniki arkhitektury prigorodov Leningrada*, pp. 444–53.

53 On Schinkel's chapel see *ibid.*, pp. 450–1.

54 Il'in, *op. cit.*, 1970, p. 243.

55 TsGIA, fond 1286, opis 2, ed. khr. 123, 1819, pp. 8–10.

56 GE OR, inventory nos. 3125–54. On this see M. Korshunova, 'Arkhitektor V. Geste' (The architect W. Hastie), *Trudy Gosudarstvennogo Ermitazha* (Research papers of the State Hermitage), vol. XVIII, 1977, pp. 133–5.

57 IRIO, vol. XXIII, St Petersburg, 1878, pp. 611–12.

58 GE OR, Inventory nos 23295–8. In the note it says that they are sending a project 'executed by candidate of architecture Gasti according to the programme set, for linking that item to the book which Hastie brought with him'. That indicates the album was already in the Imperial Library when the project was done.

59 J. Summerson, *Architecture in Britain, 1530–1830*, Harmondsworth, 1970, p. 370.

60 A.G. Cross, *op. cit.*, 1988, p. 69.

61 GNIMA, no. 1220/1–2, 3801, 3803, 3806, 1711/1–4.

62 Georges Loukomski (*sic*), *Charles Cameron . . . his life and work in Russia . . . at Tsarskoye Selo and Pavlovsk*, adapted into English by N. de Gren, London, 1943, p. 57.

63 TsGIA, fond 1399, opis 1, ed. khr. 545, pp. 5–10.

64 M. Korshunova, *op. cit.*, 1977, p. 137.

65 TsGIA, fond 1286, opis 2, ed. khr. 123, 1819, p. 9.

66 A.G. Cross, *op. cit.*, 1988, p. 66.

67 TsGIA, fond 1286, opis 2, ed. khr. 123, 1819, p. 9.

68 A. Punin, *Povest' o leningradskikh mostakh* (A tale of Leningrad bridges), Leningrad, 1971, p. 45.

69 TsGIA, fond 1286, opis 2, ed. khr. 123, 1819, p. 10.

70 M. Korshunova, *op. cit.*, 1977, pp. 137–8.

71 M. Blek and A. Rotach, 'Chugunnye arochnye mosty v Leningrade' (Cast-iron arched bridges in Leningrad), *Arkhitekturnoe nasledstvo* (Architectural heritage), no. 7, 1955, p. 143.

72 TsGADA, fond 17, opis 1, ed. khr. 12, p. 7.

73 GNIMA, Inventory no. 10760/1–40.

74 TsGVIA, fond VUA, Inventory no. 22513.

75 NIMAKh, Inventory nos A–591, A–592 (projects by Hastie).

76 TsGIA, fond 1286, opis 2, ed. khr. 123, 1819, p. 11.

77 *Ibid.*

78 S. Bronshtein, *Arkhitektura goroda Pushkina* (Architecture of the town of Pushkin), Moscow, 1940, pp. 41–2.

79 *Pamyatniki arkhitektury prigorodov Leningrada* (Architectural monuments of the Leningrad outskirts), Leningrad, 1983, p. 149 (for the Kanobio house).

80 TsGIA, fond 1286, opis 2, ed. khr. 123, 1819, p. 11.

81 See my discussion in T.F. Savarenskaya, D.O. Shvidkovsky and F.A. Petrov, *Istoriia gradostroitel'nogo iskusstva* (History of the art of town planning), Moscow, 1989, p. 164.

82 *Sobranie fasadov . . . dlya chastnykh stroenii v gorodakh Rossiiskoi imperii*, St Petersburg, 1809; also TsGIA, fond 1286, opis 1, 1809, ed. khr. 252, pp. 1–5, 16, 22, 34 *et al.* PSZRI, vol. XXX, no. 124061 of 31 December 1809. For a general discussion in English see also A.J. Schmidt, *The Architecture and Planning of Classical Moscow: A Cultural History*, Philadelphia, 1989, pp. 135–9.

83 *Razdelenie gorodskikh kvartalov na obyvatel'skie mesta*, St Petersburg, 1811; also TsGIA, fond 1286, opis 2, 1811, ed. khr. 316, pp. 1–5; PSZRI, vol. XXXII, no. 24989 of 8 February 1812.

84 TsGIA, fond 1286, opis 2, ed. khr. 123, 1819, p. 11.

85 M. Korshunova, *op. cit.*, 1977, p. 141; Ye. Beletskaia *et al.*, *Obraztsovye proekty russkikh gorodov* (Model projects for development of Russian towns), Moscow, 1961.

86 J. Summerson, *op. cit.*, 1970, pp. 381–5.

87 *Ibid.*, pp. 390–92.

88 *Ibid.*, pp. 506–8.

89 S. Ozhegov, *Tipovoe i povtornoe stroitel'stvo v Rossii v XVIII–XIX vekakh* (Standardised building designs in Russia in the eighteenth and nineteenth centuries), Moscow, 1984, p. 84; L. Chernozubova, 'Obraztsovye proekty planirovki zhilykh kvartalov i ploshchadei nachala XIX v' (Model plans for the development of residential quarters and squares of the early nineteenth century), *Arkhitekturnoe nasledstvo* (Architectural heritage), no. 15, Moscow, 1965, pp. 188–92.

90 See my own discussion in Savarenskaya, Shvidkovsky and Petrov, *op. cit.*, 1989, p. 162.

91 KOGA, fond 2, opis 3, ed. khr. 3085; TsGIA, fond 1286, opis 2, ed. khr. 37; V. Pilyavsky, 'Iz istorii planirovki i zastroiki Kieva v nachale XIX veka' (From the history of Kiev's planning and development at the beginning of the nineteenth century), *Zodchestvo Ukrainy* (The architecture of Ukraine), Kiev, 1954, pp. 197–213.

92 TsGIA, fond 1286, opis 2, 1811, ed. khr. 60.

93 *Ibid.*

94 Quoted from the book *Frantsuzy v Rossii* (The French in Russia), Moscow, 1912.

95 M. Budylina, 'Planirovki i zastroiki Moskvy posle pozhara 1812' (The planning and development of Moscow after the fire of 1812), *Arkhitekturnoe nasledstvo* (Architectural heritage), no. 1, Moscow, 1951, pp. 138–42; P.V. Sytin, *Istoriya zastroiki i planirovki Moskvy* (History of the development and planning of Moscow), vol. III, Moscow, 1972, pp. 40, 41, 44, 46–62, 64–75, 106, 111–19, 140; V.A. Lavrov, *Razvitie planirovochnoi struktury istoricheski slozhivshikhsya gorodov* (Development of the planning structure of historically evolved towns), Moscow, 1976, p. 71; A.J. Schmidt, 'William Hastie. Scottish planner of Russian cities', *Proceedings of the American Philosophical Society*, CXIV, 1970, pp. 226–43; A.G. Cross,

op. cit., 1988. Also GIM OPI fond 131; MOPA, fond 163.

96 Quoted from *Otechestvennaya voina v pis'makh sovremennikov* (The Patriotic War in letters of the time), St Petersburg, 1882, p. 499.

97 TsGVIA, fond VUA, opis 1, ed. khr. 22183, pp. 1–23. For further detailed description of Hastie's proposals in English, see A.J. Schmidt, *The Architecture and Planning of Classical Moscow*, pp. 129–32.

98 V.A. Lavrov, *op. cit.*, 1976, p. 69.

99 *Ibid*.

100 TsGIA, fond 1293, opis 166, ed. khr. 480(2), p. 1.

101 TsGIA, fond 1286, opis 2, 1816, ed. khr. 6, pp. 1–33.

102 O.A. Shvidkovsky, *Dnepropetrovsk*, Moscow, 1954.

103 TsGIA, fond 1986, opis 2, 1819, ed. khr. 123, p. 1.

104 TsGIA, fond 1286, opis 2, 1819, ed. khr. 123, p. 10.

105 *Ibid*, p. 11.

106 V. Kochedamov, 'Proekty pervogo postoyannogo mosta cherez Nevu' (Projects for the first permanent bridge over the Neva), *Arkhitekturnoe nasledstvo* (Architectural heritage), no. 4, Moscow and Leningrad, 1953, pp. 210–11.

107 TsGIA, fond 1293, opis 168, ed. khr. 17, on Tomsk region (*guberniya*); fond 1293, opis 166, ed. khr. 2, on Asmolinskaya region; fond 1286, opis 3, 1824, ed. khr. 313, on Krasnoyarsk; and fond 1286, opis 3, 1824, ed. khr. 317 on Omsk.

108 A. Osyatinsky, *Stroitel'stvo gorodov na Volge* (Building of the towns on the Volga), Saratov, 1965, pp. 62–77.

BIBLIOGRAPHY

No general works have been published dealing specifically with architectural contacts between Russia and Great Britain. The fullest studies of cultural connections across a broader front are: A.G. Cross, *Anglo-Russian Relations in the Eighteenth Century*, Norwich, 1977, and the same author's more substantial work, *By the Banks of the Thames: Russians in Eighteenth-century Britain*, Newtonville, Mass., 1980. Literary contacts have been studied in these volumes by Cross, and also by the Russian scholar M.P. Alekseyev, most notably in his 'Russko-angliiskie literaturnye svyazi XVIII vek – pervaya polovina XIX veka' (Russo-English literary links of the eighteenth century and the first half of the nineteenth century), *Literaturnoe nasledstvo* (Literary heritage), no. 91, Moscow, 1982.

1 On Charles Cameron and His Works

IN ENGLISH AND FRENCH

Catalogue d'une Biblioteque . . . de feu . . . Mr. Ch. Cameron, St Petersburg, 1812

Cross, A.G., *Anglo-Russian Relations in the Eighteenth Century*, Norwich, 1977

Cross, A.G., *By the Banks of the Thames: Russians in Eighteenth-century Britain*, Newtonville, Mass., 1980

Cross, A.G., *The 1780s: Russia under Western Eyes*, Norwich, 1981

Cross, A.G., 'Charles Cameron's Scottish workmen', *Scottish Slavonic Review*, Spring 1988

Colvin, H., 'Cameron, Ch.' in his *A Biographical Dictionary of British Architects 1600–1840*, London, 1978

Cox, B., 'Charles Cameron's work in eighteenth-century Russia', *Architectural Association Quarterly*, no. 2, 1979

Hautecoeur, L., *L'Architecture classique à St-Petersbourg à la fin du XVIII siècle*, Paris, 1912

Hayden, P., 'Imperial culture at Pavlovsk', *Country Life*, vol. CLXXXI, no. 24, 1987

Hayden, P., 'Pavlovsk', *The Garden*, vol. 107, 1982

Hayden, P., 'Cameron, Ch.', in *The Oxford Companion to Gardens*, Oxford, 1987

Loudon, J.C., *An Encyclopaedia of Gardening*, London, 1827 edn

Loukomski (*sic*), G., *Charles Cameron . . . his life and work in Russia . . . at Tsarskoye Selo and Pavlovsk*, adapted into English by N. de Gren, London, 1943

Palladio, A., *Les Thermes des Romaines . . . poubliés par O. Bertotti Scamozzi . . . d'après l'exempler de lord comte de Burlington*, Vicenza, 1785

Rae, I., *Charles Cameron. Architect to the Court of Russia*, London, 1971

Richardson, A., 'Classical architecture in Russia', *Architectural Review*, vol. 38, 1951

Robertson, J., 'A Dazzling adventurer: Charles Cameron's lost early years', *Apollo*, n.s. vol. 135, 1992

Salmon, F., 'Charles Cameron and Nero's Domus Aurea: "una piccola esplorazione"', *Architectural History*, vol. 36, 1993

Shvidkovsky, D., 'Cameron discoveries', *Architectural Review*, no. 2, 1982

Tait A., Talbot Rice T. *et al.*, *Charles Cameron*, exh. cat., London, 1968

IN RUSSIAN

Alpatov, M.V., 'Khudozhestvennoye svoeobrazie Pavlovska' (The aesthetic originality of Pavlovsk), in *Etyudy po istorii russkogo iskusstva v 2-x tt* (Studies in the history of Russian art in two volumes) Moscow, 1967, vol. I

Arkhangel'skaya N.E., *Pavlovsk*, Leningrad, 1936

Baranovskaya, V.I., and Voronov, M.G., 'Kvarengi ili Kameron?' (Quarenghi or Cameron?), *Leningradskaya panorama*, no. 1, 1983

Bartenev, I.A., and Batazhkova, V.N., *Russkyi inter'er XVIII–XIX vekov* (The Russian interior of the eighteenth and nineteenth Centuries), Leningrad, 1977

Belyavskaya, V.F., *Rospisi russkogo klassitsizma* (Wall paintings of Russian classicism), Leningrad and Moscow, 1940

Benua (Benois), A.N., *Tsarskoye selo v tsarstvovanie Yelizavety Petrovny* (Tsarskoye Selo in the reign of Elizabeth Petrovna), St Petersburg, 1910

Bronshtein, S.S., *Arkhitektura goroda Pushkina* (Architecture of the town of Pushkin), Moscow, 1940

Bur'yanov, V., *Progulki s det'mi po Sankt Peterburgu* (Walks with children around St Petersburg), part IV, St Petersburg, 1842

Chekalevsky, P., *Rassuzhdeniiya o svobodnikh khudozhestvakh, s opisaniem nekotorykh proizvedenii rossiiskikh khudozhnikov* (Discussions on the free arts, with a description of certain works of Russian artists), St Petersburg, 1792

Dyad'kovskaya, T.A., 'Neizvestnye portreti Charl'za Kamerona' (An unknown portrait of Charles Cameron), *Arkhitektura SSSR* (Architecture of the USSR), 1939, no. 2

Fomin, I.A., *Istoricheskaya vystavka arkhitektury* (A historical exhibition of architecture), St Petersburg, 1911

Glushkov, I., *Ruchnoi dorozhnik* (Travelling diary), Moscow, 1802

Gollerbakh, E.F., 'Kameronova gallereia' (The Cameron Gallery), *Zhizn iskusstva*, no. 182–3, 1919

Gollerbakh, E.F., *Detskosel'skie dvortsy, muzei i parki* (Palaces, museums and parks at Detskoye [formerly Tsarskoye] Selo), Petrograd, 1922

Gollerbakh, E.F., *Gorod muzei. Detskoye selo, kak literaturnyi simvol i pamyatnik byta* (Town-museum. Detskoye [formerly Tsarskoye] Selo as a literary symbol and a monument to a way of life), Leningrad, 1927

Gollerbakh, E.F., *Literatura o Detskom sele* (Literature on Detskoye Selo), Leningrad, 1933

Gollerbakh, E.F., and Lansere, N.E., eds, *Charl'z Kameron*, Petrograd, 1924

Gornostaev, F.F., 'Stroitel'stvo grafov Razumovskikh na Chernigovshchine' (Construction work by the counts Razumovsky at Chernigov), *Trudy XIV Arkheologicheskogo s'ezda v Chernigove 1908* (Papers of the XIVth Archaeological Congress in Chernigov, 1908), Moscow, 1911

Grabar', I.E., *Istoriya russkogo iskusstva* (History of Russian art), Moscow, 1910–14, vols III, VI

Grashchenkov, V.N., 'Nasledie Palladio v arkhitekture russkogo klassitsizma' (The legacy of Palladio in the architecture of Russian classicism), *Sovetskoe iskusstvoznanie* (Soviet art history), 1983

Grimm, G.G., *Arkhitektura perekrytii russkogo klassitsizma* (The architectural design of floors in Russian classicism), Moscow, 1939

Gruzinsky, K.K., *Pavlovsk: Istoricheskii ocherk i opisanie s planom Pavlovska i kartoyu okrestnosti* (Pavlovsk: A historical note and description with a plan of Pavlovsk and map of the environs), St Petersburg, 1911

Istoriya russkoi arkhitektury (History of Russian architecture), Moscow, 1951

Istoriya russkogo isskustva (History of Russian art), vol. VI, Moscow, 1967

Kameron, C., *Termy rimlyan* (The Baths of the Romans), Moscow, 1939 edn, with introductory essay by V.N. Taleporovsky, and commentary by V.P. Zubov

Khrapovitsky, A.V., *Dnevnik* (Diary), St Petersburg, 1874

Koz'mian, G.K., *Charl'z Kameron*, Leningrad, 1987

Kuchumov, A.M., *Pavlovsk, Dvorets i park* (Pavlovsk: Palace and park), Leningrad, 1976

Kuchumov, A.M., *Pavlovsk*, Leningrad, 1980

Kurbatov, V., *Pavlovsk. Khudozhestvenno-istoricheskii ocherk* (Pavlovsk: An art-historical study), St Petersburg, 1911

Kurbatov, V.Ya., 'Podgotovka i razvitie neoklassicheskogo stilya' (The creation and development of the Neoclassical style), *Starye gody* (The Olden days), July–September 1911

Kurbatov, V.Ya., 'Klassitsizm i empir' (Classicism and empire), *Starye gody* (The olden days), St Petersburg, July–September 1912

Kurbatov, V., *Sady i parki* (Gardens and parks), Petrograd, 1916

Kurbatov, V.Ya., *Detskoye selo*, Leningrad, 1925

Kuznetsov, A.V., *Svody i ikh dekor* (Vaults and their decoration), Moscow, 1938

Lemus, V.V., Yemina, L.V., Gladkova, E.S., and Baloch, G.N., *Muzei i parki Pushkina* (Museums and parks at Pushkin), Leningrad, 1980

Likhachev, D.S., *Poeziya sadov* (The Poetry of gardens), Leningrad, 1982 de Lin', Sh., *Pis'ma* (Letters), vol. II, Moscow, 1809

Linkovsky, V.G., 'Arkhitekturnye modeli v Rossii' (Architectural models in Russia), *Starye gody* (The olden days), December 1910

Lukomsky, G.K., *Baturinskii dvorets, ego istoriya, razrushenie i restavratsiya* (Baturin Palace, its history, ruination and restoration), St Petersburg, 1912

Lukomsky, G.K., *Yekaterinskii dvorets-muzei* (The Catherine Palace Museum), Petrograd, 1918

Lukomsky, G.K., *Tsarskoye Selo*, Munich, 1923

Matveyev, A.A., *Pavlovskii dvorets-muzei* (The Pavlovsk Palace and Museum), Moscow and Leningrad, 1931

Myuller, A.P., *Byt inostrannykh khudozhnikov v Rossi* (The life of foreign artists in russia), Leningrad, 1927

Petrov, A.N., *Pushkin: dvortsi i parki* (Pushkin: Palaces and parks) Leningrad and Moscow, 1969

Petrov, A.N., *Gorod Pushkin* (The town of Pushkin), Leningrad, 1977

Petrov, A.N., Petrova, Ye.N., Raskin, A.G., and Krasheninikov, A.F., *Pamyatniki arkhitektury prigorodov Leningrada* (Monuments of architecture in the environs of Leningrad), Leningrad, 1983

Petrov, P.N., 'Znachenie arkhitektora Kamerona' (The significance of the architect Cameron), *Zodchii* (The Architect), no. 3, 1885

Pilyavsky, V.I., 'Novoe o Kamerone' (New information on Cameron), *Stroitel'stvo i arkhitektura Leningrada* (Construction and architecture of Leningrad), no. 7, 1981

Pushkarev, I., *Opisanie Sankt-Peterburga i uyezdnykh gorodov S-Peterburgskoi gubernii* (A description of St Petersburg and the related towns of Petersburg district), parts I, II, St Petersburg, 1839

Pylyaev, M.I., *Zabytoye proshloe okrestnostei Peterburga* (The forgotten past of the environs of St Petersburg), St Petersburg, 1889

Razodeyev, B.A., Soshina, R.A., and Kletseyeva, L.S., *Kronshtadt*, Leningrad, 1977

Sapozhnikova, T.V., 'Kameron v Pavlovske' (Cameron at Pavlovsk), *Sredy kollektsionerov* (Amongst the collectors), no. 5, 1923

Sbornik Imperatorskogo Russkogo istoricheskogo obshchestva (Collected papers of the Imperial Russian Historical Society), vol. XXIII, St Petersburg, 1878

Semenpikova, N.V., *Pushkin: dvortsy i parki* (Pushkin: Palaces and parks), Leningrad, 1985

Semevsky, M., *Pavlovsk: ocherk istorii i opisanie 1777–1877* (Pavlovsk: Notes of history and description, 1777–1877), St Petersburg, 1877

Shtorkh, P., *Puteshestvie po sadu i gorodu Pavlovsku* (Guide to the gardens and town of Pavlovsk), St Petersburg, 1843

Shvarts, V.S., *Pavlovsk: dvortsovo-parkovyi ansambl' XVIII–XIX v* (Pavlovsk: The palace and park ensemble of the eighteenth and nineteenth centuries), Leningrad, 1980

Shvidkovsky, D.O., 'Kameron v Rossii' (Cameron in Russia), *Arkhitektura*, no. 2, 1980

Shvidkovsky, D.O., 'Molodost' Kamerona' (The youth of Cameron), *Yunyi khudozhnik* (The young artist), no. 2, 1980

Shvidkovsky, D.O., 'Zabytyi gorod' (The Forgotten town), *Arkhitektura*, no. 1, 1982

Shvidkovsky, D.O., 'Charl'z Kameron. Arkhitektor Admiral'teistva' (Charles Cameron: Architect of the Admiralty), *Arkhitektura SSSR* (Architecture of the USSR), no. 2, 1983

Shvidkovsky, D.O., 'Gorod Sofiya' (The town of Sofiya), *Dekorativnoe iskusstvo SSSR* (Decorative Arts of the USSR), no. 6, 1985

Shvidkovsky, D.O., 'K voprosu o rekonstruktsii Tsarskogo sela arkhitektorom Charl'zom Kameronom' (On the question of the reconstruction of Tsarskoye Selo by the architect Charles Cameron), *Arkhitekturnoe nasledstvo* (The architectural heritage), 1985, no. 33

Shvidkovsky, D.O., 'Ideal'nyi gorod russkogo klassitsizma' (The ideal town of Russian classicism), in *Deni Didro i kul'tura ego epokhi* (Denis Diderot and the culture of his era), Moscow, 1986

Shvidkovsky, D.O., 'Ot litseya do Litseiskogo pansiona' (From the lycée to the Litseisky pension), *Dekorativnoe iskusstvo SSSR* (Decorative arts of the USSR), no. 6, 1986

Shvidkovsky, D.O., 'Poslednyi period tvorchestva arkhitektora Ch. Kamerona v dokumentakh Admiral'teistva' (The last period of Charles Cameron's professional career, as recorded in the documents of the Admiralty), in *Pamyatniki kul'tury; Novye otkrytiya. Pis'mennost'. Iskusstvo. Arkheologiya (Yezhegodnik)* (Monuments of culture: New discoveries. Belles lettres. Art. Archaeology (Annual)), Moscow, 1986

Sobko, N.P., *Slovar' russkikh khudozhnikov* (Dictionary of Russian artists), vol. I, St Petersburg, 1893

Solov'ev, K.A., *Russkii khudozhestvennyi parket* (Russian decorative parquet), Moscow, 1953

Taleporovsky, V.N., *Pavlovskii park* (The park of Pavlovsk), Petrograd, 1924

Taleporovsky, V.N., *Charl'z Kameron*, Moscow, 1939

Taleporovsky, V.N., 'Arkhitekturnyi ansambl' Pavlovskogo dvortsa' (The architectural ensemble of Pavlovsk Palace), in *Pamyatniki iskusstva, razrushennye nemetskimi zakhvatchikami v SSSR* (Monuments of art, destroyed by the German invaders in the USSR), Moscow and Leningrad, 1948

Taleporovsky, V.N., *Russkie arkhitektory* (Russian architects), Moscow and Leningrad, 1953

Uspensky, A.I., *Impertorskye dvortsy* (Imperial palaces), vol. II, Moscow, 1913

Uspensky, A.I., *Pavlovskii dvorets i dvortsovyi park* (Pavlovsk Palace and royal park), Moscow, 1913

Vigel', F.F., *Zapiski* (Notes), vols I, II, Moscow, 1928

Vil'chkovsky, S.N., *Tsarskoye Selo*, St Petersburg, 1911

Voronov, M.G., 'K istorii sozdaniya Ch. Kameronom Agatovykh komnat' (Towards a history of the creation of the Agate Rooms by Charles Cameron), in *Nauchnye soobshchenniya GIOP Leningrada* (Research reports of GIOP, Leningrad), Leningrad, 1959

Voronov, M.G., and Khodasevich, G.D., *Arkhitekturnyi ansambl' Kamerona v Pushkine* (Cameron's architectural ensemble at Pushkin), Leningrad, 1982

Vrangel', N.N., 'Inostrannye khudozhniki v Rossii XVIII veka' (Foreign artists in eighteenth-century Russia), *Starye gody* (The olden days), July–September 1911

Yakovkin, I.F., *Istoriya sela Tsarskogo* (History of the tsar's village), parts I–III, St Petersburg, 1829–31

Yakovkin, I.F., *Opisanie sela Tsarskogo ili sputnik obozrevayushchego onoe s planom* (Description of the tsar's village or guide to looking around it, with plan), St Petersburg, 1830

Zelenova, A.I., *Pavlovskii park* (Pavlovsk Park), Leningrad, 1954

Zemtsov, S.M., *Pavlovsk*, Moscow, 1947

Zgura, V.V., *Kitaiskaya arkhitektura i ee otrazhenie v zapadnoi Evrope* (Chinese architecture and its reflection in Western Europe), Moscow, 1929

2   On Orientalism in Russia

IN RUSSIAN

Bolotov, A., 'Nekotorye zamechaniya o sadakh v Kitai' (Some notes on gardens in China), *Ekonomicheskii magazin* (The economic magazine), parts 23, 25, 1786

Bolotov, A., 'Nekotorye zamechaniya o sadakh nyneshnikh parkov i nekotorykh drugikh narodov' (Some notes on gardens of today's parks and of certain other nations), *Ekonomicheskii magazin* (The economic magazine), part 25, 1786

Dakhnovich, V., *Oranienbaum*, Moscow and Leningrad, 1932

Fomin, I.I., *Kitaiskii teatr i kitaiskie zatei v Detskom Sele* (Chinese theatre and Chinese follies at Detskoye Selo), Leningrad, 1935

Gollerbakh, E.F., *Detskosel'skye dvortsy, muzei i parki* (Palaces, museums

and parks at Detskoye Selo), Petrograd, 1922

Grabar', I., *Istoriya russkogo iskusstva* (History of Russian art), Moscow, 1910–14, vol. III

Kazhdan, T., 'Arkhitekturnye pamyatniki v sele Vishenki' (Architectural monuments in the village of Vishenka), *Soobshcheniya instituta istorii iskusstva* (Research reports of the Institute for the History of the Arts), Moscow, 1960

Korshunova, M., *Yuri Fel'ten* (Yuri Velten), Leningrad, 1982

Kurbatov, V.Ya., *Strel'na i Oranienbaum* (Strelna and Oranienbaum), Leningrad, 1925

Kyugariants, D., *Antonio Rinal'di*, Leningrad, 1979

Kyugariants, D., *Khudozhestvennye sokrovishcha goroda Lomonosova* (Artistic treasures of the town of Lomonosov), Leningrad, 1985

Makarov, O., *Oranienbaum*, Leningrad, 1928

Petrov, A., *Gorod Pushkin* (The town of Pushkin), Leningrad, 1977

Popova, Z., 'Rospisnaya mebel' (Decoratively painted furniture), in *Sokrovishcha russkogo narodnogo iskusstva* (Treasures of Russian vernacular art), Moscow, 1967

Raskin, A., *Gorod Lomonosov* (The town of Lomonosov), Leningrad, 1979

Shamurin, Yu., *Podmoskovie* (The environs of Moscow), Moscow, 1914

Vasil'ev, B., 'Arkhitektory Neyelovy' (The architects Neyelov), *Arkhitekturnoe nasledstvo* (The architectural heritage), no. 4, 1953

Yevangulova, O., 'Turetskaya seriya zhivopistsa N. Mattarnovi' (The Turkish series by the painter N. Mattarnovi), *Russkoe iskusstvo pervoi chetverti XVIII v* (Russian art in the first quarter of the eighteenth century), Moscow, 1974

See also books on Tsarskoye Selo in the bibliography for Charles Cameron's works

3   On Neo-Gothic in Eighteenth- and Early Nineteenth-Century Russia

IN RUSSIAN

Arkhitekturnyi al'bom, predstavlyayushchii otlichneishie geometricheskie fasady soborov, monastyrei, tserkvei (Architectural album showing the most outstanding geometrical façades of cathedrals, monasteries and churches), vols I, II, Moscow, 1832

Beletskaya, Ye.A., compiler, author of Introduction and Commentary, *Arkhitekturnye al'bomy M.F. Kazakova: Al'bomy partikulyarnykh stroenii: Zhilye zdaniya Moskvy XVIII veka* (M.F. Kazakov's architectural albums: Albums of particular buildings: Housing buildings of eighteenth-century Moscow), Moscow, 1956

Bartenev, S.P., *Kaluzhskii gostinnyi dvor* (The Gostinyi Dvor [Trading Yard] of Kaluga), Kaluga, 1929

Bolotov, A.T., *Zhizn' i priklyucheniya Andreya Bolotova, opisanye samim im dlya svoikh potomkov* (The life and adventures of Andrey Bolotov, described by himself for his descendents), vol. III, Moscow and Leningrad, 1931

Bondarenko, E.Ye., *Arkhitektor Matvei Fedorovich Kazakov* (The architect Matvei Fedorovich Kazakov), Moscow, 1938

Bondarenko, I.Ye., 'Podmoskovnye dvortsy XVIII veka' (Eighteenth-century palaces in the Moscow region), *Starye gody* (The olden days), no. 3, 1914

Borisova, Ye.A., *Russkaya arkhitektura vtoroi poloviny XIX veka* (Russian architecture of the second half of the nineteenth-century), Moscow, 1979

Borisova, Ye.A., 'Russkaya arkhitektura i angliiskaya psevdogotika (k voprosu o meste angliiskikh khudozhestvennykh traditsii v russkoi kul'tury serediny XIX v)' (Russian architecture and English pseudo-gothic (on the question of the place of English artistic traditions in Russian culture of the mid-nineteenth century)), in *Vzaimosvyaz' iskusstv v khudozhestvennom razvitii Rossii vtoroi poloviny XIX veka* (Interrelationships between the arts in Russia's artistic development of the second half of the nineteenth century) Moscow, 1982

Budylina, M.V., Braitseva, O.N., and Kharlamova, A.M., *Arkhitektor N.A. L'vov* (The architect N.A. L'vov), Moscow, 1961

Domshlak, M.I., 'Arkhitektura starinnogo prazdnika' (Architecture of the ancient festivals), *Dekorativnoe iskusstvo SSSR* (Decorative arts of the USSR), no. 12, 1965

D'yakonov, M.V., 'K biograficheskomu slovaryu moskovskikh zodchikh' (Towards a biographical dictionary of Moscow architects), in *Russkii gorod* (The Russian town), no. 1, 1976; no. 2, 1979; no. 3, 1980; no. 4, 1981; no. 5, 1982

Fekhner, M.V., *Kaluga*, Moscow, 1971

Gamaburtsev, V.A., 'V. Bazhenov i M. Kazakov, russkie zodchie XVIII v. Ikh zanyatiya arkheologicheskogo kharaktera, Drevnosti' (V. Bazhenov and M. Kazakov, Russian architects of the eighteenth century. Their activities of an archaeological character. The ancient world), *Trudy imp. Mosk. Arkheologicheskogo Obshchestva* (Proceedings of the Imperial Moscow Archaeological Society), vol. XVIII, Moscow, 1901

Glumov, A.N., *N.A. L'vov*, Moscow, 1980

Golitsyn, D.A., 'O pol'ze, slave i prochnykh khudozhestv. Istoriya estetiki' (On utility, glory and other arts. A history of aesthetics), in M.F. Ovsyanikov *et al.*, *Pamyatniki mirovoi esteticheskoi mysli* (Monuments of world aesthetic thought), Moscow, 1964

Grabar', I.E., *Istoriya russkogo iskusstva, v 6 tt* (A history of Russian art in six volumes), Moscow, 1910–14, vol. IV: 'Istoriya arkhitektury: Moskoskoe zodchestvo v epokhy barokko i klassitsizma. Russkoe zodchestvo posle klassitsizma' (History of architecture: Moscow architecture in the epoch of the baroque and classicism. Russian architecture after classicism)

Grabar', I.E., ed., *Istoriya russkogo iskusstva v 13 tt* (A history of Russian art in thirteen volumes), Moscow, 1953–64, vol. VI: 'Iskusstvo vtoroi poloviny XVIII veka' (Art of the second half of the eighteenth century); vol. VIII: 'Russkoe iskusstvo pervoi treti XIX veka' (Art of the first third of the nineteenth century)

Grimm, G.G., compiler, author of Introduction, etc., *A.N. Voronikhin. Chertezhi i risunki* (A.N. Voronikhin. Drawings and sketches), Moscow and Leningrad, 1952

Grimm, G.G., *Arkhitektor Voronikhin* (The architect Voronikhin), Moscow and Leningrad, 1963

Gun'kin, G.I., *K arkhitekturnomu naslediyu V.I. Bazhenova. Neizvestnye i predpolagaemye postroiki V.I. Bazhenova* (V.I. Bazhenov's architectural legacy. Unpublished buildings of Bazhenov's and new attributions), Moscow, 1951

Il'in, M.A., 'Psevdogoticheskaya usad'ba Moskovskoi gubernii' (The pseudo-gothic country house of Moscow region), *Trudy etnograficheskogo muzeia* (Proceedings of the Enthographical Museum), Moscow, 1926

Il'in, M.A., 'Eskizy V.I. Bazhenova dlya Tsaritsyna' (Bazhenov's sketches for Tsaritsyno), *Arkhitekturnyi arkhiv* (Architecture archive), no. 1, Moscow, 1946

Il'in, M.A., *Bazhenov*, Moscow, 1954

Il'in, M.A., *Kazakov*, Moscow, 1955

Iz istorii Preobrazhenskogo kladbishcha (From the history of the preobrazhenskoe cemetery), Moscow, 1862

Karamzin, N.M., *Zapiski o moskovskikh dostopamyatnostyakh* (Notes on Moscow sights), Moscow, 1986

Karamzin, N.M., *Zapiski starogo moskovskogo zhitelya* (Notes of an old Moscow resident), Moscow, 1986

Kirichenko, Ye.I., *Russkaya arkhitektura 1830–1910x godov* (Russian architecture from the 1830s to the 1910s), Moscow, 1978

Kirichenko, Ye.I., *Arkhitekturnaya teoriya XIX veka v Rossii* (Architectural theory of the nineteenth century in Russia), Moscow, 1986

Korshunova, M.F., 'Graficheskoe nasledie Yu.M. Fel'tena' (The graphic legacy of Yu.M. Velten), in *Pamyatniki kul'tury: Novye otkrytiya. Pis'mennost'. Iskusstvo. Arkheologiya (Yezhegodnik)* (Monuments of culture: New discoveries. Writings. Art. Archaeology (Annual)), Moscow, 1976

Kozhin, N.A., 'V.I. Bazhenov i problema arkhitektury rannego romantizma' (V.I. Bazhenov and questions of architecture of early Romanticism), *Akadamiya arkhitektury* (Academy of architecture), no. 2, 1937

Kozhin, N., *Pamyatnik russkoi psevdogotiki XVIII veka sela Znamenki, Tambovskoi gubernii* (A monument of eighteenth-century Russian pseudo-gothic in the village of Znamenka in Tambovsk district), Leningrad, 1924

Kozhin, N., *Osnovy russkoi psevdogotiki, 1: Selo Krasnoe Ryazanskoi gubernii* (The foundations of Russian pseudo-gothic. 1: The village of Krasnoe in Ryazan district), Leningrad, 1927

Kozhin, N.A., 'K genizisu russkoi lozhnoi gotiki' (On the genesis of Russian false gothic), *Akademiya arkhitektury* (Academy of architecture), no. 1–2, 1934

Kozhin, N.A., 'Novye materialy ob arkhitektore M.F. Kazakove i ego uchenike arkhitektore A.N. Bakareve' (New materials on the architecture of M.F. Kazakov and his pupil architect A.N. Bakarev), *Akademiya arkhitektury* (Academy of architecture), no. 1–2, 1935

Krasheninnikova, N.L., *Ansambl' Golitsynskoi bol'nitsy* (The ensemble of the Golitsyn hospital), Moscow, 1955

Levshin (pseud. of Grigoriev, Alexander), *Istoricheskoe opisanie pervoprestol'nogo v Rossii khrama Moskovskogo bol'shogo Uspenskogo sobora i vozobnovleniya pervykh trekh Moskovskikh soborov Uspenskogo, Blagoveshchenskogo i Arkhangel'skogo* (A historical description of Russia's principal cathedral, Moscow's Great Dormition Cathedral, and the restoration of the three main Moscow cathedrals of Dormition, Annunciation and Archangel), Moscow, 1783

Maikov, V., *Opisanie raznykh uveselitel'nikh zrelishch, predstavlennykh vo vremya mirnogo torzhestva . . . bliz Moskvy na Khodynke 1775 goda iyulya 16 dnya* (A description of various festive spectacles presented at the time of the peace celebrations . . . near Moscow on Khodynka field on 16 July 1775), Moscow, 1775

'Materialy dlya istorii bespopovshchinskikh soglasii v Moskve: 1: Fedoseyevtsev Preobrazhenskogo kladbishcha. Sobrany Nikolaem Popovym . . .' (Materials for a history of the 'preistless' sect of Old Believers in Moscow: 1: Fedoseyevs of the Preobrazhenskoe cemetery. Collected by Nikolai Popov), *Chteniya v Obshchestve istorii i drevnostei rossiiskikh* (Readings at the Society of the History of Russian Antiquity), book 2, Moscow, 1869

Mineyeva, K.I., *Tsaritsyno: Dvortsovo-parkovyi ansambl'* (Tsaritsyno: The ensemble of palace and park), Moscow, 1988

Mikhailov, A.I., *Bazhenov*, Moscow, 1951

Mikhailov, A.I., *Arkhitektor D.V. Ukhtomskii i ego shkola* (The architect D.V. Ukhtomskii and his school), Moscow, 1954

Nikolaev, Ye.V., *Po Kaluzhskoi zemle. Ot Borovska do Kozel'ska* (Around the Kaluga territories. From Borovsk to Kozelsk), Moscow, 1970

Nikulina, N.I., *Nikolai L'vov*, Leningrad, 1971

Opisanie vseradostnogo torzhestvovaniya mira s Ottamanskoyu portoyu, byvshee v Moskve 1775 goda iyulya 10 i v poslednovavshie za tem chisla (Description of the joyous celebration of the peace with the Ottoman Porte, held in Moscow on 10 July 1775 and on the days following), Moscow, 1775

Pilyavsky, V.I., *Zodchii Rossi* (The architect Rossi), Moscow and Leningrad, 1951

Pisarev, A., *Nachertanie khudozhestv ili Pravila v zhivopisi, skul'pture, gravirovanii i arkhitekture . . .* (The profile of the arts, or rules in painting, sculpture, engraving and architecture), St Petersburg, 1808

'Pis'ma Yekateriny Vtoroi k Baronu Grimmu' (Letters of Catherine the Second to Baron Grimm), *Russkii arkhiv* (Russian archive), no. 9, 1878

'Pis'ma i drugie dokumenty V.I. Bazhenova o stroitel'stve v Tsaritsyne' (Letters and other documents of Bazhenov's on the construction of Tsaritsyno), *Arkhitekturnyi arkhiv* (Architectural archive), no. 1, Moscow, 1946

Putevoditel' k drevnostyam i dostopamyatnostyam Moskvy (A guide to the ancient sites and sights of Moscow), Moscow, 4.1–4.7, 1792

Rusakovsky, I.K., 'Ansambl' za Preobrazhenskoi zastavoi kontsa XVIII–nachala XIX vekov' (The ensemble beyond the Preobrazhenii gates at the end of the eighteenth and beginning of the nineteenth centuries), in *Pamyatniki russkoi arkhitektury i monumental'nogo iskusstva* (Monuments of Russian architecture and monumental art), Moscow, 1985

Sedov, A.P., *Yegotov*, Moscow, 1956

Shalikov, K., 'Tsaritsyno', *Vestnik Yevropy* (Courier of Europe), no. 11, 1804

Shemshurina, Ye.N., *Tsaritsyno*, Moscow, 1957

Slavina I.A., *Issledovateli russkovo zodchestva: Russkaya istoriko-arkhitekturnaya nauka XVIII–nachala XIX vekov* (Researchers of Russian architecture: Russian architectural history of the eighteenth and early nineteenth centuries), Leningrad, 1983

Snegirev, V.L., *Arkhitektor V.I. Bazhenov. Ocherk zhizni i tvorchestva* (The architect V.I. Bazhenov. An outline of his life and work), Moscow, 1937

Snegirev, V.L., 'Goticheskaya chasovnya na Preobrazhenskom kladbishche v Moskve' (The Gothic chapel at the Preobrazhenskoe cemetery in Moscow), *Arkhitekturnoe nasledstvo* (The architectural heritage), no. 9, Moscow, 1959

Taranovskaya, M.Z., *Karl Rossi. Arkhitektor. Gradostroitel', Khudozhnik* (Karl Rossi: Architect, town planner and artist), Leningrad, 1980

Tartakovskaya, Ye.A., 'Chesmenskii dvorets' (Chesmensky Palace), *Izobrazitel'noe iskusstvo* (Fine art), 1927

Timofeyev, L., Alupka, Simferopol, 1983

Tikhomirov, N.Ya., *Arkhitektura podmoskovnykh usadeb* (The architecture of country houses around Moscow), Moscow, 1955

Turchin, V.S., and Sheredega, V.I., 'Psevdogotika v sisteme khudozhestvennoi kul'tury rubezha XVIII–XIX vekov' (Pseudo-gothic in the system of artistic culture at the turn of the eighteenth and nineteenth centuries), *V okrestnostyakh Moskvy. Iz istorii russkoi usadebnoi kul'tury XVII–XIX vekov* (In the surroundings of Moscow.

From the history of Russian country-house culture from the seventeenth to the nineteenth centuries), Moscow, 1979

Turchin, V.S., *Epokha romantizma v Rossii. K istorii russkogo iskusstva pervoi poloviny XIX stoletiya: Ocherki* (The era of Romanticism in Russia. Towards a history of Russian art of the first half of the nineteenth century. Notes), Moscow, 1981

Vagner, G.K., 'Ischeznuvshii pamyatnik shkoly M.F. Kazakova (ograda 'Starogo arsenala' v Ryazani)' (A disappearing monument of M.F. Kazakov's school (the railings of the 'Old Arsenal' in Ryazan)), *Arkhitekturnoe nasledstvo* (The architectural heritage), no. 16, 1967

Valitskaya, A.P., *Russkaya estetika XVIII veka* (Russian aesthetics of the eighteenth century), Moscow, 1983

Vail'ev, B., 'Arkhitektory Neyelovy' (The architects Neyelov), *Arkhitekturnoe nasledstvo* (The architectural heritage), no. 4, 1953

Vlasyuk, A.I., Kaplun, A.I., and Kiparisova, A.A., *Kazakov*, Moscow, 1957

Voronikhin, L.N., *Serviz s zelenoi lyagushkoi* (The dinner service with the green frog), Leningrad, 1962

Yevangulova, O.S., *Dvortsovo-parkovye ansambli Moskvy pervoi poloviny XVIII veka* (The palace and park ensembles of Moscow from the first half of the eighteenth century), Moscow, 1969

Yevsina, N.A., *Arkhitekturnaya teoriya v Rossii vtoroi poloviny XVIII–nachala XIX veka* (Architectural theory in Russia in the second half of the eighteenth and early nineteenth centuries), Moscow, 1985

Yeremin, G., *Veka istorii Tsarityna. Vstrechi s istoriei: Nauchno-populyarnye ocherki* (Centuries of history at Tsaritsyno. Encounters with history: popular historical notes), Moscow, 1987

Zgura, V.V., 'Tsaritsyno', *Podmoskovnye muzei* (Museums of the Moscow region), no. 6, Moscow, 1925

Zgura, V.V., 'Novye pamyatniki psevdogotiki' (New monuments of pseudo-gothic), *Trudy Obshchestva izucheniya russkoi usadby* (Proceedings of the Society for Study of Russian Country Houses), Moscow, 1927

Zgura, V.V., 'K voprosu o tvorchestve Bazhenova' (On the question of Bazhenov's creative work), *Trudy sektsii iskusstvoznaniya* (Proceedings of the Section for Art History), Moscow, 1928

Zgura, V.V., *Problemy i pamyatniki, svyazannye s V.I. Bazhenovym* (Problems and monuments, connected with V.I. Bazhenov), Moscow, 1928

4 On Adam Menelaws, and on the Palace at Baturin formerly attributed to Charles Cameron

IN ENGLISH

Cross, A.G., 'Cameron's Scottish Workmen', *Scottish Slavonic Review*, no. 10, 1988

Cross, A., 'In Cameron's Shadow. Adam Menelaws: stonemason turned architect', *Scottish Slavonic Review*, no. 17, 1992

Shvidkovsky, D., 'Adam Menelaws', *Apollo*, n.s. vol. 135, 1992

IN RUSSIAN

Alekseyeva, T., *V.L. Borovikovskii*, Moscow, 1975

Arkhiv gosudarstvennogo soveta (Archive of the State Council), vol. 2, St Petersburg, 1888

Arkhiv knyazya Vorontsova (Archive of Prince Vorontsov), book 13, Moscow, 1878

Benua (Benois), A., and Lansere, P. 'Dvortsovyoe stroitelstvo Imperatora Nikolaya I' (Palace construction work by Emperor Nicholas I), *Starye gody* (The olden days), July–September 1913

Budylina, M., et al., *Arkhitektor N.A. L'vov* (The architect N.A. Lvov), Moscow, 1961

Fomin, I.A., *Istoricheskaya vystavka arkhitektury* (A historical exhibition of architecture), St Petersburg, 1911

Gornostaev, F.F., *Dvortsy i parki yuga* (Palaces and parks of the south), Moscow, 1914

Gornostaev, F.F., 'O Baturinskom dvortse' (On the Baturin Palace), *Drevnosti: Trudy komissii po sokhraneniyu drevnikh pamyatnikov* (The ancient world: Proceedings of the Commission for Preservation of Ancient Monuments), vol. v, Mosow, 1914

Il'in, M.A., *Moskva*, Moscow, 1970

Lukomsky, G.K., 'Dva tainstvennykh dvortsa Razumovskikh' (Two secret palaces of the Razumovsky's), *Stolitsa i usadba* (Capital and country house), 1914, nos 16, 17

Lukomsky, G.K., 'Pis'ma grafa A. Razumovskogo k M. Gudovichu' (Letters of A. Razumovsky to M. Gudovich), *Starye gody* (The olden days), March 1914

Pamyatniki arkhitektury Moskovskoi oblasti (Monuments of architecture in Moscow region), vols I, II, Moscow, 1975

Pamyatniki gradostroitel'stva i arkhitektura Ukrainskoi SSR (Monuments of urbanism and architecture in the Ukrainian Soviet Republic), vol. IV, Kiev, 1986

Smik, O., 'Baturinskii palats' (Baturin Palace), *Arkhitektura radyanskoi Ukraini* (Architecture of Soviet Ukraine), no. 1, 1938

Shimansky, A., and Geichenko, S., *Kottedzh Nikolaya I* (Nicholas I's Cottage) Leningrad, 1930

Sytin, P., *Istoriya zastroiki i planirovki Moskvy* (History of the development and planning of Moscow), vol. III, Moscow, 1972

Tenikhina, V., *Kottedzh* (The Cotage), Leningrad, 1986

Tsapenko, M.P., *Po ravninam Desny i Seima* (On the plains of Desna and Seim), Moscow, 1967

Vasil'chikov, A., *Semeistvo Razumovskikh* (the Razumovsky family) St Petersburg, 1912

See also the Tsarskoye Selo section of Cameron bibliography, above

5   On William Hastie

IN ENGLISH

Colvin, H., 'Hastie, W.', in his *A Biographical Dicionary of British Architects*, London, 1980

Cross, A.G., 'Cameron's Scottish Workmen', *Scottish Slavonic Review*, no. 10, Spring 1988

Korshunova, M., 'William Hastie in Russia', *Architectural History*, vol. XVII, 1974

Schmidt, A.J., 'William Hastie: Scottish planner of Russian cities', *Proceedings of the American Philosophical Society*, 1970, vol. XIV

Shvidkovsky, D., 'William Hastie and classical Edinburgh: Scottish architects abroad', *Architectural Heritage of Scotland*, no. 2, 1992

IN RUSSIAN

Beletskaya, Ye., et al., *Obraztsovye proekty v zastroike russkikh gorodov* (Model projects in the development of Russian towns), Moscow, 1961

Blek, I., and A. Rotach, 'Chugunnye arochnye mosty v Leningrade' (Cast-iron) arched bridges in Leningrad), *Arkhitekturnoe nasledstvo* (Architectural heritage), no. 7, 1957

Bronshtein, S., *Arkhitektura goroda Pushkin* (Architecture of the town of Pushkin), Leningrad, 1940

Budylina, N., 'Planirovka i zastroika Moskvy posle pozhara 1812 g' (The planning and development of Moscow after the fire of 1812), *Arkhitekturnoe nasledstvo* (Architectural heritage), no. 1, 1951

Chernozubova, L., 'Obraztsovye proekty planirovki kvartalov' (Model projects for the development of urban quarters), *Arkhitekturnoe nasledstvo* (Architectural heritage), no. 15, 1965

Korshunova, M.F., 'Arkhitektor V. Geste' (The architect W. Hastie), *Trudy Gosudarstvennogo Ermitazha* (Research papers of the State Hermitage), no. XVIII, Leningrad, 1977

Kochedamov, V., 'Proekty pervogo postoyannogo mosta cherez Nevu' (Projects for the first permanent bridge over the Neva), *Arkhitekturnoe nasledstvo* (Architectural heritage), no. 4, 1953

Lavrov, V., *Razvitie planirovochnoi struktury istoricheski slozhivshikhsya gorodov* (Development of the planning structure of historically evolved towns), Moscow, 1977

Ozhegov, S., *Tipovoe i povtornoe stroitel'stvo v Rossii v XVIII–XIX vekakh* (Standardised building designs in Russia in the eighteenth and nineteenth centuries), Moscow, 1984

Petrov, A.N., Petrova, Ye.N., Raskin, A.G., and Krasheninikov, A.F., *Pamyatniki arkhitektury prigorodov Leningrada*, Leningrad, 1983

Punin, A.L., *Povest' o Leningradskikh mostakh* (A tale of Leningrad bridges) Leningrad, 1971

Sytin, P., *Istoriya zastroiki i planirovki Moskvy* (A history of the development and planning of Moscow), vol. III, Moscow, 1972

See also the items on Tsarskoye Selo in the
Cameron section, above.

INDEX

Academy of Architecture, French   45
Academy of Arts, Russian   108, 227
Adam, E. (engineer)   239
Adam, James (architect)   1, 10, 237
Adam, Lambert (sculptor)   52
Adam, Robert (architect)   1, 10, 237, 244
Aeschylus   33
Akhmatova, Anna Andreevna (1889–1966, poet)   41
Aksakov, Sergei Timofeevich (1791–1859, writer)   7, 181
Alexander I, Tsar (formerly Grand Duke Alexander Pavlovich, grandson of Catherine the Great)   3, 34, 36, 37, 117, 218, 227–8, 234, 239, 241–2, 245, 248–9
Alexander II, Tsar (son of Nicholas I)   236
Alexander, Shaw (plasterer)   226
Alexandra Fedorovna, Tsarina (wife of Nicholas I)   158
Alexandra Pavlovna, Grand Duchess   228
Alexandria Park   4, 223, 234, 236
    Chapel of Alexander Nevsky   236
    Kottedzh (Cottage Palace)   4, 234–5
Alexandrov bridge (over Vvedensky canal)   239
Alexandrovsk   245
Alexei Mikhailovich, Tsar (father of Peter the Great)   168
Alnwick Castle, Northumberland   4
Alpatov, Mikhail Vladimirovich (art historian)   133
Alupka   223
Annensky, Innokenti Fedorovich (1856–1909, poet)   41
Antinous   66
Apraxin, General Admiral Fedor Matveevich (1661–1728)   142
Apuleius: The Golden Ass   33
Arakcheyev, General Count Alexei Andreevich (1765–1834, confidant of Alexander I)   241
Archangel   36
Ardatov   245
Arkharova, Ekaterina Alexandrovna (grandmother of Count Vladimir Sologub)   164
Athens
    Academy   61
    Erechtheon   61
Atticus   22
Augustine, St   22

Bablovo, Prince Potemkin's castle at   1, 190–1
Bakarev, Alexei (Moscow architect)   217
Bakhchisaray   173, 238
Bakhmut   245

Bakhtin, Mikhail Mikhailovich   14
Balashov, Alexander Dmitrievich (Minister of Police, Moscow)   246
Barry, Sir Charles (1795–1860, architect)   223
Bath   244
Baturin Palace   34, 229–31, 232
Bazhenov, Vasily Ivanovich (1737 (?38)–99, architect)   9, 26, 27, 44, 192–3, 194, 196, 199–206, 207, 213, 214, 215–17, 219
Bernini, Gian Lorenzo (architect and sculptor)   182
Bernovo, church   213
Betankur, Avgustin Avgustinovich di Molina (1758–1824, Spanish engineer in Russian service)   38
Betsey and Brothers (ship)   30
Betskoy, Ivan Ivanovich (1704–95, head of the Academy of Arts)   108
Bezborodko, Count Alexander Andreevich (1747–99, personal secretary to Catherine the Great)   30, 31, 110–11, 113, 227
Blore, Edward (architect)   223
Bobrinsky, Count   8
Bogdanovich, Ippolit Fedorovich (1744–1803, poet)   41, 46
Bogoroditsk   8
Bologna   24
Bolotov, Andrei Timofeevich (1783–1833, estate manager and publisher)   8, 171, 192
Borovikovsky, Vladimir Lukich (1757–1825, artist)   227
Boullée, Etienne-Louis (architect)   33
Bove, Osip Ivanovich (1784–1834, architect)   248
Braunstein, Iohann (architect to Peter the Great)   42
Brenna, Vincenzo (1745–1820, architect)   34, 118, 119, 126, 127, 130, 142, 144, 153, 155
Bristol, Clifton Hill estate   17
Brown, John (stonemason and master bricklayer)   114
Brown, Lancelot (Capability)   5, 100, 160
Browne, John (bricklayer)   225, 226
Bruce, Margaret (wife of William Hastie)   238
Bryansk   7
Bryus, Yakov Velimovich (Governor General of Moscow)   203
Bryzgalov, Ivan Semenovich (warden of Mikhailovsky Castle)   38
Bulatnikov estate   1, 209
Burlington, Lord   22, 24, 64
    Fabriche Antiche di Andrea Palladio   17–18

Buryatia, Buddhist monasteries   167
Bush, Catherine (wife of Charles Cameron)   4, 32
Bush, John (né Johannes Busch)   4–5, 32, 34, 100, 117
Bush, Joseph   4, 100
Bush, Mrs   32
Buxton   244
Bykovo, church   213–15
Byres, James   13
Byron, George Gordon, Lord   236

Calcutta   168
Cameron, Dr Archibald   13–14
Cameron, Charles (architect, son of Walter Cameron)   10
    as Admiralty architect   34–9
    album of drawings   14–17
    arrival in St Petersburg   25
    The Baths of the Romans   12, 19–20, 21–5, 52–3
    and Baturin   34, 230, 231
    and Catherine see Catherine II, and Cameron
    and Catherine Palace   70–96
    death   39
    dismissal by Paul I   33
    early life   11–14
    and Hastie   237, 239, 251
    interests   33
    invites British craftsmen to Russia   30, 223, 225–6
    in Italy   18–21
    marriage   32
    and park design   100, 133–61, 164–5
    and Pavlovsk   7, 26, 33, 34, 116, 117–32, 164–5, 236, 237–8
    reputation   3–4, 8, 11
    and Sofiya   1, 26, 106–16, 240, 241
    and Tsarskoye Selo   1, 11, 26–8, 30–2, 41–69, 101, 104, 116, 130, 171, 175–80, 182, 183
    and Isaac Ware   17–19
Cameron, Charles, of Lochiel   12–13
Cameron, Charles (son of Dr Archibald Cameron)   13–14
    Histoire de Jean de Calais   14
Cameron, Donald   12
Cameron, Sir Donald, of Lochiel   13
Cameron, Jenny   11–12
Cameron, Walter   12, 13, 25
Campbell, Alexander (mason)   114
Carpenters' Company   12, 14, 17
Carr, Sir John   5

Catherine I, Empress (wife of Peter the Great) 42

Catherine II (the Great), Empress
  and Alexandrov *dacha* 228
  and Charles Cameron 11–12, 14, 25, 26, 28, 30–3, 91, 132, 185, 225, 237
  and 'caprices' 172
  and Chambers 171
  and Chesmensky Castle 187–9
  death 227, 238
  dogs 101
  and Gatchina 4
  and gothic architecture 185, 186
  and hermit at Pavlovsk 118
  and Joseph II 5, 226
  letters 44, 64, 65, 89–90, 98, 102, 108, 112, 192–3, 203, 237
  and Orlov 4, 8
  and parks 7
  and Pavlovsk 117, 148
  and Potemkin 103–4
  and Rinaldi 169
  and Sofiya 114, 240, 241
  and town planning 242
  and Tsaritysno 197, 200, 203–6
  and Tsarskoye Selo 1, 41, 44, 45, 61, 89–90, 92, 106
Catherine Ioannovna (niece of Peter the Great) 168
Cato 22
Cave, Elizabeth (wife of Adam Menelaws) 227
Chalgrin, J.-F. T. 9
Chambers, Sir William 1, 88, 148, 169, 175, 181, 182, 183
  Designs of Chinese Buildings . . . 33, 100, 170
  Plans . . . of the Gardens and Buildings at Kew in Surrey 100
Chantilly 5
Chereshenky estate 181
Cherkassy 248
Chernaya, River 3
Chernaya Gryaz estate 196
Chernyshev, Count Zakhar Grigorievich (1722–84) 2, 181
Chesma, Bay of, victory over Turks 102, 189–90
Chesmensky Castle 1, 2, 187–9
  church 189–90
Chesterfield, Lord 17
Chevakinsky, Savva Ivanovich (1713–80, architect to Elizabeth I) 25, 42
Chichagov, Admiral Vasily Yakovlevich (1726–1809) 37
Chigirin 248
China 167
Chufarovo estate 181
Churassov family 181
Cicero 22, 33, 66
Clement XIII, Pope 20
Clérisseau, Charles-Louis (1722–1820, architect) 12, pls 16, 17, 45
Cochrane, John (mason) 225
Code of Laws of the Russian Empire 242
Collection of Façades Approved by His Imperial Majesty for Private Construction in Towns of the Russian Empire 242
Condé, Prince de 5

Constantinople, Hagia Sophia cathedral 104, 106, 112, 227
Cornwallis, Lord 13
'The Country Gentleman' *see Selskaya Zhizn*
Craig, James (planner of Edinburgh New Town) 244
Crimea 5, 167, 173, 238
Cross, Anthony G. (historian) 8, 100, 225
Culloden, battle of 12
Cunningham, David (stonemason) 4, 225, 226

Dante Alighieri 13
Dashkova, Princess Ekaterina Romanovna (1743–1810, president of the Academy of Sciences, St Petersburg) 13
Decker, P.: *Chinese Architecture* 100
Demosthenes 1, 65, 66
  Philippics 33
Denmark 25
Denois (cabinetmaker) 31
Derzhavin, Gavrila Romanovich (1743–1816, poet) 41, 46, 52, 61–4, 66–7, 179, 227
Devkalion Second Class (masonic lodge) 203, 204–6
Dick, Andrew (stonemason) 114, 225
Dimsdale, Elizabeth 253*n*
Dimsdale, Thomas 4
The Division of Urban Quarters into Habitable Sites 242–4
Drottningholm 173
  Chinese Palace 180
Du Tertre, Jean: *Selected History of Investigations, Conspiracies and Revolutions* 33
Dukhovshchina 248, 249
Dupré de Saint-Maure, Emile (poet) 147

Edinburgh 244
Egremont, Lord 12
Ekonomicheskiy magazin (*Economic Magazine*) 8, 192
Elizabeth I, Empress (formerly Grand Duchess Elizabeth Petrovna) 168, 229, 231
Elsinore 25
Erdberg, Eleanore von 173
Etupes estate, France 117, 118

Feodosiya 238
Ferdinand IV, King of Naples 169
Fischer von Erlach, J.B. 33
FitzHerbert, Alleyne (British ambassador in St Petersburg) 225, 226
Flaxman, John 91
Fomin, Ivan Alexandrovich (1872–1936, architect) 3, 253*n*
  'Historical Exhibition of Architecture' 228
Forrester, Francis (workman) 30
Fox, Charles James 1, 66
Frederick II (the Great), King of Prussia 33
Freemasonry 39, 203–6
Fulton, R. (engineer) 239

Gambs furniture factory, St Petersburg 236
Garting (engineer) 38
Gascoigne, Charles (British industrialist in Moscow) 239
Gatchina
  Palace 4–5, 135

Priorat Castle 221
Prioratsky park 5
St Kharlampia monastery 221
Gerard, Ioghan (Ivan) (architect) 173–5
Gloucester, cathedral 217
Goethe, Johann Wolfgang von 21, 236
Gogenheim Park, Württemberg 117
Golitsyn, princes 233
Gollerbakh, Erich (early 20th-century critic and art historian) 46, 68
Golovina, Vera (lady-in-waiting at Tsarskoye Selo) 96
Goncharov family 212
Gonzago, Pietro di Gottardo (1751–1831, theatre and garden designer) 3, 100, 118, 126, 156, 163–4
Gordon, Henry (stonemason) 225
Gorenki estate 7, 229, 233
Gornostaev, Fedor Fedorovich (1867–1915, architectural historian) 229
Gould, William (pupil of Capability Brown) 5, 7
Grabar, Igor Emmanuilovich (1871–1960, art historian and critic) 12, 183
Grabtsevo, church 213
Granada, Alhambra gardens 223
Gray, John (plasterer) 225
Greig, Captain (later Admiral) (1736–88, Scot serving in Russian navy) 102, 103
Griboyedov, Alexander Sergeevich (1795–1829, writer) 9
Grimm, Baron Friedrich Melchior (confidant of Catherine the Great) 44, 66, 89, 192–3, 203, 237
Guarini, Guarino 33
Gumilev, Nikolai Stepanovich (1886–1921, poet) 41
Gzhatsk 248, 249

Hackett, James (gardener at Gatchina) 4, 5
Hadrian 66
Halfpenny, John 2, 117, 118, 169, 188, 228
Halfpenny, John and William
  Chinese . . . Architecture Properly Ornamented 100, 173
  Rural Architecture in Chinese Taste 170–1, 173
Halfpenny, William 1, 2, 117, 118, 169, 188, 228
Hamil-Bey (Turkish vizier) 102
Hamilton, John (plasterer) 225
Hampton Court 100
Hastie, William (*c.*1755–1832, architect) 3–4, 30, 42, 113, 116, 226, 237–51
Heber, Reginald (Archbishop of Calcutta) 168
Helmholtz, F. (German gardener) 5
Heraclitus 66
Hirschfeld, C.C.L. (author of garden book) 171
Homer 65
  Odyssey 23

Inverary Castle 188
Iona, Metropolitan 216
Irvine, David (stonemason) 226
Ismailov, Lev 167
Italy 13; *see also* Rome
Ivan III (the Great), Tsar 217

Jerome, St   22
Jones, Inigo (architect)   33
Joseph II, Holy Roman Emperor   5, 148–9
Julius Caesar   66

Kagul, battle of   102
Kaluga   244
Kamensky, Field Marshal Mikhail Fedotovich
    (1738–1805)   211
Kantemir family   196
Kapnist, Vasily Vasilievich (1738–1823, writer)
    227
Karl Leopold, Prince of Mecklenburg   168
Kasimov, mosque   167
Kazakov, Matvei Fedorovich (1738–1812,
    architect)   27, 206–9, 213, 217, 221, 248
Kazan   181
  mosque   167
Kazan province   245
Kedleston Hall   1, 238
Kent, William (architect and garden designer)   1,
    33, 100, 217
Kerchi   238
Kew Gardens, Surrey   1, 2, 100
  pagoda   175, 182
Kherson   36
Khodynska   1, 199
Khrapovitsky, Alexander Vasilievich (1749–1801,
    secretary to Catherine the Great)   1, 66,
    103–4
Kiev   9, 245, 248, 249
  province   248
Knobelsdorff, Hans Georg Wenceslaus, Baron
    von (1699–1753, German architect)   85
Kochubey   253n
Kolpino   239
Konkovo estate   1, 209
Konstantin Pavlovich, Grand Duke   226
Korobov, Ivan Kuzmich (1700–47, architect)
    36
Krasnoy   248, 249
Krasnoyarsk   250
Krasnoye estate   211
  church   213
  stables   212
Kroniort, General (Swedish general in 1702
    battle)   142
Kronstadt   25, 30
  St Andrew's cathedral   36
Kuchelbecker, Karl Ivanovich (d. 1809, estate
    manager at Pavlovsk)   117, 132–3, 153, 162
Kuskovo estate   180
Kutaysov, Count Ivan Pavlovich (d. 1834, valet
    to Paul I)   144
Kvasov, Andrei Vasilievich (1744–72, architect)
    113
Kyuchuk-Kainardzhi, Treaty of   191

La Mothe, Jean-Baptiste-Michel Vallin (or
    Vallen) de (1729–1800, architect)   8, 26, 44
Langley, Batty (1696–1751, architect)   33
Lansere, Nikolai Evgenievich (architectural
    historian)   3, 10, 12, 253n
Lanskoi, Alexander Dmitrievich (favourite of
    Catherine the Great)   191
Lavrov, Vitaly Alexeevich (1902–89, Soviet
    architect and historian)   247

Le Blond, Jean-Baptiste-Alexandre (1669–1719,
    architect)   113
Le Rouge, G.L.: Détails des Nouveaux Jardins à la
    Mode   33
Ledoux, Claude-Nicolas (1736–1806, architect to
    Louis XVI)   203
Lefort, Francis (1656–99, Swiss favourite of Peter
    the Great)   168
Leim, Ivan (German architect in Russian service)
    113
Ligne, Charles Joseph, Prince de (1735–1814)
    107
Little, Isaac (bricklayer and mason)   114, 226
Livy   22
Lomonosov, Mikhail Vasilievich (1711–65, poet)
    41, 43, 66
London   55
  Chiswick House   1
  Foreign Office   225
  Grosvenor Square   244
  Hanover Square   25
  Red Lion Square   244
  St George's Hospital   17
  Society of Arts   25
  White Horse Street   12
Longus: Daphnis and Chloe   33
Loudon, John Claudius   171, 229
  Encyclopaedia of Gardening   160, 229
Louis XIV, King   9
Louis XV, King   9
Lucian: 'Hippias, or the Baths'   23, 53
Lukin, Pavel (architect)   32
Lukomsky, Georgi Kreskentevich (1884–1952,
    architectural critic and historian)   238
Lund (jeweller)   256n
Lvov, Nikolai Alexandrovich (1751–1804,
    architect and poet)   26, 27, 217, 221,
    226–7, 228, 230–1, 233
  'A study of Russian antiquities in Moscow'
    217
Lyalichi (estate of Count Zavadovsky)   7
Lyon, William and George (plasterers)   114, 226

Mably, Gabriel Bonnot de   33
Macleod, John (plasterer)   226
Makaryev (town on the Volga)   245
Maria Fedorovna, Grand Duchess (formerly
    Princess Sophia Dorothea of Württemburg,
    later Tsarina; wife of Paul Petrovich, later
    Tsar Paul I)   26, 70, 75, 117, 118, 127,
    128, 131, 132–3, 135, 137, 149, 153, 155,
    158, 161, 162
Maria Theresa, Holy Roman Empress   149
Marino (estate of Prince Bariatinsky)   7
Marlborough, John, Duke of   33
Marshall, John (plasterer)   226
Martial   24
Martos, Ivan Petrovich (1745–1835, sculptor)
    136
Maryinka estate, stables   212
McVay, James and John (stonemasons)   226
Meader, James (gardener)   4, 7
Memori per le Belle Arti   13, 14
Menelaws, Adam (1763–1831, architect)   3, 4,
    30, 34, 42, 114, 116, 221–3, 225–7, 228–9,
    231–7
Menshikov, Alexander Danilovich (favourite of

Peter the Great)   42, 168
Mey, Lev Alexandrovich (1822–62, poet)   41
Michurin, Ivan Fedorovich (1700–63, architect)
    248
Mikhalkovo estate   212
Mironov, Alexei (architect)   180
Mironovsky, Ivan (Moscow architect)   217
The Modern Builder's Assistant   188
Mogilev, cathedral of St Joseph   149, 226–7
Molière (Jean-Baptiste Poquelin)   33
  Tartuffe   33
Montbéliard, Prince (owner of estate in Alsace)
    168
Montferrand, August Rikar (1786–1858,
    architect)   35
Mordvinov, Admiral Nikolai Semenovich
    (1745–1845)   34
Morris, Roger (architect)   100, 188
Moscow   4, 9, 34, 167, 173, 185, 186, 191–6,
    209–10
  Boulevard   247, 248
  Building Committee   248
  Devichye Field   247
  Dormition cathedral   192
  Earth Rampart   247
  English Club   237
  Garden Ring   248
  Khodynskoye Field, temporary buildings
    192–6, 203, 207, 211
  Kitai-gorod   217, 221
    church of Nikolai Mokrovo   217
    Synod of the Orthodox Russian Church,
      printing works   217
  Kremlin   192, 196, 215, 217, 220–1, 247,
    248
    Borovitsky Gate   217
    Catherine Church of the Assumption
      Monastery   217
    Nikolsky Gate   217
    Uspensky cathedral   217
  Lefort Palace   168
  Lefortovo   199
  Novodevichy Convent   247
  Palace of Amusements   217
  Petrovsky Castle   234
  Preobazhensky Cemetery   206, 218–19
  Razumovsky Palace   232–3
  rebuilding   246–8
  Red Porch   192
  taken by French   245–6
  Tverskaya Street   247
Mostsipanov, M. (architect)   259n
Moyka, River, bridges over   35, 239
Muir, Robert (plasterer)   226
Mullender, Isaac (bricklayer)   225
Munro, John (gardener at Tsaritsyno)   5, 203

Naples   169
  Caserta palace   169
Napoleon I, Emperor   4, 39, 163, 239, 245–6,
    248
Nartov, Andrei Konstantinovich (1680 (or
    1694)–1756, engineer and inventor)   98
Neva, River   25, 35, 41, 250
Neyelov, Ilya Vasilievich (1745–93)   2, 9, 27,
    100, 175, 190
Neyelov, Peter Vasilievich (1749–?, architect)

100, 167, 171
Neyelov, Vasily Ivanovich (1721 (or 1722)–82, architect)   100, 101, 108, 175, 185, 186–7
Nicholas I, Tsar (formerly Grand Duke Nicholas)   4, 158, 223, 234
Nikolaev   36
Nikolskoye, Lvov estate   7, 228
Nizhegorodskaya province   245
Nizhny Novgorod   9, 244
Novikov, Nikolai Ivanovich (1744–1818, writer, publisher and Freemason)   8, 203–6

Obvodny canal   239
Ochakov
   fortress   102, 104
   mosque   167
Old Believers   206, 218
Olenin, Alexei Nikolaevich (1763–1843)   227
Omsk   250
Oranienbaum   85, 180, 182, 185
   Chinese Bedchamber   169
   Chinese Palace   169
   Large and Small Chinese Studies   169
   maritime hospital   36–7
   palace   168, 169
   park   169
Order of Malta   33
   Burning of Bonfires festival   163
   Grand Priory of   5
Orel   7
Orlov, Count Alexei Grigorovich (1717–1808)   103, 144
Orlov, Prince Grigory Grigorievich (1734–1827, favourite of Catherine the Great)   4, 8, 103, 104
Orlovsky, Alexander (artist)   38, 39
Osterley Park   100
Ostrovski, Prince Potemkin's castle at   191
Over, Charles (writer on gardening)   2
   Ornamental Architecture in the Gothic, Chinese and Modern Taste   100, 171, 173
Ovid   66
   Art of Love   23
Oxford, town hall   17
Ozerki, Prince Potemkin's castle at   191

Paine, James   33, 238
Palermo, Villa Favorita   169
Palladio, Andrea   17–19, 22, 24, 39, 64–5, 126
   design for Basilica, Vicenza   65
   Four Books on Architecture   17
Panin, Count Nikita Ivanovich (1718–83)   149
Paris   24, 25
Patricola, D.   169
Paul I, Tsar (formerly Grand Duke Paul Petrovich)
   accession   33, 227
   and Charles Cameron   33
   and Catherine Palace   70, 75
   and Commission on Stone Construction   242
   death   34, 37, 162
   and Gatchina   5, 221
   and Pavlovsk   26, 108, 117, 131, 132, 135, 137, 142, 149, 155, 161–4
   and Tsaritsyno   197, 203–6
Pavlovsk   1, 2, 7, 11, 13, 26, 33, 35, 37, 108, 116–65, 167, 237–8

Apollo Colonnade   26, 131, 146, 147, 155, 162
Aviary   26, 137–40
Bedchamber   131
Billiards Room   131
Bip citadel   135, 142
Boudoir   131
Dairy   135, 136
Dancing Room   131
Dressing Room   131
Elizabeth Pavilion   34, 155–6
French Drawing Room   131
Great Star area   133, 155
Grecian Hall   130–1
Hermitage Pavilion   117–18, 147
'Holland' building   144
Italian Hall   128–30, 131
Large Dining Room   131
Marienthal   117, 142, 155, 160, 161
Memorial to Parents (formerly Memorial to Sister Frederika)   26, 135–6
Menagerie area   133, 155
New and General Studies   131
obelisk   26
Old Cottage or Chalet   117, 147
Old Drawing Room   131
Old and New Sylvia   155
Palace (Palladian villa)   119–26
   interior   126–33
Parade Ground   135
park   133–40
Paulust   117, 161
Pil tower   155
Private Garden   156
Red Valley   155, 156
Rose Pavilion   163
Round Lake   153–4
Silver Birch area   133, 155
Slavyanka valley   7, 133, 141–54
Small Drawing Room   131
Study-library   131
Swiss Hills   142, 144, 145
Temple of Friendship   26, 148, 155
Three Graces Pavilion   34, 145, 158–9
Pekhra-Yakovlevskoye (estate near Moscow)   233
Pella, palace   108
Pembroke, Lord   1
Perrault, Claude (architect)   33
Peter I (the Great), Tsar   9, 33, 42, 142, 167, 168, 183, 187, 196, 240, 248
Peter III, Tsar   4, 168, 169, 204
Peter, Metropolitan   217
Peterhof   4, 7, 223, 226, 234
   Cottage Palace   234–6
   Mon Plaisir   168
Petersburg (province)   221
Petronius   52
Petrov, Vasily (1736–99, poet): *Ode to Ochakov*   104
Petrov, P. (architectural historian)   3, 258*n*
Petrovsk   245
Petrovsky Castle (or Palace)   1, 207–9, 245
Philip, Metropolitan   216
Pilnitz, Palace of   182
Pindar   21
Piranesi, Giambattista   12

Pitt, William   1
Plato   65, 66
Playfair, William (Edinburgh planner)   244
Pliny   33
Podol   245
Podzhigorovo, church   213
Pokrov   245
Polovtsev   253*n*
Poltoratsky, Mikhail   191
Polybius   33
Pompeii   24
Pope, Alexander   100
Popov, Vasily Stepanovich (1745–1827, chancery secretary to Catherine the Great)   237
Porechye   249
Posadnikovo, church   213
Poshman, Alexander (engineer and state counsellor)   38–9
Potemkin, General Field-Marshal Prince Grigory Alexandrovich (1739–91, favourite of Catherine the Great)   1, 5, 31, 103–4, 149, 160, 190–1
Pototsky, Prince Stanislav   130
Potsdam   85
Prioratsky Palace   5
Prokofyev, Ivan Prokofyevich (1758–1828, sculptor)   128
Pskov, Lanskoi estate   191
Pushkin, Alexander Sergeevich (1799–1837)   41, 46, 61
   The Captain's Daughter   106, 114

Quarenghi, Giacomo (1744–1817, architect)   3, 4, 26, 27, 35, 38, 44, 46, 115, 126, 144, 230–1

Rachet, Jean (French sculptor)   51
Radishchev, Alexander Nikolayevich (1749–1802, writer and philosopher)   102, 106
   A Journey from St Petersburg to Moscow   106, 113–14
Rae, Isobel   12
Rainsford, Charles   13
Rastopchin, Count Fedor Vasilievich (1763–1826, Commander-in-Chief of Moscow)   246
Rastrelli, Bartolomeo Francesco (1700–71, architect)   25, 41, 43, 44, 45, 46, 61, 69, 178, 217
Ravenna   13
Razumovsky, Count Alexei Grigorievich (1709–71, founder of family; favourite of Elizabeth I)   229, 231
Razumovsky, Kirill Grigorievich (1728–1803, *hetman* of Ukraine)   229, 230–1
Razumovsky family   34, 228–33
Reed (Read or Reid), Francis (gardener at Tsaritsyno)   5, 203
Reval   36
Reykhel (artist)   38
Riga   36
Rinaldi, Antonio (*c.*1710–1849, architect)   26, 85, 100, 103, 168, 169, 172, 175–6, 178, 182, 230
Robert, Hubert   12
Rodomysl   248
Rogachev, Nikolai, architect   32

Rogerson, John   4
Rome   13, 20–5, 39, 52, 182
  baths   20, 24, 25, 45
  Palace of Augustus   24
  tomb of Sestius   100
  Villa Madama   24
Rossi, Karl Ivanovich (1775–1849, architect)
  35, 126, 217, 221
Rostovtsev, Ivan (architect)   32
Rousseau, Jean-Jacques   33
Rumyantsev, Count Nikolai Petrovich
  (1754–1826; son of Count Peter, director of
  Imperial Department of Water
  Transport)   239
Rumyantsev, Field-Marshal General Count Peter
  Alexandrovich (1725–96)   102, 106, 181,
  192, 211
Ruska, Luigi (1758–1822, architect)   31, 242
Ryurik, Tsar   188

Sablukov, General Nikolai Alexandrovich
  (1776–1848, retainer at Pavlovsk)   135, 162
Saburovo estate   211–12
St Petersburg   1, 4, 25–6, 33, 35–9, 167, 209,
  221–3
  Academy of Arts   26
  Admiralty   4, 11, 35, 36, 37
  bridges   239–40
  Hermitage   26, 108
  Kazan cathedral   3, 35, 127
  Marble Palace   26
  Mikhailovsky Castle (Engineers' Castle)   34,
    37–8, 234
  Nevsky Prospekt   239
  Palace Square   35
  Police Bridge   239
  Public Library   38
  Senate   35
  Stock Exchange   35
  Synod   35
  Tauride Palace   5–7, 108
  Vasilevsky Island   35, 36
St Petersburg and Moscow Commission on Stone
  Construction   242
Sallust   22
Samborsky, Andrei Afanasevich (1732–1815,
  priest at Russian Embassy, London)   115,
  227–8
Samoylov, Vasily Vasilievich (1813–87, actor)
  163
Sans Souci, palace   182
Saratov   244, 245
Saxony   182
Scamozzi, Ottavio Bertotti (architect)   25
Schiller, Friedrich   236
Schinkel, Karl Friedrich (1781–1841, architect)
  223, 236–7
Schlutter, Andreas (c.1665–1714, architect to
  Peter the Great)   42
Scott, George (publisher)   21
Scott, Sir Walter   236
Ségur, Count (French ambassador)   101
Seliger, Lake   221
Selskaya Zhizn ('Country Life' or 'The Country
  Gentleman')   171, 192
Semenova, Nimfodora (1787–1876, soprano and
  actress)   163

Seneca   22, 52
Seskar island, lighthouse   37
Seym, River   229
Shadrinsk   245
Shaftesbury, Anthony Ashley Cooper, Earl of
  22
Shishkov, Admiral Alexander Semenovich
  (1754–1841, State Chancellor)   161
Shmidt, Alexander (architect)   32
Shubin, Fedot Ivanovich (1740–1805, sculptor)
  188
Siberia   250
Simferopol, hospital   238–9
Skvira   248
Slavyanka, River   117, 119, 131, 133, 135, 160;
  see also Pavlovsk, Slavyanka valley
Smith, Mrs M.   13
Smolensk   244, 248, 249
Society for Encouragement of the Arts, Industry
  and Trade   228
Socrates   66
Sofiya   1, 26, 64, 106–16, 228, 240–1
  Angliiskaya Linaya   226
  Arcade   106
  market   114
  Office Buildings   106
  Post Office   106, 113–14
  St Sophia, church of   106, 108–12, 226, 227
Sologub, Count Vladimir Alexandrovich
  (1813–82, writer)   118, 164
  Tarantass   164
Sophocles   33
Soufflot, Jacques-Germain (1713–80, architect)
  33
Soymanov, Major-General Mikhail Fedorovich
  (d. 1804, head of Mining Institute)   31
Sparrow, James   4, 5
Spassk   245
Spengler (engineer)   38
Spiridonova (actress)   163
Staritsa (town on the Volga)   244
  Poltoratsky estate   191
Starki-Cherkizovo church   213
Starov, Ivan Egorovich (1745–1808, architect)
  5, 9, 26, 27, 31, 44, 109, 167, 191
Stewart, Charles (stonemason)   226
Stone Island   253n
Stowe   1, 100, 156
  Temple of Pan   148
Strabo   22
Strawberry Hill, Twickenham   1, 191
Strekalov, Stepan Fedorovich (1728–1808, privy
  counsellor)   30, 31
Strelnya estate   234
Stroganov dacha   3
Stuart, Charles Edward (the Young Pretender)
  11, 12, 13
Sukhanovo (estate of the Volkonsky princes near
  Moscow)   233
Sukhtelen, General Peter Kornilievich (d. 1836,
  soldier, engineer and bibliophile)   38
Sukhtelen, Ruff Kornilievich   38
Summerson, Sir John   1
Suvorov, Field-Marshal General Alexander
  Vasilievich (1730–1800)   102, 104
Svinin, Pavel Petrovich (1787–1839, writer,
  collector, art-lover and art historian)   161

Syon House   100
Sytny Dvor   217

Tacitus   22
Taleporovsky, Vladimir Nikolaievich (d. c.1960,
  architectural historian)   12, 75, 89, 118–19,
  130, 155, 255n
Tambov province   245
Taylor, D.   256n
Teplovka (estate of the Rasumovsky counts in
  Ukraine)   232
Tertullian: 'On Sights'   22
Theodore   22
Thomas, A.   256n
Thomon see Tomon
Tivoli, Hadrian's Villa   24
Tomon (Thomon), Thomas de   8–9, 35
Tomsk   3, 244, 250
Torzhok, cathedral of St Boris and St Gleb   227
Trezini, Domenico Andrea (c.1670–1734,
  architect to Peter the Great)   42, 113
Triscorni, Paolo (d. 1832, sculptor)   158–60
Troitskoye-Kainardzhi estate   210
Trombara, Giacomo (architect)   44
Tsaritsyno   1, 5, 196–206, 225
  Bread House   198, 206
  Grape Gates   198, 206
  Small Palace   198
Tsarskoye Selo   1, 2, 4, 7, 13, 25, 26–34, 35,
  39, 41–69, 132, 167, 182, 225, 226, 228,
  231, 239
  Admiralty   100, 186–7
  Agate Pavilion   26, 27, 52, 54–61, 67, 96
  Alexander Park   221–3, 233
  Arsenal   222
  Baths   45–54
  Bedchamber   26
  Cameron Gallery   1, 3, 11, 45–6, 61–9, 96,
    108, 112, 226
  Catherine Palace (Great Palace)   69–96, 178,
    180
    Arabesque Hall   26, 79–85
    Bedchamber   90–2
    Blue Drawing Room   75–6
    Chinese Blue Drawing Room   75–6
    Chinese Hall   26, 31, 70, 85–8, 92, 96
    Domed Dining Room   88–90
    Grand Ducal Bedchamber   76–9
    Green Dining Room   71–5
    Lyons Hall   26, 85, 92
    Mirror Room   95–6
    Palm Room   95–6
    Silver (or Red) Study   89–90
    Snuff-box Room   92–5
  Chapelle   221–2
  Chinese Opera and Pavilions   255n
  Chinese Theatre   178
  Chinese Village   27, 171–81, 226
  Creaking Pavilion   175, 179
  Double Chinese Bridge   255n
  farm buildings   222
  Gatchina Gates   27
  Great Pond   97, 100, 102, 103
  Green Dining Room   26
  Hanging Garden   1, 67
  Hastie at   240–2, 244
  Hermitage Pavilion   41, 100, 186–7

House of Antiquity (design by Clérisseau) 45
Kitchen 187
Large and Small Caprices 172, 174–5, 178–9
Little Chinatown 172–3
Menagerie 178
Menelaws at 233, 234
Orangery 4, 32, 33, 34
Pagoda 176
Park 97–106, 169
Pavilion of Arts and Sciences (design by
    Wailly) 45
Pensionerskiye Stables 222
pyramid 26, 100, 101
Red or Turkish Cascade 104
Roman baths 11
Rostral Column 103
Ruined Tower 102, 104
Rumyantsev Monument 102
School of Practical Agriculture 115, 227–8
Siberian Bridge 100, 258n
Temple of Memory 27, 32, 34, 102, 237
Triumphal Gates 103–5
Turkish Pavilion 104
White Tower 222
Zubovsky wing 46, 85, 95, 96
  see also Sofiya
Turkey 191
Tver 7, 221
Twickenham, Pope's villa in 100
Typographical Company 203
Tyzva, stream 142

Ufa 244, 245, 248, 249
Ukraine 229, 231–2, 250
Ungebauer, Karl (German gardener) 5
Ushakov, Admiral Fedor Fedorovich
    (1744–1817) 102, 104

Utkin, Fedor (artist) 32

Vanvitelli, Luigi (architect) 169
Vasilkov 248
Velten, Yuri Matveevich (1730–1801) 2, 9, 26,
    27, 46, 100, 102, 104, 171, 173–5, 179,
    187–9
Versailles, Palace of 12, 108, 234
  Trianon de Porcelain 175
Vicenza 24
Vigel, Filip Filippovich (1786–1856, writer) 35,
    37, 38
Vilno 248, 249
Viollet-le-Duc, Eugène (1814–79,
    architect) 223
Vishenki estate 210
Vitruvius Britannicus 19
Volga region 250
Volkonsky, princes 233
Voltaire, François Arouet de 11, 33, 64, 98,
    108
Voronikhin, Andrei Nikoforovich (1759–1814,
    architect) 3, 35, 126, 127, 155, 163
Vorontsov, Count Semen Romanovich
    (1744–1832, Russian ambassador in London)
    31, 223
Vorontsovo estate 212
Vvedensky canal 239
Vyatka 245
Vyatskaya province 245
Vyazmitinov, General Count Sergei Kuzmich
    (1749–1819, Minister of Police) 248

Wailly, Charles de (architect) 9, 44, 45
Walpole, Horace, 4th Earl of Orford 1, 191
Ware, Isaac (1704–66, architect) 17–19, 24, 25,
    33, 39, 64

Watson, Andrew (plasterer) 225
Wedgwood, Josiah 1, 91, 189
Wilson, Alexander (smith) 226, 239
Wilson, D. (metalworker) 256n
Wilson, James (smith) 225, 226, 239
Wilton estate 1, 2
  Palladian bridge 100, 258n
Winckelmann, Johann Joachim 12
Windsor Castle 100
Wölfflin, Heinrich 127
Wright, William: Grotesque Architecture 171,
    181
Württemberg 45
  Duke of 135

Yagotin (estate of the Razumovsky counts in
    Ukraine) 231–2
Yaropolets estate 2, 7, 181, 212
Yegotov, Ivan Vasilievich (1756–1814, architect)
    217, 221
Yekaterinoslav (now Dnepropetrovsk) 3, 239,
    248, 251
  Treasury and prison 238

Zakharov, Andreyan Dmitrievich (1761–1811,
    architect) 9, 35, 36, 37, 221
Zemtsov, Mikhail Gregorovich (1688–1743,
    architect to Peter the Great) 42
Zhukovsky, Vasily Andreevich (1783–1852, poet,
    tutor to Alexander I): Slavyanka 141–2,
    154, 236
Znamenka estate 210
  church 213
Znamenskoye-Rayok 7
Zubov, Field-Marshal General Count Platon
    Alexandrovich (1767–1822, last favourite of
    Catherine the Great) 46, 238, 239